THE MAN FROM MISSOURI

The Life and Times of

HARRY S. TRUMAN

THE MAN

The Life and Times

Alfred Steinberg

FROM MISSOURI

of HARRY S. TRUMAN

G. P. Putnam's Sons   New York

In memory of another Harry—my father

Author's Note

THIS book had its beginning during the Truman Administration, when I covered President Truman and his era for various publications. It was my good fortune to have interviewed on numerous occasions persons who played important roles in the Truman period but who have since passed away. My talks with them provided the material for an integral part of this book. Belatedly, I should therefore like to express my gratitude to Charles G. "Charlie" Ross, David K. Niles, Mon C. Wallgren, Alben W. Barkley, Patrick A. McCarran, Joseph R. McCarthy, Matthew M. Neely, William "Wild Bill" Langer, Walter F. George, James D. "Sunny Jim" Preston, John Peurifoy, Percy Priest, and Harley M. Kilgore. In most instances, the quotations from these gentlemen which appear in the book were made directly to me.

The number of persons I interviewed along the way runs into the hundreds and cannot possibly be listed by name. I should like, however, to single out the following: Leslie L. Biffle, Charles W. Watkins, Harry H. Vaughan, Mize and Lucy Peters, Tom L. Evans, Spencer Salisbury, John L. Miles, Tom Connally, Theodore Francis Green, Eben Ayers, Lindsay C. Warren, George Elsey, Paul H. Douglas,

George A. Smathers, John J. Williams, Oscar L. Chapman, Margaret Chase Smith, Eliahu Elath, Francis Rosenberger, Victor Messall, Roger Tubby, Irving Brant, and Harold Miller.

For extending me every courtesy, and for their aid, I owe a great debt to Dr. Philip C. Brooks, Director of the Harry S. Truman Library, and his excellent staff. I am also indebted to Mr. and Mrs. Howard Carvin of Independence, Missouri, for their many kindnesses. Herman Kahn, Director of the Franklin D. Roosevelt Library at Hyde Park, New York, and Mrs. Franklin D. Roosevelt were especially helpful in making available various research materials on my visits a few years ago. At the Library of Congress, Stewart Dickson has always been of immeasurable aid.

Last, but certainly foremost, has been the help of my wife, Florence. From her "cross-examination" of Mr. Truman, to her research and editorial talents, this book is in truth a collaboration.

A. S.

THE MAN FROM MISSOURI

The Life and Times of

HARRY S. TRUMAN

1

ON January 5, 1952, an aging Winston Churchill climbed aboard the Presidential yacht *Williamsburg* at the Washington Navy Yard for a political conference. Only the previous October he had been returned to the office of Prime Minister of Great Britain after having been voted from that post in July of 1945. His host on the vessel was Harry S. Truman, who was finishing out the last year of a tempestuous period of office as President of the United States.

After dinner aboard the yacht, the two men remained seated at the dining room table, where they planned to discuss the affairs of the world.

Roger Tubby, who was then Truman's press secretary, was an eyewitness to the scene that followed. Churchill seemed to have dozed off, his chin drooping against his chest. His empty whisky and soda glass was at his elbow, and an unlit, long black cigar was cradled in the V of two fingers. Then, slowly, he raised his eyelids and studied the grinning face opposite him.

Finally he spoke. "The last time you and I sat across the conference table was at Potsdam, Mr. President."

Truman nodded agreement.

Churchill's tone changed. "I must confess, sir, I held you in very low regard then. I loathed your taking the place of Franklin Roosevelt."

Truman's wide grin vanished.

"I misjudged you badly," Churchill went on after a long pause. "Since that time, you, more than any other man, have saved Western Civilization.

"When the British could no longer hold out in Greece, you, and you alone, sir, made the decision that saved that ancient land from the Communists.

"You acted in similar fashion with regard to Azerbaijan when the Soviets tried to take over Iran. Then there was your resolute stand on Trieste, and your Marshall Plan which rescued Western Europe wallowing in the shallows and indeed easy prey to Joseph Stalin's malevolent intentions. Then you established the North Atlantic Treaty Alliance and collective security for those nations against the military machinations of the Soviet Union. Then there was your audacious Berlin Airlift. And, of course, there was Korea."

Truman's grin returned.

What was there about Harry Truman that gave the impression he was too small for his job? Throughout his long political career, friends and opponents continually underrated him. Although he stood five feet ten inches tall, associates referred to him as being "below average height." Even his mother-in-law, the imperious Mrs. Madge Gates Wallace, frankly told her friends in Independence, Missouri, that it was sheer wasted effort for him to campaign against Tom Dewey in 1948.

Early in Truman's career, Joseph Shannon, a Kansas City Democratic boss, wrote off the possibility that he might enjoy a long and successful stay in politics. "The fellow's always grinning and he's too quick with his mouth," he observed. "He talks off the cuff at the wrong time; doesn't stop to consider what he's saying before out pops the words." When Truman first ran for the United States Senate in 1934, under the sponsorship of the Kansas City Pendergast machine, old Tom Pendergast was reported to have raised his black derby and scratched his bald head as he bragged, "Frankly, it was a matter of pride to me to name *just any man* and beat Bennett Clark's candidate."

In 1940, after Truman had spent a Senatorial term as a vociferous New Dealer, President Roosevelt supported his opponent in the Demo-

12

cratic primary. Roosevelt's contention was that Truman's opponent was "progressive." Four years later, when FDR told Admiral William D. Leahy that he had decided on the Missouri Senator as his running mate, Leahy turned to the President and scornfully asked, "Who the hell is Truman?"

No matter how momentous his actions or how unswerving his dedication to basic principles, many politicians failed to take Truman seriously. Some could not accept the fact that he was President. On one occasion, after he was in the White House, he telephoned Jesse Jones, the Federal Government's lending czar. "Hello, Jesse," he said. "The President has sent John Snyder's name to the Senate for confirmation as Federal Loan Administrator."

"Did the President make that appointment before he died?" Jones asked curtly.

Truman fumed. "No—*he* made it just now."

In Truman's case the form lay heavily over the substance. In fact, it tended to hide the truth that there was any substance at all. For example, Joseph Alsop, the journalist and cousin to the Franklin Roosevelts, wrote a letter to Eleanor Roosevelt following a visit to Truman's White House. FDR's White House, he declared, had been a seat of power. But Harry Truman's, he moaned, was like "the lounge of the Lion's Club of Independence, Missouri, where one is conscious chiefly of the odor of ten-cent cigars and the easy laughter evoked by the new smoking room story." Yet the courageous decisions to face up to the massive Communist threats emanated from this same atmosphere.

Harry Truman was also victim of a marrowy way of speaking that made some people feel that he was vulgarizing the great office of the Presidency. In words, letters, his choice of sports clothing and associates, and in his mannerisms, he found it difficult to separate Truman the man from Truman the President.

He could welcome Princess Elizabeth of England with heartfelt dignity when she visited the United States. Yet a few hours later he could throw his head back and laugh uproariously at a bawdy story. He insisted that the pomp attending the Presidency be maintained to the hilt, and the military band greeted him in the morning with "Hail to the Chief." Yet at night, once he was away from the limelight and within his own quarters, his valet sometimes found him washing out his own socks and underwear.

Franklin Roosevelt worked hard at establishing himself as a father

13

image. The great, wide public could relax, his vocal tone and facial expression seemed to say: things were in capable hands. Dwight D. Eisenhower also projected a father image, although he once told me of his distaste at being regarded as "the great papa to the American people."

But Truman never projected himself as the "great papa." Where Roosevelt and Eisenhower held themselves aloof, Truman liked to be with people, no matter what their station in life. He did not feel it beneath him to talk politics to passers-by. Once, while on his early-morning two-mile hike before beginning his Presidential day, he started across Memorial Bridge leading to Arlington Cemetery. Toward the center of the bridge he spied a door and a stairway that led to the bridge tender's workroom. A short time later, Secret Service men found him sitting on the floor in that room with Charles Barnhill, the bridge tender. The two were sharing Barnhill's meal and were talking politics between bites.

Truman had an enormous faculty for attracting loud, often coarse, supporters and hangers-on. Whenever his old war mates of World War I showed up, he immediately reverted to the role of Captain Harry of Battery D. Down the street he marched in their parades with long, jaunty strides—not as President Truman but as one of the boys.

Neither his enemies nor his friends could forget that he had once lost his shirt in the haberdashery business, that he was the product of a nefarious political machine, and that he had been elevated to the national scene from a minor local office. This was the indelible image they used as reference in judging him.

And when the nation was stunned by Franklin Roosevelt's death on April 12, 1945, part of this emotional shock was attributed to the realization of who had succeeded him. Yet within Harry Truman's lifetime, historians agree that he must be ranked with the strongest of American Presidents.

2

ON one occasion I remarked to Harry Truman that his father, John Anderson Truman, had led a sad, frustrating life and had been a failure.

Truman's eyes flashed behind his thick glasses and his jaw set angrily. "My father was not a failure," he snapped. "After all, he was the father of a President of the United States."

John Anderson Truman came of a family that had migrated to the United States from Nottingham, England, in 1666. The family had built the largest brewery in England, and Joseph Truman, the initial American Truman, earned his livelihood in the New World as a carpenter. He was also the first Truman to become a politician, winning election to the office of constable in New London, Connecticut. In time, the growing Truman clan moved south to Kentucky, settling in the general area of Shelby County, located in the north central part of the state. Then in the 1840's another migration occurred when Harry Truman's grandparents were among the first to settle at a place where the Kaw met the Missouri River, a town called Westport Landing, later renamed Kansas City.

The Truman heritage was one of long life and strong-willed women. Harry Truman's grandfather, Anderson Shippe Truman, had eloped with Mary Jane Holmes because her widowed mother disapproved of a son-in-law who did not own slaves. That he did not want to own slaves was beside the point to the old lady, Nancy Tyler Holmes, a forceful personality who always wore a fine lace cap to cover her scarred head, which she claimed was the result of an Indian scalping when she was nine years old. She was also a direct descendant of the uncle of John Tyler, the first Vice-President to become President upon the death of a Chief Executive.

On the western edge of Missouri, where Anderson Truman took his bride from Kentucky, he was first a school director and then a farmer. By necessity he and his wife Mary Jane were a quiet couple because his mother-in-law first gave them slaves to "legalize" their marriage and then moved in with them to dominate their lives until her death at ninety-four in 1875.

Although Anderson Truman was a strict Baptist, he nevertheless revealed a strain of humor. At one time he lived in a farmhouse which straddled two counties, and he avoided jury service by hurrying from one part of the house to the other whenever a call to jury duty came. Later on, he gleefully repeated this story to his five children: the eldest, William, whose son became a general in World War II; his three daughters, known in the house and neighborhood as Matt, Ella, and Emma; and his second son, John Anderson Truman, father of Harry.

Born in 1851, John Anderson Truman was a short man who answered throughout his life to the nickname of "Peanuts." Despite his father's background as a school director, John evinced little interest in formal education and was a desultory pupil at a rural school for a few years before he finally quit. Later in life, however, he professed great regret for his early stand against book learning, and he and his son Harry saved dimes in order to buy a set of Shakespeare's works.

Nor did John Truman enjoy plowing a field. A family story relates that one day his father took him aside and asked how he planned to support himself.

"Be a mule trader," John replied.

His father was unhappy to learn this. "Well, you know, John," he said after his initial shock, "mule trading isn't always considered the highest calling a man can aspire to. But always tell the truth and no one will believe you."

16

John liked to pull off a good wisecrack now and then and had an inordinate interest in politics. At one place where he lived, old residents later recalled him as "a little and wiry man who joked a lot and knocked people's hats off when they weren't looking." He was warmhearted and neat in his person to an extreme—two characteristics that also distinguished Harry—but when he was aroused, he revealed a violent temper.

"If my father's honor was impugned," Harry Truman recalled, "he'd fight like a buzzsaw." Not even his opponent's size gave him pause. On one occasion, said Harry Truman, his father was a witness in a case being tried in Judge James H. Slover's courtroom in Independence. John Truman sat in the witness box while an unfriendly attorney, who weighed 200 pounds, cross-examined him. Just as he finished answering a question the lawyer leaned close to his face and shouted, "Now, John, you know that's a damn lie!"

Truman leaped from the witness chair and chased him down the courtroom aisle and out of the building.

According to Harry Truman, when his father walked back alone into the courtroom a few minutes later, old Judge Slover leaned over the bench and asked, "Did you get him, John?"

"No, he got away. He ran inside a building across the street."

"Too bad," Slover said. "That fellow really had a good beating coming to him."

In 1881, at the age of thirty, John Truman was still living at home. His mother had died in 1879, and he and his father worked the 200-acre family farm near Grandview. A local history of Jackson County, Missouri, noted that "John Anderson Truman resides with his father and manages the farm: he is an industrious and energetic young man and one that bids fair to make a success in life."

This history was soon outdated, for only three days before Christmas, 1881, John Truman married Martha Ellen Young, the prettiest of neighbor Solomon Young's five daughters. After the wedding ceremony, he borrowed a carriage from his father-in-law and he and his bride traveled a hundred miles south to Lamar where he intended to try his skill at mule trading.

John had known Martha Ellen almost all his life. Their parents had been neighbors in Kentucky and their last Missouri farms were only three miles apart. A year younger than John, Martha was considered an old maid at twenty-nine when she finally consented to marry him.

17

While the Trumans had to struggle to stay solvent, the Youngs led a comfortable life. Martha's father, Solomon Young, owned a 600-acre farm not far from Kansas City. The sprawling colonial house that he had built was ample for his family of nine plus servants, farm hands, and an ever-changing assortment of relatives. Maple trees ran from the front door to the dirt road a quarter of a mile away and there were large herds of cattle and mules, prize hogs and sheep, orchards, wheat, corn, and hay fields, and all the other appurtenances of a thriving establishment.

Unlike Harry Truman's paternal grandfather, who died when Harry was only three, Solomon Young and his wife Louisa were to play an important role in his life. Off and on he lived in their house until his marriage at the age of thirty-five.

Sol Young was of German ancestry with chiefly a Methodist background. Yet years later Truman's political enemies spread the false rumor that since his grandfather was named Solomon, he was Jewish. "My Grandfather Young belonged to no church," Truman said, "but he supported many of them—Baptist, Methodist, Campbellite, and Presbyterian. They all met in the old church out in front of the house on the family farm on Sunday." When Harry was six and grew inquisitive about which sect was best, Grandpa Young told him, "All of them want to arrive at the same place, but they have to fight to see who has the inside track with the Almighty. When a man spends Saturday night and Sunday doing too much howling and praying you had better go home and lock your smokehouse."

Solomon Young was a handsome, muscular man with a full beard and a weatherbeaten face. From the 1840's until the 1860's, he served as wagon train master to the unsettled Far West. Leader of more than a dozen ventures, he ran Conestoga freight trains and herds of cattle numbering as many as 1,500 head through wild Indian territory and across mountains and deserts to Salt Lake City, Colorado and California. He was an awesome figure to the barefoot boys of the neighborhood who chased after his massive sixteen-hitch ox teams as he set out on each journey. Across the nearby prairies, Martha Ellen watched him crack his long snake whip and shout "Gee!" and "Haw!" like a general going to battle. Records of the Church of the Latter Day Saints show that he once did business with another man named Young, the Mormon leader Brigham Young in the Utah Territory.

Harry's maternal grandmother, Harriet Louisa Gregg Young, was a vivacious, red-haired woman who bore her husband nine children, seven of whom grew to adulthood. Harry's mother was next to the youngest in the family of five girls and two boys.

Martha Ellen Young was a slender, tiny girl with dark hair parted in the middle and eyes alive with laughter and mischief. An outdoor girl who rode a horse as if she were born on a sidesaddle, she was also a voracious reader who in later years adopted the appalling pastime of reading the *Congressional Record* from cover to cover each day that Congress was in session. At the Baptist College for Women in Lexington, she revealed strong talent in music and art and an ability to flaunt Baptist decree with impunity by attending dances. "I'm a lightfoot Baptist," she explained laughingly. She enjoyed talking and spoke in the same positive way that became a trademark of her son. For example, it was her firm belief that "anyone who could live on the west line of Missouri in those days and not be a Democrat was just a fool for lack of brains."

When John Truman brought his bride to Lamar at the beginning of 1882, he purchased a tiny frame house for $685. For a man who was just starting out on his own, the little house was not as important as the yard and big barn behind, because he hoped to conduct an animal-swapping business there. The property seemed to reflect his low status, for it was without a number and sat on a street that had no name. Accustomed to better living, Martha Truman nevertheless closed her mind on her past and considered only the present and bright hopes for the future. "Lamar was a pretty country village then," she recalled. "It was built around a square with a courthouse in the center and elm and maple trees." The chief distinction of Lamar was that Wyatt Earp had served as constable there before moving on with his long-barreled Colt .45 Buntline Special.

In 1883, Martha carried a stillborn child. This depressed her for months afterward, although she was soon pregnant again. And on May 8, 1884, she gave birth in her 6½-foot-wide bedroom to a squalling son who was destined one day to become the thirty-third President of the United States.

3

MARTHA Truman's baby had hardly come into the world when he became a center of controversy. "I was supposed to be named Harrison Shippe Truman, taking the middle name from my paternal grandfather," he later explained. The Harrison was in honor of his mother's older brother, Harrison Young, but by family compromise it was shortened to Harry. "Others in the family wanted my middle name to be Solomon, taken from my maternal grandfather. But apparently no agreement could be reached and my name was recorded and stands simply as Harry S. Truman."

John Truman was so excited on becoming a father that after he paid the doctor $15 for the delivery, he planted a pine tree at the side of the white cottage to signify the event. Then he nailed a horseshoe over the front door for good luck. Two days later, Martha Truman proudly reminisced, the celebrated Baptist Circuit Rider, the Rev. Washington Pease, "took him out to the farm gate and held him up to the sun and said what a sturdy boy he was."

Mule trading proved poor in Lamar and when Harry was a year old his family moved north to the village of Harrisonville, only a county below the Kansas City area. Here he first became conscious of the world about him. "My first memory," he recalled, "was that of chasing a frog around the back yard." He was by then a slender little boy with brown hair, very white skin, and hazel eyes that changed color according to his moods. Every time the frog jumped, Harry slapped his knees and laughed uproariously. He remembered hearing his Grandmother Young telling his mother, "It's very strange that a two-year-old has such a sense of humor." Another memory was of the day Uncle Harrison came to see his infant brother Vivian, who was born in April, 1886. "I remember when my mother dropped me from an upstairs window into the arms of my Uncle Harrison," Truman said, as if this were an everyday occurrence.

By the time he was three Harry knew a third place of residence when the mule trading-business failed again at Harrisonville. This time the family moved in with Grandpa and Grandma Young at Grandview, where his father agreed to manage the farm. Grandpa Truman, who lived with his son, also went along to the Young farm, but he died shortly after their arrival, at the age of seventy-one. His three daughters, who were standing about his deathbed, remembered how little Harry pulled at his beard in an effort to arouse him.

At an early age Harry Truman absorbed a strong sympathy for the Confederate cause from his Grandmother Young and his mother. Repeatedly and bitterly they spoke of their experiences during the late war. As a border state, Missouri was a center of bloody turmoil between Confederate and Union regulars and guerrillas. Early one morning in 1861, while Sol Young was out West, they told Harry, a dirty man with wild hair came riding into the Young farmyard in front of a mean-looking crew wearing red morocco leggings. He was Jim Lane, a United States Senator and leader of the Kansas Abolitionist gang known as "Red Legs."

At gunpoint, Harry's grandmother was forced to light her stove, fry meat and bake biscuits for this villainous gang. By the time the Red Legs had their fill her hands were a mass of blisters. Then Lane's crew killed 400 of Sol Young's Hampshire hogs, hacking off only the hams to cart away. Martha was so frightened that she buried herself under a feather quilt. "They shot our hens out of sheer cussedness. Then they burned all our hay and set fire to our stock barns," she told her son. Grandma Young added, "They also stole the silverware and would have taken the big iron kettle and the rock crusher, but those were too blamed heavy."

21

Two years after Lane's raid, William Clarke Quantrill's equally villainous Confederate Raiders sacked Lawrence, Kansas, and slaughtered 183 defenseless persons. Martha Truman shrugged off Quantrill's depraved deed with the comment that he had only "repaid the Jayhawkers in kind."

Her opinion of the Union cause was reinforced in August, 1863, when General Thomas Ewing issued his Order Number 11, under which Confederates were barred from remaining in several Missouri counties, including Jackson County. This meant that on a sweltering afternoon, a laden oxcart left the Young farm and behind it, trudging eastward into exile, went Louisa Young and six of her children.

It was little wonder that throughout her life Martha Truman insisted, "I thought it was a good thing that Lincoln was shot." She recalled vividly for reporters how on Lincoln's assassination "Emery, Bird [Kansas City's largest department store] was all draped in black." Decades later, when she ninety-two, she broke her hip and shoulder after tripping over a rug on her kitchen floor. Major General Harry Vaughan, who was Harry Truman's White House Military Aide, said that the next morning he and the worried President visited her. She lay bandaged and splinted in bed, but her eyes were bright and angry. "I don't want any smart cracks out of you," she snapped. "I saw your picture in the paper last week putting a wreath at the Lincoln Memorial."

In August, 1889, when Harry's sister, Mary Jane, was born, the Young household was bursting at the seams. Besides the Youngs and five Trumans, there were servants, farm hands, waifs adopted by Grandma Young, and several relatives, including Harry's first cousin, Sol Chiles, whose father was known as "Jim Crow" Chiles because of his hatred of Negroes.

By now the din was too much for John Truman. Furthermore, he was eager to make another try at animal swapping. As for Martha, watching Harry approach school age, she believed it was time to move on to a larger town where he was more likely to get a decent education than at Grandview.

The following year, when Harry's father collected his share of Anderson Truman's small estate, he and Martha decided to make a new start at private family life. The town of Independence seemed just the place for them. It had 6,000 people, and was not too far from either Grandview or Kansas City. Besides, it was a lively business community and had a good school system.

Six-year-old Harry found Independence exciting. Even the origin of its name was colorful. To the north, supporters of Henry Clay had named their area Clay County and their chief town, Liberty. Not to be outdone, the followers of Andrew Jackson in the county below had named theirs Jackson County and their county seat, Independence. As a result, Andrew Jackson became Harry's lifelong hero. Independence was also the jumping-off point for both the Santa Fe and Oregon Trails. Whittling away in the courthouse square were old-timers who talked with authority about those romantic days when the town was the busiest in America west of St. Louis. Also, Independence had served as the New Zion for the Mormon sect under Prophet Joseph Smith, its founder, until violent mobs and the state militia drove the Mormons from Missouri in 1838. Still another feature of the town was that it had been a home base for the Jesse James gang after the Civil War. There was even a cell in the Independence jailhouse which Frank James had once occupied.

In Independence, Harry's father purchased a house with a barn and a large lot on Chrysler Street for $4,000 and once more plunged into the animal business. Harry was old enough now to notice that his father was the "kind of man who never passed a cow but what he stopped and tried to buy her. He could tell a mule's age by a glance and did not have to examine his teeth."

Shortly after the Trumans settled in Independence, a singular event took place in Harry's life. When the Rev. Addison Madeira, pastor of the First Presbyterian Church, went out of his way to welcome the Truman children to town, Martha Truman decided to send Harry to his Sunday school despite her Baptist upbringing. On his first visit, a little girl with golden curls and blue eyes arrested his attention. She was Elizabeth Virginia Wallace, or "Bess," as everyone called her. "I was too backward to look at her very much," Truman recalled. "And I didn't speak to her for five years."

Although he learned to read the big print in the family Bible before his fifth birthday, Harry did not start school until he was past eight. Shortly before he began, his mother discovered he was unable to read small print or recognize objects close up. With mounting concern she took him to a Kansas City oculist who noted that the boy's eyeballs were oddly flat and that he suffered from severe hyperopia. The result was a prescription for a pair of extremely thick-lensed glasses. "I was blind as a mole without them," he admitted. "But I've been

23

'fine-printed' many a time since I've been able to read it," he added many years later.

Harry's schooling started out well in Miss Myra Ewing's first-grade class. But when he was in Miss Minnie Ward's second-grade class he came down with diphtheria and almost died. Earlier he had shown a tendency toward being accident prone. One time, while combing his hair, he fell out of his chair and broke his collarbone. Another time he swallowed a peach pit and only the quick thinking of his mother saved his life when she forced the seed down his throat with her fingers. When diphtheria struck their house, Harry's younger brother Vivian was also affected, but he recovered quickly. Harry, however, developed a paralysis in his arms and legs. For several months Martha Truman had to push her nine-year-old son about town in a baby carriage until he suddenly recovered. But hardly had he got back on his feet when he sliced off the end of one big toe by slamming the cellar door on it. Dr. Twyman, the local physician, managed to press the two pieces together with a coating of crystalline iodoform and Truman said later, "It stayed put and got well!"

By the time Harry recovered from his mishaps and illness, Martha Truman had grown unusually attached to him. Friends of his brother Vivian noted that she pushed far more chores on him than on Harry. She kept Harry close to her side, taught him to cook and help her and their maid, Aunt Caroline, in the kitchen. "Harry was 'old' even as a little boy," relatives recalled. He was also closely attentive to his little sister, Mary Jane. Every night before bedtime he held her in his arms in the rocking chair and sang her to sleep. He also braided her hair and kept watch over her outdoors. Long afterward Mary Jane said, "Harry used to take me everywhere. Perhaps that's why I'm an old maid, because he was such a nice beau." Martha Truman thought she discerned something special about her older son. "Say, I've known that boy would amount to something from the time he was nine years old," she said with pride. "He never did anything by halves."

Although his mother adored him, his father often found him irritating. He never laid a hand on Harry, though he could scold him unmercifully, which, according to Truman, "hurt worse than a good spanking." On one occasion, he bought Harry a Shetland pony and the two went for a ride with John Truman astride a lead horse. When Harry fell off the pony, his father would not permit him to climb back in the saddle but insisted that he walk the half mile home. John Truman was closer to Vivian, whose facial features and mannerisms

24

resembled his own. He also admired Vivian's ruggedness and his love of the outdoors. When Vivian was only twelve, John Truman took him into his animal-swapping business and let him have a checking account in his own name.

Nevertheless, Harry shared a common interest with his father when it came to politics. In 1892, his father was a loud booster of Grover Cleveland when he ran for a second term against Benjamin Harrison. This was the first election in which Harry took an interest. "I had a white cap with a visor on it saying 'Grover Cleveland and Adlai Stevenson,' " he recalled. When word came that Cleveland was the winner, his father climbed to the roof of his house and tied an enormous 44-star flag and bunting to the gilded rooster weather vane. And in the torchlight parade, he rode by astride a large gray horse. During the local election contests, John Truman was noted for his fisticuffs. When he ran out of arguments at the courthouse square, he would sting opponents with his fists. Several times he limped home bruised and bloodied.

Harry secretly admired his father's fighting ways because he did not have a single fist fight in his entire youth. When he was ten, his mother bought him a set of biographies by Charles Francis Horne titled *Great Men and Famous Women*. These four red volumes, from which he never parted, became his prize possession. He also began to haunt the Independence Public Library, which contained about 5,000 books. "I read everything I could get my hands on—histories and encyclopedias and everything else," he said. By the time he was twelve, he had finished his second reading of the Bible. This was all to the good, his mother explained. "For we all belonged to different churches in our family. There were Baptists, Presbyterians, and Methodists. When anybody got into an argument, they always said Harry was best posted in the Bible because he read all the history and the stories in it."

In 1896, John Truman sold his Chrysler Street house at a profit and moved to another place on Waldo Street along the road to Independence's old river port. During his six-year stay on Chrysler Street, he sometimes kept as many as five hundred goats at one time in his fenced-in back yard. He had also drilled the first natural-gas well in the area and piped the gas into his and a neighbor's house for fuel. Besides mule swapping, he had branched into the real estate business and begun to speculate on the Kansas City grain futures market. He had it figured out that he would one day make a killing and retire a millionaire.

On Waldo Street, Harry became a sort of peripheral member of what was known in town as the "Waldo Street Gang." Close by was a pond where the children swam and skated. There was also a field where the gang played baseball and other games. "Harry could not play many of the games because of his glasses," his mother said. "The boys made me umpire," he added. There were the Allen brothers—Pete and Phog—who later became nationally known for their basketball prowess; Elmer Twyman, later a physician; Charlie Ross, who would become a well-known journalist and Truman's press secretary; and three of the Wallace children—Frank, George, and Bess. From a distance, Harry watched Bess, a small, but well-coordinated tomboy. "We had a wonderful time in the neighborhood from 1896 to 1902," he said.

There was another activity that took up much of Harry's time. Martha Truman had an old upright piano and when he was about ten she became his first piano teacher. She also tried to teach Vivian, but "Mama couldn't get a lasso big enough," he said proudly. When Harry revealed first-rate ability, she sent him for a short time to a neighborhood teacher and then to Mrs. B. C. White, a Kansas City teacher who had studied under Theodor Leschetitzky, the renowned European master. Charlie Ross said, "He didn't lack spunk when he braved the jeers of the boys to go regularly to his music teacher, carrying his music roll."

Twice a week Harry went to Mrs. White's house for lessons and he rose at five A.M. each morning to get in two hours of practicing before school. He continued this routine until the age of fifteen when he suddenly quit, to the consternation of both his mother and Mrs. White, who had visions of him as a concert pianist. Harry, however, was more realistic. "I missed being a musician," he once said, "and. the real and only reason I missed being one was because I wasn't good enough. But the foundation was good. I had a lot of Bach fugues, Clementi's *Gradus ad Parnassam,* some Beethoven, Carl Maria von Weber and Liszt."

In the spring of 1898, after the United States went to war with Spain, Harry began taking a more active part in his gang's carryings-on. When the boys organized the Independence Junior Militia, he quickly joined them. "There were a dozen or more of us, all in our early teens," he recalled, "and we liked to think we would join the armed forces in a unit if the Spanish-American War would only wait for us to get old enough." The boys drilled, camped on the banks of the Little Blue River, and shot helpless backyard fowl with their .22-caliber rifles. But the Spaniards had the effrontery to surrender that summer and in the fall Harry returned to the unexciting life of the schoolboy.

At this time, he also landed his first job. Every morning before school, at six-thirty, he reported to Jim Clinton's Drug Store on the square where he mopped the floor, then swept the sidewalk, washed windows, and dusted counters, cases, and bottles for three dollars a week. "There must have been a thousand bottles to dust," he complained. This was his first acquaintance with the cynicism of the adult world and it left him confused. Jim Clinton kept some liquor bottles behind the prescription case and every morning, while Harry was in the store, the town's leading churchgoers and Anti-Saloon Leaguers trooped in one at a time and hurried behind the case. "They had come in for their early-morning drink," he observed, "and would wipe their mouths, peep through the observation hole in front of the case, and depart."

John Truman's luck as a grain speculator was on the upgrade. When the Democrats held their national convention in Kansas City in 1900, he sat in the special box with Bill Kemper, a banker and lieutenant of the growing local political machine headed by Jim Pendergast. His father helped Harry land a job as a convention page. "I remember that there were seventeen thousand people in the old convention hall when William Jennings Bryan spoke," he said. "His appeal that day was like nothing I have ever heard. He had a bell-like voice that carried well and he knew how to use it."

In those days few boys remained in high school long enough to graduate. (Of the 41 students in Harry's graduating class of 1901, only 11 were boys.) He was well liked in school for his pleasing personality and warm grin, and though his teachers ranked him as a good student he was not the best. This honor was reserved for his friend Charlie Ross, son of the town jailer, who was class valedictorian. Harry's favorite subjects were history and Latin, and for a month of afternoons, he, Charlie Ross, and Elmer Twyman whittled a model bridge patterned precisely on a description of one of the bridges built by Caesar across the Rhine which they found in the *Commentaries*.

Latin also brought Harry into the company of Bess Wallace. Twice a week he went to the house of Aunt Ella Noland, his father's sister, ostensibly to study this subject with Bess and his Cousins Nellie and Ethel. But Aunt Ella recalled that he did little studying when Bess was present. "From the fifth grade in school, which was taught by her

Aunt Nannie, until I graduated from high school we were in the same classes," Truman said. "If I succeeded in carrying her books to school or back home for her I had a big day." Aunt Ella said that she first became aware of Harry's mooning over Bess when he composed a piano piece. Bess had a special whistle to signal her closest girl friends and they used another whistle in reply. In Harry's composition, Aunt Ella said, the whistles provided the dominant theme.

Miss Tillie Brown, who taught English, enjoyed telling stories about the class of 1901. She remembered Harry as the boy who always squared his shoulders before speaking, while Charlie Ross swayed as he spoke. "Harry wasn't as brilliant," she said, "but a determined and hard worker." Charlie was editor of the *Annual* and Harry worked under him. At the graduation exercises, she kissed gangling Charlie. The rest of the class crowded around her and one boy asked, "Aren't you going to pass that around, Miss Tillie?" She said she would when the others did something worth while. "I hope yet to kiss a President of the United States," she added, certain that the remark was the most preposterous she could make.

4

SHORTLY after Harry Truman received his diploma, his father suffered serious financial reverses. For years John Truman had plunged heavily in the Kansas City grains future market with notable success. By 1901, he was worth more than $30,000, a tidy sum in those days. But now the tips began going awry and losses accumulated.

This was a double tragedy for Martha Truman because she had set her heart on college for Harry. Charlie Ross was soon to enter the University of Missouri to study journalism and Elmer Twyman was planning to follow in his father's footsteps at medical school. But with money tight, college for Harry was out of the question.

At first he made his own effort to gain a college education at no expense to his parents. Miss Maggie Phelps, one of his high school teachers, offered to tutor him and Fielding Houchens, son of a preacher, to prepare them for West Point. But after a short period of study, Harry stopped in at an Army recruiting station in Kansas City and learned he could not pass the West Point physical exam because of his eyes.

Yet even had his eyesight been better, he could not have gone. For by the fall of 1901, John Truman's money was so tied up that Harry had to get a job to help keep Vivian and Mary Jane in school. His search brought him a six-day-a-week job paying $35 a month as time-keeper with a contractor named L. J. Smith, who was building local trackage for the Santa Fe Railroad. It was not a pleasant job because he had to associate with 400 gandy dancers, or railroad hobos. Twice a day he pumped a handcar between Smith's three camps to fill out their time tickets, and he lived with them in dirty tents and ate grubby food. Whatever foul language he had not heard before, he learned now from the gandy dancers—"not by ear but by note."

Every two weeks on Saturday night he had to pay the men in a saloon either in Independence or Sheffield. The gandy dancers drew about $11 for two weeks' work and drank their earnings away before showing up on the job again on Monday. When the contract ended in June of 1902, the foreman made the following comment about the young timekeeper: "Harry's all right. He's all right from his navel out in every direction."

John Truman now needed cash desperately to stave off ruin. Some time before, he had bought forty acres sight unseen in Oregon County in southern Missouri, and one day he and Harry went there by buggy to see if he could sell it. "We crossed a little river by fords, thirteen times in eight miles," Harry Truman said, "found the forty acres running up the side of an Ozark mountain. It wasn't worth a nickel." Upon return-ing home, he took a job paying $7 a week in the mail room of the Kansas City *Star,* a Republican paper his father looked upon with distaste.

Next John Truman sold the Waldo Street house and kept only enough to make a small down payment on a cheap little house at 2108 Park Avenue in Kansas City. Not long afterward he sold the 160-acre farm Solomon Young had left to Martha when he died in 1892. This was a farm that had been in the family more than half a century. Then, suddenly, he had no money left and could not meet his debts. "He lost everything at one fell swoop and went broke," Harry Truman recalled.

John Truman, now fifty-one, never recovered from the shock of this experience. Shortly after his failure he took a dismal job as night watchman with the Missouri Elevator Company in Kansas City and his sons went to work as clerks with the National Bank of Commerce.

At a beginning salary of $35 a month, Harry worked in the "zoo," or caged section in the bank's basement, which served as a clearing-house for checks drawn on country banks. All day long he made nota-tions in longhand and he found the job dull. "I don't have enough responsibility," he complained to a fellow employee. "I don't have anything to decide." He was ambitious to get ahead but was stifled by the bank's vice-president, who believed in the *status quo*. "He was an artist at it," Truman said. "He would always remember a trivial mistake when a clerk asked for a raise." In 1904, he quit and went to the Union National Bank as a bookkeeper at $60 a month.

Harry Truman was on his own for the first time in his life that year when his father traded the Kansas City house for a down payment on an 80-acre farm near the town of Clinton and moved there with his wife. At first Harry lived with his father's sister, Aunt Emma Colgan. Then he moved to Mrs. Trow's boardinghouse where one of his fellow roomers was Arthur Eisenhower, a bank clerk who hailed from Abilene, Kansas. "Harry and I only had a dollar a week left over for riotous living," the older brother of Dwight D. Eisenhower recalled.

But Harry made that dollar go a long way. He played the piano at evening songfests for the young people in the house, and he rode into the country on wagon picnics with the other young men and girls. He paid Mrs. Trow $5 a week for a room and two meals a day. Lunch cost him ten cents and he ate it in the dark at a nickel movie. On Saturday afternoons he worked as an usher at the Grand Theater at Seventh and Walnut Streets where he had a free view of such vaudeville headliners as Weber and Fields, Lillian Russell, the Floradora Girls, Eva Tanguay and the Four Cohans. He also treated himself to a peanut-gallery seat at the old convention hall during the classical concert series and was a devotee of Josef Lhévinne, the pianist.

Anything could happen in Kansas City. When Teddy Roosevelt came to town in 1904, Harry ran from the bank to Tenth and Main Streets to stare at this awesome phenomenon who was President of the United States. "I was disappointed to find that he was no giant, but a little man in a long Prince Albert coat to make him look taller."

It was also in Kansas City that he began his military career. When Battery B of the Missouri National Guard was organized on Flag Day in 1905, he became a charter member of this 60-man outfit and served two three-year hitches. Battery B met once a week at the armory where each man paid a quarter for the privilege of drilling. For outdoor training on weekends, the battery rented horses from a local moving firm, and for their summer encampments the men went to Cape Girardeau. Private Truman served as No. 2 man on the 3-inch light gun, learned to handle Army horses and gained a smattering of the art of fencing and jujitsu. He was especially proud of his blue dress

31

uniform. However, the first and only time he wore it on a visit to his grandmother at Grandview she ordered him out of the house. "This is the first blue uniform to enter this house since the War Between the States" she scolded him. "Don't you ever come here wearing it again, Harry."

In the meantime John Truman had failed again. This time his ruin was brought on by a flood that washed away the entire corn crop on his Clinton farm. In October of 1905, therefore, he and Martha Truman moved back again to the farm of her widowed mother at Grandview, where he remained until his death nine years later.

At twenty-two, Harry Truman was enjoying life in Kansas City when his father asked him to quit his bank job and help manage the Young farm. Uncle Harrison, who was still a bachelor, wanted to leave the farm for the easier life in the city, and the elder Truman could not handle the acreage alone. Since he never disobeyed his parents, Harry returned to Grandview in the summer of 1906, and left the gay town behind.

If he was disappointed to leave Kansas City, he never admitted it. For more than ten years he followed the routine of climbing out of bed at 4:30 A.M. in summer and at 6:30 in winter. There were long days, he recalled, in which he "plowed, sowed, reaped, milked cows, fed hogs, doctored horses, baled hay and did everything there was to do on a 600-acre farm." Vivian had returned to the farm, too, but he went back to the bank the next year and, after returning again to the farm for a short stay, moved away in 1911 when he married.

Martha Truman often said, "It was on the farm that Harry got his common sense. He didn't get it in town." She also claimed he could "plant the straightest row of corn in the whole county." "I had to," he said. "If I didn't my father would force me to hear about it for a whole year afterward."

The original spacious colonial house built by Sol Young had gone up in flames in 1893, due to the carelessness of a servant girl. Grandma Young had put up a small temporary residence and it was here that the Trumans lived. Harry planned almost monthly to rebuild the big place, but he never found the time or money to do so.

Solomon Young's farm was extremely fertile, but Harry increased its productivity by crop rotation, soil conservation and weed control. He vaccinated his hogs against cholera and became an expert at sticking cows for clover bloat and at castrating pigs. Many of his neighbors were suspicious of his farming ways, scoffing at his attempt to keep

32

records of actual cost per acre on his various crops. Others questioned his use of labor-saving equipment instead of employing more farm hands. There was also talk in the area that the Young farm was jinxed. This began after a woman came visiting and broke her leg when her horse overturned her buggy. Then one winter day, when John Truman was bridling a mule, the animal yanked a timber loose and broke his leg. In the spring of 1913, Harry was setting fence posts when a calf ran into him and broke his leg, too. Brownie Huber, one of his farm hands, said, "Harry just took it kind of easy and grinned, and kidded the neighbors who came to see him."

Harry Truman had too much energy to restrict himself to farming. In 1908, he became a member of Beltown Masonic Lodge No. 450, and after rising to Junior Warden, he organized Grandview Lodge No. 618 in 1911 and became its Worshipful Master Under Dispensation. In addition, he helped organize the Jackson County Farm Bureau and the first farm club for boys and girls in western Missouri. Until 1911, he continued drilling with Battery B in Kansas City.

With Harry running the farm, John Truman felt at liberty to indulge in local politics. He attached himself to the Pendergast machine which was reaching into rural Jackson County from Kansas City and he supported it against rival Democratic factions. As a reward, he was appointed an elections judge in the Grandview precinct in 1906 and Harry got his start in politics by serving as his clerk. Two years later John Truman went as a county delegate to the Missouri State Democratic Convention at Joplin. By 1910 he was friendly with the Pendergast-backed county judge for the Eastern District of Jackson County who named him as one of thirty-six road overseers. This gave him a sense of political authority, for the road overseer felt out the local political pulse for the machine, collected taxes and bossed a crew that repaired bridges and culverts and dragged the dirt roads.

Life on the Young farm remained on an even keel until 1909. Grandma Young, who was born only a year after President Monroe took office, reached her ninety-first birthday that year. Then, hardly more than a month later, she took ill and died.

Although the Young family almost made a hobby of arguing, all previous disagreements were minor compared with the storm that broke when Grandma Young's will was read. Harry Truman estimated that her farm was then worth about $150,000, or close to $300 an acre, even though it provided an uncertain annual income. The old lady gave her property jointly to Harry's mother and Uncle Harrison and cut off Uncle Will and Aunts Ada, Sally, Laura and Sue with five dollars apiece. Grandma Young's view was that Martha and Harrison, unlike the others, had given a large part of their lives to the farm. Moreover, her husband Sol had helped the others out financially during his lifetime.

The five who were cut off by Grandma Young began legal action that lasted a decade. In the end, Martha settled with them out of court by assuming a series of onerous mortgages to pay them cash in exchange for quitclaims. "The lawyers got most of it," Vivian said bitterly. "All we got was debts."

There was even worse trouble during this period. As a rule, road overseers did little work. But John Truman was different. One summer day in 1914, while inspecting a road, he found a boulder barring traffic. Foolishly, he removed the huge rock himself instead of delegating the job to his crew. That night he suffered agonizing stomach pains and had difficulty breathing, but he refused to see a doctor. Days passed while he developed an intestinal block and finally Harry took him to a Kansas City hospital where he underwent an operation. Afterward, he returned home to convalesce. "Harry had just begun to stock the farm with Black Angus cattle," said Mary Jane, "but he had to sell them to pay the doctor bills and other expenses."

John Truman seemed on the mend that November, though Harry remained suspicious of his condition. He recalled a fateful evening: "I had been sitting with him and watching a long time. I fell asleep for a short time and when I woke up he was dead."

His father's death made Harry the man of the house at thirty. Not only did he run the 600-acre farm but he also leased and operated another 300-acre farm owned by his Uncle Harrison.

Now that his father was dead, he stepped up his own political activities. For sentimental reasons, Judge Robert Mize of the Eastern District of Jackson County gave him his father's old post as road overseer of Washington Township. When Harry proposed an ambitious road-overhaul program, however, he provoked an argument and lost the job. Then, in 1915, Congressman William P. Borland named him postmaster of Grandview. This job paid $50 a month, which Harry turned over in its entirety to Ella Hall, his assistant.

By now Harry Truman had developed an appetite to get behind the façade of politics and take part in the activities of the machine. According to Tom Evans, who became his closest friend in later life: "Harry began coming to the Thursday night meetings of the Kansas

City Tenth Ward Democratic Club about 1914. Mike Pendergast was the boss of the Tenth Ward Goats and he was the mild Pendergast compared to his brothers Tom and Jim. During the meetings when we talked about the elections and our political problems, we drank Irish beer and afterward we drifted over to the nearest saloon for more. I first noticed Harry because he stood out from us roughnecks and he always left right after the meeting. We were all there for fun, but Harry seemed to be different. If anyone there had been asked then if this quiet fellow had a political future, it would have got a big horse laugh."

5

IN the years between Harry Truman's graduation from high school and his return to the farm, a tragedy occurred in Bess Wallace's life. People in Independence liked her father, David W. Wallace, a tall, good-looking man who sported long sideburns and a drooping mustache. He was easygoing and popular. When he was only thirty-one, he was already the Eminent Commander of the Knights Templar of Missouri. Bess's mother, Madge Gates Wallace, was known for her royal bearing and, in fact, held the reputation as "the queenliest woman Independence ever produced." No one ever saw her in a house dress and few in town could bear up under her withering glance and frosty manner.

Dave Wallace's trouble was that he could not provide adequately for Madge and their four children. For a while, he worked as the deputy county recorder in charge of issuing marriage licenses. Later he was employed by the Customs Office in Kansas City. But with nagging debts piling up, he turned for solace to alcohol. Then one day in 1903, when he was forty-three, he sat in the bathtub and killed himself with a pistol.

After her father's death, Bess had moved with her family to her grandparents' large old-fashioned house at 219 North Delaware. George Gates, her grandfather, was the pillar of the local social set and the miller of Queen of the Pantry flour, a well-known product throughout the Midwest. While Harry toiled as a bank clerk, Gates sent Bess to the Barstow School for Girls, a finishing school in Kansas City. Here in voluminous blue-serge bloomers and white middy blouse she won the shot-put contest in the school's annual field day. She was also the star forward who led the Barstow basketball team to a 22–10 victory over the Independence girls' team.

She attended Barstow for two years, after which her doting grandfather bought her a handsome black horse and two greyhounds. When he purchased the first Studebaker in town, he taught her to drive it. Her life was one of ease except for the fact that her widowed mother leaned heavily on her for companionship, a relationship that was to remain until Madge Wallace's death in December, 1952.

Bess Wallace had not considered Harry Truman as her beau in high school. Nor had she seen him in the intervening years. But one evening after a day of farming, he rode horseback into Independence and paid a call on his father's sister, Aunt Ella Noland, who lived across the street from the Gates house on North Delaware. That very morning Bess's mother had sent a cake to the Nolands. After Harry helped finish it, Aunt Ella asked her daughter Nellie to return the cake plate to Mrs. Wallace. Upon hearing the name, Harry seized the plate from Nellie's hand and said he would be right back.

Two hours later, when he strolled into Aunt Ella's house, he announced with a broad grin, "Well, I saw her." This was the beginning of his courtship.

When Harry began seeing Bess, he was aware that her mother did not approve of him. As one of his friends put it: "Harry was about the most unpromising prospect for a husband we had around here then." He had no money, no college education, and he lacked a future. It was preposterous to Madge Wallace that her daughter would marry a dirt farmer, and even worse, one who did not even own the farm he worked.

Nor was there any indication that Bess took him seriously during the first five years or so after he began courting her. Yet even though they were opposites in many ways, she found his company enjoyable. She was the town's best woman tennis player and skater, and liked to dance, fish, play the current card game called High Fives, and go to ball games. All these activities bored him. He liked to talk about history and battles, play the piano, go on picnics, and attend vaudeville shows and concerts. He prided himself on his unwillingness to learn how to dance. One thing they had in common was that they both loved to tease and ribbed each other constantly.

The trip from the Grandview farm to Independence was a long one. Sometimes Harry traveled the twenty miles by horseback. On other occasions he went by train or buggy. He also started a voluminous correspondence with Bess. Decades later, their daughter Margaret related how her father walked into the living room after he had left the White House and found Bess burning papers on the hearth. When he asked what she was doing, she replied, "I'm burning your letters to me."

"Bess!" he told her. "You oughtn't to do that."

"Why not? I've read them several times."

"But think of history!" he protested.

"I *have,*" said Bess.

In 1913, Harry tried to ease his travel problem and at the same time impress old Mr. and Mrs. Gates and Madge Wallace by purchasing a secondhand Stafford for $600. When new, this four-door touring car sold at a list price of about $2,500. Harry's used Stafford could still do sixty miles an hour, and before long, Bess's brothers George and Frank brought their girl friends along when Harry and Bess went on picnics. Some of Harry's friends credited his Stafford with helping to make him slightly more acceptable at 219 North Delaware Street.

After his father died, Harry was determined to make himself financially independent so that George Gates and Madge Wallace would take him seriously. Early in 1915 he met Jerry Culbertson, a smooth-talking, extroverted man who had been prosecuting attorney of Cass County and had promoted several gold mines, none of which ever paid off. Now Culbertson was promoting a lead and zinc mine at Commerce, Oklahoma, just below the border from Missouri. When he claimed that the mine, supposedly played out, contained rich veins that had been overlooked, Harry put up $2,000, as did Tom Hughes, one of his neighbors.

With visions of wealth, Harry commuted between the mine and the farm. He found Commerce thriving because of the growing demand for lead and zinc following the outbreak of the European War in 1914. Enormous piles of slag and waste rock surrounded the town and on its outskirts was the famous, but played out, Turkey Fat Mine. For all his months of effort, however, he found no trace of metal. "I undertook to run it along with a red-haired hoisting engineer by the name of Bill Throop," he said. "But we couldn't make our mine pay." After they gave up, Throop asked him to raise another $2,500 to purchase a drilling machine "and go up north of Picher, Oklahoma, and prospect the land up there for lead and zinc." But Harry had lost his $2,000 and could not raise an additional $2,500. "If I'd done it we'd be rolling in wealth," he said.

The following year his Uncle Harrison died and left his own farm as well as his half-interest in the Grandview farm to Martha Truman, Harry, Vivian and Mary Jane. Theoretically, Harry was a fairly well-to-do property owner now, but he still lacked cash. Despite the mine fiasco, Jerry Culbertson came around shortly afterward with the proposition that Harry go into the oil business with him and an old oilman named David Morgan. Culbertson's promotional skills were to be his contribution in exchange for a third of the profits; Morgan was to contribute 1,500 acres of land he owned in eastern Oklahoma; and Harry was to put up $5,000. In order to raise this sum, Harry obtained a loan in the form of five notes, each for $1,000 and all due in ten months. His shaky financial state was reflected in the wording of the company contract, where his partners required that the "notes shall also be signed by Martha E. Truman, the mother of said Harry S. Truman."

As a former bank clerk with some understanding of financial matters, Harry became treasurer of Morgan & Company. Morgan, who served as president, spent his time in the field checking and leasing oil properties and handling the drilling of test wells. The firm was like dozens of other small combines that had suddenly become aware of the vast potential of oil for the growing automobile industry. All hoped that one of their test wells would uncover an enormous underground field and bring in millions of dollars. Like the others, Morgan & Company was distinctly in the great American tradition of gambling for high stakes against enormous odds.

As treasurer, Truman kept track of the money and assisted Morgan at meetings with lease owners, salesmen, scouts and drillers. Dave Morgan once described his enthusiasm: "Harry was greatly interested in the oil-development business. He liked the element of chance (he called it Hazard)." Truman soon discovered that there was plenty of hazard in the business. Next door to a Standard Oil well in Louisiana

39

that produced a thousand barrels a day, Morgan's test well drew "some of the finest salt water in the entire area." In addition to owning Morgan's 1,500 acres in eastern Oklahoma, the company raised $200,000 and bought leases covering 10,000 acres in Texas and 20,000 acres in Kansas. Although the company earned a profit on its manipulation of leases, its own test wells, Truman said, "unfortunately proved to be dry holes."

After a few months, Culbertson, who was secretary, sold out his interest at a profit to an Oklahoma oilman and at the beginning of April, 1917, the company was reorganized as a common-law trust under the name Morgan Oil and Refining Company. In a splashy ad in the Kansas City *Star* on April 1, the company offered to sell to the public 10,000 shares of common stock at $25 a share. The ad referred to Truman as a "native of Jackson County, Missouri; widely known in Kansas City."

Time was running out on Truman now. World War I was just a week away and soon he would be heading for an Army camp. "At the time the war came," he said, "we had a well down nine hundred feet on a three-hundred-and-twenty-acre lease at Eureka, Kansas." For years afterward, the mention of this well in the northwest corner of Greenwood County made him sad. It was the one-in-a-million gamble that would have brought him great wealth.

Morgan remembered that "due to World War emergencies, loss of operating personnel and with Harry Truman enlisted and training at Fort Sill, Oklahoma," he decided to "sell and dispose of the Morris No. 1 well and equipment" as well as the acreage leased by his company. Truman's interpretation was different: "My partners got into a fuss and let that lease go to pot. Another company took it over and drilled a well on it and there was never a dry hole found on that three hundred and twenty acres. It was the famous Teeter Pool." Morgan estimated that if he had only continued drilling another nine hundred feet, he would have hit the jackpot. Instead, this fortune was reserved for the Empire Company, which later became the Cities Service Oil Company. Three decades later, Truman wrote to Morgan: "Maybe I wouldn't be Pres if we'd hit."

6

So far as its effect on Harry Truman was concerned, World War I released the genie from the bottle. Just after the United States declared war on Germany on April 6, 1917, Truman ran into some of his old National Guard buddies in Kansas City. Several had been sent to the Mexican border in 1916 under General James J. "Black Jack" Pershing to chase Pancho Villa, and they had many rowdy stories to tell of their experiences. It was like old-home week to Truman, even though he had quit the National Guard in 1911. But there was more to come. With World War I on, Battery B of Kansas City, his old outfit, and Battery C of Independence were to be expanded into a six-battery force called the 2nd Missouri Field Artillery.

When Major John L. Miles of Battery C asked Truman to join up and help recruit enough men to activate the 2nd, he was on a spot. He liked the camaraderie of the old bunch and he had a strong patriotic urge. But his mother's mortgages on the Grandview farm now totaled $25,000 because she was still settling with her relatives in exchange for quitclaims on the property. In addition, she had taken out a mortgage on her brother Harrison's farm to give Harry the cash he needed in the oil business. In exchange, he had given her a free deed eliminating him from any share in his uncle's farm. Then there was the oil company in which he was heavily involved as treasurer. Most important of all was his desire to establish himself financially and marry Bess Wallace.

After much thought, he finally decided to join Miles and his old buddies. When he went to the farm and broke the news, Truman said, "It was quite a blow to my mother and sister." Mary Jane was now twenty-eight and he arranged for her to run the farm with the help of farm hands.

The effect on Bess was immediate. She wanted to get married without delay, but he insisted that they wait until after the war. In case he came home a cripple, he told her, he did not want her tied down. They could, however, consider themselves engaged. Later, when Truman's mother was asked why the courtship had gone on so long, she said, "Maybe she wouldn't have him until then."

Recruiting for the 2nd Missouri Field Artillery went on at a hectic pace. The old convention hall in Kansas City was soon filled with drilling artillerymen. Not only did Truman play an aggressive role in rounding up would-be soldiers for the 2nd, but he also helped raise a battery for the St. Louis National Guard regiment. Enthusiasm and patriotism engulfed Kansas City, and Truman belonged—as he had never belonged before.

On August 5, 1917, the 2nd Field Artillery was sworn into the regular Army in a body and became the 129th Field Artillery of the 35th Division. Truman hoped that he might become a section sergeant, but the men of Battery F did more than that for him. In those days the enlisted men elected their officers. When the tally was recorded, he found himself a first lieutenant. "I remember the red roadster best about the Truman of 1917," said Eddie Jacobson, one of the boys of Battery F. "He dashed about town wearing his first lieutenant's uniform." The lieutenant liked to cock his head and grin. He could also spout Army lingo. Once when he held a dance to raise money for the officers' mess, he told Jacobson and another assistant, "I know two candidates for the guardhouse if the show doesn't earn a lot of money for the boys."

Toward the end of September, the 129th left Kansas City in a heavy downpour for Camp Doniphan located at Fort Sill, Oklahoma. Hardly had the boys unloaded their gear when Truman was notified that he had been named regimental canteen officer with Eddie Jacobson as his assistant. This was in addition to taking his turn as officer of the day, equitation officer and firing-instruction officer for Battery F.

Truman knew nothing about merchandising, but fortunately Jacobson had worked as a salesman and understood something about running a store or canteen. First they collected two dollars from each man in the 129th. Then with the $2,200, they went on a shopping spree in Oklahoma City. Next they opened a barber and tailor shop and stocked their store with cigarettes, pens, writing paper and other items which were not government issue. They recruited a clerk from each battery and company, and took the precaution to prevent stealing by sewing up each man's pockets.

"Harry Truman was a sharp one in a deal," said Captain Harry Jobes of the 129th. "He had some sweaters that weren't moving. One day he passed word around giving us to understand he was doing us all a special personal favor with an unusual bargain in sweaters at six dollars each. We mobbed the canteen like women at a piece-goods sale. Before the day was out, Lieutenant Truman had unloaded his entire stock of sweaters. Later when I audited the books, I found those sweaters had cost him only three dollars each, for a neat 100 per cent profit."

Truman's canteen was unique. All other canteens at Fort Sill showed heavy losses, but his did so well that after only six months he paid back the $2,200 investment and showed a profit of $15,000, or a dividend of 666 per cent.

His life at Camp Doniphan was bound with that of Brigadier General Lucien G. Berry, a martinet of the old Army school. When Truman's captain sent Berry a glowing recommendation to promote him to captain, it came back with the notation, "There isn't anybody that good." When Berry finally did examine him for promotion in February, he made Truman wait outdoors an hour with the temperature at −10°. Then Berry pulled on his handlebar mustache and bellowed, "It will be a disaster to the country to let you command men!"

On another occasion, Berry had found some waste paper on the floor of the canteen and was in the midst of roasting Truman at officers' call when the sound of loud, laughing voices came from outdoors. Then through the doorway strolled four officers, who froze at sight of Berry.

"What is your name, mister?" Berry screamed at the biggest officer.

"Lieutenant Vaughan, sir. Harry Vaughan."

43

"How long have you been an officer?" Berry bellowed.

"Three days, sir."

Vaughan recalled that Berry then proceeded to give him unshirted hell for several minutes. "Meanwhile Harry Truman stepped back into the ranks and made himself thin. And when the meeting was over, he joined me as we were leaving. 'Thanks a lot, mister,' he told me. 'You got me off the hook.' " This was the beginning of an important friendship for both men.

Early in March, 1918, Truman received orders to leave Camp Doniphan in a group of 10 officers and 100 men for special artillery training in France. The rest of the 129th Field Artillery was to leave later and he would rejoin his outfit at the completion of his training. On his way east he convinced a railroad switchman at Rosedale, Kansas, to let him use the company telephone to call Bess. "If she doesn't break the engagement at four o'clock in the morning, she really loves you," the switchman teased him. Once he reached the East Coast, he spent the better part of a 24-hour leave in New York buying three extra pairs of glasses. The optometrist refused any payment on the ground that Truman was doing his bit for his country. Then on March 30, he was one of 7,000 men who crowded aboard the *George Washington* for the trip to France.

There was an imminence to American military activities in France that spring of 1918. The German objective was to end the war before General Pershing could move the 2,000,000 doughboys of his American Expeditionary Force against the German Army.

Truman was one of the many undergoing training while the Germans prepared their drive. After landing at Brest on April 13, he boarded a train for the 2nd Corps Field Artillery School at Montigne-sur-Aube. Back in the States his training as a field artilleryman had been on a 3.2 gun, but at the 2nd Corps School the guns were French .75s mounted on high wooden wheels. His teacher was Dick "By God" Burleson, a hard-bitten character who was not afraid of General Pershing himself because he was the nephew of President Wilson's Postmaster General. Burleson not only punctured every sentence with a few "By God's," but he also favored Truman with the most profane language heard in the A.E.F. After World War II, Truman remembered this virtuoso display and sent "By God" Burleson "to Russia with Ed Pauley and he outcussed them all."

After five weeks under Burleson, Truman rejoined the 129th Field Artillery which had meanwhile arrived in France. He had read in *The*

New York Times that he had been promoted to captain on April 23 and he added another bar to his shoulder insignia. Official word of his promotion did not reach him until October, however, and when he requested retroactive pay his claim was rejected on the ground that he had not "accepted" his commission earlier. Nevertheless, as a captain he was named adjutant of the 129th's Second Battalion and accompanied the outfit to Angers in Brittany for further training at Camp Coetquidan, which he knew from boyhood reading as an old Napoleonic artillery base.

Two important events occurred at Camp Coetquidan. It was here that he met John W. Snyder, a captain in the 57th Field Artillery of the 32nd "Red Arrow" Division. Each was too busy then to spend much time with the other. Yet this initial meeting set a basis for the close personal friendship that was to develop after the war.

The second important event took place on July 11. Throughout the 129th, Battery D of the Second Battalion had a reputation as a wild, rowdy outfit, untamed and unmanageable. Most of the men in Battery D came from the tough neighborhood around Rockhurst College, a Jesuit school in Kansas City, and were "fighting Irish." "In those days," said one of Battery D's sergeants, "we'd land somewhere, get into a fight and then we'd go to Mass." They drank their whisky straight and played infantile pranks on officers and other enlisted men.

Battery D had already run through three commanding officers when Colonel Karl Klemm, in charge of the 129th, asked Truman to take charge. One of its former officers had been thrown out of the Army because of his failure to control the men; another had suffered a breakdown. When Truman took over Battery D at six-thirty A.M. on July 11, he said, "I was the most thoroughly scared individual in that camp. Never on the front or anywhere else have I been so nervous."

That first day the men staged a fake stampede of their horses. Then after taps, they got into a fight among themselves, broke cots and chairs and sent four men to the regimental infirmary. In the morning, following these escapades, Truman called in his noncommissioned officers. "Men," he told the sergeants and corporals, "I know you've been making trouble for your previous commanders. From now on, you're going to be responsible for maintaining discipline in your squads and sections. And if there are any of you who can't, speak up right now and I'll bust you back right now."

Truman was still trying to browbeat his way to control of Battery D, or "Dizzy" D, as it was commonly called, when the Germans

45

started a major attack in the Champagne-Marne area on Bastille Day, July 14, 1918, in an attempt to crash into Paris. This drive was blunted and, in mid-August, the 129th Field Artillery started toward the front. A few days later Captain Truman had his men in position high in the Vosges Mountains on Mount Herrenberg in Alsace, reputedly one of the quietest sectors of the front.

On the night of September 6, unfortunately for those who considered this a dead sector, Truman got orders to fire a gas shell barrage at the enemy. What followed became known as "The Battle of Who Run."

About a half hour after his guns fired 500 rounds at the German lines, Truman climbed on his horse only to have it fall into a shell hole and roll over on him. By the time he scampered unhurt to his feet, the Germans had begun to lay down a murderous barrage on the American lines. Shells rained close to Dizzy D's position and a sergeant yelled, "Run, boys, they got a bracket on us!" It was hard to believe that this brawling gang of fighting Irish would go to pieces under fire, but the men panicked and all except five ran for their lives into the forest. "I got up and called them everything I knew," said Truman. The curses that poured out contained some of the vilest four-letter words heard on the Western Front. Said Father Curtis Tiernan, the regiment's Catholic chaplain, who was on the scene, "It took the skin off the ears of those boys." The effect was amazing, Padre Tiernan recalled with pleasure. "It turned those boys right around."

The Battle of Who Run did much to establish Truman as boss of Battery D. In a forgiving mood, he refused to take the advice of Colonel Klemm to court-martial the offending sergeant. Instead, he "busted" him and sent him to another battery.

Shortly after Who Run, the 129th moved north to the St. Mihiel front. This was the first time that an army composed entirely of American divisions faced the Germans. Since 1914, the Germans had occupied a triangular-shaped salient twenty-five miles long and fifteen miles deep into French-held territory. Fierce action against the head of the triangle began on September 12. Hero of the eight-day battle was Brigadier General Douglas MacArthur of the 42nd "Rainbow" Division, who might have ended the war at this time had General Pershing permitted him to assault Metz. During this struggle, Truman's men and the rest of the 35th Division were in reserve of the First Army. Afterward his outfit moved on by train to the Meuse-

Argonne sector, where more than 1,000,000 Americans of 27 divisions were attempting to smash the Germans' last-ditch defenses at the Hindenburg Line.

Drawing close to the Meuse-Argonne sector, the train hauling Battery D pulled into a siding and Truman jumped off to make unloading arrangements. At one end of the station, he spied two dead horses. As he stared, a lieutenant colonel approached him and introduced himself as Bennett Clark, the son of House Speaker Champ Clark.

"Captain," Clark yelled when Truman continued to stare at the dead horses, "the Huns are putting interdictory fire here every hour on the hour. You ought to unload and get your men under cover as soon as you can. Here are your orders and maps." Quickly, he handed them to Truman and added, "I don't want you to suffer the fate of those poor horses."

Truman glanced at his watch and saw that he had only forty minutes before the Germans began firing again. Frantically, his men unhitched their gear and teams of horses hauled away their big guns. Battery D was under cover by the time the expected German shelling was to start.

But no shells exploded. Finally, after a long interval, Truman walked back to the station and found Clark standing there, grinning. "The joke's on you, Captain," Clark roared. "The Germans haven't fired here at all." When Truman inquired about the dead horses, Clark told him, "Oh, those? The vet had to shoot them. They had glanders." This was Truman's introduction to the man who would help provide his major political opposition when he ran for the United States Senate in 1934.

The large American force deployed through the Argonne Forest where the major drive got underway shortly after midnight on September 26. Truman had ordered his men to eat breakfast before the fighting began and afterward Father Tiernan sat on a tree stump and heard confession from the Irish lads of Dizzy D. Then, said Truman, "I stood behind my battery and fired three thousand rounds of .75 shells from four A.M. to eight A.M. and then went forward for more trouble than I was ever in before."

Dizzy D made up for the Battle of Who Run with its fighting in this sector. Truman, too, added to his reputation among his men with his many narrow escapes. One night he slept at the edge of a forest next to his battery's position. He woke especially early the next morning, and this was fortunate, for hardly had he walked away when a German barrage landed directly on the spot. On another occasion, a French 155 battery to the rear of his own fired shells that just cleared the top of his head. Furious, he hurried to the rear and blistered the ears of the French captain in language as fierce as he had used to his own men at the Battle of Who Run. Still another time, on the night of September 28, he had placed his battery in a position behind the infantry on the road between Chépy and Varennes. In directing the firing of the barrage, he rode his horse past low-hanging branches which swept his glasses from his face. Almost panicky at being unable to see at such a critical time, he turned about in desperation. Moonlight shone on the glasses sitting on the horse's back just behind the saddle.

As a rule, Truman himself reconnoitered for his outfit. Once, when he was far ahead of his troops, German machine-gun fire pinned him down in a ditch for several hours. His men had given him up for dead when he reappeared to lead them across the barbed-wire field of no-man's-land. It was his custom during the artillery shelling to advance alone toward the German lines. Here, with powerful field glasses, he spotted the enemy's positions, then telephoned the information to his gun crews to help them correct their fire. On one occasion, when shells lobbed all about him, a worried infantry sergeant crept up beside him. He let Truman know that his support had been forced back a few hundred yards and that he would be safer if he did not make a target of himself and returned, too. "I did," said Truman.

Dizzy D became heroes one night when Truman was up front transmitting firing data by field telephone to his gunners in an apple orchard. He was under strict orders to fire at German batteries facing the 35th Division. While scanning the zone through field glasses, however, he spied a large German force moving around the flank of the 35th and approaching the 28th Division next to it. He had no time to report this situation to headquarters, for the 28th, unaware of the danger, would soon be overrun by the Germans. Nor was there time to request permission to fire outside of his assigned sector. He telephoned new orders to his own crews to swing their guns around and fire outside their sector. The result was that one German battery was destroyed and two others were knocked out of commission. Despite his quick action, which saved the 28th Division, Colonel Klemm was furious at his violation of orders and threatened him with court-martial. But Truman refused to be intimidated and said he would do the same thing again in the same situation. Nothing came of Klemm's threat.

During this period of fighting, the weather was bad, the air foul with gunsmoke, and the men, unshaven, tired and dirty. Occasionally Lieutenant Harry Vaughan, who commanded Battery D of the 130th Field Artillery, ran into Truman at the front. What impressed him most about Truman, he said, was that "dirt and cooties didn't seem to stick to him the way they did to the rest of us. Harry Truman hadn't had his clothes off his back for two weeks and yet he was immaculate. Moreover, he was clean-shaven. He must have shaved with coffee because we didn't have plain hot water."

On October 3, the 129th Field Artillery moved slightly north where it fell into position facing Verdun in the Sommedieu sector. The A.E.F.'s new objective was to capture the city of Sedan, where the French had suffered their most ignominious defeat in the War of 1870. If Sedan fell, the entire Hindenburg line was bound to collapse. Truman's men were sent hedge-hopping from one front line to another throughout that month. On October 27 the French edition of the New York *Herald* was passed out to the men while German 150 mm. shells exploded all about Dizzy D. The paper's headline announced that an armistice was on. "Captain," a sergeant called to Truman as a shell burst, "those goddamned Germans haven't seen this paper."

By the end of the first week in November, 1918, Truman's men were firing barrages at Metz. With Sedan having fallen on the sixth, the German Army disintegrated. It was not until five o'clock on the morning of November 11, however, that the regimental operations officer called Truman and told him there would be a cease-fire at eleven A.M. Under orders, he continued firing until 10:45 when Dizzy D lobbed a final round at a small village near Verdun. Finally, at the hour of eleven, came the silence of peace. "It was so quiet it made your head ache," said Truman.

Dizzy D began a celebration that lasted all night. French soldiers nearby drank themselves into peace on endless bottles of wine and trooped steadily through Truman's pup tent. *"Vive President Wilson! Vive le capitaine d'artillerie américaine!"* they roared, saluting each time they lurched past his cot.

With the coming of peace, Truman said, "we spent our evenings playing poker and wishing we were home." Roger Sermon, of Independence, Truman's fellow captain in the 129th, said, "To keep from going crazy we had an almost continuous poker game." Truman was a fairly constant player in these marathon sessions and he later admitted, "I learned to play poker in France—but it was a costly education."

Aside from the long wait to go home, postwar military life was good. Truman moved with his men from the mud of the front to Courcemont, a village near Le Mans, southwest of Paris. Here he lived with other officers at a handsome château once owned by Lillian Russell. It came complete with floating white swans and a mirrorlike lake. At the beginning of 1919, when President Wilson came to Paris for the Peace Conference, Captain Truman went to see him as he rode down the boulevard. He attended the opera to hear *Carmen* and *Manon* and saw the Folies Bergère, where he professed to be disgusted. He also went to Nice and Monte Carlo.

At the beginning of February, the 129th was still in France playing marathon poker. In a spirit of brotherly feeling, medals were distributed in rather generous fashion among the troops. Colonel Klemm refused to give Truman any on the ground that no man was going to get a medal for what he was supposed to do. Nevertheless, Truman was singled out by the regiment's historian who wrote: "How many of the men of the infantry, digging in on the open hillsides overhanging Charpentry and Baulny, owe their lives to the alertness, initiative and efficiency of Captain Truman and to the quick responsiveness and trained efficiency of his men at the guns!"

Diversion came on February 17 when General Pershing and the young Prince of Wales, who was later to be Edward VIII and then the Duke of Windsor, reviewed the regiment at Courcemont. It rained relentlessly that day and, standing in the downpour close to the prince, one of Dizzy D's band of Irishmen yelled out: "Hey, Captain Truman! What did the little S.O.B. say about freeing Ireland?"

It was not until April 9 that the 129th boarded the German passenger liner *Zeppelin* at Brest for the voyage back to civilian life. The trip across the Atlantic was so rough that before the *Zeppelin* docked at New York on Easter Sunday, April 20, Truman lost fifteen pounds from the rolling and tipping of the ship. Nevertheless, the return voyage produced one happy memento. Dizzy D played craps endlessly and set aside a kitty to buy Captain Harry, as the men referred to him, an engraved silver loving cup.

As his train rattled across the continent toward Missouri, Harry

Truman had time to consider what his war service had meant to him. He had been gone from the United States barely a year, yet it seemed like a decade. He had left the farmer behind and was returning with a wealth of experience and dozens of friends. "I've always been sorry I did not get a university education in the regular way," he said later. "But I got it in the Army the hard way—and it stuck."

7

DURING World War II, when Harry Truman was a United States Senator, he often got letters from farmers who wanted his help to obtain deferrals from the military draft for their sons. Truman would not intervene for them on the ground that he himself had sought no favors in World War I and had suffered serious consequences as a result. A typical reply to these requests reads: "I operated a 600-acre farm myself in the last war and had to leave it to go to France. When I came back it was in pretty bad shape." Actually, his war service was not without beneficial effects. It brought him an escape from a lifetime as a farmer; it won him a bride and gave him a firm basis for his political career. The war also taught him that he could win the respect of other men and that he was a leader.

Truman was discharged from the service with the rank of major at Camp Funston, Kansas, on May 6, 1919. Two days later he celebrated his thirty-fifth birthday at the Grandview farm. Beyond his decision not to return to farming, he had no idea how he would earn his livelihood. Nothing mattered at this time, however, except marrying Bess Wallace.

Although Bess's mother still had some misgivings, the wedding took place on June 28, 1919, at the small, red-brick Trinity Episcopal Church in Independence. Truman's best man was Ted Marks, a native of England who had served in the 129th as a captain of Battery C and was now a Kansas City tailor. In later years, when Marks was asked why Truman picked him among all his friends to be his best man, he replied somewhat jocularly, "The reason was that he could get a suit of clothes on credit from me."

After the wedding a reception was held on the lawn of the Gates house. Then Martha Truman, who had had her boy with her for thirty-five years, kissed him good-by and went home to the Grandview farm without him. Following the reception, the newly married couple left on a short honeymoon trip to Chicago and Detroit.

When they returned to Independence, they did not rent or buy a house of their own. Instead they moved into the Gates house at 219 North Delaware with Bess's mother, Madge Wallace, and her grandmother, Elizabeth Emery Gates. (Grandfather George Gates had passed away while Truman was overseas.) Madge Wallace, the *grande-dame* who was dubious about Truman as a son-in-law, nevertheless preferred that he live with her rather than lose Bess altogether.

The Gates house was certainly a more elegant place than Truman could afford. Even though it was built during the 1860's, the house was in excellent condition and contained fourteen large rooms with high ceilings. There were seven bedrooms—six upstairs and one on the ground floor—three marble-manteled fireplaces, a large old-fashioned parlor, a music room, a dining room capable of accommodating thirty persons, and a long porch that stretched across the rear of the house where Sunday supper was customarily eaten. The walls were covered with damask wallpaper, some of the windows had colored glass borders, and most of the furniture was a collection of antiques, including dainty chairs with petit-point seats. This was hardly the setting for a former dirt farmer and soldier, but Truman never expressed a complaint.

His greatest concern at this time was how he would support himself and Bess. His old oil company was still in existence, though it was neither making nor losing money. After he and Dave Morgan, his partner, had a talk, the two agreed to dissolve the firm.

One morning in July, shortly after he moved into the Gates house, Truman went to Kansas City. By chance he ran into Eddie Jacobson, who had helped him manage the regimental canteen at Camp Doniphan. "Maybe we ought to go into business together, and have a partnership again," Truman remembered saying while they reminisced about their canteen and its huge success.

His words spurred them into action. Eddie did not want to return to his old job of selling shirts on the road. Why didn't they set up a sort of civilian canteen—like a men's furnishings store? Eddie knew his merchandise and Truman could no doubt become a crackerjack salesman. Besides, he could handle the books.

It sounded like an excellent idea to Truman. His oil bubble had collapsed, though without loss; he would never take Bess to live on a farm; and he could not picture himself working for someone else. "All right, you bald-headed so-and-so," he told Eddie fondly.

Eddie had some savings which he was willing to put into the business. To raise his share, Truman arranged to sell the stock and equipment on the Young farm for $20,000, giving his mother, sister and brother a quitclaim on his quarter share of the farm. He used $5,000 to buy a Kansas City flat, which he rented out, and invested the remaining $15,000 in his partnership with Jacobson.

They signed a five-year lease on a store on the ground floor of the old Baltimore Hotel at 104 West Twelfth Street in downtown Kansas City across the street from the Muehlebach Hotel. Times were good and they expected little difficulty in moving the $35,000 worth of men's furnishings that filled cabinets, drawers and counters. Nor were they disappointed when TRUMAN & JACOBSON started business on November 29, 1919.

"We opened the store at eight o'clock in the morning and closed at nine at night," Eddie told a reporter. "Twelfth Street was in its heyday and our war buddies and the Twelfth Street boys and girls were our customers. Those were the days when the boys wore silk underwear and silk shirts. We sold silk shirts at sixteen dollars. Our business was all cash. No credit. Harry and I worked reverse shifts and we had a clerk all the time. Harry did the bookkeeping and I did the buying. We both did the selling."

The men of Dizzy D found the store a haven for swapping wartime reminiscences and they walked out with ties, socks and underwear. On a central cabinet in the store, Truman placed the loving cup the men had given him inscribed *To Captain Harry from Battery D*.

The men of the battery refused to accept him as a mere shopkeeper. Eddie Jacobson recalled that "the boys who had been in the 129th used to come into the store to see Harry. He was their financial adviser, legal adviser and everything else." Later on, Truman admitted that the easiest thing to give others was advice. But at the time he felt like a father to the boys who had served under him and he involved himself in their personal problems. "I used to drive the boys who hung around the store pretty hard, especially the Catholics," he said. "I used to make them go to Mass."

He went out of his way to encourage Albert Ridge, once a private under him and now a law school student, to do his studying at the store. "We had a balcony up over the store," Truman recalled, "and I used to send him up there to work on his books nights when the other boys were just horsing around." He took a proprietary interest in Ridge's law career and many years later when Truman was a United States Senator he won an appointment for Ridge as a Federal judge. "Ridge liked to talk," Eddie said about the old store days, "but Harry would make him get busy and study. Harry really kept Al's nose to the grindstone." Truman also tried to broaden Ridge's outlook beyond the confines of his lawbooks. One time he handed Ridge a list of ten books which, he said, "any person wanting to get ahead should read." Among the books that Truman considered so essential, Ridge later remembered, "were the Bible, Shakespeare, Plutarch's *Lives, Bunker Bean, Missouri's Struggle for Statehood,* Benjamin Franklin's *Autobiography* and Creasy's *Fifteen Decisive Battles of the World.*" Truman also recommended Plato—"Especially the parts about the old fellow who took hemlock."

During the first year of operation the haberdashery store sold over $70,000 worth of goods and the two owners earned a high return on their initial investment. With visions of still greater profits to come, the two partners plowed their earnings back into stock and kept their shelves piled high with goods.

The store was a six-day-a-week proposition, and Truman seldom got back to the Gates house in Independence before midnight. Occasionally Bess helped take inventory and went over the books. But their home life was meager during this hectic period. Even on Sunday, Truman's only day for relaxation, he seldom stayed home but took Bess to Grandview to visit his mother. After dinner, he and his sister Mary Jane played classical duets on Martha Truman's upright piano for the old lady and Bess. Then it was back to TRUMAN & JACOBSON for another hard week.

During Truman's second year in business, the happy glow of prosperity abruptly vanished. At the beginning of 1921, the store's books showed an inventory of $35,000 at cost. The partners had an offer to sell out at this price, but they rejected it, because they were doing well. Their success, however, was short-lived. After the Harding Administration took office in March, farm prices fell drastically. Like a chain reaction, prices of goods began dropping. Truman and Jacobson, who had bought their inventories at the high prices prevailing before the slump, were gradually forced to cut their selling prices until their margin of profit disappeared.

Only for a brief period that year did the haberdashery business pick up. This was in the fall of 1921 when the American Legion burst upon Kansas City for its national convention. Truman was an early member of the Legion as well as the founder and president of the first Officers Reserve Corps. Legionnaires considered it only right that they patronize the store of one of their boys. They provided the partners with a brisk trade as they poured into the store to swap war stories. "That was when we took the Baltimore Hotel to pieces," said Harry Vaughan, who marched through the haberdashery store with a long snake line of merrymakers. Vaughan, a graduate of Westminster College at Fulton, Missouri, was then working as a chemical engineer. This was his first meeting with Truman following their wartime service, but there was little time for them to talk because of the convention's noise and horseplay.

After the Legion pulled out of Kansas City, however, business hit a new low. Truman took to reading at the counter to pass the time. "You were always reading books and pamphlets, and a lot of them were about Jackson," Eddie Jacobson reminded him years later. His reading was interrupted by veterans who had lost their jobs and wandered into the store. "Instead of buying, the boys came in for loans," Eddie remembered. "When they came in asking for Captain Harry, I knew it was for a touch. But if they asked for Captain Truman then I knew we had a sale."

By early 1922 it was growing more difficult for Truman to concentrate on his reading. The inventory, valued at $35,000 only the year before, had now shrunk below $10,000. For the first time, creditors grew curt in their demands for payment. Crisis was upon the partners as they tried to borrow money to pay off the more clamorous creditors. This was a trial by fire almost as bad as Truman's experiences on the front lines. In one sense, it was even worse, for he was a helpless pawn in the economic chess game.

In January, 1922, the Twelfth Street Bank lent the partners $2,500.

This was soon in the hands of creditors. Truman then negotiated a $5,000 loan from the Security State Bank. In 1921, he had sold his Kansas City flat to make a $5,000 down payment on a $13,800 farm of 160 acres in Johnson County, Kansas. The Security State Bank insisted that he put up his farm as security on the $5,000 loan.

At last the day came when the money from the Security State Bank was paid out and the partners could not continue in business. All about them small businessmen were in the identical plight and their recourse was to go into bankruptcy to wipe out their debts. Neither Truman nor Jacobson, however, wanted the stigma of bankruptcy.

Instead, they wrote to each creditor and explained their situation. Rather than go through a costly liquidation, Truman proposed returning the remaining stock to the creditors, deducting the value from the total bills and making future payments on the balance until all the debts were wiped out. The creditors agreed to this plan.

When TRUMAN & JACOBSON finally closed its doors, the two partners owed about a thousand dollars to their suppliers, in addition to the two outstanding bank loans. Their predicament was made worse by the fact that their landlord refused to waive what was left of their five-year lease and insisted on his $3,900. In total, Truman estimated that his haberdashery experience had cost him about $30,000, including the $15,000 he originally put into the business.

The price for not accepting bankruptcy was steep. By the end of 1924, the two had paid off in full the $2,500 loan from the Twelfth Street Bank, paid the Security State $1,200 and had made small payments to merchandise suppliers. Eddie Jacobson had gone back on the road as a shirt salesman, but by February, 1925, he could no longer stand the pressure of his continuing debts. That month he filed a petition in bankruptcy, listing the total remaining store debts as $10,058.50. The chief debts were the $3,900 balance on the lease and $5,600 owed the Security State on the original $5,000 loan, even though $1,200 had already been repaid.

Lawyers advised Truman to file a petition in bankruptcy at the same time as Eddie. But he refused. Instead, he insisted upon paying off all the debts he and Jacobson had incurred, although Eddie was now free of them.

Truman's indebtedness grew more complex as the years went by. Later he made a settlement on his lease. As for his $5,000 bank loan, the Security State failed and its assets were taken over by the Continental National Bank. Truman's note was one of the transferred assets, and on April 30, 1929, the bank obtained a court judgment against him for $8,944.78, counting principal and interest. The bank also took over the 160-acre farm he had deeded to it as security. Then the Continental National Bank failed during the depression when Truman was in the Senate. When the bank's receiver put his note up for sale at $1,000, he purchased it through his brother Vivian and thus ended the years of financial misery that had grown out of his connection with the haberdashery store. Eddie Jacobson later reimbursed Truman for half the debts he repaid.

It was symbolic that after Jacobson went into bankruptcy he met Truman one day. Eddie's shirt and suit were frayed and Truman insisted that he take the few dollars in his billfold to buy new clothes. All that remained in Truman's wallet was the worn fragment of Tennyson's poem "Locksley Hall" which he had carried with him since his last year in high school. The first two lines read:

> For I dipt into the future, far as human eye could see,
> Saw the Vision of the world, and all the wonder that would be.

8

WHILE standing behind the counter in his haberdashery store amidst piles of unsalable silk shirts and underwear, Harry Truman had plenty of time to contemplate his future. He was nearing thirty-eight at the beginning of 1922 and sinking deeper in debt with each passing month. Although a friend had offered to take him into his profitable building and loan business, thus solving his financial problems, he had by this time decided on a new career and rejected the offer.

What he had in mind was politics. Colonel Bennett Clark was dabbling in politics on the other side of the state in St. Louis. Captain Jacob "Tuck" Milligan, who was in the 140th Infantry with Clark, had already had a taste of Washington, D. C., when he filled out a part of Congressman Josh Alexander's term after President Wilson made Alexander his Secretary of Commerce. Other veterans were beginning to win political offices in Missouri and elsewhere. Certainly politics seemed to be a promising field for ex-soldiers if one only knew how to break into it.

The boys of the 129th enjoyed listening to Truman's opinions about political issues and politicians, especially when he explained current political matters in terms of past events in American history. Just who first suggested that he run for office is unknown. But Captain Spencer Salisbury of Battery E, who was one of his earliest supporters, said that Truman was bound to come to politics because "he had an exceedingly pleasing personality and made a nice impression."

To enter politics in Jackson County, however, required more than making an announcement. Only a man sponsored and supported by one of the political machines could get anywhere. Fortunately, one of the boys who dropped into the haberdashery store was Jim Pendergast, whom Truman had known at Camp Doniphan. A lieutenant in the 129th before he was transferred to another outfit, Jim was the son of Mike Pendergast who headed the Pendergast machine in the rural part of Jackson County as well as the old Tenth Ward in Kansas City. Truman had known Mike casually before the war when he attended the Thursday evening meetings of the Tenth Ward Democratic Club. Mike was not considered by the machine's top pistons to be a big brain. But almost all who came in contact with him found him fair and congenial, though when he was hitting the bottle he liked to brawl. His pockets bulged in the summertime with tickets to the baseball games of the minor league Kansas City Blues and he passed them out as he strolled down the streets in his bailiwick. Often he presented a picture of frustration because his brother, Thomas J. Pendergast, or T. J., who was the real boss of the machine, would nullify his work. Nevertheless, without Mike's support a politician in the farm area of Jackson County could not hope to win his brother's favor.

It was during one of his conversations with Jim Pendergast that Truman confided his political ambition—to run for county judge for Eastern Jackson County. Jackson County elected three county commissioners, or judges, as they were officially called, even though they did not preside over a regular court. Kansas City proper elected a county judge for Western Jackson County; the rural remainder of the county elected the eastern judge; and the entire county voted on the presiding judge. The judges' duties included levying taxes and caring for roads and county buildings.

Jim did not laugh at Truman. Instead, said Truman, "Jim went to Mike with the suggestion that he and the other men of the Battery would like to have me on the county ticket for judge of the Eastern District of Jackson County in the County Court."

This provided Truman with an opening wedge. But he realized that he would have to bring pressure on Mike before he would get his support. One of Bess's brothers had married the daughter of Colonel William M. Southern, editor of the Independence *Examiner* and an important man in local Democratic politics. One morning Truman walked the few blocks from the Gates house and paid a call on Southern at the office of the *Examiner*. "Colonel," said Truman, "who are the Pendergast and Shannon bosses whom I need to see in Independence if I am going to run for office?"

"Harry, what in thunder are you talking about?" he replied.

"I mean to run for county judge from the Eastern District."

Southern tried to give him some fatherly advice. "Look, Harry, I know you're discouraged over your business failure and I'm sorry. But there's no reason to be as downhearted as that. Don't mess up your whole life by going into politics. It's no disgrace to have failed in business. Many good men have done that. You'll make good at some other business. Cheer up, Harry."

But Truman would not change his mind. "I abused him like a pickpocket for an hour," Southern later said. "I told him all the bad effects a life of chronic campaigning could have on a man. I told him how poor were its rewards, how will-o'-the-wisp its promises, how undermining the constant need for popular approval could be to a man's character. I told him how hard it was on a man's family to have him in politics. Still he smiled and shook his head and repeated he intended to make a career in politics."

By coincidence or not, Colonel Southern was just the man for Truman to see. For Mike Pendergast's Eastern District lieutenant, a loud, tough Irishman named Nick Phelps, had earlier asked Southern to suggest a good prospect for that very post. Shortly after he saw Truman, Southern met Phelps at the Independence public square. "Well, Colonel," Phelps said, "who are we going to nominate for judge from the Eastern District?"

Southern said his reply was: "We are going to nominate Harry Truman."

"And who in the hell is Harry Truman?" Nick asked.

Nick Phelps reported what Southern said about Truman to big Mike Pendergast. There were also the strong demands from his son Jim. Finally, one day, Mike drove to the haberdashery store. Truman said he was "standing behind the counter feeling fairly blue when Mike Pendergast came in. He didn't know I was busted." Mike asked him point-blank: "How would you like to be county judge?"

"I don't know," Truman answered shrewdly.

"If you would, you can have it," Mike said.

In June, big Mike called a meeting of his Tenth Ward Democratic Club. Every township in the county sent its top local bosses and the beer flowed freely. Mike had also invited Truman to the gathering. After the routine business was disposed of and the crowd had settled down, Mike stood up and rapped on the table. "Now I'm going to tell you who you're going to support for county judge," he announced.

Truman reported that one man began accepting congratulatory handshakes from his neighbors. "It's Harry Truman," Mike shouted, and the handshakes went limp. "Harry Truman is a returned soldier, a captain 'over there' with a fine record and whose men didn't want to shoot him!"

There were resounding backslaps and handshakes as Truman accepted Mike Pendergast's support. It was good to belong and to feel wanted.

A few days later, however, Truman awoke to the fact that his first race would probably be his last. Arrayed against him in the Democratic primary slated for August 1 were four opponents: Emmett Montgomery, a banker from Blue Springs; Tom Parent, a road overseer; James Compton, at one time an appointed judge in the Eastern District; and George Shaw, whom Truman characterized as "a road contractor who was honest." Much more disturbing, had he known about it then, Tom Pendergast had made a deal with the Shannon Democratic machine in the county to support Shannon's man for the Eastern County judgeship in exchange for Shannon's support of his man in the Western District. At best, Truman's candidacy was a token proposition, a sham, for the Pendergasts were committed to throw their machine vote behind Montgomery, the Blue Springs banker. The truth was that Montgomery's backers considered the naming of Harry Truman or anyone else as a candidate by Mike Pendergast to be a case of double-dealing.

Not long after Mike Pendergast's big meeting, Truman walked into the garage owned by formed Lt. Edgar G. Hinde of the 129th. Hinde recalled the conversation, though Truman did not remember it. He came in with a big smile, said Hinde. "What do you think I've done?" he asked. "I filed for judge of the Eastern District."

"I think you're crazy," Hinde told him, "but we'll see what can be done."

When Truman began his campaign, he bought a battered old Dodge roadster. The last few county courts had let the roads disintegrate so badly that he had to load the back of his jalopy with bags of cement to keep from being pitched through the windshield every time he hit a bump as he sped from village to village. He drove into each of the seven townships, spoke at picnics and political meetings and made a house-to-house canvass. Even though he had self-assurance, he was a notoriously poor speaker.

Montgomery and his supporters did not like his cocky attitude and tried to destroy him early in the campaign. Delving into his past, they found that he had actively supported a Republican for county marshal in 1920. This was true, for the candidate was Major John Miles, a battalion leader of the 129th.

Miles said: "I was a Republican in a Democratic county, yet Harry Truman worked hard in my behalf in 1920. It was our war association that made him do it, even though I was running against the Pendergast machine. He took me out to Grandview and told a large crowd of Democrats to vote for me and they looked at him as if he were crazy. Then he took me to see his mother. She was all smiles when he told her I had been his major in France. But when he said, 'Mamma, Major Miles is a Republican but I want you to vote for him anyway,' her mouth fell open and she looked thunderstruck."

Truman was confronted with his support of Miles at a picnic in Oak Grove, but turned the charge to his own advantage. "You have heard it said that I voted for John Miles for county marshal," he told the crowd. "I'll have to plead guilty to that charge, along with some five thousand ex-soldiers. I was closer to John Miles than a brother. I have seen him in places that made hell look like a playground. I have seen him stick to his guns when Frenchmen were falling back. I have seen him hold the American line when only John Miles and his three batteries were between the Germans and a successful counterattack. He was of the right stuff, and a man who wouldn't vote for his comrade under circumstances such as these would be untrue to his country. I know that every soldier understands it. I have no apology to make for it."

Besides the support of his wartime buddies, Truman counted on the votes of his Masonic brothers and also on those of neighboring farmers who had known him during his ten years on the Young farm. In addition to the strong Democratic faction that opposed the Pendergasts, there was another group that worried Truman. This was the Ku Klux Klan, which had again sprung into action as a result of the tensions and unemployment of the postwar years. White-robed and hooded gangs appeared throughout Jackson County, burned fiery crosses and claimed to be the dominating factor in the county's existence.

Two of Truman's opponents in the primary, Tom Parent and George Shaw, had Klan support. Truman and the other two candidates were besieged by Ku Kluxers to join up. Truman's natural inclinations were to oppose the Klan, but Spencer Salisbury and Edgar Hinde, who were working actively in his behalf, urged him to become a member. In the end, he reluctantly gave Hinde ten dollars in cash to pay his entrance fee. Hinde did so and returned with the news that the Klan's Kleagle would soon initiate him into the local Klan.

There are two conflicting versions of the events that followed. Spencer Salisbury, who later became his bitterest enemy, said, "Harry Truman and I went to Kansas City one morning where we met a fellow named Jones, the Kleagle of the Independence Klan, and the rest of the initiations committee. All of us went over to the Baltimore Hotel and among those present for his initiation were Edgar Hinde, a local man named Allen, and Harry Hoffman, who had taken over the Klan in the eastern part of the county. I remember Harry had to have special dispensation before they let him go through with the initiation because his grandfather, Solomon Young, was a Jew. After the initiation, Harry was never active; he was just a member who wouldn't do anything."

Truman and Edgar Hinde related something entirely different. According to an interview Hinde later gave the Kansas City *Star,* Truman was asked to hold a conference with the Kansas City organizer at the Baltimore Hotel. He went there, Hinde recalled, and the organizer said to Truman, "You've got to promise us that you won't give a Catholic a job if you belong to us and we support you."

Truman blew up at this. "I won't agree to anything like that. I had a Catholic battery in the war and if any of those boys need help, I'm going to give them jobs."

"We can't take you then," the organizer said. "Here's your ten dollars back and get out of here."

"Not long afterward," said Truman, "I joined with others and we ran Harry Hoffman out of the county."

Out of favor with the Klan and with the bosses tacitly agreeing on Emmett Montgomery, Truman did not appear to have much hope for winning the August 1 primary. In addition, he met with unexpected opposition at home. "Someone sent my wife mean letters about what

I'd been saying in the campaign," he said. "One day after she got another of those mean letters she said to me, 'Why don't you keep your mouth shut?' "

Early returns showed a close race between Montgomery and Truman. Late that afternoon word reached Truman's Dizzy D supporters that Montgomery's backers planned to steal the ballot box in a precinct at Mt. Washington and stuff it with sufficient ballots to ensure the banker's victory. Judge Henry Bundschu, a childhood friend of Vivian Truman's, described what followed:

"John Miles, the County Marshal, sent his brother George and a young soldier, John Gibson of the 129th Field Artillery, out to the precinct to preserve peace. Gibson said that George Miles took a stand on the north side of the front porch, which ran along the entire front of the cottage which housed the precinct polls, while he took a stand on the south side of the porch. They had not been there long before three or four taxicabs pulled up in the street in front of the house and out of these cabs a lot of tough fellows emerged. Gibson said he became scared, but soldierlike, he resolved that when he went out he was going to take somebody with him. So he reached in his holster and pulled out his .45 caliber revolver. He cocked it and stuck it into the stomach of the man nearest him. He said the man turned pale, raised his hands and said, 'Come on, boys, let's go!' After that, things quieted down, and the judges and clerks counted the ballots.

The man young Gibson had scared off turned out to be Joe Shannon, Tom Pendergast's chief opponent for leadership of the Democrats.

After this episode, counting the returns was almost anticlimactic to the boys of Dizzy D. But it was important to Truman, for he beat Montgomery by approximately five hundred votes. His primary campaign cost his backers $524.80 and the post he won paid only $300 a month. But it was worth all the effort, because when he defeated his Republican opponent in the election that November, he reached the first goal of his political career.

9

IN January, 1923, when Truman was sworn into office, people began calling him Judge Truman. He liked the sound of his new title, even though he was not a judge in the real meaning of that term. Several of his friends said that he spoke about his political office as if it were the apogee of success. Actually, even then, he harbored much broader political ambitions. It was not until 1934, after he had won the Democratic primary nomination for the United States Senate, that he acknowledged this to a reporter for the Kansas City *Star*.

He admitted at that time that the first rung on his political ladder was county judge for the Eastern District of Jackson County. The next step was to become presiding judge of the three-man county court. Then he wanted to be elected to the United States House of Representatives for a term or two. After this, he hoped to go to Jefferson City as the governor of Missouri. The top of his ladder—his final objective—was the United States Senate.

At the outset of his career he was well aware that his future depended on continued support from the Pendergast machine, as well as the growth of that machine beyond the confines of Jackson County.

When Truman became a county judge, Tom, or "T. J.," Pendergast hardly knew of his existence. T. J. was then in a major struggle to wrest control of the Kansas City and Jackson County Democrats from the competing machine of his rival, Joseph Shannon. To Pendergast, who had already spent a quarter of a century in politics, Truman could not have been more than just another faceless little machine stalwart who would be trampled upon if he ever got out of line. Moreover, Truman was one of his brother Mike's boys, and not his concern.

No man fitted the stereotyped picture of the American political boss more than Tom Pendergast. With a black derby atop his almost bald head, a deep bass voice that boomed and lashed, the master of ruthless decisions and publicized Christmas charities, he was the epitome of the political czar, the Irish ruler of the big city. He stood only five feet nine inches tall, though his broad back, barrel chest, wrestler's neck, enormous thick-featured face and hamlike hairy hands made him appear bigger.

Tom Pendergast came well schooled to bossism. His older brother Jim, who was a brilliant student of human nature, was a practitioner of the art long before Tom bulled his way onto the scene. Originally the large Pendergast clan, which had emigrated from Tipperary, Ireland, settled in St. Joseph, Missouri, after a short stay in Ohio where Jim was born in 1856. Tom was a St. Joe product of 1872. His father, old Mike Pendergast, was a teamster who raised his nine children to be God-fearing Roman Catholics and laid down the law at home in a thick, ringing Irish accent. All of his children were hustlers, most of all Jim, who was already an iron puddler in a Kansas City foundry when he was twenty.

But Jim was meant for better things than to remain a puddler his entire life. One day he bet all his savings on a horse named Climax at the local track. Climax was a long-shot winner and Jim used the money to buy a saloon and a "barrel house," a combination roominghouse and restaurant. Kansas City was a booming place. Even though its population was then only 35,000, it was lively and wide open.

Jim had an easy smile that settled almost permanently beneath his thick black mustache. For a saloonkeeper, he had a strange hobby of confronting heavy drinkers with a priest, pen and paper and exacting declarations of temperance—and Heaven help those who violated these pledges, which Jim kept in his saloon safe. He also stood ready to help anyone in need, and passed out half dollars to any seedy-looking person who stood before him with a hangdog quivering expression. It was in 1884, when Harry Truman was born, that Jim came unintentionally to politics. That year he suggested to his saloon customers in the First Ward that they vote for Leander J. Talbott, the Democratic candidate for mayor. The results proved astounding, for Talbott got a First Ward vote that was fourteen times larger than the vote of the Democratic alderman running with him. After this, Jim became known as the "King of the First Ward," the man with enough friends to swing the First Ward behind him. By 1892, he owned more than one saloon and controlled the liquor concession at the local race track. But, in addition, he had moved directly into politics as alderman from the First Ward.

Jim now sent for his brothers one by one. John came to manage his Main Street saloon. Then came Mike, who was good at setting up political clubs and handling organizational matters, even though he lacked that extra something needed for the role of heir apparent. Perhaps these qualities were to be found in baby brother Tom, who was now twenty and a clerk for the Burlington Railroad back home. Jim sent for him, and Tom came immediately.

Though he later claimed he was a college man and a big league baseball prospect, Tom had little schooling. He was adept at figuring profits, however, and Jim broke him in as bookkeeper for the saloons and cashier at the race track liquor concession. It was at the Elm Ridge track that Tom began wagering two dollars on an occasional race and acquired a thirst for betting on the horses that was to grow into a mania in later life.

When Tom was twenty-one, Jim put him on the local payroll as deputy constable in the First Ward. Jim also appointed him a precinct captain. This put Tom at the grass-roots level of politics, and he not only learned the habits of the precinct's voters but what was required to keep them loyal to his brother. Sometimes votes depended on a free bushel of coal, a job, paying for an operation—or threats and even force. Every Christmas there was a free dinner for the poor with turkey and all the trimmings and toys for the kiddies. But a day-in and day-out watch was kept on each voter. Jim's philosophy which he passed down to Tom was: "The important thing is to get the votes— no matter what." Number One on Jim's code of ethics was his belief that a real measure of a man was whether he kept his word. A man might be a thief or a swindler, but if he kept his word, Jim and Tom respected him.

In 1900, the Pendergasts took a giant step forward when they played a key role in electing James A. Reed mayor of Kansas City. To the Pendergasts, Reed was the personification of respectability—a quality notably lacking in themselves. He was tall and lean and strutted haughtily like a Roman Senator. They especially enjoyed his florid speeches, which earned him the nickname of "Woody Dell Jim." The Pendergast machine later promoted Reed to the United States Senate where he became Woodrow Wilson's chief Democratic opponent on the issue of the League of Nations.

To pay off part of his enormous debt to Jim Pendergast, Reed named Tom city superintendent of streets in 1900. This was Tom's first opportunity to boss men on a job and he found that he had the ability.

The same year Jim Pendergast supported Reed for mayor, he expanded his organization beyond the First Ward. His aim was to set up a city- and eventually a county-wide machine with himself as boss of the bosses. In August, 1900, he opened a clubroom at the Navajo Building on Delaware Street and invited local Democratic leaders to join. Within a month Tom rounded up 750 members for the club. Tom was now Jim's first assistant and he dressed the part of a man about town. He wore a bowler hat and a black coat and he encased his thick neck in a three-inch-high collar. His face had grown so large that people stared at him on the street. It looked like a pumpkin on a tree stump.

The Pendergasts soon found that they had an arch rival in the person of Joe Shannon, who also intended to have Jackson County for his very own. Shannon, then the czar of the Ninth Ward, was earnestly attempting to enlarge his domain. Born in St. Louis in 1867, Shannon was thirty-three when he began his quarter-century struggle with the Pendergasts. Though he had little formal schooling, he enjoyed a reputation as a scholar. He had been a city employee, a lobbyist, and later practiced law, regarding himself an authority on Thomas Jefferson. When Tom Pendergast bought a hotel in the old part of town and called it the Jefferson, Shannon was so irate that he insisted Tom use a name more appropriate to the Pendergasts—like the Jackson Hotel. In appearance, Shannon was tall, handsome and impressive. When Warren G. Harding was suddenly thrust into the news in 1920, it was widely remarked that Shannon was his double.

Since both the Shannon and Pendergast forces were Democratic, each required a special name to distinguish it from the other. The

69

Shannon crowd became known as "Rabbits" and the Pendergast boys as "Goats." A reporter was said to have originated the nicknames after an election involving both factions when he wrote: "The Pendergast crowd voted everything in sight, even the goats on the hillside. The Shannon forces flock to the polls like scared rabbits after the hunter has beaten the bush."

At one point Jim Pendergast decided there was no sense engaging in internecine warfare with Shannon's boys between elections. Even though the Goats outnumbered the Rabbits, Jim invited Shannon to a meeting and solemnly gave his word that Shannon would receive half the patronage spoils after each election. Shannon agreed to the pact which remained in force until 1916. Nevertheless, he continued to undermine the Goats.

After putting Reed in the mayor's office in 1900, Jim Pendergast controlled the city council for the next decade. As an alderman, he was known as a liberal and forced the others to adopt a progressive approach on many issues. This philosophy resulted from his identification with the working class. He seemed puzzled by his authority, and on one occasion he told a reporter: "That's all there is to this 'boss' business—friends. You can't coerce people into doing things for you. You can't make them vote for you."

By 1910, no politically ambitious young man in Jackson County could hope to win an election unless he was approved and supported by a machine. That year Jim Pendergast fell ill with Bright's disease and he realized that Tom would have to carry on. "Take Brother Tom," he told the press. "He'll make a fine alderman and he'll be good to the boys, just as I've been. Eighteen years of thankless work for the city, eighteen years of abuse, eighteen years of getting jobs for the push, is all the honor I want." The next year he was dead.

Of course, the Goats would never forget Jim Pendergast because he was the founder of the machine. Tom saw to it that a statue of Jim was erected in Mulkey Square. There he sat in bronze in his alderman's chair, just as he had in real life. But Tom had Jim's actual chair, for he took his place in the city council and served until 1916 when he quit. There was no trouble between Tom and his older brother Mike on the question of who would succeed Jim. Mike was satisfied to run the Goats of the Tenth Ward and the rural part of the county. The bigger task of bossing the entire area rested on Tom's beefy shoulders.

Tom Pendergast was more ambitious than Jim and had little of his brother's sentimental nature. He walked out of the city council because he realized that a boss only weakened his power by holding political office. It was best to manipulate the political puppets from behind the scene and not expose himself publicly. Jim's policy of sharing patronage with Joe Shannon also went against his grain. Since there was no percentage in rewarding an enemy for trying to do you in, Tom told Shannon in 1916 that the Goats and Rabbits were back on the warpath. In several respects Tom's machine differed from brother Jim's machine. Jim thought of politics as a game. On the other hand, Tom built a business empire for himself and this money machine depended on his continuing political power. Although he was a teetotaler, he owned a wholesale liquor firm. When his henchmen held office, the saloons had to serve his whisky or lose their licenses. He also had large interests in several road and building construction companies that were kept busy and profitable by being awarded preferential contracts. To make certain that he earned money on every side of the construction business, he became president of the Ready Mixed Concrete Company which supplied concrete to contractors. City inspectors who were Goats invariably refused to approve projects using other than Ready Mixed concrete. In addition, he was a partner in the Hasty-Speedy-Hurry Messenger, Automobile, Transfer and Livery Company. He also controlled the company that handled the removal of Kansas City's garbage, and opponents sometimes found that for weeks on end collectors would "forget" to haul away their garbage. When Roy Roberts of the Kansas City *Star* began brawling with Tom, the Goats assessed his personal property at such an outrageous rate that he was forced to reside across the river in Kansas. Tom also leased a string of business properties that he rented out to others, controlled oil companies, and was the proprietor of the six-story Jefferson Hotel.

Considering his various enterprises, it was essential that Tom Pendergast maintain political control. He viewed politics as a general did his army. The mainstay of his political machine was the precinct captain, each of whom he supplied with money to make certain that every voter in the precinct received personal attention. "We fill his belly and warm his back and vote him our way," he said. This attention to the needs of individual voters was not limited to the few weeks before an election. It went on daily, the year round. Tom's precinct captains knew that they had to deliver the necessary vote or be replaced. Sometimes, in order to make a good showing, they arranged for a vote that was actually larger than the total population of the pre-

71

cinct or ward. Tom gave them no political philosophy for enticing voters. The sole objective was to win. If not, another machine boss would win and feather his own nest. He once told a reporter: "You've got to have boss leadership. Now look at me. I'm not bragging when I say I run the show in Kansas City. I am boss. If I was a Republican they would call me 'leader.' "

As Tom Pendergast's fortunes skyrocketed, he moved his wife and children from the saloon-cluttered North Side to an imposing mansion on fashionable Ward Parkway. The house was of French Regency design and cost him about $150,000, not counting ornate interior decoration that bore all the telltale evidence of the parvenu. Tom's son and two daughters got whatever they wanted in the way of cars, trips and clothing. On one occasion, burglars broke into the house and among the reported losses were 480 pairs of silk stockings belonging to his daughter Marceline. At home he grew exacting about the minutest detail, insisting, for instance, that his bedsheets match the color scheme of the wallpaper. He was not so demanding, however, about the surroundings where he worked.

After he sold the Jefferson Hotel, he moved his headquarters to the second floor of a yellowish brick building above a retail store and café at 1908 Main Street in the poorer business zone of Kansas City. His office consisted of three rooms with secondhand furniture and floors that were seldom swept. At the top of the stairs was an entrance room featuring pictures of Woodrow Wilson and Jim Reed, the two enemies, and an oil painting of Tom Pendergast. Past this room was a waiting room containing a number of hard chairs which were occupied during his six A.M. to noon office hours by a motley crowd of politicians, lobbygows, beggars, contractors, bookies, immigrants, gamblers and anyone else who wanted a minute with the big boss. The waiting room was ruled by a muscular former river-boat pilot named Elijah Matheus, who stood six feet three inches tall. "Cap" Matheus followed strict orders to usher visitors into Tom's inner office on a first come, first serve basis. Rank made no difference.

Tom used a secret entrance to reach his office without passing through the waiting room. This office, only twelve feet square, was bare except for a worn green rug, a few chairs, a brass cuspidor and a splintered roll-top desk. On the wall was a newspaper cartoon of Brother Jim holding a ballot box. When Cap Matheus ushered in a visitor, he found Tom in his swivel chair behind the desk with his black derby jammed on his head and a look of impatience in his eyes. He wasted no time on pleasantries, but ordered callers to come right to the point. He made decisions on the spot and called out to Matheus, "All right, who's next?"

At noon, when Cap Matheus cleared the waiting room, Tom turned his attention to his many business enterprises and to his betting mania, often wagering as much on a single horse race as a county judge earned in an entire year. Tom's day ended early, for he had to make certain that he got home before nightfall. He knew his enemies were merely biding their time for an opportunity to kill him and escape in the dark.

Tom Pendergast's enemies in Kansas City extended beyond Joe Shannon's Rabbit opposition. For instance, in 1920, a small-time Democratic boss named Miles Bulger took advantage of the Goat-Rabbit feud to squeeze himself into control of the Jackson County court. Soon "Bulgerism" became a household word in Jackson County. Bulgerism meant selling patronage jobs, taking kickbacks from contractors, foisting shoddy work on the county, and pocketing money from construction jobs never undertaken but duly recorded in the county records.

Bulger was a troublesome minor rival, a nuisance more than a threat, but Tom Pendergast despised him. In 1922, Tom made a deal with Joe Shannon to boot Bulger and his crew out of the county court. The arrangement called for Tom's Goats to have a free hand in selecting the Western District county judge, and Shannon's Rabbits the Eastern District judge. The presiding judge would be decided by competition.

Blame for the failure of this deal fell on young Jim Pendergast, Mike's son and the man Tom was carefully grooming to take over the machine after he was gone. And now a mess existed because a grinning Goat named Harry Truman had not only entered the race for Eastern District county judge but had defeated Shannon's Rabbit, Emmett Montgomery.

10

WHEN Harry Truman defeated Montgomery, Joe Shannon commented angrily, "The voters preferred a busted merchant to a prosperous banker." Actually, Shannon's wrath stemmed from his own personal loss, for Truman's victory deprived him of the patronage, lucrative contracts and other emoluments that were the prerogatives of a boss. With Mike Pendergast's man, Harry Truman, as Eastern District county judge and Tom Pendergast's man, Henry F. McElroy, as Western District judge, Shannon's man, E. W. Hayes, the presiding judge, held ineffectual minority power.

Shannon attempted to browbeat McElroy and Truman into submission. But, according to Truman, the three judges "promptly managed a vicious political fight among themselves." When the smoke cleared, the Pendergast machine held decisive control over appointments to the sixty road overseer posts as well as hundreds of other petty jobs. The result was that Shannon seethed at the mention of Truman's name and was determined to prevent his re-election two years later.

In time, McElroy was to become spokesman for Pendergast's Goat machine, but at this stage of his career he, like Truman, was just starting out in politics. He had little tolerance for his fellow Goat, whom he considered a queer duck. Once McElroy tried to persuade Truman to agree to transfer the Jackson County seat from Independence to Kansas City where it would be under Tom Pendergast's personal scrutiny. Truman, however, would not sanction this historic loss for Independence. With some vehemence, McElroy told a Kansas City *Journal* reporter: "I tried to get it moved when I was on the county court. But a lot of little fellows around Independence Square made such a howl that the move failed."

One of the first projects that Truman and McElroy undertook as county judges was the restoration of county institutions to their jurisdiction. In 1919, the state legislature had placed the management and control of county institutions in the hands of circuit judges who were members of the judiciary, unlike Truman and McElroy who were actually county commissioners. To Truman this was a violation of the state constitution; to McElroy it meant that the Goats were deprived of the patronage involved in staffing these institutions.

The two hired John T. Barker, an excellent lawyer, to fight the legislative enactment. Barker chose to use the constitutional issue when the case came up before the State Supreme Court. He won and the county judges regained control. In his autobiography, Barker said McElroy told him that neither he nor Truman would have had any political future had the case been lost.

Truman attacked his job with characteristic enthusiasm. The machine controlled the staffing of county jobs, but genial Mike Pendergast permitted him broad authority over tax levies and expenditures as well as in the management of the county's charitable institutions. Not only did Truman familiarize himself with every county road, bridge and viaduct, but he also knew down to the last detail the diet and operating expenses of the homes for old people and juveniles. The roads were his biggest headache. Miles Bulger's legacy to the county was hundreds of miles of pie-crust roads. Shoddily constructed, with no attention paid to standard engineering practices, the roadbeds crumbled faster than they could be repaired. Bulger had also run the county into debt by more than a million dollars. Yet despite these burdens and Pendergast machine rule, Truman managed to improve some of the roads and cut his inherited county debt by almost $700,-000 in two years.

The Kansas City *Star*, a Republican newspaper and perennial battler against the Pendergast machine, went out of its way to praise Truman when he sought renomination. On August 3, 1924, it stated in an editorial:

> The present county court is busy paying off the debt. It paid off more than $600,000 last year. It has improved the roads. It has money in the treasury. That is the difference between county courts. The men who did this, Judge McElroy and Judge Truman, are up for renomination. Tuesday the Democratic voters of Jackson County will show whether they are interested enough in good service to renominate the men who are responsible for the remarkable showing made.

Not all of Truman's time was spent on his job. On Sundays he and Bess drove out to Grandview to have dinner with his mother and his sister Mary Jane. He also maintained his interest in his lodge. By 1924 he had become Deputy Grand Master and Deputy Grand Lecturer of the 59th Masonic District of Jackson County. He joined the Kansas City Athletic Club, where at the age of forty he finally learned to swim, using an unorthodox side stroke to keep his head clear of the water, because he insisted on wearing his glasses while swimming. Self-conscious of his lack of a college degree, he enrolled in the Kansas City Law School for evening classes. Dean Edward D. Ellison described him as a serious law student. "Truman attended the academic years of 1923–1924 and 1924–1925," Ellison said. "He made a general average of 'B' in the subjects he took." But Truman dropped out of law school after two years, blaming his old buddies of the 129th because they sought him out at the school with their problems. "They just made me quit," he said.

During this period he resumed his National Guard training. Harry Vaughan, whom he had known since Camp Doniphan days, and John Snyder, who had attended artillery school with him at Coetquidan, France, were also in the National Guard. The three formed a close trio during summer maneuvers at Camp Riley, Kansas, with Harry Truman a lieutenant colonel commanding the 379th Regiment and Captains Vaughan and Snyder the 380th and 381st. Vaughan, now a salesman for a company that made railroad ties, was full of horseplay. On the other hand, Snyder, who was with a bank, was a shy, diffident man who made it a point to read four books a week: two biographies, a history and a novel.

Because Truman was nine years older than Vaughan and twelve

years older than Snyder, both younger men looked up to him as one would to an uncle. One summer, when he came to maneuvers sporting a bristle mustache, he only managed to look younger and less authoritative. Another time he tried to raise a beard, but gave it up because "the hair on the right side of my face grew upward and on the left side it grew down."

In time a fourth member joined the group—Edward E. McKim, who had been sergeant with Battery D but was now a lieutenant in the National Guard. The four went in for gargantuan practical jokes, played poker in off-hours and drank together. "John Snyder had an interesting characteristic," Vaughan said. "He didn't smoke, but when he had his full quota of liquor he would bum a cigar from me. As soon as he asked for a cigar, we knew it was time for him to quit drinking."

The most important event during Truman's term as county judge occurred on February 17, 1924, when Bess gave birth to their only child. Ever since she broke the news to Truman the preceding spring, the Gates house had been in an uproar. Bess's grandmother, eighty-three-year-old Elizabeth Gates, waited most impatiently for the birth of her first great-grandchild and the unique situation of having four generations living together under the same roof.

When Bess's time drew near, Truman announced that the delivery would take place in a sanitary hospital. The women ignored him, however, and decided that the baby would be born at home. As things developed, Bess's labor pains came much sooner than expected and he had to rush out in search of Dr. Krimminger. Then, nervously, he paced the oriental rug until the doctor appeared with news that mother and daughter were doing very well under the circumstances.

A brief note in Colonel Southern's Independence *Examiner* proclaimed the infant's arrival: "Judge and Mrs. Harry Truman announce the birth of a daughter at the home on Delaware Street Sunday morning."

The Trumans were nearly forty years of age and should have been mature parents. In all the excitement, however, they forgot to purchase a bassinet and the infant girl had to be bedded down at first in a dresser drawer. She was named Mary Margaret Truman: the Mary for Truman's sister and the Margaret for Bess's mother.

11

WHEN Margaret was only a few months old, Truman had to stand for renomination in the Democratic primary. Joe Shannon had been biding his time to take care of this little upstart. With deliberation, he set up what he considered a fool-proof scheme. First he selected Robert L. Hood, who was highly regarded in the area, as Truman's opponent for Eastern District county judge. Then, even though he himself was a Roman Catholic, Shannon lined up the Ku Klux Klan against Truman. He also resorted to personal vilification, but Truman was not a man to take insults without fighting back. As a result, said the *Star,* "Great feeling was aroused over this race."

The strong editorial support of this paper helped Truman defeat Shannon's man in the Democratic primary by 1,300 votes. But there was still the general election in November and Shannon quietly made arrangements to deliver his Rabbits and the KKK to the Republicans.

By a strange turn of fate, there would have been no Republican candidate to run against Truman had it not been for the action of two of his friends. The chief culprit was Circuit Court Judge Henry Bundschu, Vivian Truman's boyhood friend. "The last day for filing for the office in the Republican primary was about closed," Bundschu said, "when Major John Miles called me by telephone from Independence saying that no one had filed for judge in the Eastern District. Miles said that several prominent farmers were thinking about filing but he had been unable to persuade any of them to undertake it. I suggested one of his deputies, Henry Rummell, file and Miles agreed with the understanding that Rummell would withdraw as soon as Miles could find some outstanding person qualified for the place. So without saying anything to Rummell about it, I went to the courthouse and filed him for the Republican nomination against Harry Truman."

Major Miles admitted, "Afterward when I couldn't get any really qualified person to run against Captain Truman, I told Rummell he ought to withdraw. But Rummell said he wasn't going to get out because Joe Shannon was going to support him. It was a dirty thing Henry Bundschu and I did to Harry Truman."

Truman knew Rummell as the town's harness maker. When he and Vivian were children, John Truman had once ordered a set of harnesses from Rummell so they could hitch goats to their little wagon. He was confident that he would defeat this nonpolitical opponent even if Rummell had Shannon in his corner.

However, he underestimated the power of the Ku Klux Klan. Spencer Salisbury, who claimed that he had accompanied Truman when he was proposed for initiation into the Klan, said: "The Rabbits had almost to a man joined the Ku Klux Klan in 1924. This was the high-water-mark year for the local Ku Kluxers, and when Shannon got the Klan to go after Harry by supporting Henry Rummell, Harry didn't have a ghost of a chance." Judge Bundschu, who had paid the five-dollar filing fee for Rummell, was aghast when he heard that Rummell had made a deal with Joe Shannon and the Klan, because Bundschu was a devout Catholic. Moreover, when he tried to collect the five dollars, Rummell refused to pay him.

The reputed leader of the Jackson County KKK was Todd George, who operated through an organization called the Independent Democrats of Jackson County. A *Star* reporter who interviewed George found that the focus of his Independent Democrats was on a single issue: "We are unalterably opposed to Harry Truman."

As November neared, there was talk of Klan violence and Bess Truman was greatly concerned about her husband's safety. But he was not perturbed. "They threatened to kill me," he said, "and I went out to one of their meetings and dared them to try. This was a meeting of

Todd George's 'Independents' at Lee's Summit. I poured it into them. Then I came down from the platform and walked through them to my car." Just as he got behind the wheel, his friends drove up with shotguns. "It was a good thing they did not come earlier," Truman said. "If they had, there would have been trouble."

In the end, the combination of Rabbits, Ku Kluxers and Republicans proved too much for him. Rummell defeated him by 867 votes and claimed a sort of fame throughout his long life as the only man ever to defeat Truman in an election.

By the beginning of 1925, Truman was in an uncomfortable but familiar situation. "I was broke and out of a job," he said. In February, Eddie Jacobson filed his petition in bankruptcy and the walls seemed to close in on Truman just that much tighter. He still attended law school, though he did not remain long after Rummell replaced him on the county court. At home, he and Bess found other things to worry about besides his unemployment on his forty-first birthday. Little Margaret was bald long past the age when she should have had curls, and when hair finally appeared it was as white as cotton. Also her speech was odd. When she started talking, she interchanged syllables. For instance, a word like "butterfly" came out "flutterby." But her hair and speech were of minor concern compared to her health, for in a single year she contracted the flu, pneumonia and rheumatic fever.

Truman's urgent problem of employment was resolved when he found a job selling memberships in the Kansas City Automobile Club. This was the era of Coolidge prosperity and Kansas City streets were choked with cars. Within a year, he sold more than a thousand memberships, and after deducting expenses he cleared about $5,000. This was $2,000 more than he had earned as a judge, but he would have much preferred his old seat on the county court.

The Automobile Club was not the only opportunity that came his way. Spencer Salisbury showed up one day with a scheme for them to become bankers. Salisbury was then a deputy collector of Internal Revenue. "I was tired of the job because it required too much traveling," he said. "Here was a chance to buy control of the stock of the Security State bank of Englewood for thirty thousand dollars. The beauty of it was that the bank's president was willing to take the thirty thousand in notes without our paying out any cash."

He talked with Truman and Arthur Metzger, who was constable of Independence. It looked like a foolproof plan for the three of them

80

to become bankers without investing a dime. Truman had no reason to doubt Salisbury. After all, his family was one of the most respected in Independence. His mother was not only Missouri State Regent of the Daughters of the American Revolution but her house fronted on Salisbury Road. Moreover, Spence's sister and Bess had been girlhood friends, and he had been captain of Battery E of the old 129th. As an old Pendergast Goat, he had also been a constable of Independence for six years before the war.

Why anyone would give up a profitable bank without requiring even a small cash investment was a question that Truman never bothered to ask. Nor did there seem to be any reason to question this odd way of doing business when Colonel Edward M. Stayton, who was an old Army comrade, a well-to-do local man named Hoover, and Lou Holland, president of the Kansas City Chamber of Commerce, agreed to become directors of the bank. With that, Truman, Salisbury and Metzger each signed a promissory note for $10,000 and became bankers.

It was not long before the situation was clarified. One Sunday, about two months after they took over, Truman, Salisbury, Metzger, Stayton and Holland spent the day scrutinizing the bank's records. "What we found made us ill," said Salisbury. "The bank turned out to be a Republican blind. It seems that Charles U. Becker, the Republican Secretary of State of Missouri, wanted a bank where he could borrow money for his printing business. And this was it. All the bank's cash assets were the funds from state auto licenses that were deposited here. Becker and his friends put up notes that weren't worth a damn. The only other assets we found were second mortgages and these were shaky. We didn't have a bank—we had a bank failure on our hands."

The five men immediately got in touch with the cashier's bonding company and reported the true situation. Then, said Truman, they unloaded their stock on other would-be bankers and got out of the banking business. Salisbury denied this. "We all got out except Harry. He stayed in, and that bank was the first in Missouri to go busted in the 1926 bank mess. Nothing happened to Harry. But the depositors lost between $50,000 and $100,000 and B. M. Houchens of Independence, who took over when the rest of us got out, killed himself in his garage one night."

Something about Salisbury must have fascinated Truman. At the same time they were involved in the banking fiasco, the two and

Arthur Metzger became partners in a savings and loan business. This was another venture they embarked on without investing any funds, but at least they founded the business themselves and did not have to worry that someone was trying to outwit them. They named their firm the Community Savings and Loan Association and operated out of a low-rent office on North Liberty Street in Independence. Having the most prestige, Truman became president; Salisbury was treasurer; and Metzger was attorney and secretary.

Truman's job was to promote the Association and sell stock in it. His partners agreed that he should collect commissions for his stock sales and he did well from the outset. Salisbury's job was to direct operations on a daily basis, while Metzger handled whatever legal problems arose. Even with the abrupt decline in home building that began in 1926, the company managed to earn money. Daily contact between Truman and Salisbury, however, engendered friction that was to lead one day to an explosion and mutual hatred.

In the early days of the Community Savings and Loan Association, Salisbury helped Truman become president of the National Old Trails Association, an organization dedicated to building first-rate national highways over the famous trails that shaped American history. His appointment to this position was accomplished through Salisbury's mother, who called on her D.A.R. friends for aid.

The job with N.O.T.A. entailed a great deal of traveling to inspect new trail roads as well as public speaking, which he found a chore because of his weak voice and nervous mannerisms. But he was proud of his achievement in this post. "I was president of the first transcontinental idea of a road from Baltimore to Los Angeles," he later said proudly. In 1949, he told a crowd at Cumberland, Maryland, "Fort Cumberland was the first milestone on the Old National Road . . . and I helped lay it out—me and Henry Clay."

By mid-1926, despite his varied enterprises, Truman longed to be back in politics. Bess caught signs of his restlessness as the Democratic primaries approached. But this time he had his heart set on more than re-election to his former post as Eastern District county judge. There was one county job that was low in prestige but high in salary, and he wanted it. "I wanted to be county collector, which carried an unusual remuneration of $25,000 a year in salary and fees," he recalled.

There was one major hurdle, however, in winning the nomination to this office. It required the direct approval of the top Goat, Tom Pendergast.

Truman knew the old political routine. At first he put out feelers among some of Pendergast's lieutenants that eventually reached the boss. Tom Evans, then president of the Goats Fifth Ward Democratic Club and already on his way toward establishing a drug chain empire, said that he dropped in to see Pendergast early one morning at his second-floor office on Main Street. Pendergast got right to the point. "My nephew Jim is bringing this man Truman to see me," T. J. told Evans. "Jim thinks he has a future. You knew him in Mike's Tenth Ward. What kind of a guy is he?"

Evans praised him highly and remarked that Truman had a great many friends.

"He is ornery, isn't he?" Pendergast said.

Not long after Evans' visit Truman climbed the worn, creaking stairs to Tom Pendergast's office. He had seen T. J. before, but this was his first call. After a wait in the crowded outer room, Cap Matheus ushered him into the big boss's private office. The feeling that came over him was one of awe as he watched T. J. in action.

The meeting, however, proved disappointing. When he told Pendergast that he wanted his support for county collector, the boss roared an emphatic "No!"

But Pendergast assured him that if he cared to try for presiding judge of the county court, he could count on the machine's support. This job paid an eighth of the $25,000 Truman had envisioned.

Mike Pendergast was furious with his younger brother when Truman described the interview. He insisted that Truman run for county collector anyway. "I'll suppost you regardless of Tom," he told him.

But without Tom Pendergast, Truman could not win and his political career would be finished. After talking it over with Bess, he took the only course he saw open. He ran for presiding judge.

12

TRUMAN had no Rabbit opposition when he campaigned for presiding judge in the 1926 Democratic primary. For Tom Pendergast had finally achieved mastery over Joe Shannon and Jackson County.

In February, 1925, the voters of Kansas City had gone to the polls in a special election to cast their ballots on the issue of a new city charter providing for a city manager government. It was the intent of the charter's sponsors to eliminate politics from the operation of local government by giving an appointed manager control of the city's business. They hoped to insure his independence by specifying that he could be hired or fired only by a majority vote of an elected nine-man city council.

Exponents of the charter were shocked when Pendergast emerged as its most vociferous supporter. So was Shannon, who said that T. J. was "signing his death warrant" because bosses needed the old system of controlling mayors. But Pendergast had the last laugh. Not only did the charter pass by a four-to-one margin, but when the first election was held under the charter, T. J.'s Goats won five of the nine council seats. One of those vital council seats was won by a mere 304 votes.

This slim margin in effect enabled Pendergast to name the city manager. And the man he picked was Henry McElroy, who had served on the county court with Truman. Within a few months almost half the city employees and all but two department heads were Goats. Within a year only Goats were acceptable municipal employees. Judge McElroy, as he insisted on being addressed, declared openly: "Tom and I are partners. He takes care of politics and I take care of the business. Every Sunday morning, at Tom's house or mine, we meet and talk over what's best for the city." For thirteen years this arrangement persisted without change.

Pendergast might have been vengeful toward his old foe, Shannon. But despite their many battles, he was rather fond of Uncle Joe. He went so far as to offer him a third of the patronage in the rest of Jackson County if Shannon refrained from putting up Rabbit candidates to oppose Goats. He also promised to support Shannon if he cared to run for the United States House of Representatives. Shannon was not averse to the two-to-one split of rural county jobs, but he wanted time to consider Pendergast's proposal about Congress which amounted to exile from Kansas City.

As a result of the agreement between Pendergast and Shannon on patronage, Harry Truman had no opposition in the primary. His only concern was the general election contest in November against L. L. Adams, his Republican opponent, who had Ku Klux Klan support.

During that fall campaign Truman took Bess with him to political meetings and gatherings wherever he spoke. Besides canvassing the county, he began to bring politicians to the Delaware Street house. This was not a happy experience for Bess's mother, who found the Goats a coarse lot. On one occasion a ward boss dropped in and picked up little Margaret to give her a kiss. He had a bulbous red nose and in her terror Margaret pinched it as hard as she could. He let out a yelp of enraged pain and released her. "Serves him right!" Bess's voice rang out sternly as she reclaimed her daughter.

In the November 2 election Truman won by a margin of 16,000 votes. Throughout the campaign he had promised to provide honest, economic government. Yet when he took charge of the damp and unsanitary county courthouse in January, 1927, few of his backers believed he could accomplish this goal and still satisfy Tom Pendergast and Joe Shannon.

His first test came that month when Pendergast telephoned and suggested that he come along to a meeting with Shannon. Truman had a good idea of what was about to happen because, as he recounted, "the court appointed the purchasing agent, county welfare officers, a county auditor, heads of homes, approved the budgets of elected officials, such as treasurer, county clerk, circuit clerk, county collector, county assessor, county highway engineer." The total came to 900 jobs and a multimillion-dollar budget.

It was Truman's recollection that someone must have given Pendergast a rather one-sided picture of his personality. For when he saw T. J. before the meeting with Shannon, the big boss said to him: "Now look here, Harry. They tell me you're a pretty hotheaded fellow. But I want you to understand that when we are in this meeting I don't want any fighting."

Truman stared at him openmouthed. "I won't cause any trouble, Mr. Pendergast," he said.

They sat around the table, three men who were so different from each other: the powerful boss, the faded boss, and the Goat officeholder. "There are always three sides to any question," T. J. said, brushing aside Shannon's demands for more than a third of the jobs. "Your side, my side, and the right side."

Truman did not utter a single word during the meeting, but sat back and watched as the argument waxed hot. First Shannon pounded on the table; then Pendergast's hairy fist crashed down. Shannon cajoled; Pendergast threatened. At one point Pendergast rose to his feet, his fist cocked to silence the wily Rabbit. Suddenly he glanced at Truman who had been observing the display with a broad grin on his face. Then he sat down and grinned, too.

The meeting ended with no extra spoils for Shannon. "Let the river take its course," T. J. told him with finality. Afterward, he gave Truman his orders about hiring. He was to put Pendergast's friends in the key jobs, but if they did not do the work he could fire them and appoint others.

Truman proved to be a highly controversial Goat. He accepted T. J.'s suggested appointees, but he also took him at his word. Not many weeks passed, as he himself confirmed, before he "fired people left and right who didn't work in the county interest." He also set up an inspection and audit system "which gave the crooked contractors an awful pain." Several of them, he discovered, had collected $2,000 for each of dozens of culverts they claimed falsely to have put in under the roads. In another move, he admitted proudly, "I stopped the expense account system of county road overseers, sixty of whom had

86

been employed. I cut the number of these overseers to sixteen. That was an unpopular move because it isn't good politics in any party to reduce the number of jobs. I was about as popular as a skunk in the parlor."

After he dropped several of Pendergast's original appointees, he began doing his own hiring. A few of these men were personally embarrassing, although most worked out well. Spencer Salisbury, his partner in the savings and loan business, said, "Harry gave me a job collecting the interest due on county school funds. But I got a little rough making them pay so he canned me. But I had a contract and he had to pay me $3,000 to quit. He also put his brother Viv in charge of buying cows for the boys' home and county farm."

The Goat leaders did not like what the nearsighted judge from Independence was doing. "He threw the organization into an uproar," Tom Evans laughingly recalled. "They weren't accustomed to anyone acting on his own. Any day they expected Old Tom to squelch Harry. But he never lifted a finger."

One reason for Tom Pendergast's apparent indifference was that he was then too busy working out several substantial deals with City Manager McElroy involving millions of dollars. Another was that he had little interest in outlying county affairs. But he also tolerated Truman because he honestly admired a man who would stand up to his organization without fear.

Truman had a compulsion to solve problems. "When I took over as the executive officer of the county," he said, "I found its road system a wreck, its courthouses falling down, its finances in such condition that the state was threatening to send the five or six hundred insane it was caring for back to the county and leave them on the courthouse steps."

One of the first problems he tackled was the county's chaotic borrowing system. The county had been borrowing money at 6 per cent interest from good little Goat banks in anticipation of future tax revenues. Total outstanding anticipation notes came to $2,400,000, which made the interest payments important. One night Truman left town for St. Louis and Chicago, where he bargained with bankers to lend Jackson County money on its expected tax revenues at lower interest rates. At first he pushed the rate down to 4 per cent and later to 2½ per cent.

But the big job, he realized, involved doing something about Jackson County's roads. Soon after he was in office he appointed a bipartisan two-man team of consultants to make an independent road study. The two engineers he named were Colonel Edward Stayton, a Democrat, and N. T. Veatch, a Kansas City Republican. Stayton and Veatch spent four months on their survey, and their joint report of May, 1927, was a devastating indictment of the crooked politics that had saddled the county with almost impassable roads. Among their charges was one that "there are some 350 miles of what has been aptly termed 'pie-crust' roads. The cost of maintaining these roads even in fair condition is almost an impossibility and certainly financially undesirable." The two engineers proposed the construction of 224 miles of new roads at a cost of $6,407,838. This sum could be raised only by a bond issue.

One morning that spring, Truman took their program to Tom Pendergast. Judge McElroy had prepared a $28,000,000 bond issue for Kansas City that was to be voted on in the spring of 1928. This was to cover an auditorium, city hall, traffic ways, sewer system, a bridge across the Missouri and a new water plant. Truman proposed to Pendergast that the $6,500,000 county bond issue come to a vote at the same time.

Pendergast was opposed to the plan because it would jeopardize McElroy's program. As city manager, McElroy was gaining the reputation of "a businessman's politician." He had thrilled many of Kansas City's business leaders when he eliminated the city's large deficit by transferring figures in the account books. "It's just a little country bookkeeping," he told them and announced that there would be no tax increases, as they had feared. In contrast to McElroy's growing popularity, the operation of the rural part of the county was a stench in everyone's nostrils. Voting on the county bond issue at this time, Pendergast felt, would endanger passage of the city bond issue.

Truman remembered T. J.'s reaction to his request. "You can't do it," he explained. "They'll say I'm going to steal it. Bulger tried it and every other presiding judge for twenty years."

This response only served to make Truman more determined. "I'll tell the people what I mean to do and they'll vote the bonds."

Pendergast jeered. "Go tell the voters anything you want to."

Another man might have taken T. J.'s reply as a negative answer. But Truman chose to regard it as a go-ahead signal. The Kansas City *Star* scoffed at his chances of winning approval for his bond issue so long as the money would be spent by the Goat machine. To Truman, however, the road program had become a crusade and he meant to visit every hamlet and farm in the county to explain it.

Pendergast might have stopped him early in his campaign, but he wanted to broaden himself by traveling and took his family to Europe that summer. During the three months he was gone, Truman drove all over the county to whip up support for his bond issue. He spoke about the obvious need for new roads and gave his word that a bipartisan board of engineers would supervise the program. His clincher was a promise to grant contracts only to the lowest bidders and not to the courthouse gang.

In May, 1928, his campaign paid off. The bond issue not only passed—it carried by a three-fourths majority instead of the necessary two-thirds. As for McElroy's proposed $28,000,000 bond issue for Kansas City, the voters rejected all of it except $250,000.

Truman retained Colonel Stayton and Veatch to run the road program. He realized, however, that since several of the top Goats were in the contracting business, there was bound to be trouble.

And trouble was not long in coming. His first road contract, a matter of $400,000, went to a South Dakota firm which had made the lowest bid on a proposed stretch of highway. Almost immediately Truman's phone began ringing and Tom Pendergast was on the other end of the line. T. J. said that several local Goat contractors were in his office and wanted him to drop in.

The call was a command and Truman went. When he walked into Pendergast's office, he found Bill Ross, John Pryor and William D. Boyle, whom he knew by reputation as important Goats and also as pie-crust road builders under Miles Bulger.

Truman reported the conversation.

"Ross, as spokesman, demanded that the contracts go to local bidders. They gave me the old song and dance about being local citizens and taxpayers and that they should have an inside track to the construction contracts. I said they would go to the lowest responsible bidders. Then Tom Pendergast turned to his friends and said, 'I told you, Bill, he's the contrariest man on earth.' I said I wasn't being contrary. I was proceeding in the legal and business manner. Then T. J. told them, 'Get out of here.' When they were gone he said to me, 'You carry out your commitments.' "

An interesting sidelight of the meeting was that Pendergast was actually a secret partner of the three contractors and lost a great deal of money by his decision.

Veatch and Colonel Stayton went ahead with the road program just as Truman had promised the voters. Although Veatch, who was a Republican, said that "the whole job was as clean as a hound's tooth," there were charges that Tom Pendergast's Ready Mixed Concrete Company was reaping a windfall on the program. This was true to the extent that all contractors knew from experience that they were only inviting trouble from company goons if they used any other concrete. But, as Truman pointed out: "All the county court had to do was to let contracts to the lowest and best bidders. Where they got their concrete and other material did not concern us; it was a matter of subcontracts. I know that some of the contractors experimented with the Ready Mixed and other brands and found the Ready Mixed most satisfactory, and that it was used extensively." Certainly there was nothing wrong with the quality of Ready Mixed. The problem was the monopoly that Pendergast enforced with the contractors, which earned him an estimated $500,000 a year in the Kansas City area.

As Truman's road program progressed, one of his prerequisites was that no farm was to be more than two and a half miles from a concrete road. Another was that the roadside was to be dotted with trees. Unfortunately, the farmers uprooted the seedlings almost as fast as they were planted.

There were many who tried to prove that he was part of the dishonest phalanx surrounding the top Goat leadership. After countless investigations, the Kansas City *Times* concluded that his road program "would be creditable to any county in the United States." The *Star,* which kept him under continual surveillance, admitted grudgingly that not only was he "extraordinarily honest" but there was "not a suspicion of graft involved in his road program."

It was his honest road program that gave Truman local prominence. But other activities added to his political stature. For instance, in 1928, when the Republicans staged their national convention in Kansas City, the Republican National Committee failed to raise sufficient funds to meet convention expenses. Truman helped raise the money locally for the Republicans on the ground that the convention would bring a spending crowd to town.

Truman's biggest push forward came early in September, 1929, when Mike Pendergast, his old friend and Goat sponsor, died. There was a wake for Mike to which his brother Tom and a long line of Pendergast lieutenants came to pay their respects.

Several of T. J.'s lieutenants wanted control of Mike's territory, but

Tom quietly turned over Eastern Jackson County to Truman who had worked so closely with his brother. Truman was now a hinterland boss for the Goats, a minor politician who was responsible for delivering 11,000 votes at election time. The delivery of these votes did not entail free bushels of coal, tickets to the Kansas City Blues baseball games or other minor league bribes. Nor did it depend on stuffed ballot boxes, so far as Truman was concerned. Instead, it depended on organization, issues and enthusiasm—the latter two rather prosaic concerns to the Goat leadership.

13

By mid-1930, when Truman ran for a second four-year term, he felt he had come a long way since 1926. Then he had been a hat-in-hand seeker of political alms in the upstairs room at 1908 Main Street. Now he was a successful presiding county judge, a first-rate road builder and a Pendergast lieutenant. He still had no intimate relationship with T. J., nor would he ever have one. But Pendergast knew he was alive, even though he left him to his own devices most of the time.

There was no doubt in Truman's mind that he would be re-elected in 1930. With the depression gripping the country, the Republicans were on the defensive, and, moreover, his successful road program almost certified his victory. "Even the damned old *Star* said editorially it was okay," he told a St. Louis reporter. Indeed, it was on the basis of the new road system that the Kansas City *Star* urged its Republican readers to back him.

Yet even though he expected to win the election in November, he did not know what to expect from his opposition. Missouri politicians played for keeps, and few gave up before official return totals were posted. One of the means used to discredit him was to give widespread publicity to the court judgment of $8,944.78 which the Security State Bank had obtained against him in 1929 for the failure of his haberdashery store seven years earlier. Another was a spurious tale that he was involved in an expense-account racket with county road overseers. There were even more questionable methods. One day, for instance, when he was in Kansas City, he parked his car in an alley. As he walked toward the street a colored woman suddenly approached him, grabbed his jacket and screamed, "Help! Police! Help!"

In a frenzy, he tore himself from her grasp, ran out of the alley and down a long block before pausing for breath. "Some of those so-and-sos were trying to frame me," he explained to a friend.

During the 1930 campaign, rumors spread throughout Jackson County that two top Democrats were to be kidnaped. One afternoon as election day neared, a man walked into Margaret Truman's first-grade classroom and told Mrs. Etzenhauser, her teacher, "I'm calling for Mary Truman, Judge Truman's daughter." Although Mary was her first name, she was always called Margaret and her teacher immediately grew suspicious. While she stalled the man under some pretense, she put through a call to Truman's office. Before he reached the school, however, the man sensed something was up and fled without the child.

Later there was an actual kidnaping, but no top Pendergast Goat was abducted. By election day the Goat grapevine brought word that the Republican Chairman of Jackson County had collected evidence of vote padding in Kansas City. Before he could present his findings and interfere with the voting, Pendergast's boys kidnaped him, gave him a beating and held him prisoner until the polls closed.

That year even Joe Shannon requested Truman's help. He had finally accepted Pendergast's offer of support for a seat in the United States House of Representatives and he needed all the votes he could get because he was running against an incumbent of the House. The 11,000 votes Truman could muster in the rural part of the county loomed large in his eyes. When Shannon came to Grandview, Truman ignored his mother's admonition that he refrain from helping his former enemy. Instead, he welcomed Shannon warmly at a public tent meeting, and the old politician gratefully acknowledged his support.

As it turned out, Shannon did not need his help because he won in Jackson County by a 45,000 majority. Nevertheless, Truman showed his own even stronger pulling power by acquiring a majority of 58,000 votes. This was 42,000 above his 16,000 majority in 1926.

Things would never be the same in Kansas City without their battles, Tom Pendergast and Joe Shannon sadly agreed before the top Rabbit took his departure for Washington.

When Harry Truman started his second term as presiding judge, he was intent on expanding his original road-building program. The depression was spreading and suffering had increased throughout the country. In Kansas City, apple sellers had made their appearance, bread lines were common and needy men were sleeping in doorways and begging for handouts. It was apparent to Truman that an additional public works program would not only provide employment for many of these men but would also help beautify Jackson County.

He soon devised another bond issue, this time for $7,950,000, of which $3,500,000 would be spent for additional roads, bridges and viaducts. The rest of the money would flow into a new $500,000 county hospital for the aged, a new $4,000,000 county courthouse in Kansas City, and a $200,000 renovation of the other county courthouse in Independence. (Jackson County was unique in having two county courthouses.)

This time when Truman went to 1908 Main Street to discuss his new bond issue proposal, Tom Pendergast accepted it with enthusiasm. What T. J. had in mind was a large bond issue for Kansas City. Because Truman's first bond issue had worked out so successfully, Pendergast realized that the Kansas City proposal stood a better chance of winning voter approval if it were tied to Truman's. Quickly he made a single $40,000,000 package of "Kansas City's 10-Year Plan" and Truman's new proposals. The Kansas City Plan called for a 32-story City Hall, a new police building, a city auditorium, city street paving, parks, playgrounds and a new waterworks system. Pendergast's reasoning proved sound, for the integrated bond issue won by a four-to-one majority in May of 1931.

Of all the projects on which Truman now worked, the new county courthouse in Kansas City held his special attention. The dismal old courthouse was a disgrace with its stained, worn floors, stale odors and gloomy rooms. Since Truman wanted the new courthouse to be a showplace, he set out at his own expense on a 24,000-mile tour to inspect other courthouses throughout the country. His trip included stops at Shreveport, Houston, Denver, Racine, Milwaukee, Buffalo,

Brooklyn and Lincoln. The Caddo Parish Courthouse at Shreveport impressed him most and he hired its architect, Edward Neild, as consulting engineer on his county's buildings.

From the moment the first line was drawn on the draftsman's board, Truman refused to sit idly by. The initial suggestion was for a 300-foot-high structure with a tower surmounted by a statue of Andrew Jackson.

But Truman rejected this plan because a telescope would be needed to see the statue. The building he finally approved was one of 22 stories with a statue of Jackson before its entrance. At Charlottesville, Virginia, he had seen Charles Keck's statue of Stonewall Jackson, which experts had told him was the finest equestrian statue in the United States. When the time came to hire a sculptor, he therefore employed Keck to portray Andrew Jackson on a horse. While the statue was still in the plaster-model stage, Truman journeyed to The Hermitage, Jackson's Tennessee farm, where he made precise measurements of Jackson's actual dress uniform, which had been preserved. Then he got in touch with the War Department in Washington to supply Keck with the customary equipment of a general of the army, circa 1814.

In contrast to Truman's building program, the Kansas City 10-Year Plan was taking a different turn. William Allen White, the sage of Emporia, hailed it as a miracle of man, and it was true that on the surface things looked excellent. Judge McElroy's new 32-story city hall seemed to be a grand structure. "Many times," a *Star* writer reported, "the city manager stood at his city hall window regaling reporters with the mistakes that had gone into Truman's building across the street."

Starting on the same low political rung as Harry Truman, McElroy had emerged as Tom Pendergast's alter ego. So far as he was concerned, Kansas City's 10-Year Plan was Tom Pendergast's 10-Year Plan. The money involved was most tempting.

Kansas City had a little stream called Brush Creek, which meandered through the city. McElroy used a million of the forty-million-dollar bond issue to pave Brush Creek with Ready Mixed Cement to a depth of eight inches and a width in some places fully seventy feet across. When the job was completed, Brush Creek became one of the awesome sights in town because it was the only creek in the entire United States to boast a thick concrete floor.

While Harry Truman became a problem to the Goat machine because of his unwillingness to hire an excessive number of county employees, McElroy's guide was strictly one of political need. Truman believed that Goats should be hired, but not more than were necessary. McElroy, on the other hand, maintained about 6,000 Goats on the city's payroll. According to the *Star,* about 2,000 of these were never seen doing any city work, and throughout town they were commonly referred to as "pads." Rabbi Samuel Mayerberg, who led a reform movement against the city manager, charged that in some months $100,000 was paid out by McElroy in fictitious claims for damages on public thoroughfares. Before the Kansas City 10-Year Plan was over, investigators were to find that McElroy had misappropriated more than eleven million dollars.

Many efforts were made by reform groups and Republicans to find similar evidence against Harry Truman of misusing funds in his county operations. At one point later on, FBI agents made an intensive check of county expenditures but failed to uncover a single instance of wrongdoing.

14

_____

MARTHA Truman was peeved by what she considered her son's self-righteousness. He had sliced 11 acres off her property for one of his highway projects, and he bluntly refused to pay her a dime even though he agreed that her land was worth a thousand dollars an acre.

Sitting in her rocking chair, she patted her chow dog "Sinner" and told a local reporter: "I'd have gotten eleven thousand dollars if my boy wasn't a county judge. If I could have my way I'd roll up my six hundred acres and move them a hundred miles further from the city. They've cut this farm up so much with railroads and highways and graveyards that it doesn't seem like home any more. First our house was a quarter of a mile back from the road. Then two railroads cut through it. Next U. S. Highway Number 71 separated the farm into two parts, and finally Blue Ridge Boulevard extension cut through the maples leading from the house to the Grandview Road."

Martha Truman was seventy-eight when her son was re-elected presiding county judge. Advancing years had not made her less alert. She was still the unreconstructed rebel, a rugged individualist with a sharp tongue and independent opinions. In spite of his marriage,

Truman's relationship with his mother remained very close, and he tagged her with the affectionate nickname "Boss" because he was amused by her free-wheeling advice to him even now that he was approaching fifty. On Sundays, after dinner, he drove along the new county roads from Independence to Grandview with Bess and little Margaret to see her and his sister Mary Jane. And inevitably, Margaret recalled, he and her aunt would sit down at the piano and play duets.

Truman's building program and other official duties, as well as his activities as Mike Pendergast's successor in rural Jackson County, often kept him away from home until late at night. Sometimes he could be found in Brown's drugstore on the south side of the Independence square where he drank coffee and watched the boys play the pinball machines. He was the small-time politician who was always available. Of an evening when he was home on Delaware Street, he liked to read biographies and histories. Reading sometimes required great concentration because his mother-in-law was a stickler for maintaining her house in good repair. If the floors weren't being sanded and polished, then the walls were being repapered or the curtains and draperies were down while the window trim was being painted. In addition, Madge Wallace's relatives were generally about the place. Bess's brothers, George and Frank, lived in small houses just below the big Gates house and came frequently with their wives, May and Natalie, for meals or a social evening. With all this bustle, Truman found it difficult to sit quietly near the old applewood clock in the parlor and read.

Throughout the years, his relationship with Bess remained unchanged. The boy who had first put her on a pedestal when he saw her in Sunday school continued to keep her there. No one ever heard him utter a harsh word to her, and she, on her part, served to calm him down when he was carried away with anger or excessive enthusiasm. Among their friends, Harry and Bess were still known as a pair of teases and jokesters. As her daughter put it, Bess had a "robust sense of humor." Lucy Mize, one of her friends, said: "Even though she had her bridge club with us girls in Independence, Bess was always timid with women. She was much more comfortable in the company of men." She was very much interested in public affairs, yet when she had to sit on the platform at civic functions she seemed awkward and frozen-faced.

Ever since Margaret's first years of sickness, Truman doted on her.

He called her "Marg" or "Margy," the "g" pronounced hard as in "good." On occasion he called her "Baby" and for a while he nicknamed her "Skinny" because she was growing up thin and delicate. Bess also used the hard "g" and called Margaret by her full name only when she was displeased with her behavior.

Since Margaret was the only grandchild on the Wallace side of the family, she was in danger of being spoiled. Although her Uncle Fred, who still lived at home, was some 25 years her senior, he romped with her as if they were the same age. On occasion, said Margaret, Grandmother Wallace thought they were making too much rumpus and "called us both down with equal fervor." Bess's mother was immensely fond of her energetic, saucer-eyed granddaughter, but she looked askance whenever Margaret pedaled her tricycle wildly through her antique-crowded house.

Margaret had too much energy for her grandmother or her parents. When she was not racing through the house, she was in the attic going through trunkloads of old-fashioned clothes or roaming through the many rooms and passageways in the basement which she labeled the "dungeon." She and her friends put out a paper called the *Henhouse Squawk* and staged carnivals in the half-acre yard. Years later when her father achieved prominence, she told reporters, "Even when I was a little girl, I used to think of myself as the one in the family who'd be famous."

So far as Margaret was concerned, her father was an easy mark. After she was grown, she admitted that when she did something wrong as a child, she could turn on tears like a faucet and melt his heart. He never spanked her, though he once threatened to do so in public at the dedication ceremony of Independence's rebuilt courthouse. She had been making a general nuisance of herself and he finally lost patience and grabbed her arm. "If you don't settle down, young lady," he told her in a voice that swept far out into the crowd, "I'm going to have to put you across my knee and spank you in front of all these people."

Truman often nullified Bess's attempts at discipline. Margaret recalled one occasion when she asked her mother for twenty-five cents to go to the movies and got a flat "No!" Truman, who had witnessed the scene, later slipped Margaret a quarter. When Bess learned of this, she was justifiably angry. "How am I ever going to teach this child the value of money without your cooperation?" she demanded.

Truman's idea of disciplining Margaret was to fine her for saying certain words, such as "dearie," which she used excessively. He finally told her that she would have to pay him ten cents every time she used it. At a single meal she said "dearie" four times and he collected what was left of that week's allowance. She never used the word again.

Because he loved the piano, Truman was determined that his daughter should, too. When the depression raged at its worst in 1932, he bought her a baby grand piano as a Christmas gift. This was an enormous personal sacrifice, even though he arranged to pay for the piano over a long period of time.

Margaret remembered how he tiptoed into her bedroom on Christmas morning and whispered, "Wait until you see what you've got." She hurried to the parlor in great anticipation. "Well, there it is," he told her proudly.

"Where?"

"Right in front of you, Baby." He pointed to the piano.

She burst into tears. "But I wanted a train."

He stood there stunned. Nor could he coax her to touch the keys all that day.

But later on he became her first teacher and taught her to play "The Little Fairy Waltz."

To a man like Tom Pendergast a piano was a useless ornament. So was a statue of Andrew Jackson. He could understand why a statue of his brother Jim sat in Mulkey Square. For Jim had done much for Kansas City, while Jackson was just a name out of history.

If Tom Pendergast found Judge Truman's interests in music and history incomprehensible, Truman's other interests and activities would have given T. J. even more reason to avoid bringing him into his inner circle. For instance, Truman was elected head of a regional organization in 1930 to plan civic improvements for nearby Missouri and Kansas counties. He also became a director of the National Conference on City Planning. Irving Brant, editor of the St. Louis *Star-Times,* said that he once attended a conference at the state university in Columbia on better state and county government in Missouri. "Judge Truman was one of those who was there and he far outshone the professors and practitioners present in the discussions on theory and application."

Truman, who had risen to the rank of colonel in the National Guard, hoped one day to show Harry Vaughan and John Snyder, his summertime encampment friends, a gold star on his shoulder. He was also increasingly prominent in Masonic affairs. In 1924 he had become District Deputy Grand Master and District Lecturer for the 59th Masonic District, and the Independence *Observer* later noted that he "was very proficient as a ritualist." After five years of service in this capacity, the Grand Master of the Grand Lodge of Missouri, William R. Gentry, a Republican, ignored his Pendergast connections and appointed him into the Grand Line of Officers. Not long afterward he climbed the Masonic ladder of offices until he reached the first elective post. This was only four steps below that of Grand Master of Missouri and brought on a convention row against him by Republican and anti-Pendergast Democratic Masons, but he won out after a hectic session.

During Truman's time as presiding judge of the county court, the nature of the Pendergast machine changed. Judge McElroy with his "country bookkeeping" had turned the machine's graft into big business. Now a new force emerged—Johnny Lazia, the gangster politician.

When the Kansas City bond question along with Harry Truman's first county bond issue came to a vote in May, 1928, Lazia decided to take over the North Side of Kansas City where the Pendergast boys had made their original start. Johnny Lazia was then thirty-one and highly ambitious. A short, slim man who affected spats, gloves and a twirling cane, he was unlike the other brutal gangsters of his time in appearance and manner. He laughed and chewed gum steadily and those who knew him called him charming. He spoke excellent English and conversed glibly on legal subjects, although he had never gone past the eighth grade. Actually, he had worked as a clerk in a law office where the promise by the head of the firm to make a lawyer of him was forgotten when he was arrested at eighteen for highway robbery. Although he was sentenced to 15 years in prison, he served only 8 months before he was paroled. Slowly he began to assemble a gang and by 1928 he had real estate and soft drink fronts for respectability and a bullet-proof car to protect him from other Little Italy rivals.

Tom Pendergast had made Mike Ross his Goat leader over Little Italy on the squalid North Side. But Ross neither lived there nor was he Italian, and Johnny Lazia decided the time had come to do away with absentee management and make himself king of Little Italy. He moved boldly on the day the people voted on the Kansas City and

101

Jackson County bond issues. Early that morning Lazia kidnaped Mike Ross's lieutenants and held them until the polls closed. That day his men bossed the polls and at the political meeting scheduled that evening at Ringside Hall, the band struck up "Here Comes the King" when Lazia made his appearance.

Lazia sent word to Pendergast that he was now boss of the North Side. At first Pendergast chose to ignore this upstart. He told newsmen that he was standing by Mike Ross and that he did not think much of Johnny Lazia. But Lazia quickly entrenched himself by weeding out Mike Ross's boys from the precincts and installing his own men in their places. Pendergast might have gone to war with Johnny Lazia. But he had too many projects underway and he saw no point in endangering his entire organization over this skinny little Italian. Lazia could have control over the North Side if he promised to bring in the votes for the Goats. When Lazia agreed to become Pendergast's lieutenant, he was on his way as the "Al Capone of Kansas City."

Lazia did not bother with rural Jackson County, where Truman was in charge of the Goats. But in Kansas City he was king of crime. In the past, Tom Pendergast had winked at the gambling joints, bawdyhouses and speakeasies. Now these became part of a ruthless crime syndicate ruled over by one of his lieutenants. Federal agents later claimed that Lazia's take came to more than two million dollars a year. In one of Lazia's downtown places if you ordered a highball, a nude waitress brought it to your table. When women and reformers complained to City Manager McElroy, the former county judge spoke piously about his "old Presbyterian mother who taught me to avoid gambling in all its forms along with alcohol and nicotine" and advocated a more positive home life and work by the churches "as a bulwark against evil influences."

In an editorial the St. Louis *Post-Dispatch* described the change that Lazia had brought to Kansas City:

> The underworld has got the upper hand. Organized lawlessness is the law. An irresponsible political machine concerned solely with spoils is in full terrifying control. Rackets of all kinds flourish. Saloons boastingly proclaim: "We never close." Gambling houses operate without pretense of concealment. Night clubs boom riotously. The oldest profession beckons boldly. The business of stealing automobiles is the important industry. It is so diligently conducted that insurance rates against the liability of theft in Kansas City are almost prohibitive.

Had the *Post-Dispatch* looked further it would have found that a man known as "Fat Willie" had the tire-stealing concession in Kansas City.

Lazia was helped to his eminence by McElroy. Truman's old wartime major, John Miles, had been put into Kansas City as chief of police by the state administration. Miles was a Republican, which made him *persona non grata* to McElroy and other Pendergast lieutenants. There was also the danger that he might stumble on something incriminating to the machine. McElroy fought him viciously throughout 1928 and 1929. He was slow in paying the police force and actually held up their wages for several months so that Miles's position became intolerable. McElroy also set up a clamor demanding home rule over the police.

When the Missouri Supreme Court ruled that Kansas City and not the state should control its own police department, Lazia no longer had to fear police attacks. In fact, McElroy agreed to consult him on all police appointments. Rabbi Mayerberg claimed that Lazia put 75 convicts on the police force and also charged that Lazia answered the phone on occasion in the office of the director of police. Once, after the rabbi met with McElroy, he found Lazia in the city manager's outer office. "You didn't get anywhere, did you?" Lazia laughed. Several Goat lieutenants justified Lazia's power on the ground that he was protecting Kansas City from invasion by outside gangsters.

Aside from Mayerberg's activities, the *Star* reported little public indignation toward the Pendergast machine. "Pendergast, they told themselves, was a personally honorable and honest man." McElroy was regarded as "a shrewd businessman capable of saving the city more than the cost of stealing." As for Harry Truman, he was that rural official who was building roads and courthouses.

Although he did not realize it at the time, a decisive factor in Truman's political career occurred at Jefferson City not long after he began his second term as presiding judge in 1931. The 1930 census had revealed that Missouri must lose three of its sixteen seats in the United States House of Representatives. When the state legislature passed a redistricting bill, however, Governor Henry Caulfield vetoed it because it was so patently a case of gerrymandering. With no Congressional Districts, all candidates for the House in 1932 had to run at-large on a statewide basis.

The effect of Caulfield's veto was to make Tom Pendergast the boss of the entire state and to push him onto the national scene. For without the support of Kansas City and Jackson County, no man could expect to be elected to the House. A nod from Tom Pendergast now became tantamount to victory.

No sooner did this become clear than a long line of would-be Congressional candidates formed at 1908 Main Street. They came from all over the state and Pendergast listened to each as he pleaded his case. Afterward he made public his own personal primary slate, which was duly reported in the *Star* on June 5, 1932. In addition to members of the House, Pendergast also named his candidates for United States Senator, state supreme court judges, governor and other elected state offices. Some of Harry Truman's friends hoped that Pendergast would name him for governor. But T. J. smiled upon Francis W. Wilson, a popular Missourian who was affectionately called "The Red-Headed Peckerwood of the Platte."

In the spring of 1932 Pendergast also decided to become a President-maker. His candidate was his aging hero, Jim Reed, who had left the United States Senate in 1928 after 18 years of fighting against the League of Nations, labor unions, social reforms and civil rights. Pendergast began his work for Reed that spring by dominating the Democratic State Convention at St. Louis where delegates were to be selected for the national convention at Chicago in June. Special trains carried 5,000 of his fellow Goats to St. Louis, and Judge Truman was one of those ordered to attend the state convention. Truman obeyed Pendergast even though he considered Reed a crusty reactionary.

Missouri papers reported how Pendergast took over the state convention by storm. He insisted that every delegate sent to the national convention be pledged to Reed and that they should not release their votes to other candidates at Chicago without Reed's approval. When one delegate from Greene County to the state convention objected to his tactics, Pendergast knocked him cold with a slap on his cheek. The March 29 headline of the Kansas City *Times* read: THE BOYS PUT IT OVER. St. Louis papers described how "the Kansas City Boss makes his slate" and reported: "Tom Pendergast dominates the convention."

Pendergast had not thought enough of Truman to make him a delegate to the Democratic National Convention. But in June, Truman went along with 400 Goats as a spectator. When excited floor paraders tried to steal the Missouri standard for their candidate, Pendergast snarled, "I'll brain you!" and they fled in horror. Pendergast worked hard in behalf of Reed, but he was no match for Louis Howe, Jim

Farley and Arthur Mullen who led the fight for Governor Franklin D. Roosevelt of New York.

Nevertheless, Pendergast was still Missouri's strong man, and except for a single casualty, his entire 1932 slate won election. His only failure was Charles M. Howell, a former law partner of Jim Reed's, whom he put up as a candidate for United States Senator. It was Howell's misfortune to have as his opponent in the Democratic primary Bennett Clark, whose name not only conjured up memories of his father, the late Speaker Champ Clark, but who also paraded as one of the founders of the American Legion and a fighter for the repeal of the 18th Amendment. The primary campaign turned into a bitter contest of name-calling with Clark, who was from St. Louis, concentrating his attack on Tom Pendergast. T. J.'s chagrin was made worse by the fact that Jim Reed proved himself an ingrate by coming out for Clark. Traditionally, one of Missouri's Senators came from the eastern part of the state and the other from the west. Since the state's other Senator, Roscoe Patterson, was from Kansas City, Pendergast's man, Howell, labored under a severe handicap. On primary day, the Kansas City Goats gave Howell 90,000 votes to 8,000 for Clark. But this margin was not enough because Clark got 250,000 votes elsewhere in the state and swamped Howell by 95,000 votes.

Pendergast was an angry man after that defeat. But he soon had a chance to show that he had not lost any power. His case in point was Francis Wilson, The Red-Headed Peckerwood of the Platte, who died between his primary victory for governor and the November general election. Because time was short, several Goat lieutenants expressed concern about finding a popular successor to Wilson. But Pendergast reached low into his political barrel and brought up Guy B. Park, an unknown circuit court judge. Needless to say, Park won the governor's race and Pendergast was vindicated.

When Franklin Roosevelt was inaugurated President on March 4, 1933, the Pendergast machine was a smoothly operating organization. Governor Park was so indebted to Pendergast that he let him name all appointive state officials; McElroy had complete charge of Kansas City and the millions involved in the 10-Year Plan; and Johnny Lazia kept the mobs from other cities outside of Kansas City. Tom Pendergast's office on Main Street became known as the "State Capitol," and the Jefferson City capitol as "Uncle Tom's Cabin."

One sour note, however, marred the prevailing harmony. President Roosevelt had declared war on the nation's gangsters. "When I came

105

to the Treasury," Secretary Henry Morgenthau said in an interview, "there were five famous gangsters on the Intelligence Unit's list of men to get." Johnny Lazia's name was on top of the list. Unable to find sufficient evidence of criminal activity, the Treasury went after Lazia for income tax evasion.

In March, 1933, he was charged with the violation in Federal Court. Tom Pendergast immediately set to work to save him. On May 12, he wrote to Postmaster General James Farley:

> MY DEAR JIM,
>
> Jerome Walsh and John Lazia will be in Washington to see you about the matter that I had Mr. Kemper talk to you about. Now, Jim, Lazia is one of my chief lieutenants and I am more sincerely interested in his welfare than in anything you will be able to do for me now or in the future. He has been in trouble with the income tax department for some time.... I wish you would use your utmost endeavor to bring about a settlement of this matter. I cannot make it any stronger than to say that my interest in him is greater than anything that might come up in the future."

Pendergast was unable to prevent Lazia's indictment. Only a month after he wrote to Farley, the calm exterior of his organization was split further on June 17 when five persons were slain in what became known as the Union Station Massacre. Federal agents were returning Frank "Jelly" Nash to prison at Leavenworth where he had escaped three years earlier. As seven officers were delivering Nash to a car at the Kansas City railroad station, three notorious gunmen—"Pretty Boy" Floyd, Adam Richetti and Verne Miller—opened up with machine-gun fire. In the melee, four officers and Nash were gunned down. All three thugs made their escape, though Pretty Boy Floyd was later slain by Federal agents, Miller by other gangsters and Richetti was captured and sentenced to death. No one tried to connect Tom Pendergast with the massacre. But Federal agents claimed that Johnny Lazia had arranged the meeting where Verne Miller hired Floyd and Richetti.

While public fear and indignation spread in Kansas City, Harry Truman kept himself busy constructing the courthouses, hospital and new roads and worrying about the devastating unemployment problem. In October, 1933, he accepted a dollar-a-year appointment from Federal Emergency Relief Administrator Harry Hopkins as Re-Employment Director of Missouri. He met Hopkins only a week after he took on this extra job and he looked up to the sallow New Dealer as a man on the glittering heights. Hopkins said he had the money and all Truman and other state administrators had to do was to help parcel it out. Tom Pendergast disliked Franklin Roosevelt intensely, but he was awed by the scale of his financial programs, which dwarfed his own. In a typical Pendergast comment, he barked: "You can't beat five billion dollars."

With social and economic unrest sweeping the country, this was a year of rioting and strikes among the unemployed and labor groups in Missouri. As Truman saw his job under Hopkins, it was one of "redistributing wealth that was amassed in the robust years." He told a university audience at Columbia in January, 1934, "If it is necessary to cut each working day to two hours to give everybody a job, then let's cut it to two hours and give the same wage we used to earn for a ten-hour day." Yet where his precious Kansas City courthouse was concerned, this proposal did not apply. When union workmen went out on what he considered an unjustified strike, he told them that if they did not return to work, "the job will be thrown open to the employment of labor on the basis of competence and skill at NRA wages, which are much lower than union wages."

Some of Harry Truman's friends theorized that Tom Pendergast tolerated him because he could point to him to refute the blanket charges leveled at the Goat machine. But Pendergast never expressed any such thought to his lieutenants. Even during Truman's second term as presiding judge, he was still asking them for their opinion of Truman. In 1933, Truman had a chance to explain his own connection with the Pendergast machine when he attended the National Guard encampment at Camp Pike, Arkansas, shortly after the Union Station Massacre. One morning in his tent he and Ed Schauffler, a Kansas City reporter, were sipping highballs made from a bottle of 20-year-old bourbon that Tom Pendergast had given him.

"Tell me, Harry, if you want to," said Schauffler, "how you, a clean-cut, intelligent public official with unusually progressive ideas, can remain part of a political organization which tolerates such things as this? I'm curious."

Schauffler said Colonel Truman "smiled in his candid, friendly way." Finally he replied: "I don't mind answering at all, Ed. I owe my political life to the Pendergast organization. I never would have had an opportunity to have a career in politics without their support.

They have been loyal friends. I know that the organization has countenanced some things which I believe are wrong. But I do believe this, and that is that you can get further cleaning up a political organization from the inside than you can from the out. At least, I can in the position I am in. If I came out against the organization and tried to wreck it, people would say I was a yellow dog, and they'd be right."

Actually, Truman was in no position to clean up the Pendergast organization from the inside. He had all he could do merely to protect himself from attacks by Goat regulars, such as Bill Ross, Bill Boyle and John Pryor, the big contractors.

As 1934 approached, Truman realized that he faced a major struggle to keep the machine from dumping him. The traditional length of service for a presiding judge of the county court was two terms and his second term would expire at the end of 1934. There was some talk around the Kansas City courthouse that Tom Pendergast might reward him with the county collector's post which he had refused him in 1926. The St. Louis *Globe-Democrat* reported that Truman had been "a district judge and a presiding judge for ten years. The pay originally was $3,500 a year. Then it jumped to around $6,000. He was broke, unable to pay a judgment against him. Having had his second election as presiding judge he was not entitled to another nomination." Despite the rumors that he might be handed the $25,000 collector's job, Truman knew better than to ask Pendergast for it. This plum could go only to someone closer to the boss.

As a matter of fact, Truman really yearned after another office. When Pendergast's man, Guy Parks, became governor, T. J. considered it safe to set up Congressional Districts and dispense with at-large statewide Congressional campaigns. "When the redistricting of the state for Congress came up in the 1933 legislature," Truman said, "I went to Jefferson City and worked for a Congressional District for Eastern Jackson County. I admit that I had in mind the idea of running for Congress in the new district myself. The district was created all right, but Pendergast and Shannon decided to support not me but Jasper Bell. So I was out in the cold."

Bell had been a member of the city council that gave Tom Pendergast the one-man majority he needed to make McElroy city manager back in 1926. This was enough to win a reward from the machine, even though it was Truman who had done all the work of carving out the new Congressional District.

On Truman's fiftieth birthday in May, 1934, he was completely without hope of ever winning the machine's support for a halfway decent political office. A few days later he was in the Pickwick Hotel in Kansas City and wrote a long memo to himself on the hotel's stationery in which he scrawled: *I thought . . . that retirement in some minor county office was all that was in store for me.*

15

THE year 1934 was an important one for both Harry Truman and Tom Pendergast. It brought bad news for Pendergast in February when the Federal Court found Johnny Lazia guilty of income tax evasion. Judge Merrill Otis, who in a few years would direct his attention to Pendergast himself, sentenced Lazia to jail for a year and fined him $5,000, but Lazia lost no time appealing this decision and was released on bond.

Pendergast was glad to have Lazia back in circulation because the municipal election was scheduled for March 27 and he had some doubts about the outcome. The city now had a strong Fusionist organization, composed of dissident Democratic and Republican factions, which was supporting the former president of the University of Missouri, Dr. A. Ross Hill, for mayor against the Goat candidate Bryce Smith. Pendergast was in no mood to give up his lucrative financial take and a warning went out to the precinct workers that the election "had to be won or else."

In reality, he had little to fear. On his orders, Governor Park had appointed Goat election commissioners who approved a Kansas

City registration list that included from 50,000 to 85,000 nonexistent "ghost" voters. The approved list showed that some persons were registered as many as 30 times; from 50 to 100 persons were registered as living together in tiny apartments; some voters were recorded as living on empty lots or in vacant buildings; and thousands of persons long dead were being carried as accredited voters.

Even with this enormous ghost vote, the machine refused to take chances. The Associated Press account of the municipal election began: "Big Tom Pendergast's Democratic machine rode through to overwhelming victory today after a blood-stained election marked by four killings, scores of sluggings and machine gun terrorism." Beginning at six A.M., when the polls opened that day, Goat crews roamed all over town beating up Fusionist voters and election workers with baseball bats and blackjacks. One crew drove past Fusionist headquarters and used it for rifle practice. Pendergast's margin of victory was a 60,000 majority for Smith over Hill for mayor and six council seats to two for the Fusionists.

As usual, in many quarters Pendergast was not blamed personally for the election-day mayhem and murders. He was immune to criticism, for an awe amounting almost to reverence was associated with his name. On the streets people still repeated stories about how Tom Pendergast always kept his word, and how he went to Mass every morning.

It was not long after his smashing victory in the municipal election that Tom Pendergast was carried away by his horse-betting mania. One day he bet $10,000 on a longshot and won $250,000. Before this wager, he had revealed a large appetite for betting on the horses; now he went wild.

Yet even with this compulsion to bet on the ponies, he managed to keep firm control of his machine. For he realized that only through his political organization could he acquire the money he needed at the race tracks.

Since every challenge to the machine was a personal threat, it was not surprising that he was furious when he heard that Senator Bennett Clark was proclaiming loudly from Washington that he would smash the Pendergast machine and name Missouri's next Senator to join him at the Capitol. Senator Roscoe Conkling Patterson, a Republican mossback, was up for re-election that year, and with the New Deal riding high, any Democrat who won the primary was an odds-on favorite to beat him. The mere mention of Bennett Clark's

111

name was enough to make Pendergast smash his hairy fist down on his roll-top desk, for Clark reminded him of his only real defeat since becoming the state's boss. Now Clark had the gall to announce that he would name Patterson's successor, and the man he had in mind was his wartime crony, Jacob L. "Tuck" Milligan, who had already served as a member of the House of Representatives for seven terms.

Even though he could count on his contingent of ghost voters, Pendergast looked far and wide for a strong candidate to thwart Clark. After culling the field, he decided on Jim Reed as his best possibility, although he was seventy-two now and had been out of the Senate since the 1928 election. Reed may have thumbed his nose at him two years before by supporting Bennett Clark against Howell for the Senate, but he was still Pendergast's hero.

While Reed considered Pendergast's offer, Joe Shannon in Washington did not think it would lead to anything. "Jim Reed is an able man, and one of the most difficult," he told a reporter for the Kansas City *Journal-Post*. "I've heard that he can't even get along with himself at times. He's a good vote-getter and I think he could win, if any Democrat could. But he's getting old. And he's comfortable. I don't think he'll run."

Uncle Joe Shannon was right. After stalling Pendergast, Reed finally sent word that he did not choose to run.

This created a problem, for Pendergast did not like to have things hanging in mid-air. Again the search went on, and this time he decided on Shannon himself. Uncle Joe was pleased and even went so far as to ask several Missouri papers to carry the news that "Pendergast has asked me to take the nomination for the Senate."

Shannon, however, carefully weighed his decision. At sixty-seven he saw himself the holder of a safe House seat for life. There was much to be lost in tossing this away merely to try for a seat in the other chamber. If Tuck Milligan, his House colleague, should defeat him, he would have nowhere to go. Shannon liked Washington, the many friends he had made in the House of Representatives and the reputation he had gained as a student of Jefferson. He had not been able to put across a bill to make a national holiday of Jefferson's birthday on April 13, but the Democrats had accepted his idea of Jefferson Day dinners across the country and a Jefferson memorial building in Washington. He also imagined himself an important fighter against the New Deal, and believed that if he left Congress the anti-Roosevelt Democrats would suffer an important loss.

For several weeks Shannon considered Pendergast's offer. But in the end, like Reed, he turned it down after quietly canvassing Missouri Democrats and concluding that Tom Pendergast could not possibly bring in a winner against Clark's man.

Pendergast then turned to James P. Aylward, who had got his political training under Shannon and was then Jackson County Democratic Chairman. But when former Democratic Senator Harry Hawes, who had given up the Senate seat that Bennett Clark now occupied, announced that he, too, would work for Milligan, Aylward lost little time in declining Pendergast's offer.

With his first three choices out of the picture, Tom Pendergast was in a quandary. Just when or why he decided on Harry Truman has never been determined. He had rejected Truman for county collector, governor and congressman. He had never taken him into his confidence, and had always held him at arm's length.

On May 7, when Aylward announced his decision publicly, Truman was out of town. Governor Park, who wanted to get a bond issue to rebuild the archaic state institutions, had appointed him chairman of the bond issue committee because of his success in Jackson County. "I went out speaking for it, visiting thirty-five counties," Truman told a reporter. "While I was in Warsaw [Missouri] in May, 1934, James P. Aylward called me from Sedalia and said he and Jim Pendergast were at the Bothwell Hotel."

Truman did not know why Aylward asked him to join them in their hotel. In Washington, however, Shannon was already aware of Tom Pendergast's decision and told Bill Helm, Washington correspondent of the Kansas City *Journal-Post,* that T. J. was "talking about Judge Truman."

"And who is Judge Truman?" Helm asked.

It was Shannon's opinion that Pendergast was merely filling a gap in his ticket so he could forget about it. "I don't think Truman's heavy enough for the Senate," Shannon said. "I can't imagine him there and I doubt if he can be elected."

When Truman walked into the hotel room in Sedalia, Aylward got right to the point. Tom Pendergast had decided on him for the United States Senate. "They said the organization would back me at least ninety-eight per cent," Truman recalled.

He must have been thunderstruck by the offer because it went far beyond his boldest dreams. Yet he was politician enough to play coy and plead that he did not have the money or the statewide reputation necessary for the contest. He let Aylward and Jim Pendergast talk on and on about how they would help him overcome these handicaps. Finally he agreed.

On May 14, he scribbled a note for his memory book:

> It is 4 A.M. I am to make the most momentous announcement of my life. I have come to the place where all men strive to be at my age. . . . In reading the lives of great men, I found that the first victory they won was over themselves and their carnal urges. Self-discipline with all of them came first. I found that most of the really great ones never thought they were great. I could never admire a man whose only interest is himself. . . . And now I am a candidate for the United States Senate. If the Almighty God decides that I go there I am going to pray as King Solomon did, for wisdom to do the job.

On May 17, when he drove to Jefferson City and filed for the Senate race, there was great surprise in the Kansas City area that Tom Pendergast had chosen him as his candidate. The Kansas City *Star* said: "It was agreed Pendergast had taken on a real job. To jump a man from the county court bench to a Senate nomination was quite an undertaking." People who talked to Pendergast about his selection of Truman found that he said different things to different people. Spencer Salisbury reported that T. J. told him: "I want to put him in the Senate so I can get rid of him." Tom Evans went to see Pendergast at this time and T. J. again asked him what he thought of Truman. Then Pendergast said: "I don't feel that Harry Truman has a chance."

A friend of Pendergast's said that T. J. gave the following reason for throwing Truman into the race: "The boss remarked that he had found out that the United States Senate did not represent the people; that most of its membership represented merely the big-business interests of the country, and that he had decided he wanted to have his own emissary there." This sounds egomaniacal even for a person as self-centered as Tom Pendergast. Yet Spencer McCulloch of the St. Louis *Post-Dispatch* reported later that Pendergast told him he had noticed that some Senators represented the oil industry, others the railroads, steel or utilities, and that T. J. therefore decided he would send his "office boy" to represent him in the United States Senate.

When Harry Truman opened his campaign for the Democratic nomination that July, Johnny Lazia was waiting for the United States

114

Circuit Court of Appeals to consider the appeal of his conviction for income tax evasion in the District Court. On the night of July 9, he returned to his fancy Armour Boulevard apartment hotel long after midnight with his wife Marie and his bodyguard, "Big Charley the Wop" Carolla. As he stepped out of his bullet-proof car, he was cut down by a submachine-gun fusillade. Lazia's last words were: "Tell Tom Pendergast I love him."

Although Lazia's death was the result of a gangland war, it soon became obvious to Truman that his opposition intended to tar him for Lazia's link with the Pendergast machine as well as for the bloody Kansas City election earlier in the year. "I live in Independence, not Kansas City," he said. "I've never voted in Kansas City in my life."

Milligan was not the only contender Truman had to face in the primary contest. Shortly after he filed at Jefferson City, Representative John J. Cochran of St. Louis also entered the race. Cochran was indeed a formidable foe. Praised publicly by President Roosevelt, he also had the support of Bill Igoe, the tough and wily boss of the St. Louis Democratic machine. Cochran had by far the best background of the three Senatorial contenders. He had started out as an editorial writer for several St. Louis papers, worked as secretary to Senator William J. Stone, the chairman of the Senate Foreign Relations Committee, and then became head of the Committee staff. Cochran had also served as a member of the House of Representatives since 1926, and with the coming of the New Deal had emerged as an effective work horse for FDR in the House. Not long before he jumped into the race against Truman and Milligan, Capitol correspondents had voted him one of the six most useful members of the House.

Despite Cochran's reputation, Goat strategists whooped with joy when he entered the Senatorial contest, for they envisioned Cochran and Milligan splitting the vote that would have gone to Milligan, thus insuring Truman's victory. On the other hand, Milligan foresaw Truman and Cochran splitting the vote to his advantage, while Cochran believed he would benefit from a split in the vote between his two opponents. Truman, however, was aware of some revealing evidence that Cochran was not so sure of victory as he professed to be. This important piece of information, which he later passed on to a reporter, was that "Jack Cochran came along after he had made a deal with a man in his Congressional District to take the House nomination there and withdraw if Jack didn't get the Senate nomination."

Truman formally opened his campaign on the Fourth of July. For his kick-off speech he selected the college town of Columbia in the middle of the state, far from Tom Pendergast's bailiwick. To make certain he got a warm reception, Pendergast ordered his lieutenants to send every Goat they could to Columbia with instructions to applaud and cheer their heads off at everything Truman said. He also ordered Governor Park to give Truman a rousing introduction before his speech, which would be carried by radio to every town in the state.

Columbia was bulging with visitors by the time Truman walked onto the platform. Viewers remember him that day as a spruce dresser with a friendly grin on his face, his bright eyes magnified by thick glasses. He was cocky and relaxed, unlike Bess who looked most uncomfortable. Martha Truman, approaching her eighty-second birthday, was on the platform, too, sizing up the politicians who stopped to shake her boy's hand and letting him know on the spot which men were really behind him and which were fakers.

Truman mouthed his speech as if attempting a phonetic rendition from a foreign language. But what he had to say was hard-hitting. To Bennett Clark's charge that he was the Pendergast machine's candidate, he frankly owned up that he was glad to get such support. He pointed out then, as he did throughout the campaign, that: "It will be remembered that both Mr. Milligan and Mr. Cochran journeyed to Kansas City two years ago and sought and received the endorsement of the Kansas City organization for their race for nomination as Congressman-at-Large from Missouri." Then he hit at Senator Clark as the boss behind Milligan. "Senator Clark is lending the weight of federal patronage to the candidacy of Mr. Milligan. His entire action in this campaign is obnoxious to Democratic instinct!" He went on to charge Clark with trying to set himself up as the boss of the Democrats in Missouri. He also stressed the point that he was just as loyal a supporter of President Roosevelt as his two opponents. "I follow him for his large honest intent; for his engaging democracy of thought and action; for his firm determination that life shall be made pleasant for us all; for his view that individual security is the basis of universal security."

Truman tried to demolish Milligan's assertion that he was the only rural candidate. But William Hirth, head of the Missouri Farmers' Association, ignored both farmer candidates and asked his members

116

to support Cochran. Said Truman: "I am appealing for Democratic votes in this campaign on the score that I know the farmers' problems, having been a dirt farmer for twelve years. Being a farmer by birth and experience, I believe I shall carry with me to Washington a far clearer idea of the farmer's position and his needs than either of my opponents." Then he shrewdly added, "In addition to the business and civic experience I have had."

Truman's debut called forth some of Senator Clark's special brand of sarcasm. "His opening speech at Columbia," Clark explained, "was attended almost exclusively by a mob from Kansas City (in fact, I am informed that the natives looked over the crowd to see if Dillinger was there), and by a lot of state employees ordered out by their superiors as a condition to holding their jobs. Harry fears that someone from the eastern part of Missouri may undertake to set up as a boss. Harry Truman fears a boss in Missouri—God save the mark! Harry places the intelligence of the Democrats of Missouri so low and estimates their credulity so high that he actually went into great length in promising the people if elected to the Senate he would not set up as a boss or undertake to dictate to anybody.

"Why, bless Harry's good, kind heart—no one has ever accused him of being a boss or wanting to be a boss and nobody will ever suspect him of trying to dictate to anybody in his own right as long as a certain eminent citizen of Jackson County remains alive and in possession of his health and faculties. . . . The fear that lurks in everyone's mind is that if elected to the Senate, Harry would not be able to have any more independent control of his own vote than he had as presiding judge of the county court of Jackson County."

Truman campaigned without letup during the four weeks before the primary. "I went into sixty of Missouri's one hundred and fourteen counties where I made from six to sixteen speeches a day," he wrote later. "I had become acquainted with all the county judges and county clerks in the state of Missouri and was very familiar with the operations of the so-called 'courthouse gangs' in all the country counties." Roger Sermon, a grocer in Independence, who had been a captain in the 129th Field Artillery, served as Harry's campaign treasurer and parceled out the $12,280 spent during that month to pay for ads, leaflets and meeting halls.

The Kansas City *Times* reported that "in the whole of Missouri history there have been few such spirited contests within a party."

The truth was that when the three opponents discovered they lacked any issue on which they disagreed, their campaigns deteriorated to mudslinging and vilification. *The New York Times* called it "a record low in statesmanship," while the St. Louis *Post-Dispatch* denounced the campaign as a case of "the pot, kettle and stewpan calling each other black."

Milligan called Truman the "Münchausen of Politics." Senator Clark, backing up his man, informed the voters that "Mr. Truman has been conducting a campaign of mendacity and imbecility unparalleled in the history of Missouri." Joe Shannon was called upon by Tom Pendergast to add his light to the campaign and he let go a blast at Cochran whom he labeled "Ranting John" and "the office boy of the St. Louis *Post-Dispatch*." In a speech on July 31, Truman tried to explain who was calling whom names: "With Cochran's man, William Hirth, terming me a 'Bell Boy' and Senator Clark denominating me as a 'common liar' over a statement which appeared in the *Congressional Record* covering the charges I made concerning him, the campaign has reached a 'sacrilege stage,' as Cochran has said." Even though Milligan was supported by Clark, he charged that if Cochran won the Senate seat St. Louis would have two Senators. Cochran hit back with the comment that Clark would have two Senate votes if Milligan should win. Both then turned their tongues on Truman, calling him "Pendergast's office boy," and Milligan added that if Truman were elected Senator and went to Washington, he would get "calluses on his ears listening on the long-distance telephone to his boss."

On August 4, only three days before the primary, the three candidates spoke from the same platform at the Annual Old Settlers Picnic. "I have spoken only of the public records of my opponents," Truman said, while Cochran and Milligan stared openmouthed. But he went on to say that if either beat him in the primary, he would support the winner in November.

The politicians had given Milligan the edge at the start of the campaign. But even with the loud voice of Bennett Clark behind him, he began slipping almost immediately. The race soon centered on Truman and Cochran. Throughout the Ozarks, the KKK, which had temporarily revived, blasted away at Cochran. It therefore became obvious to his backers that they would have to add to his expected margin in St. Louis. But the Democratic machine there made a real blunder when it bragged that Cochran would carry St. Louis by

125,000 votes, for this boast forced Tom Pendergast to add to the vote he planned to bring in for Truman in Kansas City.

Election day was quiet in Kansas City that August, unlike the wild day of killings and beatings during the municipal election in March. Truman, at home in Independence to vote, told a *Star* reporter: "I made the fight. I traveled all over Missouri. I drove day after day in the heat and I feel better now than I did when the campaign began. I have one reservation on that. I did have a head-on collision in my car and got a sprained wrist and some broken ribs. . . . I didn't stop. Went right on handshaking and making short speeches."

When the returns started coming in that night, it seemed that Truman was going to be badly beaten. Outside of Jackson County, Cochran had a total of 234,580 votes. Truman was far behind with 139,321 and Milligan was third with 138,702. Bill Igoe and Mayor Bernard Dickmann, bosses of the St. Louis machine, had done a big job for Cochran, for the St. Louis totals (which looked suspicious) gave him 104,265 votes; Milligan had 6,670 and Truman 3,742.

They were not smart enough, however, to match wits with Tom Pendergast. Since Cochran had won Jackson County by a plurality of 95,269 votes in his 1932 Congressman-at-Large race, they were convinced that even if Pendergast cut his vote in half, Cochran would still win the Senate primary. They did not suspect that the machine in Kansas City and Jackson County was merely waiting for them to make their totals known before disclosing the Pendergast territory vote. When it was made public, Harry Truman had a whopping total of 137,529 votes, compared with a microscopic 1,525 rounded total for Cochran and 8,912 for Milligan. In some precincts, Cochran failed to get a single vote. The final statewide figures gave Truman a plurality of about 40,000 votes, and the St. Louis machine was in no position to cry "Fraud!"

After his victory in the primary, newsmen and photographers came to Independence to interview Truman. He was asked about his religion and explained that he had joined the Baptists at seventeen. "But frankly, all the religion I have is found in the Ten Commandments and the Sermon on the Mount." One photographer wanted a picture of ten-year-old Margaret and Harry asked her to change into a pretty dress. "But everybody is waiting to play," she protested. At Grandview, Martha Truman told a reporter, "You know, there's only one man in the whole campaign I want to slap. Bennett Clark went out of his way to do Harry dirt."

119

The day after the primary, the Kansas City *Star* wrote: "Tom Pendergast today stands forth as the undisputed dictator of Missouri's democracy." Buried elsewhere in its editions were comments about Truman, including one that said: "Jackson County has found him a capable and honest public official, a man of unimpeachable character and integrity."

Although Charlie Ross, Truman's childhood friend and high school classmate, had become editor of the St. Louis *Post-Dispatch's* editorial page, the newspaper set the line that went out all over the country about the Democratic Senate nominee: "Under our political system," the paper stated, "an obscure man can be made the nominee of a major political party for the high office of United States Senator by virtue of the support given him by a city boss. County Judge Truman is the nominee of the Democratic Party because Tom Pendergast willed it so. Shades of Benton and Blair, Cockrell and Vest, Stone and Jim Reed!"

Nor did Tom Pendergast add to Truman's reputation some time afterward when he was asked by a *Post-Dispatch* writer: "Do you exact any promises in advance?" Pendergast's brusque reply was, "If a candidate hasn't got sense enough to see who helped him win and hasn't sense enough to recognize that man's friends, there is no use asking for favors from that candidate in advance."

The nation's newspapers expressed general revulsion toward the man who would go to Washington as the big boss's choice. Truman was well aware of this distaste, which temporarily dampened his joy at winning out over Cochran and Milligan. Tom Evans got friends to contribute the beer and they all had a big time at the celebration in honor of Truman's victory. Truman was there, but he was not his usual cocky self.

In the November general election, Senator Patterson was an easy mark for Truman, who was so sure of winning that he spent only $785 campaigning against his Republican opponent. This was a Roosevelt year, and the name of Roosevelt was filled with magic for anyone who claimed him as his leader. In addition, according to the newspapers, most Republican politicians in Missouri expressed dislike for their Senator. No one was surprised when Truman returned him to private life by a plurality of 262,000 votes.

Shortly after Harry Truman won election to the Senate, he went into his daughter's bedroom to see her.

"How do you think you'll like to live in Washington?" he asked, beaming.

Margaret's reaction startled him.

"I don't want to go to that mean old Washington!" she said firmly, as if nothing could change her mind.

16

HARRY Truman never shared Margaret's initial reaction to Washington. The capital was a place of excitement, abounding with the landmarks of history he had read about since early childhood. His chief concern as he embarked on his Senatorial career was whether he was worthy of his new position. How would a Jackson County judge fit into an arena where Webster, Clay and Calhoun had once debated the great issues of their day?

Late in November, 1934, the newly elected Junior Senator from Missouri decided on a quick trip to Washington to look over the place where he would reside during the next six years.

Reporters found him a strange mixture of humility and cockiness. Bill Helm, Washington correspondent for the Kansas City *Journal-Post,* remembered that Truman walked into his office unexpectedly, introduced himself and grinned like "two Chessie cats" while he referred to himself as "only an humble member of the next Senate, green as grass and ignorant as a fool about practically everything worth knowing."

When asked what he hoped to accomplish during his short visit to

Washington, Truman blandly told newsmen he was going to arrange a Reconstruction Finance Corporation loan for Jackson County. City Manager McElroy had refused to accept one so long as Herbert Hoover was President. But under Roosevelt's two-year regime none had been proffered the county or Kansas City because of FDR's unwillingness to deal with Tom Pendergast. Truman also told reporters that he had asked Senator Clark to arrange a meeting for him with Henry Morgenthau. Later he said candidly, "Senator Clark and I went around and called on the Secretary of the Treasury. He was out—or maybe he just wouldn't let us in."

When he returned to Missouri, Truman added to the confusing picture he had presented in Washington by a speech he delivered to the Kansas City Elks Club. "I won't be a James A. Reed or a Thomas Hart Benton," he said, comparing himself to two of Missouri's Senate greats. "But I'll do the best I can and keep my feet on the ground. That's one of the hardest things for a Senator to do, it seems. All this precedence and other hooey accorded a Senator isn't very good for the Republic. The association with dressed-up diplomats has turned the heads of more than one Senator, I can tell you.

"My trouble is that I probably won't find a place to live. You see, I have to live on my salary, and a cubbyhole rents for a hundred and fifty dollars a month there. The ones that are fit to live in run from two hundred and fifty to five hundred a month, and, although it's hard to believe, there are some saphead Senators who pay fifteen hundred dollars a month for their apartments."

On December 18, 1934, *The New York Times* seized upon his speech to castigate him with sarcasm. The editorial, titled "Just a Farmer Boy," considered him so insignificant that apparently no one bothered to check his first name. It read:

> Judge Henry S. Truman, Senator-elect from Missouri, is not moved as yet by the splendors of Washington or the majesty of the Senate. If the will of Tom Pendergast and the people has called him to the Senate, his heart is true to the rivers of the home county, the Kansas and the Missouri, Big Blue and Little Run. In his speech to his brother Elks and tillers of the soil in Kansas City—whose agriculturalists gave him 135,000 of his fat majority—he was "just a farmer boy from Jackson County." He wasn't going to make a splurge at Washington. He was going to "keep his feet on the ground." That, he said in language highly indecorous for a sub-freshman.

But all was not a pounding of spikes into Truman's head. On December 27 came the dedication of the new county courthouse he had built in Kansas City. It was one of his last appearances as county judge and he induced Supreme Court Justice Pierce Butler to make the chief address at the ceremony. Big-eyed, ten-year-old Margaret made her father proud when she unveiled the equestrian statue of Andrew Jackson before the building, and local papers hailed Truman both for the appearance of the new courthouse and the unique absence of graft in its construction.

The time was drawing near for Truman's departure for Washington to be sworn in as a Senator on January 3. But before he left Independence, the townspeople held a banquet in his honor at the First Christian Church. Speeches were short and the food good. Mize Peters, who was his first-grade seatmate, recalled that "Miss Anna Watson, postmistress at Marceline, got up and told him, 'Someday you will be elected President and I will be there to see you inaugurated.' He laughed louder than the whole crowd put together at her words."

Truman also climbed the stairs to Tom Pendergast's Main Street office before he left for Washington. Pendergast's advice was blunt: "Work hard, keep your mouth shut and answer your mail." Among his very last calls was one on W. L. C. Palmer, his high school principal, and Mrs. Palmer, who as Miss Ardelia Hardin had been one of his favorite teachers. He talked about books, his continuing interest in Latin, and said that he did not expect to be very busy as a freshman Senator. In his spare time, he told them, he planned to enroll at Georgetown University's night law school.

When he finally departed for Washington, he left Bess and Margaret behind. There were many details to attend to, such as hiring a staff and finding an apartment, before his wife, daughter, and mother-in-law arrived. Mildred Dryden, who had been his secretary during his terms as presiding county judge, was to continue as his secretary. What he needed most now was an experienced administrative assistant, a man who knew the ropes on the Hill.

Jim Aylward accompanied Truman to the office of Representative Frank Lee from Joplin, Missouri, who had lost out in the 1934 election. Victor Messall, who was Lee's administrative assistant, vividly recalled this first meeting. Truman impressed him as being an extremely neat tourist with sharply creased trousers, carefully combed graying hair and shiny shoes. "This is Senator Truman," Aylward told

124

Messall. "He wants you to work for him as his secretary." Truman said nothing, but smiled uncomfortably.

Messall immediately rejected the offer to become Truman's aide. The thought flashed through his mind that "Harry Truman had been sent to Washington by a man criticized throughout the country as a crook," Messall said later. "I didn't see any future in an association like that. Here was a guy—a punk—sent up by gangsters. I told myself I'd lose my reputation if I worked for him."

Truman was disappointed, but Messall agreed to help him find a place to live. After driving about Washington, Messall located an inexpensive apartment at Tilden Gardens, just off Connecticut Avenue in the northwest section of the city. It meant a drastic step down in Truman's standard of living because there would be four persons crowded into a small apartment consisting of a living room, dinette, two bedrooms, kitchen and bath. Then Messall drove him to Seventh Street where Truman bought a few cheap pieces of furniture on the installment plan. They also stopped at a music store. "He sat down at every piano in the place," Messall said. "He could really play. Finally, he rented one for five dollars a month. But right then he had trouble because he was broke." After leaving the music shop, they drove to the Hamilton National Bank where Truman went in hat in hand to talk about a loan. Years later at a bankers' dinner, he told how he had always had a high regard for the Hamilton Bank because "it was willing to float a little slow paper for me."

When his family arrived and were settled in the newly furnished apartment, Truman again asked Messall to serve as his aide.

"By now I realized that my original impression of him was all wet," Messall said. "This was a man of real integrity and brains and no Pendergast or anyone else was going to push him around. Once you got to know him you knew he had something special. So I agreed to go to work for him."

At noon on January 3, 1935, Truman walked down the Senate aisle attired in a rented morning coat and striped pants. Senator Bennett Clark, who had so recently denounced him, escorted him to the dais. It was a busy day for Vice-President John Nance Garner for he had thirteen new Senators to swear in, all Democrats. Bess and Margaret sat in the gallery during the ceremony, but Margaret did not recognize her father in his soup-and-fish outfit.

Once he was sworn in and began to work, Truman was painfully aware of his handicaps. Before coming to Washington, he had read through all the biographies and magazine pieces he could find about his new colleagues. With only a few exceptions, they were all college graduates. There were former governors and long-time members of the House of Representatives, judges of State Supreme Courts, financiers and state political leaders. It was the awestruck expression on his face that led Senator Hamilton Lewis, the Democratic Whip from Illinois, to approach desk number 94, almost at the end of the back row, one afternoon. "Mr. Truman," he advised him, "don't start out with an inferiority complex. For the first six months you'll wonder how you got here. After that you'll wonder how the rest of us got here."

But Truman was burdened with an even greater handicap than a sense of intellectual inferiority. "I was under a cloud," he later admitted. So far as the older members of the Senate were concerned he did not represent his state but one of the most corrupt political machines in the country. He knew that this was the general attitude toward him on both sides of the aisle. "I never considered him a Senator," Pat McCarran of Nevada once said. On the Republican side, Bronson Cutting of New Mexico stared through him as if he didn't exist, while George Norris of Nebraska, the Senate's fighting liberal, steered clear of him for a long time.

Truman also found himself under attack by a few columnists who tried to make much of his political origin. "There was one columnist who wrote some lie about my family," he later said. "Instead of sending him a letter, I called him on the phone and I said, 'You so-and-so! If you say another word about my family, I'll come down to your office and shoot you.'"

"Senator Truman may have come into the Senate under a cloud but he had nothing to worry about," Messall said. "In the first place, he had a good personality and made friends easily. He was always going out of his way to do favors for others and you couldn't help but like his smiling, friendly manner. This was not put on, and he was that way with everyone. I never heard him say a cross word to his staff, and that's a real test of sincerity. It was only a matter of a little while before he won acceptance from almost all the other Senators."

The ice was broken on the Republican side when William Borah, the "Lion of Idaho," now in his twenty-ninth year of Senate service, swung an arm about Truman's shoulder and treated him with a broad show of friendship. Then it was Senator Charles McNary of Oregon,

126

the Minority Leader, who ignored party labels and discussed issues and personalities with Truman. On one occasion, he pointed to one of his Republican charges and told Truman, "He's a great trial to me. He talks too much and too soon." He nodded toward another Republican. "That one—I'd say he's my number two s.o.b." Senator Arthur Vandenberg of Michigan was another Republican who befriended Truman. One day Truman entered the Chamber while a hectic debate was in progress. Vandenberg "called on me to speak," said Truman. "I happened to have the information that was needed to settle the argument completely." When he finished, Vandenberg told the Senate, "When the Senator from Missouri makes a statement like that we can take it for the truth." Truman never forgot his remark.

On the Democratic side of the aisle, Carl Hayden of Arizona, a member of Congress ever since Arizona achieved statehood in 1912, tutored him on the complex Senate procedures. Other Democrats also cooperated, but Vice-President Garner turned out to be his most important friend. "Truman was always running to Garner for advice," Messall said.

As the weeks sped by, Garner came to consider Truman one of his many protégés, even though Truman was an out-and-out New Dealer and the Vice-President was a conservative. At the old man's "dog house," where members met over bourbon and branch water "to strike a blow for liberty," Truman was often confronted with his Missouri foe, Bennett Clark, also a Garner protégé. On one occasion, when Garner was asked to state his honest opinion of Clark, Cactus Jack withdrew his soggy cigar butt from his thin-lipped mouth, rolled it between his fingers and finally replied, "If I were going to rob a train and I had to choose an accomplice from the United States Senate, I would pick Bennett Clark."

At an early stage in Truman's career, Garner frequently let him take over the Vice-President's chair in the Chamber and preside over the Senate. The first time Garner did this, Truman experienced severe stage fright. By coincidence, Margaret was in the gallery and she spied him sitting with his hand over his mouth, a characteristic gesture when he was nervous. Unable to contain herself, she began waving at him. When this failed to draw his attention, she leaned dangerously over the rail. All the while, Truman sat staring straight ahead. As her antics grew wilder, he suddenly fluttered his fingers without removing his hand from his mouth. She realized then that he had been watching her all the while and that she could expect a good talking-to later.

Truman's closest friendship was with the "Young Turks," the twelve other Democratic Senators who were sworn in with him. Among the Young Turks, Truman's special friends were Lewis B. Schwellenbach of Washington, Carl A. Hatch of New Mexico, and Sherman "Shay" Minton of Indiana. Truman later appointed Schwellenbach to his Cabinet, Hatch to the Federal District Court, and Minton to the Supreme Court.

One of the peeves of the Young Turks was Senator Huey Long of Louisiana, who was at his rowdiest in 1935 with his jeers at Roosevelt and frequent one-man filibusters. On June 13, he spoke almost sixteen hours, during which time he gave recipes for "pot-likker," fried oysters and turnip greens. After twelve hours, Schwellenbach expressed the opinion of Truman and the other Young Turks by interrupting the Kingfish and asking, "Does the Senator realize that a group of new Senators have day after day and week after week and month after month seen the Senate, which is supposed to be the greatest deliberative body in the world, turned into a circus by the Senator from Louisiana?"

Once, when Truman occupied Garner's chair and recognized Long, the other Senators present stampeded into the cloakrooms to avoid the inevitable long-winded tirade. Truman was forced to sit through several hours of ranting nonsense. Afterward, he said, when the Senate adjourned, Long walked across the street with him. "What did you think of my speech?" the Kingfish asked.

"I had to listen to you," Truman said, "because I was in the chair and couldn't walk out."

A sour sneer settled on Long's face before he hurried away. He never spoke to Truman again.

17

SHORTLY after Truman became Senator, he called the White House to make an appointment with the President. However, he was unable to get past Stephen Early, the President's press secretary, who stalled him off for five months.

Not long after his initial failure to see Roosevelt, he went with Joe Shannon and Representative Jasper Bell to see Attorney General Homer S. Cummings. This meeting seemed to buttress the view of the Kansas City *Star* that Truman wanted to create a better climate between the Administration and Tom Pendergast. But it was of little consequence because Cummings had no political influence with Roosevelt. Moreover, he had been given orders by Roosevelt to smash the Kansas City machine. As a result, the Attorney General merely shook hands with Truman and exchanged a few banalities.

Unknown to Truman, Cummings had already begun his drive to destroy Tom Pendergast. On February 3, 1934, at the request of Senator Bennett Clark, President Roosevelt had appointed Maurice Milligan as U. S. Attorney for the Western District of Missouri. Truman knew Maurice Milligan as the brother of Tuck Milligan, a pal of Clark's, who had run against him in the Democratic Senatorial primary.

Before Milligan took the job, Cummings had called him to Washington for a briefing. According to Milligan, Cummings said angrily, "Kansas City is one of the three 'hot spots' in the United States. Chicago and St. Paul are the other two. These three cities have been involved with every kidnaping that has occurred to date, either as the situs of the crime, the hideout or the place of ransom payment." It was little wonder, then, that Cummings had not shown any warmth toward Truman in their meeting.

"Actually," Vic Messall said, "Senator Truman only wanted to meet Roosevelt to say hello and for no other reason." But it was not until he was a Senator five months that Roosevelt permitted him to come to his White House office. "I went along with the Senator to the West Wing of the White House the day of his appointment," Messall said. "When we got to the appointments secretary's office, outside the President's office, Harold Ickes, Henry Wallace and other Cabinet members were sitting around on the sofas and chairs and talking government business. We were both impressed. However, none of them said hello to the Senator and he sat in silence while he waited. Finally Pa Watson, who handled FDR's appointments, told Truman he could go in to see the President. Although he had a fifteen-minute appointment, he was out in only seven minutes."

Nevertheless, Truman's initial reaction to Roosevelt was one of hero worship. "He was as cordial and nice to me as he could be," he recalled. They had not discussed any issues or legislative matters. "It was quite an event," he added, "for a country boy to go calling on the President of the United States."

About three years were to pass before Truman would consider the sight of Franklin Roosevelt a little less than breath-taking. By then, the President had evinced an unrelenting unwillingness to give him any Federal patronage, the bread and butter of any Senator's home support. When it came to making appointments to the Federal bench, or as Federal attorney, marshal or Collector of Internal Revenue, or approving homestate river and harbor projects, Roosevelt pointedly ignored Truman. Instead, FDR worked closely with Bennett Clark, even though Clark was an early isolationist and an anti-New Dealer. In fact, the more Clark came to oppose Roosevelt, the more patronage he collected. Even when Roosevelt finally barred Clark from further patronage, he did not transfer such favors to Truman but bestowed them instead on the governor of Missouri.

"Truman did manage to get a little patronage," Vic Messall said, "but only when Bennett Clark needed his help back home. The two never really hit it off. When they were obliged to be in each other's company they'd smile and do a little polite mumbling, but that was all. For very minor Federal jobs back in Missouri, Clark would come around, and he and Truman flipped a coin with the winner naming the man for the job."

The Administration also tended to ignore Truman because he was an ardent New Dealer and his vote was generally in the bag on Administration bills. In only a few recorded instances did he vote against the White House. In 1937, for instance, he voted for a resolution condemning the sit-down strikes of that year in automobile plants as an unfair labor practice.

He also opposed the Walsh-Healey Bill of 1936, which required government contractors to pay prevailing wages on contracts involving $10,000 or more. On this issue he joined Bennett Clark to see to it that the bill did not pass the Senate. On the last day of that session, the two realized that a final effort would be made to squeeze the Walsh-Healey Bill through under the unanimous consent rule. This meant that if a single Senator objected to the measure when it came up, the bill was automatically killed.

All that day Truman and Clark remained on the Senate floor, waiting for the bill to be brought up. By eight P.M., Truman was famished, for he had gone without food since breakfast. He told Clark he would run down to the Senate dining room for a sandwich and hurry back to the floor. Clark was to hold the fort until he returned.

"I wasn't gone twenty minutes," Truman told a reporter. "When I came back I saw that Clark wasn't in the Chamber. I then found out that Walsh had called up the bill meanwhile and that it passed without objection, only a minute or so before I got back." Clark had gone to the men's room and Senator Walsh had called up his bill as soon as he disappeared. "To make it worse," Truman added, "some of our friends were sitting in the gallery and saw the whole thing. I can imagine how they felt."

Not until Truman began showing minor signs of independence did White House aides maintain a close watch on his voting. Even then, however, they did not pressure him by offers of patronage but solely by demands that he remain loyal to the New Deal. After a while, this treatment began to irritate Truman. "The explosion came in 1938," Viv Messall said. "That summer he was driving back to Kansas City when Jimmy Byrnes called me. Byrnes said that the New Dealers had only a tie vote on a major bill and FDR needed Truman back at the Capitol to break the tie.

"I called the highway police and they picked Truman up and brought him back to Washington. He was mad clean through when he walked into the office. 'Who do those so-and-sos think they are? he yelled. 'I haven't been recognized by the White House, but they think they can use me to vote for Roosevelt! Get Steve Early on the phone!' "

Early tried to mollify Truman. "What's troubling you, Senator?"

"I'm sick and tired of being the White House office boy!" Truman shouted. "This is the third time I've come back here to bail you guys out on a vote. You tell that to the President!"

Not long afterward Truman told reporters that he did not favor three terms for any President.

18

———————————

TRUMAN quickly established a routine in Washington. Every day he rose at 5:30 and read the two Washington morning papers through from cover to cover, including the want ads and comic strips. He was careful not to crease the sport pages, because Bess was an ardent baseball fan. Then he shaved with a safety razor, stropping dull blades on the palm of his hand in order to get a few extra shaves from each blade.

After dressing, he left the apartment house for a brisk walk in nearby Rock Creek Park, always marching along at the old infantry pace of one hundred and twenty steps a minute. On his return to the apartment, he generally found his womenfolk up and he ate breakfast with them.

"At seven every morning," Messall said, "Truman called me to report he was leaving his place to walk down Connecticut Avenue. I picked him up en route and drove him to the Senate Office Building." Once in his office, Truman went over the mail, talked to visitors and called various government agencies on behalf of constituents. "No lobbyist could ever demand anything from him or tell him how to vote,"

Messall said. "If anyone put pressure on him, he immediately turned stubborn. On the other hand, he never made demands on others. When he wanted me to do something he'd ask, 'Don't you think we ought to do it this way?'"

During the early days of the New Deal, Senators spent a great deal of time calling government agencies on behalf of businessmen back home about work projects and government contracts and licenses. Truman, however, found that he had little influence at most New Deal agencies. "I always liked Harry Hopkins," he once told Jonathan Daniels. "He was one of the few people who were kind to me when I first came to Washington." He also had good relations with Secretary of Labor Frances Perkins, whom he joined in a luncheon group that met occasionally at the Allies Inn cafeteria "and talked over common problems." But with Jesse Jones, boss of the RFC, "terrible-tempered" Secretary of the Interior Harold Ickes, and others in the Administration's hierarchy, his arguments carried no weight.

Despite his lack of major influence, requests for aid poured into his office. When he could do something, his approach was to favor the underdog. "One morning," Messall said, "I brought him fifty folders of applications for appointments to West Point from Missouri boys. The folders were thick and contained recommendations from judges, state legislators, mayors, et cetera. We went through each folder methodically and finally we got down to a folder that contained no letters of recommendation—only a single-page application written in pencil on a sheet of cheap, rough paper. Truman read it and then he turned to me and ordered, 'Give him the appointment.'"

At ten A.M., Truman usually hurried out of his office to committee. The Senate Democratic Steering Committee had assigned him to two major committees, Appropriations and Interstate Commerce, as well as to two minor committees, the Printing Committee and Public Buildings and Grounds. Since each major committee was fragmented into as many as a dozen subcommittees, a Senator often had two subcommittee hearings in process at the same time.

By noon Truman was at his back row desk in the Senate Chamber. Although some of his freshmen colleagues entered the debate almost as soon as they were sworn in, he took the advice of Garner to learn the score before he spoke. After a few weeks, Truman labeled the Chamber "the cave of the winds." He did not introduce his first bill until he had served four months. This was a measure to provide insurance on farm mortgages by the Farm Credit Administration. Vice-

President Garner assigned his bill to a committee that promptly pigeonholed it. Six months after he was sworn in, Truman rose for the first time to speak, saying only: "I move to reconsider the vote by which the amendment offered by the Senator from Pennsylvania was rejected."

He explained his reticence to join Senate debate in a press interview. "I'm not going to demagogue until I have something to demagogue about." But even later, when he began making Senate speeches, he found it a torture. Vic Messall said: "I used to feel sorry for him. Every time he had to make a speech he'd tell me, 'I can't do it.' He just couldn't talk worth a damn in front of people and had to steel himself to open his mouth. When he finally spoke, he never did so extemporaneously but always read prepared statements generally filled with statistics." Early in his Senatorial career, Pathé News sent a crew to his office to record a speech. Retake after retake followed with the cameraman shouting angrily, "Senator, speak up!" Finally the head of the crew told the cameraman, "Let's call it off. This guy can't even talk. Let's get our equipment and get out." Messall prevailed on the crew to try once more and this time Truman did a passable job. "He ain't no Roosevelt," the sound man said in Truman's presence before they left.

After a long afternoon at the Capitol, Truman returned to his office in the Senate Office Building across the street where he occupied Room 248, a three-room suite that looked into the grass inner court of the building. This was to be his office until he moved into the White House in 1945, though he could have claimed larger and more convenient suites as he gained seniority. These late sessions in his office were generally devoted to signing correspondence. He was ambidextrous and his signatures with either hand differed only in slant. On occasion, he wrote nasty letters, but Messall made it a practice to hold them a few days. Almost invariably on second reading Truman tore them up.

During the thirties the Senate still numbered among its members frock-coated gentlemen from the deep South and Westerners in ten-gallon hats and string ties. By contrast, Truman, in his neat double-breasted business suit, had little color. In fact, he was seldom recognized as a Senator. Once when telephone repairmen were working in his office, Messall told them to help themselves to drinks from the liquor stocked in the office icebox. Messall was gone an hour and when he returned he asked, "Did anyone come in?"

135

One of the repairmen replied, "Yes, one guy did and I told him, 'Look, you want a drink? We'll give you one but don't tell the Senator we did, because if the Senator finds out we'll be fired.' He drank one with us and then he left."

Messall asked for a description of the man. It was Truman.

As a rule Truman returned home for dinner at about seven-thirty. Sometimes, after eating, he went to the grocery with Bess or helped do the dishes. When it rained, Margaret liked to skate indoors and the racket she made filled Truman with concern. Finally one day he knocked on the door of Paul Wooton, a Washington correspondent who lived directly beneath him, and falteringly apologized for Margaret's roller skating. Truman was certain that Wooton would give him hell, but instead Wooton assured him that the noise didn't bother him at all. Truman returned glumly upstairs where Margaret was still skating.

After some months, Truman had Margaret's piano shipped to Washington from Independence and returned the one he was renting. He enjoyed playing the piano after dinner and occasionally he and Bess went to concerts at Constitution Hall. But more often than not he spent his evenings on Senate work. Margaret remembered that he "brought home mountains of work and long after I was in bed he would be reading and studying his problems." He would spread his papers on the dining room table and go through them methodically. Often he fell asleep reading and Bess had to shake him awake and tell him to go to bed.

He managed to get in an enormous amount of reading, not all of it on Senate business. There was always a voracious appetite for biographies of political and historical figures and for military analyses. Truman had a passionate interest in the Civil War and he and John Snyder, his wartime friend and National Guard companion who was then working in Washington for the Comptroller of the Currency, studied Civil War battles and argued about them as if that holocaust still raged. On September 30, 1939, Truman wrote a letter to a Mr. Foster in New York:

> I am still studying battlefields. If you haven't done it you ought to compare Hillaire Belloc's outline of the Battle of Austerlitz with Chancellorsville. You will be surprised at the similarity of the two maneuvers.

One of the chief forms of Senatorial recreation came around the poker table. Truman enjoyed poker but he seldom played. Yet years later those who served with him in the Senate liked to conjure up tales about him at the poker table. Vic Messall said that he played well but had certain failings. One was a cautiousness that sometimes irritated other players. One night Truman was in a game at a friend's apartment. Al Holland of Pathé News sat at his left. When Truman dawdled and studied his hand interminably, Holland yelled at him with unbridled impatience, "All right, double-focus, what are you going to do?"

"Truman had another poker-playing peculiarity," Messall said. "He never wanted to beat anyone. I saw him turn down four aces one night so someone who wasn't doing well could win a pot."

Truman was friendly with Senator Joseph F. Guffey of Pennsylvania, who had the reputation of being one hundred per cent for anything Roosevelt wanted. Other Senators used to say, "Guffey doesn't know what his position is on this bill because Roosevelt's line is busy." Guffey owned a game preserve and one time he invited Truman to do some hunting. But when caretakers herded game in front of the hunters, Truman refused to shoot.

As a firm believer in the sanctity of marriage, Truman was never touched by scandal. "Harry Truman never had a Mrs. Peck," Charlie Ross once said, referring to Mrs. Mary Hulburt Peck, the friend of Woodrow Wilson, who was responsible for his becoming the target of a national whispering campaign in the 1916 election. Vic Messall described Truman's odd behavior at Washington cocktail parties. "When he went alone and there were women present, he'd keep his coat on, take a drink and say, 'I've got to go on to dinner.' Then he'd walk out fast." He liked a good off-color story, but he did not approve of any vulgarity when women were present.

Drinking was a special problem on the Hill during New Deal years. Truman was never known to be drunk, but he liked his bourbon and branch water, although Mrs. Truman did not approve of drinking. Ed Halsey, Secretary of the Senate, maintained a superb stock of liquor in his office. During the day when tension rose on the Senate floor, members would saunter across the hall to Halsey's office for a tension reliever. Funmaker of the group was Nate Bachman, Senator from Tennessee, whom Truman considered the best storyteller and mediator in the Senate. "Bachman could get any controversy on the Senate floor settled," he said, "by stepping out of the Chamber and asking

137

someone to say to the troublemaking Senator, 'Nate Bachman wants to see you in the Secretary's office.' "

When the Trumans first arrived in Washington, Bess enrolled Margaret at Gunston Hall, a private school established in four old Washington houses. Margaret was then in the fifth grade. Every morning Bess drove her to school and picked her up late in the afternoon. Because most of the girls lived at the school, Margaret was an outsider. She said, however, that she was finally accepted by the other girls when she won a school contest for screeching the loudest.

While Truman worked hard to master his job, Bess and Margaret did a great deal of sightseeing. Bess took her to the usual places—the Lincoln Memorial, Mount Vernon, the Lee Mansion and the Tomb of the Unknown Soldier. Margaret said that they went to the Smithsonian Institution "exhaustively." One time they joined the tourists at the White House, and gawked through the elegant Green Room, Blue Room, East Room and State Dining Room. That first year Mrs. Roosevelt invited Margaret along with the daughters of other Congressmen to a dancing party at the White House. Mrs. Truman declined the invitation by writing to Mrs. Roosevelt that her daughter was only eleven. Not until four years later did Margaret get another White House invitation, this time to a reception. But when she pestered her father to let her go, he told her, "You're too young. You're only fifteen." When she continued to argue, he added the clincher. "And besides, your mother has decided against it."

In the summer, when school let out, Bess, Margaret and Mrs. Wallace returned to Independence. As soon as Congress adjourned, Truman went home, too, and there were frequent trips to Grandview to see the "Old Rebel," as he affectionately called his mother. During the Congressional sessions, she wrote him frequently, giving her views on pending legislation. She also wrote to other Senators to prod them into supporting her hero, Franklin Roosevelt. She read the daily *Congressional Record* and congratulated her son when she thought he voted right and criticized him when he did not.

During this period Truman maintained his colonelcy in the National Guard. For a few weeks each summer he and John Snyder, Harry Vaughan and Eddie McKim donned uniforms and went through the rigors of the summer encampments. As in the old days their practical jokes were broad. One of their pranks took more than a decade to develop.

138

It began one summer day during the mid-twenties when McKim served as Vaughan's adjutant. After a photographer had taken a picture of the officers, Vaughan ordered McKim to carry his chair back to the porch. "You've ruined my record," McKim complained. "This will be the first work I've done."

Twelve years went by when, one day in St. Louis, John Snyder called Vaughan and suggested that the two meet Senator Truman and McKim, coming in at 1:20 P.M. on the Baltimore and Ohio. It was a July day with the temperature at 110 degrees. On arrival, the 235-pound McKim was obviously drunk and swayed precariously. "John, you take the Senator to the club and I'll get Eddie there separately," Vaughan said, embarrassed. At the St. Louis Athletic Club, Vaughan somehow raised McKim's body to his shoulder and staggered to Truman's suite, where he threw him onto a couch. "Lay there and sober up, you drunken s.o.b.," Vaughan panted.

Suddenly McKim opened his eyes and said soberly to Vaughan, "You would make me carry that chair to the porch at Fort Riley!" Truman threw back his head and laughed until he was almost in tears. He and McKim had concocted the gag.

In the Senate, Truman seemed an unlikely choice to participate in such horseplay. Even though he was widely accepted by his colleagues, he lacked the easy casual manner of those who were not dependent on their salaries. Indeed, he had great difficulty getting along on his $10,000 a year. "He always had a loan going at a Washington bank," Vic Messall recalled. Some years later when Truman was a guest at the home of Donald Richberg, one-time head of the NRA, he made an unusual admission. Lord Halifax of Great Britain had asked him how he got along on his pay and Truman replied candidly, "I could not live on my salary. So I just put my wife on the payroll." Bess was down for $4,500 a year.

As time went on, although Truman was well versed in the Senate's history and impressed with its importance, he no longer considered himself inferior to other members. An old colored doorkeeper at the Senate once led one of Truman's constituents onto the floor and pointed out the seats that had been occupied by Missouri Senators Francis Cockrell and George Vest. "When they represented your state," the doorkeeper said, "the seats were most ably filled with statesmanship." Then he added in a tone of sorrow, "I cannot say so much for your later Senators." Truman was furious when he heard about this incident.

The esteem in which Truman held the Senate was revealed at a banquet he attended in St. Joseph, Missouri, where several judges were present. According to John Barker, a Missouri lawyer, when the master of ceremonies called the judiciary the most important branch of the government, Truman leaped to his feet. "The legislature is!" he shouted. "It's close to the people and provides the money to run the government. I can say anything I want to about judges," he added in a softer tone, "because I have no license to practice law. Therefore, no license can be taken away from me. Besides, I can't be sued because I haven't anything."

19

_____

To Harry Truman, the most interesting part of his Senate day came in committee, where a stream of witnesses testified and faced sharp interrogation. It did not take him long to realize that his background as a county administrator was vastly different from that required of a good committee operator. As he told a joint session of the Missouri State Legislature on March 21, 1939: "I found out very soon after I settled down to a study of my duties that the business of a good legislator is not to get things done quickly and efficiently as a good administrator has to do; but to prevent, if possible, the enactment into the law of the land many crazy and crackpot measures."

Truman's service on the Appropriations Committee gave him insight into government operations and Federal financing. Here government officials argued for money they insisted was needed to carry out their work. Many found it an imposition that Congress determined what money they could spend. At the same time, some committee chairmen considered themselves bosses of the agencies they judged. Truman early observed that "the chairmen of the Military and Naval Affairs Committees, especially in the House, where appropriations originate, tended to become Secretaries of War and Navy" and "had to have seventeen-gun salutes, parades, et cetera, as often as they could find excuses to visit Army posts and naval bases."

The chairman of the Appropriations Committee was doughty little Carter Glass of Virginia, father of the Federal Reserve System. With deference to his fighting manner, committee members called him "The Old Rooster." Senator James F. Byrnes of South Carolina, who ranked high in seniority on Glass's committee, had the enviable position of being Roosevelt's messenger in the Senate. Byrnes was the Senator who buttonholed his colleagues in the cloakroom and passed along FDR's promises for patronage and support of pet projects in exchange for support of the President.

As the bottom man in seniority on the Appropriations Committee, Truman steered clear of arguments for a few years. He had much to learn but he was fortunate in having Senator McNary, the Republican leader, as a tutor. "He and I used to discuss at great length . . . matters that were pending in the Appropriations Committee," he later wrote. Though the total annual Federal budget in the middle New Deal years was only slightly higher than the single appropriation for Marshall Plan aid after World War II, the squabbles over its contents were just as hectic as they were later when the budget was six times as great. The wrangling was especially acute when it came to the budget for the armed services. Because of his own military experience and interest, Truman specialized in defense and military spending on the Appropriations Committee and came to be known as an exponent of a big army. Nevertheless, as he put it, the armed forces "do a good job on the waste side. They throw money around by the scoop shovelful."

On the Printing Committee, where Senator Hayden was chairman, Truman helped supervise the Public Printer in charge of the Government Printing Office. Problems involving the *Congressional Record,* which the GPO printed, came before this minor committee. Among these problems was the complaint of several Senators that some of their colleagues altered the Senate debates before they were printed so that the written record differed from what was actually said.

When Truman first came to the Senate he was assigned to the District Committee, which handles the affairs of the Nation's capital. This committee spends hours considering such matters as the fee to charge for dog licenses and the minimum size of fish sold at the Washington market. Truman soon resigned from this committee on the ground that the city was entitled to home rule. "I didn't come to the Senate to be a local alderman," he argued.

He also served on the Public Buildings and Grounds Committee with Senator Tom Connally as chairman. From his reading, he had learned that the Capitol architect during Lincoln's first administration had urged moving the central stairway of the Capitol forward several yards, setting it in proportion to the stairways leading to the Senate and House Chambers. Together, Truman and Connally pushed this 1863 proposal through the Senate, although, said Truman, "a little pinhead Congressman from Iowa interested the Washington *Star*, and the House beat the bill."

There is no question that his services on the Senate Interstate Commerce Committee did more to bring Truman into prominence than any of his other Senate activities before World War II. And the man most responsible for this was Senator Burton K. Wheeler, chairman of that committee. Vic Messall said, "Truman often admitted that if it hadn't been for Wheeler, he never would have moved along the road to the White House. Wheeler put him in the right spot at the right time."

The two men were opposites in many respects. Wheeler was vitriolic and gesticulating; Truman, friendly and quiet. Wheeler loved nothing better than a good fight; Truman was a peacemaker. Wheeler was a born prosecutor, with a slashing style that wore witnesses down until they made incriminating admissions. He was also a champion of the underdog, and as U. S. Attorney for Montana from 1913 to 1918, he went after the copper and railroad moguls with a determination to end their political and economic domination of his state. When he came to the Senate in March, 1923, he immediately won nationwide fame for his attacks on big business. Only a year later he was the Senate prosecutor of the Teapot Dome scandal involving several of the late President Harding's close associates. In 1924, when the Democrats nominated John W. Davis, a Wall Street lawyer, for President, Wheeler deserted the party to run for Vice-President on the Progressive Party ticket with Senator Robert M. La Follette of Wisconsin. The platform they ran on was a forerunner of the New Deal.

In 1935, when Truman came to the Senate, the first phase of the New Deal was already over. Signs of an economic upturn were appearing and the business community, which had fallen into a state of shock with the onslaught of the Great Depression, gave indication that it was eager to do battle against further New Deal measures. Many

143

New Dealers in the government feared that Roosevelt lacked courage for a row with industrialists and would abandon much of his yet unfulfilled program.

Roosevelt, however, had no such intention. The first attack in 1935 was to be against the public utilities. On January 22, FDR announced that there would be "no quarter with the utilities." Shortly afterward, the White House sent Congress the Public Utility Holding Company Bill, known as the Wheeler-Rayburn Bill, with Wheeler sponsoring it in the Senate and Sam Rayburn in the House. The heart of the bill was Section XI, called the "Death Sentence" clause, which dissolved all public utility holding companies unless they could prove their continuance was necessary. What had happened in the United States was that holding companies had acquired control of the voting stock of several hundred operating electrical power companies. The Administration took the position that the holding companies were "milking" the operating companies by draining off profits, raising rates and putting operating company property on their books at excessive valuation in order to pyramid their own holdings. The holding companies maintained that they were necessary to finance operating companies.

The Public Utility Holding Company Bill created a furor. As a member of Wheeler's committee, Truman was caught in the middle of the fight. The hearings conducted by Wheeler, said Truman, "were the most remarkable that I ever had anything to do with." The parade of public utility champions included Wendell Willkie, president of Commonwealth and Southern, the former Democratic Presidential candidate John Davis, John Foster Dulles, and the Whitneys who ran the New York Stock Exchange. Wheeler and Willkie tangled in mammoth arguments, with both men ill-tempered and unwilling to make the slightest concession to the other.

Leaders of the public utility lobby called on Truman, demanding that he vote against the bill. When he refused, he said, "The lobby sent people out to Missouri to get the Democratic organization there to exert pressure on me. That failed also." Next, the lobby induced Missourians who owned public utility securities to flood Truman's office with letters and telegrams urging that he vote against the bill. During the heat of the fight, a total of 30,000 such demands crossed his desk, and he ordered all of them burned. The Kansas City *Journal-Post*, though pro-Pendergast, was owned by Henry Dougherty, president of Cities Service. When Truman refused to support the holding companies, the *Journal-Post* ran a two-column editorial on page one denouncing him. The lobby's power was so extensive that on June 11, when the "death sentence" section came up for a Senate vote, it passed by a whisker, 45–44. The total bill then passed the Senate 56–32, with Truman paired in favor.

As Truman's committee service lengthened, Wheeler let him help run hearings on other matters. In 1937, for instance, a Truman bill passed the Senate requiring operators of motor vehicles engaged in interstate commerce to take Federal driver's examinations. The trucking industry strenuously attacked this measure, charging that Truman was in collusion with the optical industry to promote the sale of eyeglasses. Although he had little trouble winning Senate approval, the House twice rejected the bill.

"What was funny about the Senator's concern about driving standards," Vic Messall said, "was that he was the worst driver I knew. He always ignored speed limits and he passed cars on curves and hills. You sat there praying you wouldn't get killed."

On one occasion, when the Trumans were driving back to Washington from Independence, he ran a red light at Hagerstown, Maryland, and plowed into another car. Then his own car bounced off and was demolished when it rammed a lamppost. "Part of the lamppost fell down on the car and gave Bess an awful jolt," Truman said. "Her neck has never been quite right since." Truman escaped with only a strained back. Highway patrolmen who arrived at the scene took him to the mayor. But when the mayor learned that Truman was a United States Senator, he was so upset that instead of handing him a stiff fine, he gave him the keys to the city.

In addition to his committee work on Federal driver's examinations, Truman was also assigned to a three-man subcommittee to determine what should be done to regulate the fast-sprouting civil aviation industry. At that time Truman did not enjoy flying because of an experience in World War I when he was ordered to go aloft in France. "It was an old 'Jenny,' " he recalled, "and the pilot didn't want me to ride with him any more than I wanted to take the ride. I became very sick, due to all the gyrations he gave the plane. I was sick for many years after that whenever I took a flight in a plane."

Although Truman was only the subordinate Democrat on the civil aeronautics subcommittee, when the chairman failed to attend the hearings, he and Warren Austin, the Republican Senator from Vermont, ran the entire show. What emerged was a bill later known

145

as the Civil Aeronautics Act of 1938. The heart of this bill established an administrative boss for the Civil Aeronautics Board to conduct the quasi-judicial work for the CAB, which involved economic regulation, safety controls and accident investigation.

Before the bill became law, however, Truman was almost robbed of authorship by Senator Pat McCarran of Nevada. After the Interstate Commerce Committee reported the Truman-Austin Bill out favorably, it went on the Senate Calendar. McCarran then quietly removed it from the Calendar and reintroduced it as a new bill. By the time Truman got wind of what had happened, Vice-President Garner had already referred the so-called McCarran Bill to the Senate Commerce Committee.

When the bill emerged from McCarren's committee, it differed from Truman's bill by making no provision for an independent CAB administrator and keeping the Board under the thumb of Congress, instead of functioning as an independent agency under the President's appointive power. Truman was furious when the McCarran version passed the Senate; and his anger increased when he was omitted from the conference committee to iron out differences between the Senate and House versions of the bill.

At this point Bennett Clark entered the picture. In 1938, fearful that he might not win re-election without Truman's support, he hurried to Garner and staged a scene of violent outrage. "If you don't put Harry on the conference committee, you can have my resignation from the Senate!" he bellowed. Garner heard him out with his crooked smile, knowing that the only way Clark would leave the Senate was in a box. Then he quietly added Truman's name to the list of conferees.

In the conference committee sessions, Truman carried on a running dog fight with McCarran, who had no intention of retreating from his position. The other members, however, reinserted the main points of Truman's original bill. This version passed both houses and was signed by the President, although McCarran maintained to his death that he was the father of the Act.

Truman's most significant activity during his first term in the Senate came about by accident. This work not only established him as a top-ranking Senator but also gave him the important background for his War Investigating Committee of World War II. In February, 1935, Wheeler introduced a resolution to investigate railroad finances. The American railroad system was a "sick" industry with several roads either bankrupt or on the verge of going under. Wheeler proposed to examine the financial management of this multibillion-dollar industry and come up with remedial legislation to protect stockholders and rehabilitate the carriers.

The Senate showed little interest, however, and it was not until the following year that he won the small budget of $10,000 to undertake his investigation. Although Truman desperately wanted to serve on the subcommittee, Wheeler did not make him a member when he opened his investigation in December, 1936. But noting Truman's disappointment, Wheeler permitted him to sit in on the hearings.

Reporters who covered the investigation said that "for two years this inquiry plodded along through some of the dullest hearings ever recorded on Capitol Hill." Yet Truman never missed a session. Hundreds of witnesses representing various railroads appeared to discuss and argue the complex financial matters. To gain a better understanding of what was going on, Truman began his own private study of the railroads. Often he spent evenings at the Library of Congress, scanning old newspaper files on the industry's financial morass. He also arranged for the Library to send him 50 volumes on the railroads which he read methodically. Senators who observed his strange pastime referred to him as "eccentric."

When one of the Democratic members of the subcommittee finally withdrew because he found the hearings too dull, Wheeler promptly named Truman to replace him. Then, in the spring of 1937, Wheeler became one of the leaders opposing FDR's court-packing proposal and was soon so involved in the battle that he stopped attending the railroad hearings. Other subcommittee members also got into that historic battle, and Truman found himself alone at the investigation. To maintain the status of the hearings, Wheeler elevated him to vice-chairman of the subcommittee. The promotion was swift and sudden, but from his observation of Wheeler and from his own intense reading, Truman proved himself a master investigator.

One of the first railroad lines he looked into was the bankrupt Missouri-Pacific in his own state. Subtle threats came from railroad lobbyists, and bags of mail poured in from Missouri demanding that he call off the investigation. But Truman refused to be intimidated. "Don't ease up on anything," he told the subcommittee staff. "Treat this investigation just as you do all the others." Although some staff aides did not believe he meant what he said, he was soon accusing the

Missouri-Pacific of false bookkeeping and fradulent stock transactions and proving his points from the railroad's own financial records.

Max Lowenthal, whom Wheeler had appointed counsel to the sub-committee, was one of those who doubted Truman's intentions when the Missouri-Pacific investigation began. But he later told a reporter, "There were not two other Senators who would have withstood such political pressure as Senator Truman did."

"Lowenthal was a mystery man," Vic Messall said. "He exercised power behind the scenes and had a great deal of influence on Wheeler, and subsequently on Truman. Truman was a good listener to what Mr. Lowenthal had to say." Lowenthal was a protégé of Louis D. Brandeis, Associate Justice of the Supreme Court, who functioned for years as a dissenter on the conservative court. To the public, Brandeis personified the scholar on the bench as well as the intrepid fighter to safeguard basic civil rights and curtail the "Curse of Bigness." Roosevelt referred to him as "Isaiah."

Then in his eighties, Brandeis held weekly teas in his Victorian apartment on California Street for New Deal intellectuals. Lowenthal was a frequent guest and on one occasion he asked Truman to come along. The elderly Justice took an immediate liking to the Senator with the flat Missouri twang and from that time on Truman was a regular visitor. It was an experience for Truman to hear Harvard lawyers expound on constitutional law and to listen to discussions of the philosophy behind the New Deal.

But after a few calls at the Brandeis apartment, said Truman, "the old man would back me into a corner and pay no attention to anyone else while he talked transportation to me. He was very much against the control of financial credit—hipped on a few insurance companies controlling too much of the country's credit."

Chiefly as a result of Brandeis's influence, Truman's Midwestern agrarianism and suspicion of Wall Street blossomed. In June and then in December of 1937, he made his first important speeches in the Senate, speeches that were distilled Brandeisese with a dash of Missouri for flavor. Railroad receiverships became "the greatest racket on earth"; railroad financiers the "wrecking crews"; and Wall Street lawyers the "highest of high hats" who pulled "tricks that would make an ambulance chaser in a coroner's court blush with shame." So far as he was concerned, the Carnegie libraries were "steeped in the blood of Homestead steel workers" and the Rockefeller Foundation was "founded on the dead miners of the Colorado Fuel and Iron Company and a dozen other similar performances."

In his June 3 speech, he made his first preliminary report of the railroad investigation. "Some of the country's greatest railroads have been deliberately looted by their financial agents," he told the Senate. "Speaking of the Rock Island reminds me that the first railroad robbery was committed on the Rock Island back in 1873 just east of Council Bluffs, Iowa. The man who committed that robbery used a gun and a horse and got up early in the morning. He and his gang took a chance of being killed and eventually most were. That railroad robber's name was Jesse James. The same Jesse James held up the Missouri Pacific in 1876 and took the paltry sum of seventeen thousand dollars from the express car. About thirty years after the Council Bluffs holdup, the Rock Island went through a looting by some gentlemen known as the 'Tin Plate Millionaires.' They used no guns but they ruined the railroad and got away with seventy million dollars or more. They did it by means of holding companies. Senators can see what 'pikers' Mr. James and his crowd were alongside of some real artists."

In his December speech, Truman pitched his talk to a plea for a return to a simpler way of life. "I believe the country would be better off if we did not have sixty per cent of the assets of all insurance companies concentrated in only four companies. . . . I also say that a thousand county-seat towns of seven thousand people each are a thousand times more important to this Republic than one city of seven million people. Our unemployment and our unrest are the result of the concentration of wealth, the concentration of population in industrial centers, mass production and a lot of other so-called modern improvements. We are building a Tower of Babel."

Brandeis was one of the first to congratulate him on his speeches.

The railroad investigation droned on throughout 1937 and 1938, with Truman singlehandedly cross-examining dozens of witnesses. Occasionally, Wheeler dropped in and the sparks flew because he was judge, jury and prosecutor rolled into one. Truman's approach was courteous and mild, though during the investigation of the Kansas City Southern Railroad he bluntly told a witness, "The purpose of this hearing is to find out whether wholly owned subsidiaries and railroad holding companies are of any use and benefit to the general public. Personally I do not think they are."

In January, 1939, when Truman finally completed the hearings, he presented the Senate with reasons why a new law was needed to regulate the finances of the railroads. Then he and Lowenthal sat down and wrote it. As Truman put it: "When investment bankers continually load great transportation companies with debt in order to sell securities to savings banks and insurance companies so they can make a commission, the well finally runs dry."

Truman proposed major changes in the regulation of railroad financing, but the industry brought such tremendous lobbying pressure to bear on Congress that a year passed without Senate action. In May, 1940, a discouraged Truman wrote to an attorney in St. Louis: "I feel as if my four years and a half hard work has been practically wasted, but we will be ready for a new start when Congress next meets."

Even when the Senate finally approved his bill, a long deadlock resulted because the House passed a different version and stubbornly refused to compromise. Not until September were Truman and Wheeler able to effect a satisfactory agreement with House conferees. The bill then won quick acceptance in both houses and became law when President Roosevelt signed it. Its title was the Transportation Act of 1940.

20

IN 1934, when Harry Truman became a Senator, Tom Pendergast was the strongest political boss in the United States. But from that moment on, a Greek tragedy began to unfold. The future held downfall, prison and disgrace for Pendergast; for Truman, the White House. The man who was to bring Pendergast down and elevate Truman was Franklin D. Roosevelt.

In that year of 1934, Pendergast's passion for the horses began to take over his existence. One of his lawyers later explained the extent of his disease to a judge: "He told me that when the afternoon was here, he would go into a little room, and there he would take the form sheet and handicap these horses and then he would sit with the telephone at his ear and he would hear a call—'They're at the post!' Later: 'They're off!' And so over that telephone by ear and not by eye, he watched those horses run to the finish line—all the thrill that can ever come to any man for that which possesses him and which he cannot down."

Pendergast literally gave his kingdom for a horse. Despite the enormous take from his various enterprises, his betting losses exceeded his business profits. His friends pleaded with him to stop his wild betting, but Pendergast had no more control over this compulsion than an alcoholic has over liquor.

With the help of City Manager McElroy, he had already milked Kansas City to its financial limits, and by the time Truman was elected to the Senate, he was at the point of desperation because of his gambling losses. At no time, however, did he give any indication of his plight to Truman, whom he never considered more than a minor underling in his organization. Although Truman's victory in the election was also a triumph for his machine, Pendergast did not bother to attend the swearing-in ceremony, for at the beginning of 1935 he was deeply involved in the graft scheme that would lead to his ruin.

Back in 1929, 137 insurance companies had raised Missouri fire insurance rates by 16⅔ per cent. The Missouri state insurance superintendent objected to the increase, however, and a Federal court impounded the additional money the insurance companies had collected until its disposition could be determined. By 1935, the amount that had been impounded was almost $10,000,000.

As Pendergast grew more panicky over his racing losses, he greedily eyed these funds. Emmett O'Malley, who was now his hand-picked state superintendent of insurance, got in touch with the insurance companies and asked if they would pay "someone" for a settlement in their favor.

There was no turning back when Pendergast walked into the Palmer House in Chicago on January 22, 1935, and agreed to a bribe that eventually totaled $750,000. After T. J. received the first $100,000, O'Malley made a settlement which the Federal Court accepted on February 1, 1936. The court's order awarded 80 per cent of the impounded money to the insurance companies and returned the other 20 per cent to policyholders. Not long afterward Pendergast collected his next bribe installment of $250,000.

Since all the bribes had been paid in cash, he was certain no one would ever find out what had happened. And no one did for a while. As for the money he received, it was soon thrown away on the horses. Government records later showed that he bet $2,000,000 in 1935 and lost $600,000.

Involved as he was in bribes, business and local politics, Pendergast made few political demands on Truman. In June, 1935, the Kansas City *Star* quoted Truman as saying that Pendergast frequently sent him telegrams requesting him to vote for or against various legislation.

Truman told the *Star* reporter: "I don't follow his advice on legislation. I vote the way I believe Missourians as a whole would want me to vote."

Vic Messall could not recall any telegrams to Truman from Pendergast. "In fact," Messall said, "he never even sent the Senator a single letter on legislation. His demands were much more insignificant. He would tear off a scrap of paper from a grocery bag and scribble a note in red pencil asking Truman for a favor. And his requests were never more important than for Truman to help find a little clerk's job for people from Missouri. I remember a note that read, 'Please help my friend, J. C. Smith.—T. J.' "

From time to time Pendergast went to New York where he occupied a luxurious suite on the twenty-ninth floor of the Waldorf-Astoria. His political brethren and well-wishers in Washington were expected to appear and pay him homage in this plush atmosphere so unlike the drab curtainless office on Kansas City's Main Street. In the summer of 1935, while the First Session of the 74th Congress was winding up its work, Pendergast and his wife were at the hotel preparing to sail on the *Normandie* for Europe.

Truman was one who went to New York at this time and took Vic Messall with him. "T. J.'s penthouse looked just like a stockbroker's office," Messall said. "It was a madhouse with ticker tape machines bringing him race-track news and results and the place was filled with jockeys and bookies. He told us that some jockeys had double-crossed him with wrong tips and he almost killed a few of them."

Actually, this was more than a social call for Truman, who had been besieged by Lloyd Stark, a fellow Missourian, to help him win Pendergast's approval as the Democratic gubernatorial candidate in the 1936 election. "Bennett Clark and I took Lloyd Stark up to New York to see Pendergast and urge him to support him for governor," Truman told Jonathan Daniels. "Pendergast kept saying to me, 'He won't do, Harry. I don't like the so-and-so. He's a no-good.' " But T. J. was in a jovial mood because of his coming trip and the fact that he had already collected part of his insurance company bribe. "Finally," said Truman, "he agreed if Stark would get some country support, he would support him, too. The old man had better judgment than I did."

Made in retrospect after Pendergast's downfall, this last statement reflected Truman's sense of guilt for promoting a man who contributed to T. J.'s sorry end. Lloyd Stark had first approached Pendergast in 1932 for approval to run for governor. But T. J. had rejected him even though Stark would have made an attractive candidate, for he came from a well-known family, had a fine war record, was clean-cut in appearance and he headed the multimillion-dollar Stark nursery, the largest in the entire United States.

Far from being discouraged by Pendergast's rejection, Stark grew even more determined to become governor of Missouri. In 1934, he attempted to stay on Pendergast's good side by supporting Truman for the Senate, although he did not contribute to his campaign fund. And the next year, when Truman was exhilarated by his first session in the Senate, Stark played on his good will to help him with the Democratic boss. After Pendergast made his reluctant commitment to back Stark if he could get support outside of Jackson County, Truman worked hard in Stark's behalf. "I lined up the country and T. J., too," he said ruefully. The result was that Pendergast finally told reporters he would support Stark because "ten spoke for Stark when one spoke for all other Democratic candidates."

In June, 1936, when the primary campaign in Missouri was beginning to take shape, the Democrats were staging their national convention at Philadelphia. This was Truman's first participation in a national convention. He was designated a delegate-at-large and one of the 48 honorary vice-presidents of the convention, but Tom Pendergast, of course, was the undisputed boss of the Missouri delegation. That spring, after receiving his third bribe installment, Pendergast had again taken his wife to Europe. On June 2, he returned to New York on the *Queen Mary*'s maiden voyage to attend the convention.

He was not well, however, as he left the ship for the Waldorf. As June moved along he suffered agonizing stomach pains. Nevertheless, late that month he went down to Philadelphia to take charge of his delegation, intending to commute daily between New York and the City of Brotherly Love. But on his first day in Philadelphia the weather was humid and Truman and the other delegates thought he looked ill. That evening Truman brought him back to the Waldorf, with Pendergast groaning about excruciating pains in his stomach during the entire trip to New York. Doctors diagnosed a coronary thrombosis. They barred him from returning to the convention, and ordered him to take a six months' rest if he wanted to live.

But Tom Pendergast could not relax in New York. The Missouri primary was on and he felt that he could not trust any of his lieutenants to take charge in his absence. By August, when the primary was at hand, he was haggard, having lost 40 pounds. To a Kansas City *Star* reporter who visited him at the Waldorf, he said, "I guess the people at home are saying I have stayed back here to dodge a fight."

Despite his absence, his boys outdid themselves. When the majority of Missouri's 114 counties revealed an anti-Goat total, the Jackson County Pendergast machine trotted out ghost votes in full force. For instance, Kansas City's Second Ward, with a population of 18,478, gave Stark 19,202 votes to 12 for his opponent. Stark's total vote in Kansas City was almost 170,000. Statisticians later figured that this total was possible only if Kansas City had 200,000 more adults than the census revealed.

After the primary, the *Star* began a private investigation of the heavy ghost vote and U. S. Attorney Maurice Milligan decided to make his first move as soon the November general election was over.

Tom Pendergast wanted to get back to Kansas City to lead his forces in the fall election. But when his pains grew more severe, doctors discovered an intestinal cancer and operated to remove the malignancy. "If he had died there in New York," said Truman, "he would be remembered as the greatest boss this country ever had."

But Pendergast did not die. In mid-September he was back in Kansas City to handle the defense of his machine, for there were reports that a dozen or more FBI agents were quietly investigating the August primary. Milligan turned up here and there in the Pendergast wards gathering evidence and *Star* reporters working with the Citizens League were amassing affidavits through interviews.

An ominous air hung over the November general election in which Stark defeated Jesse W. Barrett, the Republican gubernatorial candidate, by 264,199 votes. With FDR's backing, Milligan acted swiftly and, on December 14, Federal Judge Albert L. Reeves instructed a grand jury to search for election frauds.

Tom Pendergast, an old pro, remained unperturbed. "I have been investigated for forty years," he told a reporter. "If Reeves and Milligan can find anything wrong, I'll not squawk." At this, Milligan moved to seize the ballots as evidence. In Washington, Truman was disturbed by this attempt to ruin the Pendergast organization. He was convinced, however, that the machine had overreached itself. "The registration was crooked in 1936," he admitted, "and that was what made Stark Governor. I don't believe Tom Pendergast knew anything about it or that he was ever involved in that sort of thing.

It was due to overzealousness of his workers, the desire to make a big showing."

Early in January, 1937, the Grand Jury indicted 20 persons. Pendergast, who had earlier believed that Milligan would take no action, saw now that he was in an all-out fight to save his organization. For those indicted, he supplied bail money and his own lawyers. Milligan's next move was to attempt to implicate Pendergast directly in the elections fraud. When this failed he went after other Goat underlings.

The trials dragged on for two years. In all, there were 39 indictments involving 278 defendants, of whom 259 were convicted. Truman might have kept clear of the proceedings, for he was not personally involved. But he had a stubborn sense of loyalty to the machine that had raised him from obscurity to the United States Senate. From Washington he said, "It looks like he [Milligan] is trying to put the whole Democratic Party in jail." He called the court action "a persecution of innocent women and men."

Despite his battle with Tom Pendergast, Roosevelt tried to get him to use his influence on behalf of the Administration in 1937. This was the year of his Court reorganization plan, better known as the "Court Packing Plan." After the Supreme Court had declared a number of his New Deal measures unconstitutional—the NRA, the Railroad Retirement Act, the Frazier-Lemke Farm Bankruptcy Act, the Connally "Hot Oil" Act, the Guffey Bituminous Coal Act and the Agriculture Adjustment Act—Roosevelt proposed to change the complexion of the Court so that it would endorse the New Deal and not act as a wrecking crew of "Nine Old Men." His plan called for adding a new justice for every one already on the Court who was over seventy and would not retire.

The proposal divided the Senate Democratic majority into warring factions. As a loyal follower of the President, Harry Truman supported Roosevelt's plan even though most of his friends, including Senator Wheeler and Vice-President Garner, opposed it. Senator Joseph T. Robinson, the Majority Leader, led the fight for approval chiefly because Roosevelt had promised to reward his efforts by naming him to fill the next vacancy on the Supreme Court. It was a six months' struggle for Robinson, one that Garner felt should have been abandoned in April when the Supreme Court upheld the Wagner Act. In May, when Justice Willis Van Devanter retired, FDR had the opportunity to put Robinson on the Bench but insisted that he continue to work for the court-packing plan. Finally, in July, overworked and dispirited, Robinson died of a heart attack in his Washington apartment.

The problem immediately arose as to who would succeed Robinson as Senate Majority Leader. Garner's choice was Pat Harrison of Mississippi, who viewed the job of Majority Leader as that of Democratic Senate manager. Roosevelt, however, wanted a Majority Leader who would function primarily as his agent in the Senate. To his mind, the man who would do this was Senator Alben Barkley of Kentucky.

The struggle between Garner and Roosevelt began the day after Robinson's death when Roosevelt made public a letter to Barkley in which he addressed him as "My Dear Alben" and designated him "Acting Majority Leader of the Senate." Garner smarted at this blatant interference by the Executive Branch in the internal affairs of the Senate. But the White House ignored him and campaigned actively for Barkley by promising Senators patronage and election help.

Alben Barkley once said, "I knew the vote was going to be awfully close in the caucus. When the fight began I ascertained that Harry Truman would vote for me. But he came to me before the vote and said that homestate pressure on him was so great that he wanted to be relieved of his promise to me. I let him off the hook."

The truth was that from the outset Truman was committed to Harrison. When White House strategists learned this, they decided the best way to make him switch to Barkley was to have Tom Pendergast put pressure on him. Pendergast was in Colorado Springs when he received a call from Jim Farley. The reason he telephoned, Farley said, was to get Pendergast to "line up Harry on the right side."

Shortly afterward, Pendergast called Truman. "Look here, Harry, Jim Farley just called and asked me if I couldn't talk to you about voting for Barkley. Can't you do that?"

"No, Tom, I can't," Truman replied. "And I'll tell you why. I've given my word to Pat Harrison."

This was enough for Pendergast. "Well, Harry," he said, "I told Jim you were the contrariest guy in the world. So I guess that's that."

Seventy-five Democrats voted in the secret caucus and Barkley squeaked through by a vote of 38 to 37. Afterward he said, "I have often wondered how I would have felt about Harry Truman if I had lost the majority leadership by one vote!"

Truman had taken a brave stand in the face of pressure both from the White House and from Tom Pendergast. Yet the press tried to paint him as a willing tool of the bosses. Missouri papers spread the

157

story that he had voted for Barkley after being ordered to switch from Harrison. "That report is a lie and everyone knows it," he said angrily to a Kansas City *Star* reporter. "I voted for Pat and can prove it by Senator Clyde Herring of Iowa who sat next to me when we voted. I showed him my ballot."

In July, 1937, Pendergast's troubles finally came to a head when he clashed with Governor Lloyd Stark. Since Stark had not expressed horror when he succeeded to the governor's mansion at Jefferson City with the help of the fraudulent election of 1936, Pendergast firmly believed that it was his prerogative to expect Stark to obey his commands with the same alacrity as his predecessor, Governor Guy Park.

After Pendergast had put through his call to Truman at Jim Farley's behest, he asked Stark to come to Colorado Springs for a conference. On July 26, Stark arrived for a summit meeting accompanied by several newsmen. Pendergast made two requests: the naming of an election board friendly to the Goats then being harassed by Milligan and the reappointment of Emmett O'Malley as state superintendent of insurance for another four years. With O'Malley in control of that office, Pendergast reasoned, there was little likelihood that the insurance bribe, in which both were involved, would ever be exposed. Stark, however, minced no words in telling Pendergast that he had no intention of appointing a friendly election board. As for O'Malley, Stark said, he would be kept on only for a year at most.

Not long after this meeting, Stark appointed a new election board. Within a few months, the board struck 60,000 ghost voters from Jackson County's rolls and set up a records system to control registration and voting. This was a crushing blow to Pendergast because it vindicated Milligan's prosecution of his machine. Another blow came in October when Stark fired O'Malley.

Milligan's four-year term as U.S. Attorney for the Western District of Missouri was to end early in 1938 and Stark now wanted him reappointed to another term. As a loyal Pendergast man, Truman met with Attorney General Homer Cummings to inform him that he opposed Milligan's reappointment. He also mentioned his opposition in one of his rare appointments with Roosevelt.

Afterward, FDR wrote a memo to Cummings in which he said that he had "heard indirectly that there is a good deal of opposition to him [Milligan] amongst the powers that be in Missouri."

Cummings replied on November 1: "Answering your question specifically, I can say that I have not heard one word from either

158

Senator on the subject, or from any other person in authority adverse to Mr. Milligan."

Roosevelt's memo to Cummings on November 3 carried the game further: "Thank you for the information about Milligan. I have very good reason to believe that he ought to be reappointed and I think if you and I from now on take the position that we have heard no valid reason against his reappointment, it will help him to be confirmed next February."

With that, he sent Milligan's name to the Senate for confirmation. The Kansas City *Star* reported early in 1938: "Truman returned to his office today after a trip to Kansas City and St. Louis. While in Kansas City he conferred with Thomas J. Pendergast, the Democratic political leader, and they discussed the Milligan appointment. After the conference, Pendergast announced that anything to be said, regarding Milligan, would be by Truman on the floor of the Senate, leading to the belief that the Senator would actively oppose the reappointment."

The Senate code was such that when a Senator declared the nomination of an individual from his home state as "personally obnoxious," the Senate generally rejected the nominee. President Roosevelt knew that if Truman objected to Milligan, the nomination would be lost. As a result, when Truman stopped off at Chicago on the way back from his Kansas City meeting with Pendergast, he received a telephone call from a White House aide. The President was requesting him to abandon his fight and to refrain from rising in the Senate to declare Milligan "obnoxious" to him. Truman agreed and said publicly, "Since the President wants this, I shall not oppose the confirmation, although politically and personally I am opposed to Mr. Milligan because I do not think and never have thought he was fit for the place."

Truman was in a tight spot. If he said nothing when Milligan's nomination came to a Senate vote, he would be a traitor to the Pendergast dynasty. If he did make a strong speech against Milligan, even though he refrained from calling him obnoxious, it would make him look like Pendergast's bellhop.

When Milligan's nomination came to the Senate floor on February 15, 1938, Truman decided that whatever the consequences he had to speak out. After rewriting his speech several times, he rose and read it in an angry voice:

159

"The President has appointed him and the President wants him confirmed because of a situation in Kansas City due to vote-fraud prosecutions in the Federal Court. Mr. Milligan has been made a hero by the Kansas City *Star* and the St. Louis *Post-Dispatch* because of these prosecutions.

"The implication has been that any capable lawyer I would recommend for district attorney in western Missouri would not do his duty in regard to the vote-fraud prosecutions. Every good lawyer and decent citizen in Jackson County is just as strongly opposed to vote frauds as the Kansas City *Star* and Mr. Milligan. The detail work and the actual trial of the vote-fraud cases have all been done by Mr. Milligan's two able deputies and not by Mr. Milligan. If the district attorney's office was to have been rewarded for vote-fraud prosecutions by a reappointment, one of those able deputies should have been appointed."

Truman also pointed out that "Mr. Milligan has accepted emoluments in the form of fees in bankruptcy proceedings in the Federal Court of western Missouri. In fact, he has received more money in fees in one case than his salary has been from the Federal Treasury for a whole year."

Had Truman stuck to this line of attack he might have swayed his colleagues. But he could not refrain from an unreasonable attack on the election frauds judges. He said:

"The Federal Court at Kansas City is presided over by two as violently partisan judges as have ever sat on a Federal bench since the Federalist judges of Jefferson's Administration. They are Merrill E. Otis and Albert L. Reeves. Mr. Reeves was appointed by that great advocate of clean, nonpartisan government, Warren G. Harding, and Mr. Otis was named by that other great progressive nonpartisan, Calvin Coolidge. These two judges have made it perfectly plain to Mr. Milligan—and he has been able to see eye to eye with them, due to bankruptcy emoluments—that convictions of Democrats are what they want. . . .

"I say this to the Senate, Mr. President, that a Jackson County, Missouri, Democrat has as much chance of a fair trial in the Federal District Court of western Missouri as a Jew would have in a Hitler Court, or a Trotsky follower before Stalin. . . .

"Because the President asked for him, I have not attempted to exercise the usual Senatorial prerogative to block his confirmation. I think, however, I would not be doing my public duty if I did not tell the Senate just what he is doing."

The reaction of Truman's colleagues to his speech ranged from icy indifference to outrage. Vice-President Garner, friendly toward both Truman and Bennett Clark, left the dais when Milligan's nomination came up and sat in the back row, listening attentively with an unlighted cigar in his mouth. Clark had not only suggested Milligan in the first place, but Milligan's older brother "Tuck," who ran against Truman in the primary campaign of 1934, had been a protégé of Garner when he was Speaker of the House. Garner feared that Clark and Truman would clash angrily in debate. Clark, however, challenged Truman only on his remark that Milligan was not morally fit for the job. Truman quickly explained that he was speaking of private, not public, morals.

In the call for the vote the only "No" came from Truman. As soon as Milligan was safely confirmed, Garner shouted, "Hey, Bennett, you and Harry go out and have a drink!" Then, putting his arms around both men, he led them from the Senate chamber.

This defeat in the Senate was not the end of the trouble Truman brought on himself by opposing Milligan. The day after his speech, the Federal grand jury, the two judges and the Kansas City lawyers' association bitterly denounced him. Judge Reeves called his Senate address "the speech of a man nominated by ghost votes, elected with ghost votes and whose speech was probably written by a ghost writer." The St. Louis *Post-Dispatch* printed a Fitzpatrick cartoon depicting Truman as a dummy on a ventriloquist's lap with a caption reading: "Charlie McTruman Does His Stuff." An accompanying editorial called his speech "a scurrilous attack upon good government."

A month after Milligan was reconfirmed, Tom Pendergast had to stand a big test. The city election was scheduled for the last Tuesday in March and the Pendergast machine was weakened both by the loss of ghost votes and the consequences of the election frauds trials. If he lost now, it meant the end of the Pendergast-McElroy administration that had controlled Kansas City since 1925. The local papers made much of Pendergast's discomfort. But when the votes were counted they showed that Mayor Smith, T. J.'s local aide, had won re-election by more than 40,000 and seven of the eight city councilmen were Goats. Flushed with success, Pendergast taunted Governor Stark with the challenge: "Let the river take its course."

And the river took its course. After the municipal election, Senator Clark began courting Tom Pendergast and Harry Truman. He was up for re-election that year and feared he would not win the Democratic nomination without their help. Pendergast said he would not only support Clark and forget their enmity of 1932, but for good measure he would also support him for President in 1940. Truman spoke twice for Clark during the primary. The first time was in April at Marysville, Missouri. Clark had emerged as an isolationist leader in the Senate, and when Truman endorsed him, he was met with a barrage of boos. Within the week he made a second speech in Clark's behalf at Springfield, but this time with happier results.

Clark won the primary, but Pendergast's candidate for the State Supreme Court lost to Stark's man. Nevertheless, T. J. looked forward to further battles with Stark. And from past experience he confidently assumed he would eventually force him into political oblivion. But in mid-1938 his secret insurance bribe came to light.

The first move in exposing the scandal was made by a minor employee of the Internal Revenue Bureau. He told a reporter of the Kansas City *Star* a vague story about five insurance company checks having been cashed in Chicago and the money turned over to an unidentified Missouri politician. Internal Revenue, he said, had traced the checks to Charles Street, vice-president of the General American Insurance Company. But when Street refused to say whether any of the money had reached Tom Pendergast, the Bureau closed the case.

The *Star* reporter repeated the story to Governor Stark, who called Milligan and told him the details. Shortly afterward Stark telephoned Milligan again from Washington and asked him to attend a conference with Treasury officials.

When Milligan arrived in Washington, Stark said that he had gone to the White House to tell the story to President Roosevelt. FDR had called Secretary of the Treasury Morgenthau and ordered him to get to work on the matter without delay. Stark and Milligan then went to the Treasury to discuss the case with officials.

Since Street had died the preceding February, there seemed to be no way to tie Tom Pendergast to the bribe. But in the end A. L. McCormack, the St. Louis insurance man who had also played a key role in the affair, broke under questioning by Milligan. When the story was made public, Pendergast's underhanded activity became known as the "Second Missouri Compromise."

By early 1939, Pendergast was aware that the Government was nearing court action. Only direct intervention at the White House could save him, he believed, but he did not send Truman to intercede for him with Roosevelt. Instead he dispatched Kansas City's chief of police, Otto P. Higgins. Although Higgins spent a week in the capital in an attempt to make an appointment, FDR refused to see him. Pendergast then sent his nephew Jim on the same mission, but Jim also failed.

At the end of March, when Truman was in Kansas City, it was obvious to him that Pendergast was in serious trouble, although T. J. would not discuss it with him. On April 4, Attorney General Frank Murphy and FBI Chief J. Edgar Hoover flew to Kansas City. Three days later, while Truman was on has way back to Washington, Pendergast was indicted.

A *Star* reporter recorded the bizarre courtroom scene when the boss was arraigned. It was Good Friday and Pendergast appeared unruffled by the proceedings. When one of his lawyers tried to help him remove his overcoat, he pulled away and said in a loud voice, "I'll take it off. There's nothing the matter with me. They prosecuted Christ on Good Friday and nailed Him to the Cross." He was furious only when news photographers took his picture as he was being fingerprinted. "Hell, they have a million!" he shouted. He was then subjected to personal questions.

"You are five feet nine, aren't you?"

He chuckled. "I've grown shorter. They say, you know, that age shortens a man."

"Your hair is gray?"

"What's left of it is gray."

He was released on $10,000 bond and told to appear in court at the end of the month when the trial date would be set.

Truman was shocked en route to Washington when a reporter told him of the indictment. This was his opportunity to cast off the machine and denounce Pendergast. But his sense of loyalty and feeling of debt were too strong. "I am very sorry to hear it," he told the reporter. "I know nothing about the details, nor why the indictment was voted. Tom Pendergast has always been my friend and I don't desert a sinking ship."

Action was swift in Kansas City. City Manager McElroy, who had started his career at the same time as Truman when they both served on the County Court, resigned a few days after Pendergast's indictment. He aged perceptibly when proof was found that in a ten-year period he had received kickbacks of more than $10,000,000 from salaries of city and county workers. He had also diverted an $11,000,-000 water bond sinking fund and spent an additional $5,800,000 on what he called emergency purposes. Soon confined to a wheel chair, he suffered a fatal attack just before his impending arraignment.

On May Day, Pendergast and his insurance superintendent stooge, Emmett O'Malley, went before Judge Otis and pleaded not guilty. But on May 22 Pendergast had a change of heart and threw himself on the mercy of the court. Otis wanted to know why he had so foolishly destroyed his life. The answer, of course, was his horse-betting mania. "I don't know what it is, but it has been with me all my life since I came from St. Joseph here."

Judge Otis looked down at him standing before the bench and said, "I can understand the feeling that has been expressed for him here by his friends. I believe if I had known him, I, too, might have been one of his friends. I think he is a man of the character that makes friends."

The judge then sentenced him to serve 15 months in Federal prison, fined him $10,000 and agreed to settle his tax evasion charge for $434,000. The St. Louis *Post-Dispatch* cried out that he "merited a far heavier sentence."

Accompanied by his son, Tom, Jr., and his nephew Jim, Pendergast went by car to Leavenworth Penitentiary. He arrived at the east gate at 8:45 A.M. on May 29. Clutching a small handbag, he walked quickly to the gate without looking back. It was the end of his dynasty.

Truman said: "When Tom Pendergast was down and out, a convicted man, people wanted me to denounce him. I refused. I wouldn't kick a friend."

One aftermath of Tom Pendergast's fall from power was its effect on Truman's relationship with Spencer Salisbury, wartime captain of Battery E of the 129th Field Artillery and his business partner in the mid-twenties. After the Englewood banking venture collapsed in 1926, the two men had continued in their other enterprise, the Community Savings and Loan Association of Independence. Here Truman doubled as president and general manager while serving as presiding judge of the Jackson County Court. But when his duties on the court and his county road construction program began to take up so much of his time, he turned over the management of the association to Salisbury.

"In 1928," Salisbury said, "we began to have a falling out." According to Salisbury, "Harry took down Al Smith's picture in the courthouse and when I asked him why, he said, 'It isn't good business to have him in the courthouse.' Then in 1931 or '32 we had an argument about his commissions. He also wanted to give Jim Pendergast control of the business so Jim could tie it in with his own building and loan association in Kansas City. So we just threw Harry out.

"He didn't like it a bit when I supported Bennett Clark against the machine in 1932. But our real trouble came in 1934 when I worked for Tuck Milligan against him in the Democratic primary. After that primary, I went out and got affidavits proving election fakery."

In the years that followed, Salisbury became a minor thorn in the sides of the Pendergast machine. After Governor Stark began action against Pendergast, he became one of Stark's champions. When T. J. went to prison, he blasted the machine and announced, "We're mighty tired out in this part of the country of being dominated by Pendergast appointees." In August, 1939, Truman finally took action against Salisbury by sending a telegram to the head of the Federal Home Loan Bank System, demanding an investigation of the Community Savings and Loan Association and of Salisbury. "They were out to get me after that," Salisbury said.

The following December the board of the association kicked Salisbury out. Early in 1941 he was brought to trial for having filed a false affidavit in 1939 claiming that the association had no lawsuits pending against it. Salisbury pleaded guilty to this charge and got a 15-month prison sentence. He came out of jail as Truman's bitterest enemy. Twenty years later, he still bristled at the mention of Truman's name.

21

TOM Pendergast's downfall had a profound effect on Truman's career. On one hand, he felt that without the organization's aid his chances for re-election in 1940 were slim. On the other, he knew that his loyalty to Pendergast had weakened his standing with independents.

By innuendo the newspapers attempted to tie him to every election fraud of the decade in Jackson County. As 1940 approached, they demanded that he lash out at Pendergast, although it was obvious that they would not support him even if he did. "The Kansas City and St. Louis papers demanded that I denounce him," he told a reporter. "I refused and they denounced me. But in public office you can't let the newspapers dictate your life and thought."

Franklin Roosevelt, a master in public relations, tried to get Truman to extricate himself from the Pendergast web. "Shortly after the indictment of Pendergast," Maurice Milligan said, "I called upon President Roosevelt. After complimenting our office in its recent work the President said, 'I told Harry Truman the other day that he had better get away from that crowd out there.'"

Actually Truman's relations with President Roosevelt were still distant. In 1938 he told a *Star* reporter that FDR had "ignored me from the start" and admitted that the President had not talked to him in months. There was also resentment on Truman's part, because FDR was giving Governor Stark patronage that normally went to a Senator. "One time," Jim Farley related, "I reported that Senator Truman wanted to name the United States Marshal in the Western District of the state. Roosevelt said he would have to consult Governor Stark. I protested that I did not think Stark should be consulted because it was a Federal appointment." Roosevelt ignored Farley.

When Tom Pendergast was sentenced to Leavenworth, newspapers pointed to Stark as Truman's successor and began referring to him as the "Tom Dewey of Missouri." The Kansas City *Star* went so far as to hail him as "a good bet, as a compromise Presidential candidate" in 1940. During 1938 and 1939 Stark's name showed up among those invited on the Presidential yacht for cruises down the Potomac, and he was the subject of rumors regarding possible appointment to Roosevelt's Cabinet. Columnists mentioned him frequently as the successor to Claude Swanson, Roosevelt's ailing Secretary of the Navy.

"A mighty big straw in the wind," said Vic Messall, "was that President Roosevelt tried to get Truman to accept an appointment to the Interstate Commerce Commission. He told him he didn't have a chance to be re-elected." Truman said the offer came "in a roundabout way," and added, "I sent him word, however, that if I received only one vote I intended to make the fight for vindication and re-election to the Senate."

Despite Truman's refusal to disavow Tom Pendergast, Stark continued to act friendly and paid him courtesy calls when he visited Washington. One hot day in 1939, Stark came into Truman's office and told him, "Some folks back home are trying to push me to run against you next year, Harry. But I'll never run against you for anything."

As soon as Stark left, Truman buzzed for Vic Messall. "That dirty blankety-blank is planning to run against me!" he fumed.

In September, 1939, shortly after the European war broke out, Stark announced himself as a candidate for Truman's seat. Messall said, "Senator Truman sat down and wrote Stark a blistering letter. He reminded him he was responsible for his political career and called him everything in the goddamned book."

Disturbed by Stark's candidacy and the President's overt favoritism for the governor, Senator James F. Byrnes said that he "went to the President and urged him to remain neutral." But, Byrnes added, "the President told me that while he did not know much about Mr. Truman, Governor Stark was an intimate friend, was very progressive and would make a great Senator."

At this point it seemed that Stark would have no trouble winning Truman's seat. Maurice Milligan, however, considered that his own work in breaking Tom Pendergast's rule was worthy of reward and he, too, announced as a Senatorial candidate. "When some of Truman's own friends asked me to run," Milligan said, "I took that as positive assurance of the then Senator's desire to stay out of the race. How could a Pendergast man get anywhere without a Pendergast?"

Truman was faced with two major problems. First, could he get substantial Missouri backing? Second, where would he get the necessary campaign funds? He had no money and could not even help his mother financially. In fact, on April 2, 1938, his man Friday, Fred Canfil, and his younger brother Vivian had had to help Martha Truman rearrange the debt on the farm at Grandview. She had given a mortgage on her property to Jackson County in exchange for a $35,000 loan from school board funds. A year later, when Truman found his family unable to meet the mortgage payments, he told a reporter, "We are having difficulty. You know how it is when you seem to owe more than you can pay."

His brother Vivian was then under a heavy mortgage on his own property and was earning only about $150 a month, according to Vic Messall. "I felt sorry for Vivian," Messall said. "One time when I was in Kansas City, I asked him how he would like to become a Federal Housing Administration appraiser. Vivian answered me, 'I couldn't hold a job like that. I'm not qualified.'

"Why not?" Messall asked. "You can do it as well as some of those FHA people and it'll pay you three or four hundred dollars a month."

Messall arranged an interview for Vivian at the FHA. "Viv was asked only one question: 'What do you know about mortgages?' "

According to Messall, Vivian replied, "I don't know a damned thing about them except that I've been on the wrong side of one all my life." He got the job.

Late in 1939, Harry Truman put out feelers back home to help determine his chances for re-election. In January, 1940, he wrote to John Snyder that Senator Tom Connally had gone out to Missouri and had spoken at a meeting at Springfield. "He said enough nice things about me to elect me (if it had been left to that crowd!). The booing of Stark was a rather unanimous affair."

Encouraged by this reaction, he wrote to 30 friends to meet him at the Statler Hotel in St. Louis that month to talk over plans for a second term. To his chagrin, only a handful of the 30 showed up. Even Richard Lacey, who was supposed to serve as his campaign treasurer, did not make an appearance. "Much worse," Messall recalled, "all those present told him he didn't have a chance of winning. Truman looked stunned."

Not long afterward, the Democratic State Convention also met at St. Louis. The St. Louis machine, controlled by Mayor Bernard Dickmann and an aspiring young political leader named Robert Hannegan, came out for Governor Stark. Truman addressed the state convention, but his speech evoked only slight applause. He occupied a complimentary suite at the Statler for entertaining delegates, but only a few dropped in to visit him. When Harry H. Woodring, Roosevelt's Secretary of War, came to the suite, Messall said that Truman told him, "I'm whipped. This is the end of me."

Woodring, an old friend, did not try to cheer him. "I have my plane out here," he said, "and I have places for you and Messall to ride back to Washington with me."

Messall declined the invitation. "I'm not going back to Washington tonight. I'm going to take the train to Kansas City to see Jim Pendergast and find out if he'll support the Senator."

Messall said that Truman was crying when he left St. Louis.

The next morning Messall saw Tom Pendergast's nephew. "I won't keep you long," Messall told him. "I just came from St. Louis. I want to know if Harry Truman files, will you support him?"

Jim Pendergast smiled. "Tell Harry that if he only gets two votes he will get my vote and my wife's vote."

This did not seem like a significant remark. But, according to Messall, it had special meaning, for Jim was implying that he would pledge the remnants of the Pendergast machine to Truman. And this meant about 100,000 votes.

Messall then telephoned Truman in Washington and told him he intended to file for him. Truman said it was no use.

"Look, Senator," Messall cut in, "if you don't file you can't be elected. What do you have to lose? If you don't run you're through in politics."

Truman took a different tack. "It takes from one hundred to one hundred and fifty dollars to file. I've got to think about it."

"There's no time," Messall said.

Truman was silent. Finally he said, "All right, Vic, go ahead and file for me."

In a February snowstorm Messall drove to Jefferson City with two of Truman's staunch supporters and friends, Colonel Frank Erhart, assistant to the head of the Veterans Administration, and Paul Nachtman, an attorney for the National Labor Relations Board. The Missouri Secretary of State was about to close his office when the three walked in just before noon that Saturday. He expressed great surprise when Messall asked for the filing documents. "I didn't think Harry was going to file," he gasped.

The first hurdle had been leaped. But now came the problem of organizing the primary campaign and raising money. Messall quit his job as Truman's secretary and took on a new one as campaign chairman. At Sedalia, Missouri, he rented an old dilapidated building as campaign headquarters. He also set up a strategic sub-headquarters in the Ambassador Office Building in St. Louis. "I helped the owners of the Ambassador get refinancing through the Reconstruction Finance Corporation and they let us have two floors furnished for nothing during the campaign," he said.

Messall had made a list of people and business firms Truman had helped as a Senator, and now he wrote to these beneficiaries for contributions. Sufficient funds came in to print some handbills and posters, but there was not enough money to create an aura of optimism. He also sought free help by establishing a committee with numerous vice-chairmen, because he knew that people liked the title.

The campaign committee lacked a treasurer. "There were a half-dozen bankers for whom Truman had done great financial favors," Harry Vaughan said. "But they couldn't be located. It was a joke when the campaign committee named me treasurer. They were looking for someone with a name or a title, and I was a lieutenant colonel in the Reserve Corps. I was then a salesman with the T. J. Moss Tie Company of St. Louis and I had a bank balance of a dollar and a quarter."

Of all the daily papers in Missouri, only the Kansas City *Journal* came out for Truman. The Kansas City *Star* wrote, "The machine is betting its chips on public apathy." The St. Louis *Post-Dispatch* needled Truman endlessly. On one occasion it ran a political cartoon by Fitzpatrick depicting two huge trucks, one labeled Milligan and the

170

other Stark. The trucks were in a head-on crash with Harry Truman caught in a child's toy car between them. The caption read: *No place for a kiddycar.*

Without newspaper support, Truman found that his campaign depended on covering the state personally to make speeches. At the outset, he had to attend to his Senate duties as well as his re-election fight, and spoke of this problem in a letter to a friend, "Mrs. Truman has gone to Missouri and I have to commute back and forth nearly every weekend on account of the campaign." But after a few trips he was forced to forget about the Senate and concentrate on the election.

Truman's opening speech on June 15 was made on the courthouse stairs at Sedalia, deep in Stark territory in the middle of the state. He could not have picked a worse time for rousing the crowd to enthusiasm, because Paris had been surrendered to the Nazis the preceding day and the town's 20,000 persons were distracted and worried by this tragic event. Truman's close friend, Senator Lewis Schwellenbach, of Washington, was present to give him a send-off, and, in an attempt to be funny, called attention to Truman's shortcomings as a speaker. Schwellenbach told the crowd, "First let me say that there has been no more loyal or better friend of President Roosevelt in the United States than Harry Truman." Then, before Truman spoke, he added, "I need not tell you that Harry Truman is not an orator. He can demonstrate that for himself."

Truman's eighty-eight-year-old mother sat proudly on the platform that day, although Dr. W. L. Brandon, one of his eleven campaign committee vice-chairmen, said he was "such a bad speaker that it was pitiful."

Truman pitched his speech toward Missouri's Negro population of 245,000. "I believe in the brotherhood of man, not merely the brotherhood of white men but the brotherhood of all men before law. . . . In the years past, lynching and mob violence, lack of schools and countless other unfair conditions hastened the progress of the Negro from the country to the city. . . . They have been forced to live in segregated slums, neglected by the authorities. Negroes have been preyed upon by all types of exploiters. The majority of our Negro people find but cold comfort in shanties and tenements."

Despite President Roosevelt's display of favoritism for Governor Stark, Truman hoped for a few kind words from the White House. The most he could get, however, was a pallid statement from Steve Early: "While Senator Truman is an old and trusted friend of the

171

President, his invariable practice has not been to take part in primary contests."

Ignoring White House rebuffs, Truman realized the importance of wrapping himself in the Roosevelt mantle. And he seldom failed to remind audiences of this. In one speech his campaign oratory got the better of him when he told the crowd, "Just the other day I spent a very pleasant hour with the President at the White House discussing various bills pending in Congress, and he expressed the hope that I would come back to the Senate next year."

Truman also asked various Federal officials for aid. On June 12, 1940, for instance, Secretary of the Interior Harold Ickes noted in his diary:

> Senator Truman telephoned me yesterday to ask whether I would pass the word down the line to any Missouri people in Interior to vote for him for Senator. My information is that Governor Stark is in the lead and personally I favor Governor Stark, although Truman has made a good New Deal Senator.

Milligan made his first campaign speech on June 22, while Stark delayed his initial public appearance. Although Truman's Sedalia speech was far from an oratorical success, his scrappiness and sincerity went over well. In contrast, Milligan's first address was a disaster. People came expecting to hear a Clarence Darrow on the hustings, but his speaking voice proved much worse than Truman's and his personality failed to project.

The reason for Stark's delay in launching his campaign soon became obvious. From conversations with Roosevelt he had got the impression that the President wanted him as his next running mate. Furthermore, *The New York Times* reported that FDR had approved him, Jimmy Byrnes, Sam Rayburn and Supreme Court Justice William O. Douglas as possible Vice-Presidential nominees.

When the Democratic National Convention got under way in Chicago on July 15, 1940, both Truman and Governor Stark served on the Missouri delegation. While Truman busied himself on the Resolutions Committee, Stark "consented" to run for Vice-President and established his headquarters, passing out "Stark Delicious" apples to all delegates. "Stark Boom Quickened," said *The New York Times* as the governors of Wyoming and Arizona came out for him, and his floor manager claimed 200 first-ballot votes. On the floor of the barn-like convention hall, Stark's people staged a demonstration, but spectators were startled to see Mrs. Henry Clay Chiles, head of the women's division of Truman's campaign organization, striding through the "Stark for Vice-President" demonstrators holding high a "Truman for Senator" banner.

Stark's short-lived candidacy died once Roosevelt won renomination for a third term, for the President insisted on Secretary of Agriculture Henry A. Wallace as his running mate. Ickes wrote in his diary that while FDR had considered Stark for Vice-President earlier, he had discarded him because "he has no sense of humor and he bores me." Stark loyally supported Wallace, but Truman saw to it that the Missouri delegation gave 28½ votes to Speaker William B. Bankhead and only 1½ votes to Wallace.

The spectacle of a man running for both the Senate and Vice-Presidency annoyed Missouri voters, as Stark learned upon his return to the state. Furthermore, the delay in beginning his campaign for the Senate had irked some important newspaper publishers. Nevertheless, he remained the frontrunner for Truman's seat.

The primary campaign, now beginning in earnest, proved to be a brawl. Later Truman called it "the bitterest and dirtiest fight I ever witnessed." Milligan's original strategy had been to debate national and state issues with Stark. But with Truman in the race, Milligan and Stark focused their entire campaigns on his connection with Pendergast. By innuendo and direct statement they tarred him with the Pendergast brush and he grew accustomed to hearing himself referred to as "Tom Pendergast's stooge."

Stark also charged that he had a "slush" fund forced from unwilling contributors to pay his expenses. In turn, Truman demanded of a crowd in Independence, "How clean are the hands of Governor Stark as to slush funds? Who put the lug on state employees? Who dipped their hands in the mud of vituperation?" (After the election, a Senate investigating committee ruled that Stark had compelled state employees to contribute money to his campaign.)

During July, Truman made a whirlwind automobile tour of 75 counties. Although the weather was oppressively humid, he maintained a schedule of ten talks a day. Fred Canfil and Harry Vaughan, both burly in build, alternated as chauffeur, but each was soon exhausted. Truman's technique was to make a short talk, shake as many hands as he could, and then catch a few winks of sleep in the car as they drove to the next town.

His basic campaign strategy was to attract support from the various segments of the population. First, he had appealed to the Negroes in his opening speech at Sedalia. Then, while he was in Chicago for the Democratic National Convention, he won additional publicity among Missouri Negroes by addressing the National Colored Democratic Association. He counted on large-scale support from veterans, but here he had to contend with the fact that Stark also had a fine war record. He knew he would have to share the farm vote with Stark, too, for almost every farmer in Missouri had Stark's apple trees in his orchard.

With regard to the labor vote the situation was hardly clear-cut because all three candidates clung to Franklin Roosevelt's coattails. But Truman gained an important advantage from his investigation of the nation's railroads. On one occasion, he had testified before a Presidential fact-finding board against a proposed wage cut for railroad labor. When the board rejected the wage cut, the Railroad Brotherhoods became Truman's champions. Now, during his fight for renomination, A. F. "Alec" Whitney, president of the Railroad Trainmen, and Alvanley Johnston, head of the Railroad Engineers, ordered their members to organize "Committees for Truman" at railroad terminals in Missouri. Two weeks before the primary, they put out a special Truman edition of *Labor,* the Brotherhoods' paper, and distributed more than a half-million copies throughout the state. The paper carried encomiums from influential New Deal Senators and did much to increase Truman's support among unions generally.

By the last week in July, Missouri politicians agreed that Milligan's campaign had gone sour. From a poor third, Truman had moved up behind Stark, but he seemed to face a losing battle because of the campaign fund shortage. Pressed as he was, Truman borrowed $3,000 on his life insurance policy to help meet some of the expenses. "Besides being rich on his own," said Harry Vaughan, "Stark was married to the daughter of the president of the St. Louis Transit Lines. We couldn't afford a seven-thousand-dollar half-hour radio broadcast, but Stark was on radio regularly. Our entire campaign funds came to only eighteen thousand dollars, a ridiculously small amount for a statewide fight."

At the start of the decisive last two weeks of the campaign, Vaughan had only $200 in cash. Desperate, he and David Berenstein, a friend of Truman's from St. Louis, hit upon an idea. Well supplied with stationery and envelopes, they spent the $200 on 1½¢ stamps and sent out 13,300 open-flapped letters with the message: *If you*

174

want to see Harry Truman returned to the Senate, send $1 immedi-
ately. Within two days $1,800 poured into the office from every sec-
tion of the state. They reinvested this sum in stamps and mailed out
more letters. Back came enough money to keep the campaign moving.

As the campaign neared its climax, Truman, gnawed by doubt,
began to feel that he could not win without Senator Bennett Clark's
support. But Clark, who stayed out of the primary fight after backing
Milligan early in the campaign, was now in Washington. Vic Messall
returned to the capital and walked into Clark's office one afternoon.
"Why can't you speak for Harry Truman?" he demanded.

"Harry Truman never made any speeches for me," Clark bellowed.
"Why should I speak for him?"

"Yes, he did," Messall said. He named the dates and places where
Truman had spoken in his behalf during Clark's re-election fight in
1938.

"The hell with Harry Truman!" Clark roared.

Dejected, Messall walked out and wandered across the street to
the bar of the Carroll Arms Hotel, where he spotted Senator Carl
Hatch sitting at a table.

Over drinks, Messall told him of Clark's refusal to support Truman.
When he finished, Hatch called Clark on the telephone. "You wait
here," he said to Messall. "I'm going over to see Bennett and I'll be
right back."

Thirty minutes later Hatch returned, smiling. "I've got it all settled, Vic. Bennett is going to support Harry."

Hatch and also Alben Barkley went out to Missouri to campaign
for Truman, although it was Hatch's private opinion that "Truman
practically has no chance." By the time Clark arrived in St. Louis and
installed himself at the Mayfair Hotel, it looked as if his support
would come too late. Nevertheless, Clark called political leaders
throughout the state and announced publicly for Truman. What Truman needed, however, was for Clark to exert his influence on the
political machine in St. Louis, for it had become evident to his backers
that St. Louis would decide the election.

At the start of the campaign, Truman had tied his candidacy to
that of Lawrence McDaniel of St. Louis, who was running for governor. The two had made a tacit agreement to support each other
even though McDaniel's chief backers, the Mayor Dickmann-Bob
Hannegan machine of St. Louis, were behind Truman's opponent,
Governor Stark.

175

Truman's strategists hoped that he might erode Stark's support in St. Louis by his show of strong support of McDaniel in other parts of the state. But when Senator Barkley attracted a measly crowd of 300 in his St. Louis rally for Truman, McDaniel's campaign committee backed away from Truman and announced that the Senate race was "wide open."

This defection infuriated Truman's backers and many threatened to switch their support from McDaniel to his opponent for governor. McDaniel was thoroughly frightened by this prospect, but Mayor Dickmann held his ground and continued to support Stark.

Although the situation in St. Louis looked hopeless to Truman's backers, they continued to pressure Bob Hannegan to come out for him in exchange for their support of McDaniel. Only two days before the primary Hannegan agreed. "The biggest break," Truman said, "was when Bob Hannegan, who had been working for Stark . . . switched his support to me." Once Hannegan announced for Truman, he ordered his precinct captains and ward men to ring doorbells and promote Truman without letup.

The newspapers were now calling the primary contest a horse race between Truman and Stark. On August 3, at his final rally in Independence, Truman not only lashed out at Stark, but also roasted the Republicans and bluntly told his audience: "Any farmer fool enough to vote the Republican ticket ought to have his head examined." The crowd of 3,500 cheered.

On election day, August 6, Truman handed his ballot to George Wallace, Bess's brother, an election judge in the third precinct of Blue Township in Independence. Early returns showed Stark far in the lead, and his margin widened during the day. By ten P.M., Truman was 11,000 votes behind and his top supporters were ready to concede. He was weary and disheartened when he heard the news. "I went to bed defeated," he later admitted.

At ten-thirty, Tom Evans called Truman from Democratic headquarters where he was counting the vote to tell him that the picture looked grim. Margaret answered the phone. "Daddy's gone to bed," she said. In the middle of the night Truman's total suddenly spurted and he continued to gain on Stark. Then came a key total. Truman, who was supposed to be politically dead in St. Louis, captured the election there by 8,411 votes. This gave him a plurality over Stark throughout Missouri of less then 8,000 votes. His margin of victory was due to Bob Hannegan's work.

When the final result became known at eleven A.M., Truman's friends were exhausted and on edge, but he was refreshed and elated after a good night's sleep. The St. Louis *Globe-Democrat* referred to his victory as the "calamitous result." Stark sent a letter of explanation to President Roosevelt: "You will be interested to see that the machine vote, backed by Bennett Clark with every force at his command, was 100,000 less than our combined vote. [He referred to his own 254,585 votes; Milligan's, 125,024; and Truman's 262,552.] I am sorry to report that virtually all the Federal appointees, including Postmasters and WPA workers, were lined up with Clark and the machine against us. Due primarily to the severe drought, etc., about 100,000 of our rural vote, which is strong for me, did not turn out."

Roosevelt, however, had no time for losers. His reply read:

DEAR LLOYD:

Your letter enclosing the clipping has been received and I was interested to read the analysis of the recent Primary fight. I am sure you understand my personal feeling toward you. I can only say that we will all have to get behind the ticket and work for a Democratic victory.

With all good wishes,
Your friend,
FRANKLIN D. ROOSEVELT

Roosevelt also wrote to Truman, congratulating him on his victory. In the flush of triumph, Truman felt charitably disposed toward Maurice Milligan even though he told a St. Louis *Post-Dispatch* reporter that Milligan had "tried to connect me with everything under the sun." Before entering the race, Milligan had resigned as U. S. Attorney and was now out of a job. Truman therefore wrote to FDR on September 14, requesting that he reappoint Milligan to his old post.

Despite victory in a hard-fought primary, there were still the Republicans to contend with in the November general election. Once again Truman was savagely attacked as a Pendergast man. There was also evidence of opposition from Democrats who were more interested in punishing him than in winning at the polls. Just as his campaign against Manvelle Davis, his Republican opponent, was about to get under way, the papers announced that anti-Goat Presiding Jackson County Judge Montgomery had foreclosed on his mother's farm. "Old man Montgomery foreclosed to embarrass me," Truman said. "They

177

sold it under the hammer without giving us any chance to refinance and moved Mamma off the farm."

The loss of the farm was used not only to point up Truman's apparent inability to achieve financial success, but, coupled with stories about the failure years before of his haberdashery business, to make him an object of ridicule. Rumors were also spread about supposed skulduggery on his part in "forcing" the county to extend his mother the $35,000 loan on the property back in March, 1938. Actually, as county officials later admitted, the property was worth more than $35,000. According to Truman, "The matter of the farm loan was done for a political purpose, getting my brother to sign the note and foreclosing in a short time, causing the loss of my mother's farm. I had nothing to do with getting the loan." After the foreclosure, Martha Truman moved with her daughter Mary Jane to a small frame house in Grandview.

As the fall campaign progressed, Manvelle Davis followed the pattern of Stark and Milligan in the primary and vilified Truman with wild abuse. "He quoted lies published in the St. Louis *Post-Dispatch* and the Kansas City *Star* and apparently had a grand time doing it," Truman said.

Shortly before the election on November 5, Truman was elevated to the rank of Grand Master of Masons in Missouri. Forrest C. Donnell, the Republican candidate for governor, was also in the Grand Lodge hierarchy. When he and Davis came to Wellsville to speak at a Republican rally, Jim Wade, one of Truman's supporters, asked Donnell if it were true that Truman, his brother Mason, had been elected Grand Master in Missouri. Donnell, who was noted for his honesty, flashed his lemony smile and acknowledged the truth of Wade's remark.

"Then how is it possible," asked Wade, "that he could be the low sort of person Manvelle Davis has been saying he is?"

"Of course he isn't," Donnell replied.

The incident was widely reported throughout the state and Truman believed that Donnell's politically naïve comment cost Davis thousands of votes. Donnell, however, suffered no damage, for when the ballots were tabulated, he emerged victorious over McDaniel by 3,613 votes, although Truman defeated Davis with a total of 930,775 votes to 886,376.

With the exhausting election campaign behind him, Harry Truman

178

viewed 1940 as the hardest year of his life. But it was also the year of vindication. He was now a Senator on his own merit.

When he walked onto the Senate floor following his grueling ordeal, his colleagues gave him a standing ovation. A reporter on the scene noted, "They behaved like boys greeting a popular schoolmate who had just got over the measles." Afterward, a score of Senators held an impromptu lunch in his honor.

He now belonged, independent and secure, no longer the creature of Tom Pendergast.

22

WHEN Truman returned to Washington after his election he found the capital stirring with activity. As a result of the war in Europe, Congress had repealed the arms embargo, Roosevelt had transferred 50 overage American destroyers to England and Selective Service had been set up to draft young men into the armed forces.

By 1941, new Army camps were being established throughout the country and the initial wave of defense contracts went out to American industry. Truman and his fellow Senators scrambled to get as many defense contracts for homestate constituents as they could extract from the War and Navy Departments. But, as Truman admitted to a reporter, he was treated as if he had leprosy. Word had gone out, presumably from the White House, Truman said, that certain Missouri politicians were to be ignored.

At the time he was meeting these rebuffs, a friend wrote him about the appalling waste in the construction of Fort Leonard Wood at Rolla, Missouri. When other letters making the same complaint poured in to his office, he decided to look into the matter himself.

At the camp he found workers dawdling, some asleep on the job, and great confusion everywhere. Valuable equipment lay unprotected from the elements. He quizzed workers, foremen and contractors and worked up tables of costs, wages and expenditures. All of it added up to enormous waste of manpower, money and material.

Before returning to Washington, he completed a tour of 30,000 miles, checking several other camps under construction as well as defense plants in a perimeter from Florida out to Texas, Oklahoma, up to Nebraska and back again through Michigan. "The trip was an eye opener," he said. Almost all projects were on a cost-plus basis: the higher the costs, the greater the profits. Nowhere did he see any sign of prior planning; everything was makeshift.

Once back in Washington, his fury at fever pitch, he discussed what he had seen with his friend John Snyder, then director of the Defense Plant Corporation. He also talked over what he should do with Bill Helm. With the Executive Branch either oblivious to or unconcerned about what was going on, he decided that the Senate must establish a committee to investigate the situation.

With this in mind, he rose in the Senate Chamber on February 10, 1941, and denounced the defense program. He pointed out that, in many instances, firms were awarded contracts because their top officials were personal friends of members of the Quartermaster General's advisory board. "When a friendship, however, dominates the selection of an inferior contractor, then that is wrong," he said. Truman also laid some of the blame on contractors. "I have never yet found a contractor who, if not watched, wouldn't leave the Government holding the bag. We are not doing him a favor if we don't watch him."

He drew applause when he said: "It is considered a sin for a United States Senator to make a recommendation for contractors, although we may be more familiar with the efficiency and ability of our contractors than anyone in the War Department." He spoke bitterly about a single company landing $300,000,000 to $500,000,000 in contracts while he was unable to obtain anything for Missouri firms. "I am reliably informed that from seventy to ninety per cent of the contracts have been concentrated in an area smaller than England."

This was fighting talk by a man who felt for the first time that he could speak with authority in the United States Senate. He introduced Senate Resolution 71, calling for a committee of five Senators to investigate the operation of the vast defense program. "It won't do any good digging up dead horses after the war is over like last time," he warned. "The thing to do is dig this stuff up now and correct it."

By coincidence, said Senator James Byrnes, President Roosevelt had telephoned him at this very time to report that Secretary of War Henry Stimson and Secretary of the Navy Frank Knox were disturbed because the House was in process of approving a resolution by Congressman Eugene Cox of Georgia to investigate defense contracts. Knox and Stimson feared a hatchet job if Cox, rabidly anti-Roosevelt, went after them. Byrnes concluded that if the Senate set up its own investigating committee, the House would probably not approve a duplicating investigation.

In sifting through the resolutions before his Audit and Control Committee, which decided whether the Senate should provide money for investigations, Byrnes came across Truman's resolution. He sought him out to ask what had prompted his action. Byrnes quoted Truman as saying, "A contractor in Missouri alleged that the War Department awarded its contracts only to the big contracting organizations."

Since Byrnes believed that Truman would not start a major investigation, he rushed to the Senate Chamber within an hour after talking to him. It was Saturday, March 1, and only sixteen Senators were present. Swiftly, Byrnes won unanimous consent to bring up Truman's resolution and secured its passage without debate. As Byrnes had anticipated, the House dropped Cox's proposal when it learned of the approved Senate resolution.

Byrnes was determined to forestall any sweeping investigation. Truman had asked for an appropriation of $25,000—not a munificent sum but large enough at least to start an effective investigation. With less than this amount, he would be forced to restrict his inquiry to the single contractor in Missouri. Byrnes therefore recommended that the investigating committee be given only $10,000. Infuriated, Truman demanded more money. But it was only "after a week of haggling," he said, that Byrnes agreed to raise the appropriation to $15,000. Byrnes refused to go beyond that amount and Truman had to accept it, even though he knew it was inadequate.

Byrnes was still not taking chances. It was all right for Truman to be the committee's chairman because it had been his resolution. But he was not to decide the committee's composition. Originally, Truman had proposed a five-man committee: three Democrats and two Republicans. Byrnes changed the total to seven: five Democrats and two Republicans. Normally, the Vice-President, acting upon the advice of the chairman, named the members to a special committee. In this case, however, the membership would be decided by Truman, Henry Wallace, Alben Barkley and the Republican leader, Charles McNary. It soon became obvious to Truman that they were suggesting men he did not want. One day he told Bill Helm, the reporter who had first suggested he introduce his resolution, "I don't want —— ——; he's an old fuddy-duddy. Then they wanted to know how I felt about —— ——. I told them No. He's a stuffed shirt." Because of this bickering, the committee was not organized until mid-March. With the exception of Tom Connally, who was put on the committee to steady it, the other members—Carl Hatch, James Mead, Mon Wallgren, Joseph Ball, and Owen Brewster—were relatively new Senators like Truman.

Byrnes lectured Truman about running his own show and not turning over the job to hired attorneys. Although Truman had no intention of relinquishing his authority to lawyer-prosecutors, he realized that he needed a first-rate counselor. One morning he visited Attorney General Robert H. Jackson and asked for his best lawyer, someone who was young, energetic, brilliant and hard-hitting.

A few days later Jackson sent him his lawyer. Truman raised his eyebrows when Hugh Fulton walked in, for he was a large, heavy man who wore a derby and spoke in a squeaky voice. But Truman's initial disappointment vanished as they talked and he discovered that Fulton had prosecuted some of the Justice Department's top cases. In turn, Fulton asked Truman bluntly if the committee intended merely to get headlines for itself.

"You get the facts," Truman snapped at him. "That's all we want. Don't show anybody any favors. We haven't any axes to grind, nor any sacred cows. This won't be a whitewash or a witch hunt."

When Fulton agreed to be committee counsel, Truman hired him at a salary of $9,000, or more than half of his committee's $15,000 appropriation. With only $6,000 left, he had to rely on an old Congressional trick to create a staff. This was the practice of "borrowing" personnel from executive agencies downtown, with the agencies paying their salaries. Thus, Tom Clark worked for the committee through the courtesy of the Justice Department; William M. Boyle, Jr., who later became Democratic National Chairman, went to work as assistant counsel; and Matthew J. Connelly became an investigator.

Just as the committee staff began to take shape, Truman was faced with the chore of finding a replacement for Vic Messall, who resigned as his secretary to become a lobbyist. This problem was solved when he asked his old friend, Harry Vaughan, to join him in Washington to take over Messall's job.

Another vital question that had to be solved was the determination of his committee's scope of action. From the outset, Truman had no intention of restricting his investigation to the charge made by the Missouri contractor, as Byrnes expected him to do. He was determined that his committee would investigate the entire national defense program. This meant procurement and manufacture of all kinds of materials and munitions, construction of aircraft, ships and military camps and operation of defense plants.

But what would the committee's approach be in conducting such sweeping investigations? Senator Harley M. Kilgore of West Virginia, who was soon to be added to Truman's committee, said: "In January, 1941, he and I went to Senator Matt Neeley's inauguration as governor of West Virgina. On the return trip, we discovered we had a mutual interest in American history. We got to talking about the disruptive committee work in the Civil War. I had a set of the voluminous *Reports of the Joint Committee on the Conduct of the War,* put out by that wretched Civil War period group of Congressmen. Not only did they interfere with military operations and strategy, prolong the war unnecessarily and at great cost in lives, but they also tried to do Lincoln in. Lee later said that the Joint Committee was worth several divisions to him.

"When we returned to Washington, Harry borrowed a copy of the hearings of the Civil War Joint Committee from the Library of Congress. And we had several further discussions on the way that Joint Committee almost ruined the Union cause with its attempt to supervise the running of the war. By the time Harry got his own committee, he knew exactly how he would run it—the opposite of the Civil War committee."

Truman said: "Vandenberg, Brewster, Taft and one or two other influential Senators tried to get me to make a Committee on the Conduct of the War out of my committee. Thank goodness, I knew my history and I wouldn't do it."

His final decision was to make the committee apolitical. "Harry functioned as a chief of staff," Kilgore said. "And he was a good one. He welded the committee members together as a team." Members were told that anything they accomplished would be presented as the findings of the entire committee and not as the handiwork of a single

Senator. All statements and conclusions would be expressed only on the Senate floor or in formal reports.

More important, the committee would never advocate changes in military strategy or in the size or disposal of the defense effort. Its sole purpose would be to investigate the operation of the defense program and to uncover graft, waste and inefficiency. It would search out facts and base conclusions on those facts.

With these standards as a guide, the Truman Committee began its investigation. It started slowly in order to ground itself in the fundamentals of the defense program. Secretary of War Stimson was the first witness to appear and provided the committee with a general picture of developments and problems. Then came officials from various government agencies who discussed their activities in ordnance requirements, contract and matériel priorities, shortages and labor problems. Truman called a dozen generals and several civilian experts of the War Department to tell the committee about the mobilization program. After this preliminary testimony, he began his investigation into the operations of the camp construction program.

As this investigation was getting underway in April, 1941, a strike threatened the entire defense program. John L. Lewis, who had broken with Roosevelt and supported Wendell Willkie in 1940, had taken his coal miners out of the pits. Normally, the Executive Branch handled such problems, but under the circumstances Truman considered the strike as falling under his committee's investigating authority. If the mines were not in operation by April 25, he announced, his committee would summon Lewis and the mine operators and "take them for a bus ride to get them together" in order to maintain coal production during the national emergency.

When both sides ignored his threat, he ordered Lewis and twelve northern operators to appear before his committee on the following Monday, the twenty-eighth. It soon became clear to him that recalcitrant southern operators were responsible for the deadlock. He lost no time sending them a message: "Your faction is holding up settlement. We know your mines are owned by northern capitalists and bankers. If you don't end this deadlock within 24 hours, we are going to send for these capitalists and bankers. We intend to put them on the witness stand and find out from them, as principals, whether the national safety or the wage dispute comes first." The threat was effective. That night the deadlock ended and a settlement was made.

This unprecedented labor mediation by a Senate committee added

185

greatly to Truman's stature. For the first time, favorable stories about him began to appear in the nation's press. But his anonymity was still so marked that the Washington *Star* ran a picture of someone else with the caption SENATOR HARRY S. TRUMAN.

The committee now resumed its investigation of the camp construction program. Nine camps were closely examined, and committee members personally observed construction and talked with workers and contractors. In addition, the military men in charge of the program were called upon to testify.

Truman was busy writing the committee's report on the camp construction program when Hitler's forces invaded the Soviet Union on June 23. Asked about this turn of events by reporters, he gave an off-the-cuff opinion that was the complete reverse of President Roosevelt's reaction and policy. "If we see that Germany is winning we ought to help Russia," he said, "and if Russia is winning we ought to help Germany, and that way let them kill as many as possible, although I don't want to see Hitler victorious under any circumstances. Neither of them think anything of their pledged word." This statement did little to enhance his reputation in the field of foreign affairs.

In contrast, Truman was on firmer and more familiar ground with his analysis of the camp construction program. In August, his 98-page report noted a "needless waste" of more than $100,000,000 in the $1,000,000,000 program. Among other blunders, he disclosed that the War Department had begun construction of camps without any plans.

Many of his charges led to belated changes by the armed forces. The Army had used "fantastically poor judgment" in choosing campsites. It was renting cars, trucks and equipment at sky-high rates instead of purchasing outright—a move, as the Quartermaster Corps grudgingly admitted, that could have saved $13,000,000. The Truman Committee also reported that payments to contractors and architectural engineers were made in "much the same way that Santa Claus passes out gifts at a church Christmas party." Nor did Truman spare labor leaders who forced workers to join their unions before getting defense jobs and charged them extortionate fees for work permits. General Brehon Somervell, whose Services of Supply caught most of the Truman Committee's fire, later said that the changes initiated as a result of the report saved the Government about $200,000,000.

Buoyed by the success of his first report, Truman was ready to move in to several areas of the defense program. He had already established his work routine. Every morning he reached his office about seven-thirty, met with Hugh Fulton, and the two then plowed through piles of reports, letters and notes, many of which supplied leads for investigations. Once the official day began, his office in Room 248 of the Senate Office Building and the committee's quarters in Room 449 were thronged with government officials, businessmen, union leaders, lobbyists and the curious. When the committee held hearings, Truman presided like a judge in court. All sessions were open to the public and, in line with Byrnes's dictum that Senators must not let hired lawyers run the show in their absence, no hearings were held if committee members were not present.

Although Truman permitted witnesses to bring their own attorneys, he refused to let their lawyers ask questions. No one was permitted to browbeat a witness. On one occasion Truman went so far as to scold a Senator for calling John L. Lewis a "charlatan" to his face. He made certain, however, that witnesses did not mistake his courtesy for weakness. Witnesses with complaints had to put up or shut up. At one committee hearing, Donald Nelson, an official of the defense program, complained that first-rate businessmen would not work for the Government because the press would malign them. "Tell me the names of those businessmen and I'll get in touch with them," Truman snapped. Nelson blanched and withdrew his complaint.

Only when an official was known to be hostile toward the committee did Truman get tough. On October 18, 1941, he had lunch with Harold Ickes and told him that Jesse Jones, head of the RFC and Secretary of Commerce, was to appear before his committee. He also mentioned that Jones had signed a "vicious contract" with the Aluminum Corporation of America (Alcoa) which had squeezed out small aluminum producers by keeping them from getting access to magnesium and bauxite, the raw ore used to produce the metal. Truman was so incensed by Jones's arrogance that he told Ickes that "Jones was going to be given the works." He insisted he would do so even though "terrific pressure had been brought on him to go easy with Jones."

Jones got "the works." After the hearing, he agreed to negotiate a supplemental contract with Alcoa which considerably weakened that company's monopolistic position in aluminum production.

Truman and the members of his committee roamed the country, going through shipyards, aircraft factories, mines, defense housing developments, machine tool plants and other defense establishments.

In 1941 alone, the committee held about 70 hearings and gathered more than 3,000 pages of testimony. Truman's favorite committee traveling companions were Harley Kilgore and Mon Wallgren. "He called Bess every night we were away from Washington," Kilgore said. "When we traveled by train, we flipped a coin each night to see who would get the lower berth. He didn't stand on his rights as chairman."

In Washington, Truman's sanctum was his "Doghouse," a room to the right of his office desk. The Doghouse was high-ceilinged and comfortably furnished with black leather easy chairs, desks and tables. Truman collected autographs and the walls were covered with inscribed photographs as well as the red-marked field artillery maps of Battery D. From time to time bottles labeled *From the Private Stock of Tom Pendergast* were noticeably in evidence.

In this room the full committee gathered several times each week for private sessions. Members, of course, served on other committees, and some were on as many as eight to ten subcommittees within those committees. Truman was deeply involved with the Appropriations, the Interstate Commerce, and the Military Affairs Committees, but the Truman Committee was his chief interest. In the Doghouse, the Truman Committee members kept each other informed of their activities and went over proposed committee reports. When a report was in preparation, each member had the opportunity to suggest changes. Since Truman insisted that all reports be unanimous, sometimes as many as five drafts were written before unanimity was reached. Republican committee member Owen Brewster was once asked to explain this curious unanimity. "Reasonable men don't differ much when they have the facts," he commented.

Defense agency heads also came to the Truman Doghouse to discuss their problems "off the record" with the committee. Here, in an atmosphere free from fanfare and publicity, they learned some hard facts about irregularities the committee had uncovered in their agencies, with the result that several important changes were made in methods of operation. In addition, before reports were made public, these officials as well as the private firms involved were given a chance to come to the Doghouse and present rebuttals. Here also came individuals who had ideas for improving the defense setup. Many were crackpots. Truman said that one excited man proposed filling planes with dirt and unloading them over enemy capitals, which, he insisted, would bury those cities and end hostilities.

Throughout the country, as 1941 progressed, there was little sense of urgency about the defense program. The continent of Europe lay in Hitler's hands; Asia seemed destined to become Japan's vassal. And despite United States aid to Britain, most Americans considered the defense program as a means to make business profitable and eliminate the widespread unemployment that had crippled the nation for a decade. To the public as a whole the role of the Truman Committee was that of a watchdog to hold down waste in the expanding economy.

On December 7, Bess and Margaret were in Washington preparing to return to Independence for Christmas. "Daddy had telephoned Saturday night," Margaret recalled, "to say he planned to spend Sunday in a small hotel in Columbia, Missouri, just resting and sleeping after a week of rugged daily schedules." When the radio announced the Japanese attack on Pearl Harbor early that afternoon, Bess put in a hurried call to the Tennant Hotel in Columbia. Truman was sound asleep, but he finally fumbled for the receiver and managed to get it to his ear. Later he admitted he was "frantic" because he was in an isolated spot and could get back to Washington only with difficulty. He had to walk across open fields to a small private air hangar, where he begged the owner to borrow a small plane and fly him to St. Louis. When he finally arrived in Washington, it was Monday noon and President Roosevelt was preparing to tell the Joint Session of Congress: "Hostilities exist. There is no blinking at the fact that our people, our territory and our interests are in grave danger." Three days later, when Germany and Italy declared war on the United States, the fighting became global.

Now there was no defense program, but a war program instead. To Truman, it was more urgent than ever that the war effort at home be properly managed. Most immediate, something had to be done about the bungling and confusion that existed at the top level of those responsible for the war effort. Truman was writing a report on this situation when several committee members came into his Doghouse to discuss their future. Some of the Senators maintained that the committee should disband because it was unpatriotic to criticize the Government during war. But Truman rejected this reasoning. Since it was never the intent of the committee to interfere with strategy or military tactics, he said, its work was wholly constructive.

Actually, Truman had wavered once about the committee and his own future. Right after Pearl Harbor, he went to see General George C. Marshall to get his permission to join the regular Army. But Marshall scoffingly told him: "Senator, you've got a big job to do right up there at the Capitol with your Investigating Committee. Besides, this is a young man's war. We don't need any old stiffs like you."

The Army, however, acted with dispatch to take Truman's secretary, Harry Vaughan, as a lieutenant colonel, and sent him to Australia to serve as executive officer to Brigadier General Arthur Wilson in charge of American troops. Truman wrote to a friend, "I rather felt they had taken off my right arm when they took him." He told newsman Bill Helm that he vowed not to drink until he and Vaughan were together again.

During December, 1941, Truman and his committee members whipped their first annual report into shape. It was to be a devastating indictment of that year's defense efforts, and especially of the Supply Priorities and Allocation Board (SPAB) and the Office of Production Management (OPM), the defense agency concerned with contracts and the priority system for allocating materials and supplies.

Roosevelt had appointed William Knudsen, head of General Motors, and Sidney Hillman, president of the CIO's Amalgamated Clothing Workers, as co-directors of the OPM. They were articulate men, although each spoke with a heavy accent, but unfortunately, they did not speak to each other. Knudsen strongly favored using dollar-a-year men and WOC's (without compensation) from the ranks of big business, whereas Hillman considered each contract that passed over his desk in terms of its effect on organized labor.

Truman was offended by the underlying philosophies of both men. On October 29, 1941, for instance, he told the Senate: "A responsible company has made a low bid. It is prepared to perform and is capable of performing if not illegally interfered with. Mr. Sidney Hillman advises that it be denied the contract and that the taxpayers pay several hundred thousands of dollars more because Mr. Hillman fears trouble from what he calls irresponsible elements in the American Federation of Labor."

In his first annual report, Truman condemned the chaotic situation at the OPM. He proposed that it be scrapped and replaced by a new war agency under a single chairman.

Before making his report public, however, he sent it to the President. Immediately after reading it, Roosevelt eliminated SPAB and the OPM and established the War Production Board (WPB) with Donald Nelson as its chairman. "President Roosevelt received public credit for establishing the War Production Board because of his advance knowledge of the committee's report," Truman said. "That was all right with me."

In January, 1942, he finally read the 146-page document on the Senate floor. Not many Senators were present as he began, but those who were formed a group around him to listen. The report was a blistering denunciation of greed, stupidity, and self-seeking. Truman censured the automobile industry for failing to convert its plants to war production while continuing to produce millions of pleasure cars. He criticized the defense program for ignoring small firms, for its "golden goose" contractual arrangements, and for purchasing whatever aircraft plane manufacturers produced instead of forcing the production of needed planes at full capacity. He examined the problems of metal shortages and their causes, from OPM's charge that "it was unpatriotic to talk about the possibilities of an aluminum shortage" to his own that eastern steel firms were preventing the construction of West Coast steel mills. He told about the waste and mistakes in the defense housing program and the inordinate profits being made by contractors. He called businessmen the "dupes of peddlers of influence," and suggested legislation to curb the Five and Ten Percenters. "The fact that the entire future of the nation is at stake," he said, "makes it imperative that there should be a constant check to ascertain that the program is actually being carried out efficiently, economically and fairly so that the necessary sacrifices are apportioned to all without favoritism."

With this report, Truman established himself in the first rank among his fellow Senators. Of even greater importance, his glacial relationship with President Roosevelt began to thaw out.

23

THE Truman Committee expanded its work in 1942, and Truman was not only involved in endless hearings but was often away from the capital on long trips. Margaret, who entered George Washington University that fall, said her father "always looked exhausted and grave." As for Truman, he told Bill Helm, "I'm as tired as a dog and having the time of my life."

After the impact of the first report, the Senate gave the committee $100,000, an increase of $85,000 over its initial appropriation. Truman became known as the "fact man" of the Senate. His head teemed with statistics which he could spout at any suitable moment.

There was little rest from his duties. When he was in town, he seldom went to social functions. "Even here," Kilgore said, "if there was a mixed affair, he always ducked out early." His avocation was the movies, and he enjoyed poor pictures because they put him to sleep. On the road, he whiled away dull evening hours playing ten-cent-limit poker with Kilgore, Wallgren and others on the committee.

During 1942, the Truman Committee uncovered even more staggering evidence of graft and waste, resulting in part from the conflict between the military and civilian agencies over who had chief authority in supervising war production. The situation had grown so bad that Truman privately rebuked Donald Nelson in his Doghouse and urged him to insist that civilians run the war production program.

The committee found that one reason for the rubber shortage was that seven separate government agencies thought they were in charge of the rubber program. In addition, the committee blamed a cartel arrangement between the I. G. Farbenindustrie and Standard Oil for the lag in the development of synthetic rubber. At the same time that many defense plants could not get materials, producers of consumer goods were manufacturing toys and games made of vitally needed metals. The steel industry was still arguing against increasing capacity because it feared a postwar oversupply. These and other matters Truman brought to the attention of the White House and insisted upon action.

Aside from exposing these conditions the committee was also responsible for saving lives. When the Curtiss-Wright Corporation passed defective aircraft engines at one plant that resulted in the deaths of several student pilots, the committee condemned four hundred engines. At the Glenn Martin plant an engineering survey, ordered by Truman, disclosed that the wingspread of the B-26 Martin Bomber was too short for stability. When Martin was summoned to testify, he told Truman that he had to go ahead with production because the blueprints were already completed and he was tooling up. Truman looked hard at him through his trifocal glasses and threatened to make certain that the Government would not purchase any of the planes. Martin immediately agreed to make changes.

As Truman's reputation increased, he discovered that the Administration was no longer antagonistic toward him. When FDR planned to bring former Governor Stark into the Government to handle labor mediation matters, Truman was still uncertain about how Roosevelt would accept his direct intervention to prevent the appointment. He therefore asked Sherman Minton, then on the U. S. Circuit Court of Appeals, to write to FDR in his behalf. "This appointment would be very displeasing to Senator Truman, who has always been our friend," Minton wrote. "The appointment would give Senator Clark, whose support we never have, an excellent opportunity to work on Truman." Roosevelt dropped Stark from consideration.

Truman was also getting a good press around the country. The

Truman Committee had become part of the American lexicon. It meant honest, forthright investigations and exposure of crooks. Even the St. Louis *Post-Dispatch,* Truman's tenacious foe, came to this conclusion. In its pages on November 8, 1942, Marquis Childs referred to him as "one of the most useful and at the same time one of the most forthright and fearless of the ninety-six." As for the Truman Committee, he declared: "There is no doubt that it has saved billions —yes, billions—of dollars."

When the 1942 elections approached, Democratic Party stalwarts for the first time considered Truman an asset in helping to elect a Democratic Congress. He joined the circuit swingers leaving Washington for the hinterlands, but, as he wrote to the postmaster of St. Joseph, Missouri, on November 9: "Nearly every District I went into went Republican. I don't know whether that was due to my inability to put it over or because of the trend against the Administration."

Truman also began to get a chance at patronage. Senator Bennett Clark had long ago been written off by Roosevelt, and with former Governor Stark retired to his apples, Truman now sat at the very top of the Missouri totem pole. He discovered, however, that government agencies still did not show him much respect when it came to placing people he recommended. "They seem to think it is a disgrace for a man to be a Democrat," he wrote to the U.S. Attorney at St. Louis. In a letter to his friend Lewis Schwellenbach, who had resigned from the Senate to become a Federal District Judge in the State of Washington, he wrote: "The President's mistaken notion he was getting co-operation by taking the enemy into the camp is something I never did believe in and I don't believe in that policy now."

Nevertheless, he did not meet with total defeat on the patronage score. When Congressman Richard M. Duncan, who had been in the House for ten years, lost out in 1942, Truman promoted him for Federal District Judge in Missouri. The Missouri lawyers' association opposed Duncan, as did Attorney General Francis Biddle. Yet Roosevelt approved the nomination. But Truman's biggest patronage success was in rewarding Bob Hannegan, who had engineered his winning margin in the 1940 primary.

After the election in 1940, Hannegan and Mayor Dickmann, joint bosses of St. Louis, had attempted a coup to put Larry McDaniel, the St. Louis saloon commissioner, into the governor's mansion, even though he had lost by 3,613 votes to Forrest Donnell, the Republican candidate. Hannegan proposed an investigation of the election by the state legislature. Since the Democrats controlled the legislature, such an investigation would inevitably end in barring Donnell and making McDaniel governor. Although Governor Stark, then in his last weeks in office, denounced Hannegan's plan as a "shameless steal," the legislature went ahead with its so-called investigation. But Donnell appealed to the courts, which ruled that he had been legally elected and must be named governor. As a result of this attempt to seat McDaniel, Mayor Dickmann was defeated for re-election in April, 1941.

Despite Hannegan's part in this unsavory affair, Truman believed that he merited a reward for his aid to him in 1940. Early in 1942, a likely spot opened up as Collector of Internal Revenue at St. Louis. When the St. Louis *Globe-Democrat* heard that Truman was promoting Hannegan for Collector, it charged that Hannegan was the "most discredited boss of a discredited political machine."

Truman told reporters, "Hannegan carried St. Louis three times for the President and for me. If he is not nominated there will be no Collector at St. Louis." Roosevelt felt the same way, and in June, 1942, he appointed Hannegan to the post.

Hannegan did not let Truman or Roosevelt down. He put in long hard days as Collector and attended night school to study taxation. Within a year, the St. Louis Collector's office, which had been rated the worst in the country, was labeled the most efficient by the Bureau in Washington. In October, 1943, with Truman's help, Hannegan moved to Washington as Commissioner of Internal Revenue.

"By the fall of 1942," Senator Kilgore said, "Harry Truman was in a respected position. Then he pulled a *faux pas*. *American Magazine* wanted to ghost write an article for him on his committee's findings. Harry had never had anything in print before, so he was quite excited. He got an agreement whereby nothing would be printed unless he initialed each page of the manuscript beforehand. But he was too trusting.

"Late one day a girl associate editor of *American* came rushing into his office with copy. She told him that the presses were ready to roll and asked him to read it right away. He told her she looked like an honest girl and that he was sure the article was proper. To help her out, he didn't bother to read the article, but merely initialed each page. He didn't know it, but what he initialed was a blistering attack on the Administration. The committee lawyers ran up to New York

195

late that night and asked Judge Ferdinand Pecora to help them force *American Magazine* to drop the article. But Pecora couldn't do anything because Harry had initialed each page.

"The article came out in November, 1942, and was titled 'We Can Lose the War in Washington.' Roosevelt was so incensed that he cut off all relations with him. Finally, after several months, I was at the White House one day and I told Roosevelt the story. He agreed to make up, though he said it grudgingly. I don't think Roosevelt ever really forgot it."

Regardless of this setback in his relations with the White House, Truman continued his work with enthusiasm. On June 23, 1943, he wrote to Schwellenbach: "We have been having a most hectic time in this Capital City and you ought to pat yourself on the back that you are out from under it. I have been spending my time running from one subcommittee to another and in the meantime trying to operate my Special Committee for the benefit of the war effort and the taxpayers, and it is a hard combination."

Throughout 1943, the Truman Committee continued to make probe after probe, looking into the seaworthiness of Liberty ships, lend-pease operations, postwar reconversion and renegotiation of war contracts. That year, Fred Canfil, who was one of Truman's investigators, chanced upon the secret work on the atomic bomb. Truman was all set to investigate the huge expenditures when Administration officials called on him and explained why he should not. James Byrnes later said, "He knew of the project generally through his Senate committee work."

On March 8, 1943, Truman appeared on the cover of *Time*. The profile story was inaccurate, but it emphasized his importance to the war effort. When the story appeared, Schwellenbach sent him a telegram: WHAT DO THEY MEAN AN OCCASIONAL DRINK OF BOURBON? James Byrnes, who had gone on the Supreme Court in July, 1941, and then resigned to become "Assistant President" as head of the wartime Office of Economic Stabilization, ribbed him about the cover picture, which portrayed his face as a series of rutted wrinkles. "It is their policy," Truman replied, "to make everyone look as ridiculous as possible, particularly if he is a public official."

Time's coverage was an important boost for Truman. Shortly afterward, several papers began mentioning him as a possible Presidential candidate for 1944. When this came to his attention, he wrote to a friend, "I can name you a half-dozen good Senators who have been absolutely ruined by the sting of that bee."

As a prominent Senator, he was now in demand as a speaker. On November 26, 1943, he made his first coast-to-coast broadcast on the work of his committee. But speaking was not his forte and he found it unpleasant. After one speech, he wrote apologetically to Leonard Reinsch of the Atlanta *Journal,* who was his speech instructor, "The talk at Philadelphia was under a very severe handicap. They had put on some half-dozen speakers before they got to me. The crowd was getting restless and I fear very much that I butchered the speech."

Reinsch, who was critical of his machine-gun style of delivery, often cautioned him to "keep it slow and remember the living room." Following one speech, he wrote: "As you got to the end of the statement, you had a tendency to hurry the last few words."

Unlike many of his colleagues, who earned several thousand dollars a year on the lecture circuit, Truman refused to accept a fee for speaking. Once when he was criticized for having his wife on his payroll, he told a reporter, "I could have made a lot more than Mrs. Truman received for her competent performance of my secretarial work. A New York man telephoned me and was very insistent I sign up with him for a series of lectures and dinner appearances at four hundred dollars and expenses for each. When I told him I wasn't interested, he raised it to six hundred. When I told him I wouldn't do it at any price, he called me a damn fool and hung up."

In the summer of 1943, Truman started his last year as head of the committee which produced a total of 32 reports. At a cost of only $400,000, Truman claimed, the investigators saved taxpayers $15,000,000,000. This sum does not include major savings resulting from action to head off troubles in specific war industries before they developed. Nor can it possibly reflect the saving in lives through improved weapons and machines of war which the committee helped bring about. In evaluating the work of the Truman Committee, Stanley High praised it in the *Reader's Digest* as "the public's most accessible court of appeals, the sharpest prod and one of the most powerful action-getting agencies in the government."

By the beginning of 1944, newspapers across the country were mentioning Truman with increasing frequency as a possible candidate on the Democratic ticket. In the spring, a poll of Washington correspondents named him as the man next to President Roosevelt who had contributed most to the war effort. Columnists conjectured on the change that had come upon him in recent years. But Truman did not see himself as having been transformed in any way through some mysterious alchemy. "I haven't changed," he insisted. "I am the same person I was five or ten years ago."

24

IN the spring of 1943, while Truman concentrated on his investigations, the Democratic political bosses began laying the groundwork for the 1944 convention. Ed Flynn, genial boss of the Bronx, chunky and large-jowled Frank Walker, Chairman of the Democratic National Committee, Mayor Ed Kelly of Chicago, the Cook County boss, and Edwin Pauley, the National Committee Treasurer, launched a series of meetings to make their plans. The off-year 1942 elections had been little short of disastrous, and there was no doubt in their minds that if President Roosevelt did not run for a fourth term, the Party would be in grave danger. They agreed that he had to be renominated.

Once this decision was made, they turned to an examination of Vice-Presidental candidates. All were opposed to retaining Vice-President Henry Wallace on the ticket. In 1940, he had been jammed down their throats by Roosevelt and had since become the darling of the C.I.O., the labor organization which threatened to vie with them for control of the Party. One of Wallace's main drawbacks was that he made no effort to cultivate his fellow politicians, because he was basically not gregarious. His entire focus was centered on issues and not on people, the heartbeat of any political party.

These, then, were the two problems confronting the Democratic bosses as they considered 1944—to convince Roosevelt he had to run again and to dump Wallace. They felt fairly confident they could persuade FDR by pointing out that his leadership was not only needed in the war effort but that he had to remain in office to insure the establishment of his postwar international organization. Regarding Wallace, the solution of the problem was incalculably more "iffy" because Roosevelt was fond of him.

The first break came in the summer of 1943. Roosevelt had named Wallace to head the Bureau of Economic Warfare (BEW), but Wallace could not get along with Jesse Jones, the Secretary of Commerce. Roosevelt sided with Wallace privately and grumbled about "Jesus" Jones, as he called him, though he remained outside the fray because of Jones's popularity on Capitol Hill. When Wallace and Jones resorted to public name-calling, however, FDR stripped them of power in the foreign field and announced "a plague on both their houses." This action gave the bosses their opening gambit.

Initially, casting about for a possible successor to Wallace, they gave no consideration to Truman. Nevertheless, they did propose him for an important post. Frank Walker was finding his dual role as National Committee Chairman and Postmaster General burdensome. In the late fall of 1943, he met with Truman and offered to make him Chairman of the Democratic National Committee. Although Truman was flattered, he realized it would interfere with his investigative work and rejected the offer. But he did make a suggestion. As patronage boss of the Executive Branch, Walker had acted on his recommendation to appoint Bob Hannegan Collector of Internal Revenue. Why not elevate Hannegan to National Committee Chairman?

There were obstacles to Truman's proposal. Hannegan had left St. Louis only a few weeks before and was new to the national scene. Besides, some of the bosses had never met him. Even worse, Roosevelt had never laid eyes on him and might look askance at anyone whose political experience did not extend beyond a Midwestern town.

Despite these drawbacks, Ed Flynn and Walker went to the White House to promote Hannegan with FDR. The President was then in the midst of such weighty matters as planning for the Normandy invasion, military operations in the Pacific, and his proposed United Nations organization. Nevertheless, he agreed to talk to Hannegan. Not long afterward, Hannegan was notified that the President wanted to see him to discuss his personal tax problems. This was only a ruse,

200

because FDR already knew his own tax situation thoroughly. After their initial meeting, Roosevelt, still uncertain, asked Hannegan to return. Following their second talk, however, FDR gave him his strong approval, and Hannegan took over the National Committee on January 22, 1944.

Hardly had he assumed his new post when the party bosses were confronted by an emergency. As Ed Flynn put it, "Signs of failing health in the President were unmistakable. . . . His usual pep and keen interest in things were missing." The bosses were certain that he could not live through another term, but they still needed him to run in order to win the national election. Ed Pauley bluntly expressed the practical, cold-blooded reasoning of the group: "You are not nominating a Vice-President of the United States, but a President." Whoever was on the ticket with FDR was bound to have a taste of the White House. The Vice-Presidency, which had always been a political sideshow, was now paramount.

In earlier White House years, FDR had sometimes been ill and looked worn out, but he always bounced back. Now, however, after returning from his North African visit in November, 1943, he remained listless and out-of-sorts. By his sixty-second birthday on January 29, 1944, his lined face made him look a decade older. As he complained to Senator Kilgore, "The details of this job are killing me." A total of 47 war agencies were reporting directly to him. In addition, there was military strategy to discuss with generals, overseas meetings with Churchill, Stalin and Chiang Kai-shek, political fences to mend and programs to promote with an obstreperous Congress, postwar planning for both the United States and the world and a multitude of other concerns.

That January, when Hannegan became National Committee Chairman, he and the other bosses went to the White House to discuss the forthcoming national convention in July. Since they agreed that FDR must run for a fourth term, they carefully centered their talk on Vice-Presidential possibilities. When Wallace's name came up, they insisted he would lose the South for the Democrats. Other names were mentioned, among them Jimmy Byrnes, Roosevelt's War Mobilization Director and Assistant President. Ed Flynn flatly asserted that labor and the North would oppose Byrnes. Furthermore, the Catholic vote would be jeopardized because Byrnes, though born a Catholic, had become a Protestant. Hannegan brought up the name of Truman, his own sponsor. The bosses agreed that he would be an excellent candidate. Roosevelt made no comment.

After the meeting, the bosses decided that stronger pressure would have to be brought on the ailing President to drop Wallace, and they evolved a plan to bring him around to their point of view. Influential businessmen visiting the White House were asked to tell Roosevelt that Wallace would be a detriment to the ticket. Edwin Pauley also had a long talk with "Pa" Watson, the President's military aide and close friend, who disliked Wallace and agreed to make it difficult for those favoring Wallace to get appointments with Roosevelt.

By spring, the relentless pounding on Roosevelt by the bosses began to have some effect. Instead of defending Wallace, he fell silent about his Vice-President. Then he grew concerned and asked Ed Flynn to canvas Wallace's strength in various key states. Flynn reported back that New York, Pennsylvania, Illinois, New Jersey and California would be lost in November if Wallace were on the ticket.

In March, 1944, Roosevelt developed a cold and a fever, although he continued at his work. "Don't press him and wear him out," Mrs. Roosevelt cautioned government officials. In April, he went south to Hobcaw, Bernard Baruch's plantation in South Carolina, for a two-week rest, but was forced to remain a month. At this point, Ed Flynn lost his nerve. First he implored Mrs. Roosevelt not to permit her husband to run again. Then he personally urged Roosevelt not to go for the fourth term, but was unable to win this agreement from the President.

In the meantime, Bob Hannegan spoke to Truman about becoming a Vice-Presidential candidate. Truman argued that the President might not favor his candidacy because his committee had made numerous attacks on war agencies. Furthermore, the Republicans would have a field day because of his association with Tom Pendergast. "I'm happy in the Senate," he said. Hannegan, however, told him not to take himself out of the race by making public statements to that effect.

"At the end of March," Senator Kilgore said, "Truman, Mon Wallgren and I were on the West Coast on Committee business. While we were in San Francisco, there was a Democratic dinner and we had a cocktail party in Harry's room before it began. Ed Pauley came around for a drink and he brought up the question of who would run with Roosevelt. I told him Truman would. Harry blushed, but I could tell that he didn't hate the idea. He was so embarrassed that he proposed a toast to Sam Rayburn as the next Vice-President."

Vic Messall commented later, "Senator Truman was always politically ambitious. I'm sure he wanted to be Vice-President. But he had to pretend he didn't."

By the end of April, the newspapers frequently mentioned Truman's name as a possible candidate along with Wallace, Byrnes, Rayburn, Barkley, Governor Robert Kerr of Oklahoma, Manpower Mobilizer Paul McNutt and Supreme Court Justice William O. Douglas. Speculation and confusion increased as rumors spread that Roosevelt favored one candidate and then another. Newsmen plagued Truman with questions about the boom surrounding his name. But he minimized his own candidacy, while carefully abstaining from taking a definite stand against running. "If Bob Hannegan is running me for Vice-President, he is doing it without my knowledge and without my consent," he told reporters.

Wallace suffered a bad break in May when Roosevelt asked him to fly on a mission to Siberia and war-torn China. This was unfortunate for his candidacy because he would be absent during a vital jousting period. But he could not refuse the President, and armed with seed and medical supplies, he left on May 20 for a 12,000-mile trip.

With Wallace gone, the bosses increased their pressure on Roosevelt and he grew more uncertain about Wallace's future. Moreover, his mind was strained by other concerns. On June 6, the Normandy invasion took place. There were doubts and critical emergencies that brought on sleepless nights. Urgent problems in the Pacific, arising from differences about strategy between Admiral Nimitz and General MacArthur, were awaiting his decision.

During this period, Hannegan had grown aware that FDR was much impressed with Jimmy Byrnes's ability. If Roosevelt dropped Wallace, he might insist on Byrnes for his running mate. Hannegan therefore planned to string Byrnes along by professing to work in his behalf. By buying time in this manner, he hoped to reduce Byrnes's natural aggressiveness and finally render him harmless. Hannegan's first move in this direction, Byrnes admitted, came on June 13, a week after the Normandy landings, when Hannegan told him that he was the right man for Vice-President and that Roosevelt thought so, too. Byrnes was flattered and did not press Roosevelt for a public statement supporting him, as he might otherwise have done.

Late in June, the Republicans nominated Governor Thomas E. Dewey of New York for President and Governor John W. Bricker of Ohio for Vice-President. If Roosevelt entertained any plan for retiring, he threw it aside after the vilification heaped upon him by the Republicans, especially by Congresswoman Clare Boothe Luce, his wife's friend. At his press conference on July 10, he read a letter he had sent to Hannegan, announcing that he was running for a fourth term "reluctantly but as a good soldier." His physician, Vice-Admiral Ross T. McIntire, stated that he was "in excellent health." But newsmen noticed that while FDR read his letter to Hannegan his hands trembled.

With the Democratic National Convention scheduled to begin on July 19, Roosevelt gave a dinner on the eleventh for top party officials. Seated about him at the White House dining room table were Bob Hannegan, Mayor Ed Kelly, Ed Flynn, Ed Pauley, Frank Walker and George Allen, Secretary of the National Committee. Uppermost in everyone's mind was the unsettled question of the Vice-Presidency.

Roosevelt, however, had no intention of letting this problem interfere with dinner. Instead, said Pauley, he maintained a running discourse on poisons in food and the various attempts to assassinate him in this way. After he exhausted this subject, he cut through the polite "buts . . ." with stories about other attempts on his life.

By this time the dinner guests were in a state of nervous tension. But at last Roosevelt invited them to his study on the second floor, where they were joined by his daughter Anna and her husband, John Boettiger. Roosevelt was listless now and offered no objection when the subject of his running mate was brought up. One by one the group canvassed the potential Vice-Presidents, George Allen said. Rayburn was ruled out because of a split in the Texas delegation. Barkley was rejected when the President noted that the Senator was almost five years older than he. When FDR mentioned John Winant, the Ambassador to Great Britain, the group maintained a stony silence. The bosses, led by Ed Flynn, objected to Jimmy Byrnes because his "hold-the-line" wage ruling had antagonized labor and because he was from the Deep South. Ed Pauley said that Roosevelt then offered the name of Associate Justice Douglas, telling the group that he "had the following of the liberal left wing of the American people; the same kind of people whom Wallace had . . . and, besides, he played an interesting game of poker." After an initial uneasiness, the bosses argued that Douglas had no visible supporters and was therefore a liability to the ticket.

Harry Truman was next put forth, and here the men showed their only enthusiasm. Ed Flynn pointed out that Truman's record was good in Congress; he was respected by labor; he had made no anti-Negro remarks; and he came from a border state and not from the South. "It was agreed," Flynn said, "that Truman was the man who would hurt him least."

FDR did not accept the group's verdict without a struggle. He referred to Truman's association with Tom Pendergast, and the bosses countered this objection by emphasizing that he had never been personally involved in Pendergast's troubles. Roosevelt then admitted that he had approved of Truman as head of the War Investigating Committee and that he had done a superior job, but he went on to say that he really did not know him well. Next, he mentioned the problem of Truman's age, saying that he thought Truman was about sixty whereas Douglas was under fifty. A crisis was at hand when Roosevelt asked John Boettiger to get a *Congressional Directory* and look up Truman's age.

When Boettiger left the room, the bosses realized that if Roosevelt learned authoritatively that Truman was sixty, it would eliminate him from consideration. But Ed Pauley saved the day. When Boettiger returned, Pauley casually took the *Congressional Directory* from him, laid it unobtrusively on his lap and started an animated conversation with Roosevelt to distract him. The ruse was successful for FDR forgot about checking Truman's age and finally said to Hannegan, "Bob, I think you and everyone else here want Truman."

At this point, said George Allen, Pauley hustled everyone out of Roosevelt's study. While they were putting on their coats, Hannegan returned to the study under the pretext of having forgotten his coat there. When he rejoined them, said Allen, he had a note scribbled on an envelope which read: *Bob, I think Truman is the right man. FDR.* Mystery surrounds this note because only one other person claims to have seen it. Truman said that Hannegan later showed him this note at the convention, that it was written on a scratch pad and not on an envelope and its message read: *Bob, it's Truman. FDR.*

Events crowded on events now with blurring speed. Wallace was back from the Orient. Worn and thin from the hardships of his trip, he was in no condition for the battle that faced him. In addition to the bosses, animosity had cropped up in unexpected quarters. Secretary of the Interior Ickes and Judge Samuel Rosenman, one of FDR's speech writers, told Roosevelt that they thought Wallace would split the Party. This was the first defection within the ranks of the New Dealers and Roosevelt was impressed. He insisted that they express their conviction to Wallace personally and on July 12 they lunched with him. Wallace was deeply hurt by what Ickes and Rosenman said. That afternoon he discussed his candidacy with FDR, and asserted that he had no intention of running unless the President thought it would aid the ticket.

Feeling cornered, Roosevelt invited Wallace to lunch the next day. This time Wallace came prepared and showed Roosevelt a list of 290 delegates who were pledged to him. Even more effective, he had a copy of the yet unreleased Gallup Poll which showed that 65 per cent of Democratic voters were for Wallace; 17 per cent for Alben Barkley; 5 per cent for Sam Rayburn; 4 per cent for Senator Harry Byrd of Virginia; 3 per cent for Jimmy Byrnes; 2 per cent for Justice Douglas; 2 per cent for Harry Truman; and 2 per cent for Secretary of State Edward R. Stettinius. Roosevelt let out a loud "Well, I'll be damned!" Wallace claimed that Roosevelt told him at this lunch that he was for him. When he asked FDR to release a public statement during the convention, stating that if he were a delegate he would vote for Wallace, Roosevelt agreed and wrote the letter, which he dated July 14.

The bald truth was that FDR was now opposed to Wallace. When Eleanor Roosevelt asked him to keep Wallace on the ticket, he growled, "Wallace had his chance to make his mark and if he could not convince the Party leaders that he was the right person, I cannot dictate to them twice."

On July 13, Jimmy Byrnes said, Roosevelt informed him that if Wallace refused to withdraw from the race, he intended to write a weak letter in his behalf saying he would vote for Wallace if he were a delegate. Byrnes was reassured by these words and believed that he was still the leading Vice-Presidential candidate. In fact, his assurance rose when Roosevelt added that Henry Wallace had no chance of winning the nomination.

But overnight Byrnes's cockiness vanished. Bob Hannegan, playing a complicated role, brought him disquieting news. With feigned concern, Hannegan told him that Roosevelt favored either Harry Truman or Bill Douglas. Hannegan mentioned a letter in which Roosevelt had expressed his views.

Roosevelt had left Washington on the thirteenth, and Byrnes anxiously telephoned him at Hyde Park. He demanded to know if there was any truth in Hannegan's report.

"We have to be damned careful about language," Roosevelt told

Byrnes. "They asked if I would object to Truman and Douglas and I said no. That is different from using the word 'prefer.' I hardly know Truman. Douglas is a poker partner." FDR added that if Byrnes went to Chicago and made a fight for the Vice-Presidency, he had his blessing.

Byrnes triumphantly called Hannegan. Innocently, Hannegan heard him through and said, "I don't understand it."

Actually, Hannegan had gone to the President before he left Washington and induced him to write a letter, dated July 19, the opening day of the convention. It read:

> DEAR BOB:
> You have written me about Bill Douglas and Harry Truman. I should, of course, be very glad to run with either of them and believe that either of them would bring real strength to the ticket.
>   Always sincerely,

Since Hannegan had hoped to get a letter praising Truman alone, he was not pleased. This letter not only mentioned Douglas—it put his name before Truman's. With Roosevelt out of town there seemed nothing Hannegan could do to correct the situation. Furthermore, FDR planned to bypass the convention, for he had made arrangements to leave for Hawaii the next week to meet with MacArthur and Nimitz.

During the Congressional recess, Truman went home to Independence to prepare for the Chicago convention. He was now head of the Missouri delegation and was to serve on the convention's Resolutions Committee to help write the Party Platform. He had not referred to himself at any time in public as a Vice-Presidential candidate, nor had he publicly declared that he would refuse the honor if it were offered. Tom Evans, his Kansas City friend, noted that "Truman understood that FDR wouldn't live out his next term." But even to Evans he said, "I'm satisfied where I am. Just a heartbeat, this little [Truman made a gesture holding his thumb and forefinger an eighth of an inch apart], separates the Vice-President from the President."

At eight A.M. on Friday, July 14, as he, Bess and Margaret were about to leave for Chicago, the phone rang. Byrnes was on the line, calling from Washington. Truman said, "Byrnes asked if I would nominate him for Vice-President, as the President wanted him to have that position on the ticket. I said surely I'll do it if the President wants it done." In view of Bob Hannegan's activities, the request was a puzzler.

But this was not the end of phone calls that morning. "Before I could get into the automobile," Truman said, "Senator Barkley called and asked me to nominate him for Vice-President." According to Barkley, Truman replied, "Why, Alben, I'd be tickled to death to do it, but I've already promised Jimmy Byrnes I would nominate him."

"Well, if you've promised Jimmy," said Barkley glumly, "that ends that."

Chicago was stifling hot when the Trumans arrived. Truman installed Bess and Margaret at the Morrison Hotel, while he took a private suite on the seventeenth floor of the Stevens Hotel.

Hannegan pulled into town on the fourteenth, to give himself five days to maneuver before the convention officially began. Before he left Washington, he had exacted a promise from Roosevelt that he would be in sole charge of the convention without any herd-riding on delegates from White House underlings. Mayor Kelly provided him with an apartment-hideaway on Chicago's North Side where the two could meet quietly with Ed Flynn, Ed Pauley and Mayor Frank Hague of Jersey City.

Truman was hardly settled in his hotel suite when Hannegan paid him a call and laid out his strategy to make him the Vice-Presidential nominee. But he was shocked when Truman interrupted to tell him he was going to nominate Jimmy Byrnes because, as Byrnes had put it, "the President wants me to have that position on the ticket."

Hannegan was so flustered that when Ed Flynn arrived in Chicago, he ran up to him and shouted, "It's all over! It's Byrnes!" Hannegan also told Flynn that Mayor Kelly had decided to shift to Byrnes. Kelly's plan, said Hannegan, was to help develop a deadlock and then slide Senator Scott Lucas of Illinois into the slot.

That day President Roosevelt was preparing to board his special train for the West Coast, where he would board the U.S.S. *Baltimore* for his Pearl Harbor conference with Nimitz and MacArthur. Fearing that his entire plan had collapsed, Hannegan called Roosevelt and insisted that he stop in the Chicago railroad yard for a final talk. Reluctantly, Roosevelt agreed.

The next morning, Saturday, the fifteenth, the plot grew more complex. Byrnes, who was then still in Washington, said that Mayor Kelly called him from Chicago to tell him that Hannegan was in his room and that they were expecting Roosevelt to arrive at the station about three o'clock that afternoon. Kelly assured Byrnes that he and Hannegan were going to give him a resounding build-up when they saw the President. Later in the day Kelly called Byrnes again and reported that they had seen FDR and the Vice-Presidency was "settled"—the President wanted Byrnes.

This was an interesting statement considering the fact that Kelly did not see Roosevelt during his Chicago stopover. Only Hannegan and Ed Pauley scampered aboard the train and closeted themselves with FDR for a secret conference. According to Pauley, Hannegan told Roosevelt that Byrnes was refusing to get out of the race. Since Roosevelt, a week earlier, had accepted the verdict of the bosses at his White House dinner to drop Byrnes from consideration, there was no argument on this score. Then Hannegan tried to get a letter from the President favoring Truman as the Vice-Presidential nominee. Instead, said Grace Tully, FDR's secretary, who was also aboard the train, Hannegan came out of FDR's private car with the "Bill Douglas and Harry Truman" letter Roosevelt had given him in Washington. "Grace," he told her, "the President wants you to retype this letter and switch these names so it will read 'Harry Truman or Bill Douglas.' "

On Sunday, Truman began promoting Byrnes for Vice-President. That evening he stayed in his hotel suite where friends dropped in for drinks and political talk. Afterward he told George Wallace of the St. Louis *Post-Dispatch:* "I've made up my mind. I'm not going to get into this thing unless the President personally wants me to. I've thought it all over very carefully and I've told Hannegan." Wallace mentioned the likelihood of Roosevelt's dying in office during his next term. To this Truman said: "Do you remember your American history well enough to recall what happened to most Vice-Presidents who succeeded to the Presidency? Usually they were ridiculed in office, had their hearts broken, lost any vestige of respect they had had before. I don't want that to happen to me."

Jimmy Byrnes arrived in Chicago on Sunday, confident he was the next Vice-Presidential nominee. He had breakfast with Mayor Kelly and Bob Hannegan, and said they told him that FDR had flatly stated, "Well, you know Jimmy has been my choice from the first. Go ahead and nominate him."

Heartened by his conversation with Roosevelt, Hannegan thought it best to withhold the truth from Byrnes for a while yet, especially since Byrnes would not intervene personally with the delegations so long as he thought the bosses and the President were behind him. Hannegan also had further assurances from the Party bosses and key delegation leaders that Wallace did not have the required 589 votes. As for Truman's campaign to nominate Byrnes, this was an excellent camouflage of Hannegan's true intent. Most important, it would bring Truman out of his Resolutions Committee smoke room and permit delegates and other politicians to observe him in action while he promoted Byrnes.

On Monday morning, Truman had breakfast with Sidney Hillman, who was bossing the C.I.O.'s Political Action Committee (PAC). Although Truman had forced Roosevelt to drop Hillman as a co-director of the OPM, Hillman bore him no grudge. While they ate, Truman pushed Byrnes's candidacy until Hillman held up his hands in protest.

"We're for Wallace," he said. "There is only one other man we could consider supporting."

"Who?" Truman asked.

"I'm looking at him now," Hillman said, smiling.

This response was typical of many voiced that day. Phil Murray, head of the C.I.O., said that his organization would not accept Byrnes, but if Wallace failed to win the nomination the C.I.O. would back Truman. Dan Tobin, head of the Teamsters Union, agreed with Murray. George Harrison and A. F. Whitney, Railroad Brotherhood presidents, took similar positions. William Green, head of the American Federation of Labor, went further and told Truman bluntly, "The A. F. of L. is for you and will support no one else."

Truman met with this reaction not only in labor circles. Senators Kilgore and Carl Hayden told him they were promoting him. When he spoke on behalf of Byrnes before the Maryland delegation and said he was not himself a candidate, Governor Herbert F. O'Conor shouted, "You're crazy as hell!"

By evening Truman was worn out as a result of all his activity. Dutifully, he reported each conversation to Byrnes, who nevertheless remained self-confident. "He would tell me each time that Roosevelt would publicly declare he was for him for Vice-President," said Truman.

Hannegan realized that his success in putting Truman across depended on perfect timing. Byrnes was still radiating self-confidence, although Truman, while professing not to be a candidate, had already made key conquests. It was time to stick a pin in Henry Wallace's giant-size balloon because Wallace was reportedly on his way west to take the convention by storm.

That Monday night Hannegan leaked the letter to the press Roosevelt had written for Wallace on July 13. Addressed to Senator Samuel D. Jackson of Indiana, it read:

HYDE PARK, NEW YORK
July 14, 1944

MY DEAR SENATOR JACKSON:

In the light of the probability that you will be chosen as Permanent Chairman of the Convention, and because I know that many rumors accompany annual conventions, I am wholly willing to give you my own personal thought in regard to the selection of a candidate for Vice-President. I do this at this time because I expect to be away from Washington for the next days.

The easiest way of putting it is this: I have been associated with Henry Wallace during his past four years as Vice-President, for eight years earlier while he was Secretary of Agriculture, and well before that. For these reasons, I personally would vote for his renomination if I were a delegate to the convention.

At the same time, I do not wish to appear in any way as dictating to the convention. Obviously the convention must do the deciding. And it should—and I am sure it will—give great consideration to the pros and cons of its choice.

Very sincerely yours,
FRANKLIN D. ROOSEVELT

This weak letter had the effect Hannegan desired. When labor leaders saw that Roosevelt was not for Wallace "do or die," Wallace support was visibly weakened.

Truman had asked his old friend John Snyder, who had left government service to become vice-president of the First National Bank in St. Louis, to accompany him to the convention. He gave Snyder orders to pass the word around that he was not a candidate, but he discovered that Snyder had been doing precisely the opposite. On Monday evening, Truman put through a call to Tom Evans in Kansas City. "Are you my friend, Tom?" he shouted into the phone. "If you are, I want you to come to Chicago right away."

When Evans walked into Truman's hotel suite, he found that Roy Roberts, managing editor of the Kansas City *Star,* was also present. "Roy was a good friend of Harry's," said Evans, "even though he blasted the Pendergast Machine in his paper."

211

Roberts, who weighed 375 pounds, greeted Evans exuberantly. "Tom, I'm Harry's manager for the Vice-Presidency."

"The hell you are," Evans replied. "You're nothing but a lousy Republican. You can't be his manager."

Truman stepped between them. "Tom," he said to Evans, "I want you to see that I don't get the Vice-Presidential nomination."

Evans promoted Truman instead.

By Tuesday, the political atmosphere in Chicago was electric. The name "Roosevelt" was hardly mentioned, forgotten in the struggle for the Vice-Presidency.

That evening Hannegan called on Truman again. The time was approaching for him to withdraw his support from Jimmy Byrnes and declare that he was a candidate. Hannegan now insisted that the President wanted him as his running mate. Truman's reply was, "Tell him to go to hell. I'm for Jimmy Byrnes."

Hannegan argued and pleaded, but got nowhere. Nevertheless, after he left Truman, he told George Wallace of the St. Louis *Post-Dispatch* to break the story that "the President would be pleased to run with Senator Truman."

Hannegan was also busy on other fronts that evening. He held a conference with Sidney Hillman, Phil Murray and A. F. Whitney to get them to solidify their opposition to Byrnes and reaffirm their friendship for Truman. Once more he met with Byrnes, this time accompanied by Mayor Kelly and Frank Walker. Afterward Byrnes said that Walker assured him they had 700 delegates lined up for him, or almost 150 more than were needed to put him on the ticket. As the meeting broke up, however, Hannegan decided that the time had come to puncture Byrnes's dream. According to Byrnes, Hannegan glanced at Kelly and said, "Ed, there is one thing we forgot. The President said, 'Clear it with Sidney.' " This expression was used extensively by the Republicans in the coming campaign in an attempt to smear the Democratic Party as being controlled by a left-wing, foreign-born labor leader. If Hannegan actually uttered these words, it was only to pretend to Byrnes that he was still loyal to him but was having trouble winning labor support for his candidacy. As a politician, Byrnes knew that labor was just another pressure group and did not control the Democratic Party. Moreover, he had not shown any concern when Truman had told him of Hillman's opposition.

The next morning, July 19, Hannegan came to Byrnes's suite and, with feigned chagrin, informed him that Hillman would not support him. Byrnes was now certain that Hannegan was not his friend.

But he was to grow even more uneasy. That day the convention opened at noon for its first session and the Chicago Stadium was in an uproar. Reporters were hunting for Hannegan, charging him with deliberately leaking a false story to the St. Louis *Post-Dispatch* that the President favored Truman.

Finally, Hannegan called a press conference and passed out mimeographed copies of the letter Grace Tully had typed for him on the Presidential train the previous Saturday. Hurrying to telephones to call their home papers, the reporters drew their own conclusions: Roosevelt wanted Truman first and Douglas second.

The confusion was now so great that the bosses called a meeting in Bob Hannegan's North Side hideaway apartment. Did the President really want Truman? What did the letter really mean? Ed Flynn reported: "We called the President, who was on his private car en route to the Pacific Coast, and I insisted that he tell these men he wanted Truman for a running mate. FDR talked to Walker, Bob Hannegan and Kelly. Kelly asked for a note and FDR sent it to Bob."

Roosevelt had finally said he wanted Truman as his running mate.

Later that day, before Roosevelt was renominated for his fourth term, Hannegan went to see Truman again. Truman was still playing coy, but Hannegan now spoke bluntly and told him about the telephone call to the President. He also showed him a note written on a scratch-pad slip which read: *Bob, it's Truman. FDR.*

An hour later, said Jimmy Byrnes, Truman came to his suite. "He told me that he had learned from Hannegan that the President had telephoned, asking that he [Truman] run for Vice-President." When Truman asked Byrnes to release him from his promise to nominate him, Byrnes had no alternative but to agree.

Before he gave up, however, he tried to reach Roosevelt, who had arrived at San Diego, but FDR would not come to the phone. His candidacy was over, neatly done in by Bob Hannegan. Byrnes now did the only thing he could. "In deference to the wishes of the President," he wrote to Senator Burnet R. Maybank of South Carolina, he was withdrawing from the Vice-Presidential race.

Senator Alben Barkley reported that Byrnes was furious when he was dumped. Byrnes stamped up to him, Barkley said, and growled,

"If I were you I wouldn't say anything too complimentary about FDR in your nominating speech!"

Roosevelt won nomination easily. But the laudatory speeches and the polling of delegates seemed a mere prelude to the important business that was to follow. On Thursday the twentieth, Hannegan hoped to win Truman's nomination for Vice-President. Truman, however, was not working hard in his own behalf and with Wallace on the scene at last there was always the possibility of an upset. Battle lines had formed and name-calling between contending forces had sunk to gutter level. Never before had a contest for the Vice-Presidency provided such rancor. Old George Norris, out of the Senate after a grand political career spanning almost a half-century, wrote to Wallace and asked, "Why this awful fight over the Vice-Presidency? . . . I am wondering if the gambling chances are that FDR is going to die before he serves out his next term if he is re-elected."

Even with his own delegation Truman did not play the part of an active candidate. When the Missouri delegation, 32 strong, met to decide on their choice for Vice-President, Truman, as delegation chairman, ruled a resolution endorsing him as being out of order. In exasperation, Sam Wear, an old supporter, called out, "There is no one out of order here but the chairman of this delegation." Finally, while Truman was at the door in a conversation, Wear sneaked the resolution through and he won unanimous approval.

When Senator Sam Jackson, the permanent chairman, called the second day's session to order, he read the letter Roosevelt had written in Wallace's behalf to the delegates. The anti-Wallace forces hooted, while the Wallace-ites hailed it as a strong endorsement. The afternoon was waning when Bob Hannegan decided that Truman was overdue in making his own strong bid.

"I got a call from Bob Hannegan that afternoon," Tom Evans said. "He demanded, 'I want you to get Harry Truman over to my suite in the Blackstone right away.' " Evans told him that Truman was in a committee meeting and did not want to be disturbed. " 'I don't give a damn!' Bob shouted. 'It's of the utmost urgency. Get him out!' I got Harry out of the meeting and over to Hannegan's suite. Harry sat on one of the beds and Hannegan on the other while he put in a call to President Roosevelt in San Diego. When the call came through, Harry refused to talk to Roosevelt. Finally Hannegan did."

Roosevelt had a habit of shouting into the telephone, so that it was necessary to hold the receiver a foot from your ear. "Bob," Roosevelt yelled, "have you got that fellow lined up yet?"

"No," said Hannegan. "He is the contrariest Missouri mule I've ever dealt with."

"Well, you tell him," Truman heard Roosevelt roar, "if he wants to break up the Democratic Party in the middle of a war, that's his responsibility!" With that, Roosevelt hung up.

"Harry was pale when the conversation ended," Evans said. After a few minutes of silence, Truman turned to Hannegan and asked, "Why the hell didn't he tell me in the first place?"

When Truman left Hannegan, he was determined to battle Wallace all the way. He told reporters who surrounded him, "I will win. I wouldn't be in the race if President Roosevelt didn't approve." The bosses now began to make pronouncements. Frank Walker loudly proclaimed that he was for Truman. Boss Hague of Jersey City declared, "If President Roosevelt is for Truman, I'm for him." Ed Pauley chimed in with a negative note: "The President in my opinion is thoroughly convinced that Truman will cost him less votes than any other candidate." The reporters quoted Truman as saying, "I never ran for a political office I wanted. But I've fought for every one I've ever had. Damn it! I've never had an office I didn't have to fight for, tooth or nail."

Truman insisted that Bennett Clark make the speech nominating him even though Clark was on Roosevelt's hate list. But little time remained before the evening session and Clark was not in his assigned room. Just as Truman was about to abandon the search, he learned that Clark had a hideaway room in another hotel. When he got there, Clark was sleeping so soundly that no amount of pounding on the door roused him. Finally, a bellboy came to deliver a suit and Truman strode into the room behind him.

That evening Roosevelt's acceptance speech was piped into the convention hall from the West Coast. His amplified voice had an eerie tone and delegates said it sounded "like a voice from beyond."

Hannegan was eager to wrap up Truman's nomination immediately afterward, but screaming Wallace supporters in the galleries threatened to stampede the delegates on the floor. Even the organist was a Wallace partisan and played endlessly, "Iowa, That's Where the Tall Corn Grows." Large signs lettered FRANK AND HANK popped up everywhere. Hundreds of the galleryites pushed their way onto the floor where they marched, milled about and sat with delegates.

The Wallace campaign was better planned than Hannegan had anticipated. The chaos was so complete that he thought it would be impossible to nominate Truman that evening. Ed Pauley tried to lessen the din by warning the organist that he would chop through the amplifier wires if he did not play other tunes. But even when the organist switched to nonpartisan songs, the ear-splitting howls and screams went on. When Arizona yielded to Missouri so that Clark could nominate Truman, a crescendo of boos rocked the rafters. Clark's speech turned out to be his usual haymaker address. He walloped Governor Dewey for showing the "insolence of incapacity" and said of Truman that he "possesses the qualities of mind and heart to make a very splendid President in the event anything happens to Roosevelt."

Because of the continuing din for Wallace, Mayor Kelly hit upon a scheme to buy time. On the ground that the stadium held a third more people than its legal capacity, he declared the place a fire hazard and forced adjournment to the following day. The Wallace forces went wild with fury at this news.

The time gained was not wasted. Before the convention assembled again on Friday, the twenty-first, Hannegan had already promised key delegations future jobs and patronage. Then Truman joined him in his office located below the speaker's platform. Vic Messall was also present and from time to time he and Truman peeked out at the trading going on among the delegations. Everywhere the talking point was that the delegates were not voting for a Vice-President but for a President.

On the first ballot Wallace failed to get the necessary 589 votes, although Hannegan died several deaths along the way. The totals stood: Wallace, 429½; Truman, 319½; Bankhead, 98; Barkley, 48; and all others, 280.

The Friday session had now been in progress more than six hours and several delegations demanded a halt for dinner before beginning the second ballot. But outside the stadium an enormous crowd of Wallace supporters waited in line with tickets for the evening session. Realizing that there was bound to be a repetition of the previous evening's demonstration if the convention adjourned and then began a new session afterward, Hannegan ordered Permanent Chairman Sam Jackson to start the second ballot immediately. Jackson pounded his gavel and made this announcement amidst cries of protest from the Wallace forces.

216

Truman was hungry and left Hannegan's office below the platform to buy a hot dog. Then, still munching on it, he joined the Missouri delegation on the floor for the second ballot.

Before balloting got underway, Ed Pauley wrangled with the Alabama delegation to switch from Bankhead to Truman. As the first state called in the alphabetical voting, Alabama's support for Truman would have tremendous psychological effect. But by the time Senator Bankhead agreed to put his state in Truman's column, Alabama had already been called and recorded its vote for Bankhead.

The second ballot vote was a thriller. Wallace took an early lead, 148 to 125, but an important break came when Maryland announced for Truman. Then Governor Kerr of Oklahoma added to the Truman thrust with 22 votes. Truman forged ahead with a vote of 342 to Wallace's 286. But Wallace gained strength and the totals became 400 for Truman and 395 for Wallace, then 477½ to 472½.

Hannegan poured it on now. At signal, states began to switch to Truman. His supporters rose to their feet and applauded; despair spread among Wallace's men. By eight o'clock it was all over. Truman's victory total was 1,031 votes.

Truman was chewing on his second hot dog when he was acknowledged the winner. The crowd surged toward the Missouri delegation and raised him high as they carried him to the platform. Delegates and spectators roared as Hannegan held up his arm. Truman finally spoke, a short acceptance speech of only 92 words. He closed with "I don't know what else I can say except that I accept this great honor with all humility. I thank you."

Margaret related that when her mother managed to reach him, she asked, "Are we going to have to go through this all the rest of our lives?" Vic Messall who was standing nearby said that Truman looked at him and muttered, "Let's get the hell out of here."

As soon as the convention was over, Truman sent his brother Vivian back to Grandview to give their mother a firsthand report. But Martha Ellen Truman had listened to the convention over the radio in the comfort of one of her four living room rockers. Wearing a blue shawl around her frail, bony shoulders, she told reporters that she would have preferred her Harry to remain a Senator where he "can do more good." She also said: "I listened to the Republican Convention, too, and tried not to hate them. They keep predicting that Roosevelt will die in office if he's elected. I hope Roosevelt fools them. I'm not a giggly woman, but I can't help smiling when people cheer at the mention of Harry's name."

From the Pacific, Roosevelt sent Wallace a wire praising him for his "magnificent fight." He also wired Truman congratulations and asked him to let him know his plans.

The morning after Truman's victory, Bess held her one and only press conference. "I'm just getting excited," she told reporters. She said she had not particularly wanted her husband to be Vice-President, nor did she think he had been in the running. "But two days ago I began to realize the boom for him might be serious. When it really hit me," she went on, "was last night when Maryland threw its votes to him." When reporters asked about her work for her husband, she replied that she went over all his speeches in advance. Urged to supply personal details about his habits, his likes and dislikes, she commented, "He is the type of person who would be satisfied to eat beefsteak and fried potatoes every night."

The plain, homespun picture she painted of her husband was in sharp contrast to the aura of sophistication that surrounded Roosevelt. Truman added to this impression by bursting into the room during the press conference and yelling, "Where's my baby? I have a telegram for her." Margaret, who was sharing the limelight for the first time with her mother, turned crimson. "It's only from a couple of fellows I go with," she stammered.

That day Hannegan packed his bags and left Chicago, his six months of labor crowned with success. Later he appraised his handiwork: "When I die, I would like to have one thing on my headstone—that I was the man who kept Henry Wallace from becoming President of the United States."

25

MISSOURI had previously had only two native sons on a national ticket and state pride ran high when Truman won the Vice-Presidential nomination. Even before he returned from Chicago, his friends in Independence staged a mammoth demonstration in his honor. Signs ten feet high proclaimed CONGRATULATIONS SENATOR HARRY S. TRUMAN, and speaker after speaker extolled him from the platform at the Independence courthouse square.

The Trumans did not return until the twenty-fourth. Bess found that there were penalties for being in the limelight. One day, while shopping in Kansas City, a woman pointed her out in an elevator and shouted, "This is Mrs. Truman." Another woman stared at her as if she were a department store dummy, then sneered, "Why, she's wearing seersucker." Bess looked blankly ahead, but later she said, "I wonder if they thought a Vice-Presidential candidate's wife should be dressed in royal purple?"

Truman remained in Missouri until after the state primary on August first. His old friends in the Pendergast machine were trying for a political comeback, and he sought to help them by announcing,

"I'm a Jackson County Democrat and I'm proud of it. That's the way I got to be a county judge, a Senator and candidate for Vice-President."

Tom Pendergast, out of jail since mid-1940, was tending strictly to his business at the Ready Mixed Concrete Company, for Judge Otis, in sentencing him, had barred him from re-entering politics for five years after his release. In the the meantime his nephew Jim Pendergast was Mr. Boss. Gone from the scene was T. J.'s old opponent Joe Shannon, the Rabbit leader, who had died in March, 1943. Bennett Clark was up for a third Senate term and although Truman supported him, his isolationism had antagonized too many people and he was resoundingly defeated in the primary.

When Truman left for Washington, applause for his victory at Chicago still rang in his ears. Local wags noted that Roy Roberts at the *Star* was running Tom Dewey for President and Harry Truman for Vice-President. The impact of Truman's success at the convention was also apparent in Washington, where the Truman Committee unanimously voted to retain him as chairman. But he believed that this would bring the committee into the "firing-line of politics," and resigned from this post on August 3.

While Truman marked time before launching his campaign, President Roosevelt was busy in Hawaii. Using the code name Mr. Big, FDR sat in a mansion overlooking Waikiki Beach, where on July 26 he heard Admiral Nimitz and General MacArthur argue their cases for the next military move in the Pacific. Although the Chiefs of Staff opposed retaking the Phillippines, Roosevelt was swayed by MacArthur's persuasive and emotional argument and rejected the alternative of a Formosan invasion. Later the two discussed the forthcoming election campaign. According to Clark Lee, a reporter covering MacArthur, Roosevelt snarled, "I'll lick that son-of-a-bitch up in Albany if it's the last thing I do!" MacArthur was convinced it would be the last thing he would do. After they parted, he told his aide, "I knew then I would never see him again."

It was not until the second week in August that Roosevelt returned, exhausted, to the United States. On August 12, he spoke at the Bremerton, Washington, Navy Yard and gave the worst speech of his career. Robert Sherwood said: "When he delivered his speech he was in such pain that he had to support himself by holding on to the lectern with all the tremendous strength of his arms and hands."

220

On his train trip east, he could no longer tolerate speed and ordered the engineers to travel no faster than 25 miles an hour.

By the time he reached Washington on August 17, the papers were publishing the results of the latest opinion polls taken after the Bremerton speech. His popularity had dived sharply, while Dewey's was soaring. With some concern, Roosevelt invited Truman to lunch at the White House on the following day.

A small table was set under the magnolia tree which Andrew Jackson had planted on the South Grounds in memory of his wife, Rachel. The day was hot and Truman and FDR ate in shirtsleeves. Roosevelt's collar was much too large for him. He was wan and sluggish. But Truman knew that his description of the President's appearance would be widely printed, and he told reporters afterwards, "The President looked fine and ate a bigger meal than I did."

While they nibbled at sardines on toast, FDR insisted that in the months ahead Truman travel by rail and not by air—"because one of us has to stay alive." He also asked that Truman campaign for both of them because he was too busy running the war and planning the peace. After lunch, FDR handed Truman table roses for Bess and Margaret. Outside the White House, Truman fanned himself with the roses and told reporters: "He's still the leader he's always been and don't let anybody kid you about it. He's keen as a briar."

On August 31, at eight-thirty A.M., Truman stood on the courthouse steps at Lamar, his birthplace, where Senator Tom Connally went through the ceremony of officially notifying him that he was the Democratic nominee for Vice-President. Truman's acceptance speech was a plea not to vote for Dewey because he lacked experience to lead the nation in the coming peace, and he emphasized that it took a new President a year or two to learn his job. In an editorial, the Washington *Post* attacked his argument for a fourth term for Roosevelt as "grossly overdrawn."

Lamar's population was only 3,000, but 9,000 Truman rooters were there to hear him. Newsmen roaming through the town came up with an interesting item. Only one person in the community remembered Truman from his Lamar days—eighty-year-old John Hart, whose white whiskers were heavily stained by tobacco. Hart had once worked for John Truman and claimed that he had seen Harry once when he was "just a little shaver."

Truman next went to Detroit for a pre-campaign Labor Day speech on September 4. Ordinarily a talk about Roosevelt and the glories of organized labor would have been no problem, but the A. F. of L. and C.I.O. leaders in Detroit were not on speaking terms and refused to sit together. Finally, Truman compromised with an afternoon speech to the C.I.O. and one in the evening for the A. F. of L. The speeches were essentially similar, the key point being to "put human welfare first and profits second."

Truman had only one other conversation with FDR on the coming struggle with the Republicans when he went to the White House on September 6 with Governor Coke Stevenson of Texas, who was worried about Texas Democrats threatening to bolt the ticket. On another afternoon he visited the White House again, this time with Eddie McKim, his old National Guard pal, but the occasion was a Presidential reception for the cast of a movie on the life of Woodrow Wilson.

As they were leaving the White House, McKim nudged him and said, "Hey, bud, turn around and take a look. You're going to be living in that house before long."

"Eddie, I'm afraid I am," Truman replied. "And it scares the hell out of me."

Although Roosevelt had no desire to conduct an active campaign, he was soon enraged by Republican insinuations about his health. Harry Hopkins explained to Robert Sherwood that FDR "told me he meant it when he said this was the meanest campaign of his life. . . . He was particularly resentful about the whispering campaign which he believed was a highly organized affair." Finally, on September 23, FDR jumped into the fray with a speech before the Teamsters Union in Washington, which Republicans sadly agreed was his best political oration. Referring to the Republican charge that he had sent a destroyer to the Aleutians to bring back his black Scotty, Fala, FDR said with withering sarcasm, "The Republican leaders have not been content to make personal attacks upon me—or my wife—or my sons —they now include my little dog, Fala." Afterward, Hannegan eagerly acquiesced when FDR mapped out a program of five more speeches.

Before his own campaign got underway, Truman returned to Independence with Harry Vaughan to help his wife and daughter pack their belongings for the trip back to Washington where Margaret was starting her junior year in college. Not long before, Colonel Vaughan had returned from Australia in battered condition. After serving as provost marshal of Brisbane, he was in a plane crash at Sydney, emerging with a fractured breastbone, a crushed foot, and three ribs pulled loose. Following his recuperation at Walter Reed Hospital in Washington, he became the War Department's liaison officer with the Truman Committee. Margaret said: "Colonel Vaughan and Daddy started for Washington in two cars, with our belongings packed inside and some of them lashed to the roofs of the cars. They looked like pioneers."

Hannegan's strategy was to have George Allen manage Truman's campaign. When Truman introduced Allen to his mother, he told her that Allen had not seen a Republican in his native Mississippi until he was twelve. The old woman snapped, "You didn't miss much."

Although wealthy Democrats offered to defray the expenses of an opulent campaign, Truman, realizing that he would be beholden to them, turned them down. Instead, he used an old combination sleeping and club car—the *Henry Stanley*—which was attached to any train traveling the Truman route. In addition to accommodations for himself, Hugh Fulton, Matt Connelly and Eddie McKim, the *Henry Stanley* was equipped with typewriters, a loud-speaker system and a recorder.

Tom Evans, assisted by Eddie Jacobson, was chairman of Truman's campaign funds committee. "Truman gave me strict orders to put all the money we raised in John Snyder's bank in St. Louis," Evans said. "He also told me, 'Before you accept any money, clear it with me. Certain people I don't want any money from.' Sometimes there was no money to get the train out of the station. But Eddie was a whirlwind in calling people and raising enough so the train could get out and keep moving."

Since the Democrats based their campaign on the necessity for keeping Roosevelt in office during the crucial postwar years, the Republicans not only had to fight this concept but also had to undermine the belief that he was healthy enough to survive the rigors of the Presidency. Because of the difficulties in conducting such a complex campaign, they concentrated their attack on Truman. Herbert Brownell, Jr., Republican National Chairman, labeled the effort "the exposure of the unfitness of the Democratic candidate for Vice-President, Senator Truman." *Time* Magazine noted that "Anti-New Deal newspapers have examined the Truman record with the zeal of ballistic experts." George Creel in *Collier's* sensed the Republican tactics when he wrote, "After long years during which Vice-Presidential candidates wore identification badges . . . now comes a campaign where . . . the competence of Mr. Roosevelt's current running mate is the nearest thing the country has to a burning issue."

For all their pains, however, at no time did the Republicans succeed in making Truman a major issue. Among their accusations was one that Bess was on his payroll. He answered quite frankly, "A Senator can't get along on $10,000 a year. After all, we're just poor folks." He also pointed out that "I never make any decisions unless she is in on them." When Clare Boothe Luce turned her acid tongue on Bess, he angrily told a reporter: "The way she talked about my wife—well, if she were a man, I would have done something about it."

There was also the rumor that he was Jewish. Truman's reply was, "I am not Jewish but if I were I would not be ashamed of it." When the country was flooded with leaflets containing the "facts" about his haberdashery store litigation and the loan on his mother's farm, he labeled it "nothing but a damned bunch of lies, just a smut sheet." There were stories that he was anti-Negro and believed Negroes had organized "push days" in Washington. He was quoted as saying, "I wouldn't let my daughter go downtown on the streetcars on Thursdays any more. They push people off the streetcars." Actually, he was popular with Missouri Negroes and the National Association for the Advancement of Colored People. In the Senate, he was a strong advocate of anti-poll tax and anti-lynching legislation.

In addition, Truman's old connection with Tom Pendergast was a recurring theme. There was also the charge, first made public by Arthur Krock in *The New York Times,* that he had been "cleared with Sydney." But these attempts to malign him did not upset him so much as front-page stories in the Hearst papers from coast to coast that he had been a Ku Kluxer. "The fact is," he told a reporter, "that the Klan fought me in the days when the Klan had political strength and that I fought back. In the State Masonic Grand Lodge, I put through a resolution condemning the organization."

But Truman was by now so accustomed to defamatory attacks that he did not let them interfere with his plans. As he traveled south in the second week of October to start his campaign, *Time* assessed him as "unsophisticated" and "homespun and plain as an old shoe." The magazine reported his statistics as height, five feet ten inches; weight, 167 pounds; waist, 33 inches—"an inconspicuous man with thin lips, steel-rimmed glasses, flatly combed gray hair and a flat, not unpleasant Missouri twang. "At sixty," *Time* concluded, "Harry Truman is very much alive." This came after the prophecy: "There is no reason to suspect that he would make a great President—and there is no reason to believe that he would be the worst."

The *Henry Stanley* pulled into New Orleans on October 12 for the official opening of Truman's campaign tour. When confronted by a roomful of servicemen's wives, each holding a baby, he lamely refused to kiss any of the infants on the grounds that he had a cold. Later he said he was afraid he might have dropped one of the babies. A New Orleans newsman, trying to make a story about Truman's reputed poker playing, got this reply: "Card games? The only game I know anything about is that game—let me see—I don't know what the name is, but you put one card face down on the table and four face up, and you bet."

The *Henry Stanley*'s tour carried Truman through Texas, New Mexico, up the Pacific Coast to Seattle, then eastward across the country to Massachusetts, down to New York and Washington and finally back home to Missouri. At every stop, local politicians scampered aboard to chew the political fat until the next stop when they climbed down to be replaced by more local politicians. At ten P.M., when the day's campaigning was over, Truman changed into pajamas, a figured silk dressing gown and beat-up kidskin house slippers. Then, grinning, he strolled into the car ahead which housed his five traveling reporters and called out, "How about it, boys? Let's have a little ten-cent ante."

Late one afternoon he stopped at Uvalde, Texas, for a visit with Cactus Jack Garner, out of politics since 1941. Garner came to the station in torn khaki work pants and a shapeless, dirty white ten-gallon hat, his hands stained black from picking his pecan crop. He struck a match across the seat of his pants, lit a Mexican cheroot and greeted his protégé. "I'm glad to see you, Harry. Bless your old soul." He apologized for his appearance. "Today I've been in the cornfield since early morning. I took the 'down row'—had to bend down, following the wagon." Then his face brightened and he said impishly, "I wish we had time to strike a blow for liberty. Somewhere in the world it must be twelve o'clock."

"Step right in, milad." Truman urged him aboard the *Henry Stanley*. "I've got it right in here."

Truman went on to California. "The toughest audience I had to deal with was in Los Angeles," he said. "It was completely hostile and

225

must have thrown more than a hundred pointed questions at me."
One of the questions was whether he supported California's Hal Styles
for Congress. Truman opened the gate to nationwide criticism when
he said he would, even though Styles had once belonged to the KKK.

The state of Washington was the true "Mashed Potatoes Circuit,"
said George Allen, and Truman was expected to prove he was a good
candidate by eating a heavy meal at each stop. In a small town in
Idaho, when the welcoming committee and total audience turned out
to be only three schoolteachers, he nevertheless gave them the political works for fifteen minutes, loud-speakers and all. Crossing into
Montana, Allen feared that Senator Burton Wheeler, who had led
the Senate isolationists, would be on hand to greet them. "Burt won't
be there," Truman assured him. Wheeler stayed away. While he was
in Butte, he received a present from Eddie Jacobson with a note that
read: *Use the enclosed liquid as a stimulant to keep you awake while
studying the art of poker playing with the enclosed deck.*

Passing through North Dakota, Truman did a war dance on a bag-
gage truck with old Chief Standing Alone and four of his Sioux
braves. He stopped in Minneapolis for a rally sponsored by young
Hubert Humphrey, who was anxious to use the publicity as a springboard into the mayor's office the following year. In Illinois, Truman
lashed out at Dewey, Hoover, and Wall Street speculators. His taunts
nettled Republicans, but audiences yelled themselves hoarse for more.

The lack of coordination between his campaign and Roosevelt's
brought on a bad crisis in Massachusetts when Truman called Senator
Walsh an "isolationist" and added, "Walsh has two more years to serve
in the Senate and there's hope for his reformation." William Hassett,
one of FDR's assistants, said that the President was stunned by Truman's comment because he needed Walsh's support to win the state's
16 electoral votes. Walsh was wild at the charge, but Roosevelt managed to placate him.

After speaking in Massachusetts and New York, where he and
Henry Wallace shared the rostrum at a huge Madison Square Garden
rally before a pro-Wallace crowd, Truman stopped in Washington,
Pittsburgh and West Virginia, then went back to Independence for
the election. Following his visit to the polling booth, he spent election night surrounded by Battery D buddies and other friends in the
Muehlebach Hotel penthouse in Kansas City.

At Hyde Park that Tuesday evening, November 7, FDR sat in his

226

dining room, listening to early returns over the radio. Friends found him dejected and on edge, certain that Dewey would win.

In the Muehlebach, Truman noted the pessimism enveloping his wartime buddies and called, "Everybody around here seems to be nervous but me." Spirits sagged even further when early Missouri returns indicated a Republican trend. "I think that calls for a concert," Truman shouted. He sat down at the piano and played Paderewski's *Minuet*.

Not until 3:45 A.M. did Dewey concede. The wait was painful, although the final result revealed a resounding Democratic victory with 432 electoral votes to only 99 for the Republicans. With relief, Roosevelt telegraphed Truman. I AM VERY HAPPY THAT THINGS HAVE GONE SO WELL. MY THANKS AND CONGRATULATIONS FOR YOUR SPLENDID COOPERATION. In return, Truman wired: I AM VERY HAPPY OVER THE OVERWHELMING ENDORSEMENT WHICH YOU RECEIVED. ISOLATIONISM IS DEAD. HOPE TO SEE YOU SOON.

But mixed with Truman's elation was his smoldering anger at the abuse the newspapers had heaped upon him during the campaign. He told a reporter, "A straw man has been constructed that you newspapers will now have to bury. Nobody told me how to do my duty, and I feel that I have served the people. But I never forget a favor. If I had been willing to forget my friends, I could have had headlines in your damn paper and plenty of other papers."

His good humor returned when Roosevelt asked him to meet him at Union Station in Washington on Friday the tenth for a triumphant ride through the streets of the Capital to the White House. "All that flying for a fifteen-minute auto ride!" he joked. "But if the Chief wants it, it's O. K."

Despite his levity, however, he realized that the day was not far off when he would become President of the United States.

26

TRUMAN'S short career as Vice-President began on January 20, 1945. At Roosevelt's insistence, the traditional inauguration ceremony was not held at the Capitol but on the South Portico of the White House. Although it was bitterly cold that Saturday, FDR refused to wear a hat or coat. That day, for the last time, his legs were encased in braces.

After Henry Wallace administered the oath to Truman, and Chief Justice Harlan F. Stone swore in FDR, the President delivered an inaugural address that lasted only five minutes. At its conclusion, he grinned at Truman and shook his hand.

Afterward, there was an official White House luncheon for 1,500 persons. Roosevelt would not attend, but Truman joined Mrs. Roosevelt to receive the guests. Mrs. Roosevelt confessed to him, "I can't get my husband to eat. He just won't eat."

Later, Truman left the White House, caught a ride back to the Capitol and telephoned his mother.

"Did you hear it on the radio?" he asked.

"Yes, I heard it all," she said. "Now you behave yourself up there, Harry. Now you behave yourself!"

"I will, Mamma," he promised.

When Truman took over as presiding officer of the Senate on January 22, Roosevelt had already left Washington for the Yalta Conference with Winston Churchill and Joseph Stalin. Just before departing, he summoned Truman to the White House to inform him that he was firing Jesse Jones as Secretary of Commerce and Federal Loan Administrator and replacing him with Henry Wallace.

"Jesus Christ!" Truman said on hearing the news, for he realized the difficulty of winning Senate approval for Wallace with Roosevelt out of the country. "I'll see every Senator I can," he assured FDR weakly.

After determining that there was no possibility of winning Senate approval for Wallace to take over both of Jones's jobs, Truman's strategy was to separate the two positions and then vote Wallace in solely as Secretary of Commerce. The separation of the two posts was embodied in a bill introduced by Senator Walter George of Georgia. Senator Barkley was to call for a vote on the George bill and after its passage, Wallace's nomination for Secretary of Commerce was to be considered.

Unfortunately, when Truman looked down from the dais, Barkley was dozing at his desk and Senator Robert A. Taft of Ohio had risen for recognition. Senate Rules called for the presiding officer to recognize the first Senator on his feet. But Truman knew that Taft would call for a vote on confirming Wallace for both jobs because he was certain it would not carry. Truman looked everywhere but at Taft. Finally, a sharp prod roused Barkley and Truman loudly recognized the Kentuckian. The rest was simple: the George bill passed and Wallace was later confirmed as Secretary of Commerce.

Truman had been Vice-President only six days when Tom Pendergast died on January 26. It might have been smart politics for Truman to ignore Pendergast's death, but instead he boarded an Army bomber for Kansas City. Before he left Washington, he told newsmen, "I'm as sorry as I can be. He was always my friend and I have always been his."

Tom Pendergast had been looking forward to his return to politics. "I've done a lot for Kansas City," he told a reporter from the St. Louis *Star-Times* on his seventy-second birthday in October, 1944. "For the poor of Kansas City—I've done more for them than all the big shots and bankers, all of them put together."

Truman was widely criticized for attending Pendergast's funeral.

But he did not care. Deserted by family and friends, T. J. had died a broken old man with debts that wiped out his estate. Truman could not forget that he owed his entire political career to Pendergast. At the funeral, he listened with bowed head as Monsignor MacDonald described T. J. as a man "with a noble heart" and said, "I have heard men say they would rather have his word than his note."

When Truman was elected Vice-President, he had told Luther Huston of *The New York Times* that he planned "to be a politician's Vice-President." Huston reported, "He will have a hand in shaping legislation and steering it through the Senate; will operate behind the scenes to keep fences patched and curb feuds; and may even be more zealous at times than Garner in championing the programs of the Administration."

There were many things wrong with this appraisal. In the first place, Roosevelt was gone over a month for the Yalta Conference and during this time Truman had few contacts with Administration tacticians. Even when Roosevelt returned, Truman saw little of him. Records show that FDR was in Washington less than 30 days of Truman's 82-day period as Vice-President. It is true that Truman attended Cabinet meetings, but only a few were held because of Roosevelt's frequent absences from Washington, and besides, Truman admitted that FDR "never discussed anything important at his Cabinet meetings." Truman had official appointments to see Roosevelt only on March 8 and March 19. He also saw him on a few other occasions, but at no time did they have a heart-to-heart talk.

As for the duties of his office, Truman knew that the Vice-President was barred from joining in debates in the Chamber and could only vote in case of a tie. This occurred only once, when his vote defeated an amendment to the Lend-Lease Act introduced by Senator Taft which would prevent postwar delivery of lend-lease goods contracted for during the war. The Vice-President also had authority to direct bills to committees, and Truman brought anguish to New Dealers when he committed the Missouri Valley Authority Bill to the Commerce Committee, which opposed it, instead of the Agriculture Committee.

Truman was restless as Vice-President. Although he enjoyed the honor, the office was a form of refined torture to a man who had worked at breakneck speed throughout the war years. Faced with little to do, he became the social lion of Washington. He, Bess, Margaret and Bess's mother, Mrs. Wallace, were still living in their small,

$125-a-month Connecticut Avenue apartment, where they could not entertain guests. But Washington social leaders peppered him with invitations. *Time* wrote: "The amiable Missourian with the touch of country in his voice and manner had conquered a schedule that had ... Capitol Society writers breathless." On some days he and Bess went to three cocktail parties and a dinner. George Dixon, the humorist, wrote in his column: "Currently, the new Vice-President is the most fed gentleman in Washington. He has guzzled at more feed troughs than Whirlaway. And the invitations continue to pour in."

Harry Vaughan, now a brigadier general and the first military aide to a Vice-President, reported on a party given for the Trumans by Evalyn Walsh McLean. Owner of the Hope Diamond, Mrs. McLean reigned as the social queen of Washington, and not only served unusual, exotic foods but also hired Metropolitan Opera stars and concert artists to entertain her guests. "At the dinner she gave for the Trumans," Vaughan said, "when Clare Boothe Luce and her husband, Henry Luce, entered, Mrs. McLean greeted them sharply. 'Mrs. Luce,' she said, in front of the other guests, 'you weren't invited to this party. I'm going to ask you to leave.' They were gatecrashers and had to suffer the embarrassment of being thrown out."

Truman also attended an affair at the National Press Club that caused him no end of chagrin. While he played the piano for reporters, Lauren Bacall, the movie actress, climbed onto the instrument. He turned his head away from her, but a photographer snapped a picture that attracted nationwide coverage. Miss Bacall's press agent insisted that Truman had been an accomplice. Bess's reaction was one of outrage. "She said she thought it was time for me to quit playing the piano," Truman admitted.

In time he grew weary of the steady round of parties and longed for some tasks to keep him busy. But the Vice-President's office was one of constitutional idleness. As Margaret Truman said, when she heard Senator Henry Ashurst of Arizona remark that he knew the names of all the Vice-Presidents, "I didn't think there was any man in the United States silly enough to fill his head with such useless information."

But Truman was well aware of the fact that there was one aspect of the Vice-Presidency that was neither silly nor useless. On February 20, while he presided over the Senate, a rumor swept the Capitol that Roosevelt was dead. Hastily, he dashed to the office of Leslie Biffle, who had succeeded Colonel Halsey as Secretary of the Senate on

February 8. "I hear the President is dead," Truman said grimly. "What will we do? Let's find out what happened."

Because he was too shaken to call the White House, Biffle did so for him. It was not Roosevelt who had died, but "Pa" Watson, who passed away on the U.S.S. *Quincy* while returning from Yalta with FDR. Truman was still Vice-President.

But he realized that Roosevelt's end was not far off when he saw him on his return a week later. "He seemed a spent man," he said. "I had a hollow feeling within me."

As Vice-President, Truman had at his disposal a government limousine and chauffeur. That winter, when the chauffeur made his morning stop at Truman's apartment to drive him to the Capitol, another man sat beside him. Truman assumed he was the driver's friend getting a free ride into town. One day, when he asked the driver about this, the chauffeur exclaimed, "He's no friend of mine. He's a Secret Service man." The Secret Service, convinced that Roosevelt was failing, had assigned a special agent to guard Truman on the streets.

On March 1, when FDR came to the Capitol to give Congress and the nation his report on Yalta, Truman sat with Sam Rayburn on the Speaker's platform while Roosevelt sat at a table in the well of the House. Apologetically, FDR explained why he did not stand. "I know that you will realize it makes it a lot easier for me in not having to carry about ten pounds of steel around on the bottom of my legs." His speech was dismal and the words came hard. Afterward he asked Truman to excuse his lackluster performance and said, "As soon as I can, I will go to Warm Springs for a rest. I can be in trim again if I can stay there for two or three weeks."

His face drawn, his skin sallow, he left for Warm Springs on March 30. Shortly afterward, Truman went on a fishing trip with Sam Rayburn and a few friends to a small lake in eastern Maryland where the bass were biting. The contrast between the healthy Truman and the dying President was never more striking. "You guys have a fifteen-thousand-dollar-a-year oarsman," Truman told Rayburn laughingly when he took over the rowing chore. On the return trip, rowing through a swift-moving river, he stopped to rest and stood up. The boat suddenly lurched and he fell into icy water. For a time it looked as if the country would be without a Vice-President, but the men finally hauled him back aboard. Wrapped in blankets, he sat shivering at one end of the boat. "You just go on and catch the fish, Sam," he said to Rayburn, "and I'll do the swimming."

On April 11, when the Senate adjourned for the day, newsmen surrounded Truman for an interview. One of the reporters called him "Mr. President."

Truman grinned. "Boys, those are fighting words out in Missouri where I come from. You'd better smile when you say that! You know right here is where I've always wanted to be, and the only place I ever wanted to be. The Senate—that's just my speed and my style." This was his last interview as Vice-President.

During the fateful afternoon of April 12, he sat on the Senate rostrum and penned a letter home. It read in part:

> DEAR MAMMA & MARY:
> I am trying to write you a letter from the desk of the President of the Senate while a windy Senator is making a speech on a subject with which he is in no way familiar. . . . We are considering the Mexican Treaty on water in the Colorado River and the Rio Grande. . . . The Senators from California and one from Utah and a very disagreeable one from Nevada [McCarran] are fighting the ratification. . . . Turn on your radio tomorrow night at 9:30 your time, and you'll hear Harry make a Jefferson Day address to the nation. . . . It will be followed by the President, whom I'll introduce.

When the Senate recessed at 5:10, Truman stepped down from the dais and headed for the House side of the Capitol. Sam Rayburn had asked him to drop over to his "Board of Education," or hideaway quarters on the first floor of the Capitol's southern end. This was a dark room with a frayed rug, a fireplace, an oil painting of Rayburn, several black leather chairs and a sofa, as well as the ingredients to "strike a blow for liberty."

When Truman marched in, Rayburn told him that the White House had telephoned and wanted him to return the call immediately. When he got the number, the switchboard operator hurriedly connected him with Steve Early's line. "Please come right over," Early said in a choking voice. "And come in through the main Pennsylvania entrance."

The men in the room saw Truman's face turn ashen and his jaw set hard. When he hung up, he muttered, "Holy General Jackson!" Then he announced grimly, "Boys, this is in this room. Something must have happened. I'll be back soon."

He ran the length of the Capitol basement and through the underground tunnel to his office in the Senate Office Building. Picking up his hat, he ordered Tom Rorty, his chauffeur, to get his car out for the drive and told Harry Vaughan, "I'll either telephone you within an hour or be back by that time."

By running through the basement of the Capitol he had eluded his ever-present Secret Service guards. And now, in his last hour as Vice-President, he was unguarded as he rode down Pennsylvania Avenue to the White House.

It was 5:25 when he arrived at the White House. A trip up the elevator to the second floor and a walk down the corridor brought him to Mrs. Roosevelt's study. When he entered, he found Mrs. Roosevelt, her daughter Anna, John Boettiger and Steve Early waiting for him with stricken faces. "Harry," Mrs. Roosevelt said, "the President is dead."

Tears flooded Truman's eyes. "Is there anything I can do for you?" he stammered.

"Tell us what we can do," she replied. "Is there any way we can help you?"

Secretary of State Stettinius came in, crying. Mrs. Roosevelt said she wanted to go to Warm Springs and asked permission to use a government plane. Her request seemed strange until Truman remembered that he was now her husband's successor and she was a private citizen. Quickly he assented.

Then he got on the phone and called Les Biffle, asking him to come to the White House at once. He also called Sam Rayburn and told him to bring other Congressional leaders. Another call went to Harry Vaughan with instructions to come with Matt Connelly, and still another to Chief Justice Stone to come immediately to swear him in.

When he called his apartment, Margaret answered the phone. "Let me speak to your mother," he said curtly.

"Are you coming home to dinner?" she asked.

"Let me speak to your mother!" he repeated.

"I only asked you a civil question," she insisted.

"Margaret!" he yelled. "Will you let me speak to your mother!"

Bess burst into tears when he told her the news. "Come right away with Margaret," he ordered. The Secret Service men who were assigned to guard their apartment led Bess and Margaret out the back door and drove them to the White House.

234

Before he took his oath of office, Truman gave his first order as President. He announced that the United Nations Charter Conference would proceed on schedule in San Francisco on April 25. There was trouble finding a Bible when the Chief Justice arrived. The Cabinet and Truman's family and friends crowded into the Cabinet Room. Truman's memory was that "everyone was crying and carrying on. None of us could believe that FDR was gone." The clock under the Woodrow Wilson portrait stood at 7:09 P.M. when Chief Justice Stone administered the oath to Truman.

Afterward, Truman asked the Cabinet to remain for a short meeting. With choking voice, he assured them he would carry out the policies of Roosevelt. When the meeting was over, Secretary of War Henry L. Stimson lingered behind to tell about the atomic bomb project. Truman later drove back to his Connecticut Avenue apartment where his next-door neighbor, General Jeff Davis, gave him a ham sandwich and a glass of milk.

Gradually, the shock and daze wore off and he realized that he was now President of the United States. From Lamar, Missouri, to 1600 Pennsylvania Avenue, he had traveled a great distance.

27

_____

WITH the exception of Abraham Lincoln and perhaps Franklin Roosevelt, no President took office in a period of greater crisis than did Harry Truman. In Europe, cannons, tanks, planes and guns continued their carnage, though the end of the fighting appeared in sight. In their wake little Caesars were popping up everywhere to take advantage of the political vacuums. Among the Big Power Allies, bombastic demands emanated that threatened the continuation of their wartime alliance. Prime Minister Churchill of Great Britain adamantly insisted on maintaining the British Empire of the pre-war period. Charles de Gaulle of France nettled his war companions with talk about a Near East French suzerainty and a grab of the Aosta Valley in northwest Italy. On the Eastern Front, Stalin brazenly installed Communist governments in the territories on Russia's western borders.

In the Pacific, the costly battles for the islands of Iwo Jima and Okinawa were over, with casualties reaching almost 70,000. General MacArthur was engaged in a mopping up effort in the Philippines. Ahead lay a frontal attack on the island empire of Japan. In China, the Nationalists under Chiang Kai-shek, exhausted from a decade of war with the Japanese, were already sparring with the Chinese Reds for domination of that weary nation. On other fronts throughout the world, the earlier whispers and pleas of colonial areas for freedom and independence were reaching screaming proportions.

On the home front within the United States, a gigantic restlessness augured trouble. There was little understanding of the responsibilities of world leadership, which the war had forced on the rich nation. There was bitter opposition to continuing price controls and rationing, smoldering resentment by labor and soldiers at the large new crop of war-made millionaires, and hysteria over an expected postwar economic depression. A vast disillusionment had already set in regarding an everlasting peace because of the antics of the Russians in Eastern Europe. World leadership demanded a large postwar military force to frighten would-be saber rattlers. But the American public wanted the boys home and out of uniform as soon as possible. Within the Government, the national fiscal affairs were in disorder with a budget of $99 billion and tax receipts of only $46 billion. Relations between the executive and legislative branches had reached the point of distrust and animosity.

To cap all these, one of the most popular Presidents in history and the leader of the Western World lay dead at Warm Springs, Georgia. When Mrs. Roosevelt put her arm around Truman's shoulder and told him that her husband was dead, he knew that FDR's prestige would be his biggest handicap. It was inescapable that he would be compared unfavorably with his predecessor, a man of different background, personality and experience. Truman also realized that, largely by unavoidable circumstances, Roosevelt had nevertheless done him a disservice by not taking him into his confidence.

He was on his own, alone and unprepared for the enormous decisions that he would have to make in the crucial months ahead. How would he make out? Charlie Ross delved into this question in an article he wrote at that time: "The rise of Harry Truman to the Presidency is one of the most amazing phenomena in American political history. Luck—or call it fate—time and time again intervened to send him down the right road when another road would have stopped him dead." Concerning Truman's attributes, Ross stated: "He is impeccably honest. He takes advice, but can be stubborn when he makes up his own mind. Perhaps he is too amiable. . . . Will Truman measure up? . . . Harry Truman has a lot of stuff, more stuff, I think, than he has generally been credited with."

Truman's first day as President began on Friday, April 13, at six-

237

thirty A.M. when he climbed out of bed in his apartment without waking Bess, Margaret or Mrs. Wallace. After his customary walk, he returned for breakfast with Hugh Fulton. Because of the housing shortage in Washington, the apartment house manager was already being besieged by callers who wanted the Truman apartment. A crowd gathered in the street, and when Truman left the building again, he told the swarm of photographers, "My, but I seem to be popular this morning." He spied Tony Vaccaro of the Associated Press and invited him to join him in his limousine.

Once in the White House, he walked into the oval office of the President and sat down for the first time at FDR's desk. The top was cluttered with knickknacks that Roosevelt had accumulated over the years. Truman ordered them removed. Secretary of State Stettinius was his first visitor and gave him a 45-minute briefing on the foreign situation. Then he met with military advisers who agreed that the war against Germany would last another six months while Japan would not be subdued until late in 1946. After the meeting Truman asked Fleet Admiral William D. Leahy, Roosevelt's chief of staff, to stay on with him in the same capacity.

"Are you sure you want me, Mr. President?" the crusty old Admiral asked. "I always say what's on my mind."

Truman assured him he was just the type of person he wanted.

When Leahy left, Truman signed his first official document as President, a proclamation of Roosevelt's death. It gave him a strange feeling to sign his name as President. Even five months later, he confided in a letter to Mrs. Roosevelt, "I never think of anyone as the President, but Mr. Roosevelt."

His first official call was to Les Biffle to invite himself to lunch in Biffle's office in the Capitol. Roy Roberts of the Kansas City *Star* dropped in for a talk, and later expounded his views on Truman:

> Humility probably would be the first characterization. Then loyalty, perhaps excessive loyalty that sometimes gets high officials into trouble; common sense; deep patriotism; and above all an abiding faith in his country and its democratic system. . . . The sheer fact he is the average man, understands the average man and his quality, is probably Truman's greatest asset as he undertakes these new overpowering responsibilities.

Biffle invited thirteen Senators and four Representatives to lunch with Truman. It felt good to be back in familiar surroundings, but

Truman recognized the importance in his new capacity of maintaining friendly relations with Congress. When a box of cigars was found in his old Vice-Presidential office, he gave it to Senator Vandenberg, the Republican leader on foreign affairs. During the meal, he asked permission to address a Joint Session of Congress on the next Monday after Roosevelt's funeral.

When lunch was over, Truman started to walk out on the Senate floor, but Biffle stopped him. "You can't go out there, Harry," he said. "You're President now."

On his way out, Truman told reporters, "Boys, if you ever pray, pray for me now. I don't know whether you fellows ever had a load of hay fall on you, but when they told me yesterday what had happened, I felt like the moon, the stars and all the planets had fallen on me."

One reporter called out, "Good luck, Mr. President."

"I wish you hadn't called me that," Truman said.

Back in the White House, he was visited by Jimmy Byrnes, who had flown from Spartanburg, South Carolina, to attend Roosevelt's funeral. He asked Byrnes to become his Secretary of State, and "he almost jumped down my throat taking me up," Truman said later. Byrnes, however, did not want to assume this post until the United Nations Charter Conference in San Francisco was completed.

During the conversation, Byrnes offered to provide Truman with the details of the atomic bomb project, but Henry Stimson had already given him the facts the previous evening after he had taken the oath of office. Truman was also briefed on the bomb by Vannevar Bush, head of the Office of Scientific Research and Development. Admiral Leahy, who was present at this meeting, scoffed at the whole idea. "This is the biggest fool thing we have ever done," he announced. "The bomb will never go off, and I speak as an expert in explosives."

Later that first afternoon as President, Stettinius returned with Charles Bohlen, the State Department's Russian expert, to discuss the Soviet attempt to force a Communist government on Poland. Following this meeting, Truman sent a cable to Churchill giving his view on this subject. Memos and reports began piling high on his desk as the afternoon wore on, and although he tried to read them as fast as they came, the pile grew. That night, when he returned to his apartment, he already had a fairly good idea of the monstrous job that had fallen upon him.

The days that followed offered no respite. On Saturday, the fourteenth, for instance, he was up at dawn for another long succession of briefings on a host of matters ranging from the nation's finances to foreign relations. That morning at ten he had to call a temporary halt in order to hurry to Union Station to meet the train carrying Roosevelt's body.

On the return ride to the White House, the streets were lined with sobbing people. And all that day, while he engaged in cramming sessions, FDR's remains lay in the East Room not far from his desk. That evening, he, Bess and Margaret boarded the train for Hyde Park where FDR was to be buried the next day in the Roosevelt family's rose garden. Then on the trip back to Washington, he closeted himself with Jimmy Byrnes to go over the speech he was preparing for Congress.

Truman's first big test came on Monday when he walked into the House of Representatives to address the Joint Session of Congress. He was so nervous that he started to speak without being introduced. "Just a minute, Harry," Sam Rayburn said. "Let me introduce you." Rayburn shouted, "The President of the United States!" and Truman began again. He read his speech from a big black notebook, his Missouri twang bearing none of the dramatic overtones of his predecessor. Nevertheless, he was continually interrupted by deafening applause. His honeymoon with Congress was on.

Afterward Truman wrote a happy "Dear Mamma and Mary" letter: "My greatest trial was today when I addressed the Congress. It seemed to go over all right from the ovation I received. Things have gone so well that I'm almost as scared as I was Thursday when Mrs. R. told me what had happened." He closed with—"your very much worried son and bro." At Grandview, his mother told reporters: "I can't really be glad he is President, because I'm sorry that President Roosevelt is dead. If he had been voted in, I'd be out waving a flag, but it doesn't seem right to be very happy or wave a flag now."

On Tuesday, Truman held his first press conference in his office, where 348 reporters crowded into the room. "They gave me a pretty hefty fifteen minutes," he wrote his mother. He made swift replies to questions and sometimes spoke so rapidly that newsmen could not copy down his words. No, he was not going to the San Francisco Charter Conference to organize the United Nations. Yes, he supported the Bretton Woods Conference—"We need an international monetary setup." No, he did not want to discuss the St. Lawrence

Waterway. Did he expect to see Soviet Foreign Minister Molotov before the San Francisco Conference? "Molotov is going to stop by and pay his respects to the President of the United States, as he should." Did he have any plans for public office for Jimmy Byrnes? No, he did not. Did he plan to lift the wartime ban on horse racing? No.

The round of briefings did not let up. At the end of one wearing afternoon, he wrote his mother, "This day has been a dinger, too." With the United Nations Charter Conference scheduled to begin in San Francisco on April 25, he met with the American delegation headed by Stettinius and including Senators Tom Connally and Arthur Vandenberg. State Department officials wanted him to butter up Vandenberg, the ranking Republican on the Senate Foreign Relations Committee. This favored treatment annoyed Connally, the Chairman of the Foreign Relations Committee, who said later, "Vandenberg had been a leading isolationist before Pearl Harbor and in his heart he was still one."

Truman also saw French Foreign Minister Georges Bidault, Philippine President Sergio Osmena, Chinese Foreign Minister T. V. Soong, and Dr. Stephen Wise, head of the American Zionist Emergency Committee. In addition, American Ambassador to Russia, Averell Harriman, flew back from Moscow for conversations. It was during a talk with Harriman that Truman's future policy toward the Soviet Union hardened. Harriman emphasized the deteriorating relations with the Russians since Yalta and insisted that the West was faced with "a barbarian invasion of Europe." The Reds, said Harriman, still wanted world revolution and believed that the postwar American economy was dependent on exports to Russia. He told Truman that he had rushed back from Moscow because of "the fear that you did not understand, as I had seen Roosevelt understand, that Stalin is breaking his word."

On April 14, the Trumans moved from their Connecticut Avenue apartment to Blair House, the old square yellow building diagonally across Pennsylvania Avenue from the White House. Mrs. Roosevelt's accumulations of thirteen years were still in the White House and Truman insisted she take her time about moving out. It was at Blair House that he discussed Soviet-American relations with Molotov on April 22 and 23.

Truman did not mince words in these talks. Coldly, he scolded Molotov for violating the Yalta Agreement to establish a freely elected government in Poland. He demanded that the Russians keep their word. "We don't want to operate on the basis of a one-way street," Truman threatened.

Molotov flushed. "I have never been talked to like that in my life," he protested.

"Carry out your agreements and you won't get talked to like that," Truman snapped.

One of the discomforts of the Presidency that bothered Truman from the beginning was his complete lack of privacy. He existed in a goldfish bowl. Every word he uttered was subjected to analysis and interpretation, reporters trailed him like bloodhounds, photographers took countless pictures. During his first few weeks in office, whenever he walked across the street from the White House to Blair House enormous crowds collected. Finally, the Secret Service ordered him to go by car from the rear of the White House to the alley entrance behind Blair House. On one occasion he walked to the Hamilton National Bank at 14th and G to examine his safety deposit box. When he came out, traffic was backed up for blocks. Once he and Bess went to a party given by the American Newspaper Women's Club at the Mayflower Hotel. When they sat in a box at the side of the ballroom, a crowd collected only a few feet away and stared silently. Finally, Truman remarked uncomfortably, "We certainly are on display, aren't we?" Back in Missouri, reporters sought out his relatives and acquaintances for color stories. Sue Gentry of the Independence *Examiner* said, "Almost everyone in town here was interviewed to exhaustion—and misinterpreted." Truman wrote to his mother and sister, "Hope you have not been bothered too much. It is terrible— I mean terrible—nuisance to be kin to the President."

Newsmen were quick to note that he was partisan to Missourians and his old war buddies. One reporter wrote, "Battery D must have at least 10,000 men in it. They all want to see Truman." The Washington *Daily News* headlined one story: ALL MISSOURI'S HERE TO SEE HARRY. When Teddy Roosevelt crammed the White House with his old Rough Rider buddies, the public found it romantic, but when Truman began bringing in Missourians and World War I buddies, newspapers found it offensive. Harry Vaughan became his military aide; John Snyder, Federal Loan Administrator; Bennett Clark, Associate Justice on the Circuit Court of Appeals; and Eddie McKim, chief White House secretary.

During his first week in the White House, McKim found some

stenographers working on the thousands of letters that had poured in to Mrs. Roosevelt after her husband's death. "So this is 'My Day,'" he growled. "Mrs. Roosevelt is no longer riding the gravy train. Stop it!" He fired the girls and ordered the work dropped. But Bess Truman heard about it and complained to her husband, who gave instructions that the work be resumed at once. Truman finally dispatched McKim to the Federal Loan Administration and out of the White House.

Truman also wanted Charlie Ross to work for him. "On April nineteenth," Ross said, "he called me up and told me to come over to his office. When I walked in, his first words were, 'Charlie, I'm going to put your feet in the fire. I want you to come here and be my press secretary.' I didn't want to do it because I wanted to cover the San Francisco UN Conference for my paper." But he agreed to take the job after the conference ended, although he asked Truman to keep it secret until then.

Truman, however, insisted upon one concession—to call their old high school teacher, Miss Tillie (Matilda Brown), and tell her the news in confidence. Steve Early, who was staying on temporarily as press secretary, opposed this move on the grounds that Miss Tillie would gossip about the appointment. But Truman, overrruling him, made the call. "Miss Tillie, I've just put Charlie in charge of my press relations," he told her. "I'm getting a great deal of fun out of Charlie calling me Mr. President."

Proud of her boys, Miss Tillie asked if he remembered their graduation night and how she had kissed only Charlie, because he was the best student in the class, while telling the others that she hoped yet to kiss a future President of the United States. Immediately after the conversation, Miss Tillie called the Independence *Examiner* and spilled the beans. "I started out by calling him Mr. President," she said, "but went right back to calling him Harry before we finished talking." The *Examiner* scooped all other newspapers in reporting Ross's appointment, and many editors grumbled about the White House giving an exclusive to a small town paper.

On April 25, the San Francisco UN Charter Conference opened. Three days later Italy surrendered just as the Western Nations saw evidence of mounting trouble with Russia both in San Francisco and Europe. In a telegram to Truman on April 18, Churchill had insisted that the British and American Armies proceed as far as they could into Eastern Europe. Churchill's desire, said Truman, was to hold on to conquered Eastern European territory until the Russians lived up to commitments. In another message to Truman, Churchill said he feared the "descent of an iron curtain between us and everything to the eastward." Churchill also demanded that the West capture Berlin and not permit the Russians to take the German capital. Truman, however, relied on General Eisenhower to determine strategy on this issue. Eisenhower's view, as reported to General Marshall, was: "Berlin itself is no longer a particularly important objective. Its usefulness to the Germans has been largely destroyed and even their government is preparing to move to another area." Truman accepted Eisenhower's opinion despite Churchill's demand.

Shortly after American and Soviet armies linked up late in April, German resistance collapsed. On May 1, when Hitler committed suicide, serious negotiations began with Nazi military leaders to effect a formal ending to the war that had cost more than 15,000,000 lives. But these were stalled for days because Truman insisted upon unconditional surrender of German forces on all fronts, including the Eastern one.

Germany's unconditional surrender, on V-E Day, was finally agreed upon by Truman, Stalin and Churchill for nine A.M. Washington time on May 8. The preceding night the Trumans had finally moved into the White House. Early on V-E Day, Truman wrote to his mother, "I am sixty-one this morning, and I slept in the President's room in the White House last night." He told her that Churchill had wanted V-E Day set on the seventh and "was as mad as a wet hen" when he insisted on the eighth.

28

V-E Day was a day of wild rejoicing throughout the country. From a White House window, Truman looked out at the immense crowd that had collected in Lafayette Park across the street. Strangers embraced and kissed each other and cheered the new President's name.

But Truman's own joy was not undiluted. He was aware that his advisers gloomily predicted a loss of a half-million American lives in an invasion of the Japanese islands. Then there were the reconversion programs, the establishment of the United Nations, the complicated details of preparing for peace with the conquered nations. Devastation, hunger and weariness spread a dark blanket over Europe, and the menace of Communism was everywhere.

In addition, vexing problems had arisen among the wartime Allies. In Germany, for instance, French forces, which had taken Stuttgart, had refused to evacuate that city despite an agreement to do so. Truman was forced to cut off American supplies to the French troops before they would get out. De Gaulle had also sent troops into northern Italy for "frontier adjustments." Here again he refused to pull out until Truman threatened to cut off supplies. At one point, Truman said, the French commander "actually threatened to have his troops fight American troops." De Gaulle later said: "The complicated problems of our Old World did not intimidate Truman, who considered them in simplified form. For him, all that was needed to satisfy a country was to apply New World Democracy to it."

On V-E Day, Leo Crowley, Foreign Economic Administrator, walked into Truman's office with a written order, which, he explained, authorized a cutback in Lend-Lease supplies to American allies now that Germany had surrendered. Truman signed the order without reading it. It was not much later when he learned from the harsh outcry raised in Moscow that what he had signed was not a cutback but an embargo on all Lend-Lease shipments to Russia. Even ships at sea with supplies bound for the Soviet Union were ordered to return to American ports. Chagrined, Truman rescinded the order Crowley had misrepresented to him, but not before Stalin had made good propaganda mileage out of it.

Coupled with the growing Soviet distrust of American intentions resulting from Crowley's order was the intransigence and continued wrangling by Molotov and his deputy, Andrei Gromyko, at the San Francisco Conference. On May 10, Truman felt lonely in his position and sought advice in an eight-page longhand letter to Eleanor Roosevelt. In her reply, Mrs. Roosevelt scolded him for wasting his time writing longhand letters. Her advice was that he should quickly get on a personal footing with Churchill. "If you talk to him about books and let him quote to you from his marvelous memory, everything on earth from Barbara Frietchie to the Nonsense Rhymes and Greek Tragedy, you will find him easier to deal with on political subjects. He is a gentleman to whom the personal element means a great deal."

The tone of her reply made it clear to Truman that he had to depend solely on himself for answers to the problems he faced. Indeed, his self-assurance grew with practice, though it took time. On May 28, for instance, when Herbert Hoover called on him to discuss the devastation and hunger in Europe, Truman kept addressing Hoover as "Mr. President," to the former President's embarrassment. One of Truman's assistants said that he developed a mania for making decisions and was unhappy when there were none to render at the moment. On his desk he placed a three-sided gadget with the motto: THE BUCK STOPS HERE.

Eager to see his mother again, Truman asked her and his sister to visit him over the Mother's Day weekend, arranging to have them flown to Washington on Roosevelt's plane, the *Sacred Cow*. Because of his crippled legs FDR had installed an elevator in the plane, but when Martha Truman used it on landing, it stuck and she said to the pilot, "I am going to tell Harry that this plane is no good and I could walk just as easily as I could ride." Surrounded by reporters, Truman greeted her at the airport. "Oh, fiddlesticks," she scolded him. "Why didn't you tell me there was going to be all this fuss and I wouldn't have come?"

Her son Vivian had told her teasingly that she would have to sleep in Abraham Lincoln's bedroom. "You tell Harry," she warned Vivian, "that if he puts me in the room with Lincoln's bed in it I'll sleep on the floor."

Truman calmed her later by assuring her that she would sleep in the Rose Room, facing Pennsylvania Avenue, where visiting queens slept. But his mother found the room too large and the bed too high and therefore slept in the small adjoining room where ladies-in-waiting were put up for the night.

The first day she was in the White House, Martha Truman went for a stroll through the building. Alone in the East Wing, she fell down a stairway, but made no mention of the fall until she was back in Grandview. She was her old peppery self, giving vent to strong opinions on all subjects. Regarding the new wartime style of women wearing slacks, she said in horror, "They look like the Jack of Clubs." About her son, she said proudly, "Harry can milk with both hands." But Truman noted that during her White House visit "she didn't seem to feel there was anything special about my being in the White House."

That spring Truman had a special present for his mother. He and Vivian put up $20,000 cash for 87 acres of the Young farm which she had lost in 1940 when she defaulted on $4,000 interest due on her $35,000 mortgage. In total, the brothers retrieved 394 acres at a cost of slightly more than $40,000. When Truman received the deed on June 15, he wrote his mother that she now had a rent-free house for the rest of her life. Martha Truman was terribly worried when the deed was published in the papers. "There is nothing they can say about me that hasn't been said all over," he assured her.

After V-E Day, when the Russians at the charter conference in San Francisco continued to fight every major position taken by the United States, Truman decided to break the impasse. Ailing Harry Hopkins, FDR's closest wartime adviser, had come to Washington for Roosevelt's funeral and told Truman that he planned to resign from the government to write his memoirs and earn some money. But Truman now pressed him into service for one last mission to Moscow to discuss deteriorating Soviet-American relations with Stalin.

Hopkins saw Stalin on May 27 and reported that he was still furious over the abrogation order on Lend-Lease shipments. In turn, Hopkins warned Stalin of the great shift in American public opinion toward Russia and blamed Stalin for ignoring the Yalta agreement to hold a democratic election in Poland. During these talks, Hopkins also got a confirmation of Russia's agreement at Yalta to enter the war against Japan three months after the German surrender.

In addition, Stalin agreed to end Soviet wrangling over the voting procedure in the proposed Security Council of the UN. The Soviet position had been that a single veto could prevent any discussion of a crisis by the Security Council, but Stalin now sent word to Andrei Gromyko to abandon this fight. At Truman's request, Hopkins also proposed a direct meeting in the near future of the Big Three—Truman, Stalin and Churchill. Stalin agreed with alacrity to a conference starting on July 15 at Potsdam, near Berlin.

With this reversal in Stalin's attitude, Truman had reason to believe that his first two months in office had been successful. He felt a slight easing of the tension that had gripped him since taking office.

Life in the White House was not an unmitigated torture. Bess Truman had found the barnlike Executive Mansion a gloomy place when she first inspected it. The big Roosevelt clan had done a lot of living in the old building. The walls were dirty and the furniture was worn. The President's office was a shambles with the rug threadbare, chair coverings ripped and springs popping through seats. She therefore went to work to make the place her own. She had Truman's bedroom painted cream and she moved his upstairs study desk to look out on the Washington Monument. Far better than the old bed in the apartment, he now had a large blue-canopied affair. Margaret's piano—the one he had bought for her during the depression—was too big for the White House doors and had to be hoisted through the second-floor living room window. Margaret's was not the only piano, however, for he received another as a gift. When his mother heard about this, she told reporters, "That was nice, but it's too bad they didn't give it to someone who had no piano."

Bess also provided quarters for her mother. Madge Wallace was not in good health and Bess explained that she had to look after her because "no one else can live with her and a hired companion is out." The old woman, imperious to the end, was still uncertain what to make of her son-in-law and his good fortune, especially since he did not assume a new personality to fit his new position. For instance, one evening at dinner, Margaret said, her father flipped a watermelon seed at her mother, who returned one in his direction. Soon a war was on, with watermelon seeds flying all over the room. The White House butler who came to clear the table also became a target of flying seeds, while the servants stood about and roared.

One discomfort of White House living was the large number of clocks. In a letter, Truman complained to his mother that "the ship's clock in Mrs. Wallace's room bangs away in that crazy sailor count of bells." The old grandfather clock in the hall had a "high squeaky voice . . . like fat tenors." There was a "hoarse" clock, a little time-keeper with a big voice "like most small people." There was also a complaint about institutional cooking, necessary in an establishment of that size. Most revolting was the frequent serving of Brussels sprouts. Once, at a party, Margaret met Elliott Roosevelt who asked, "Has Mrs. ——— succeeded in starving you yet?" Truman felt a special responsibility for keeping the White House in good working order. Every night before retiring he made the rounds checking windows and doors. One night, when a heavy rain poured into the second floor, he leaped from bed, raced barefoot in his striped pajamas to the bathroom, collected an armful of towels and went methodically from room to room mopping up the water.

Bess and Margaret were irked by being under Secret Service guard and conspired to elude the agents, but were unable to beat the game. Margaret was then in her junior year at college, and although she looked relaxed in her tweed skirt, sweater and saddle shoes, not far away was the ever-watchful eye of the Secret Service.

From the start, Bess's normally cheerful personality failed her in public and she looked stiff and frozen. When she had to christen an Army C-54 hospital plane, she timidly whacked its nose nine times with a champagne bottle without success. "Fine thing for a shot-put champion," her daughter commented. Republican newspapers claimed that she was a more proper First Lady than her predecessor, while Democratic papers compared her unfavorably with Mrs. Roosevelt, who had a strong public personality. It was only in the living quarters of the White House, away from public glare, that she was her witty and outgoing self.

In contrast, Truman loved to be on public exhibition. When he presented medals to war heroes, he read citations with such emotion that he sometimes wept. He burst with pride when he gave a dinner in honor of General Eisenhower on June 18, and wrote his mother about it. He referred to Eisenhower as "a real man," and described the dinner as "a gaudy affair if gold braid counts."

In June, when college let out, old Mrs. Wallace decided to return to Independence. Bess and Margaret accompanied her, leaving Truman alone in Washington. He wrote his mother that it was "rather lonesome in this old barn without anyone." He also told her about his many activities and mentioned receiving Hermann Goering's baton as a gift. "It's the fat Marshal's insignia of office," he wrote. "Can you imagine a fat pig like that strutting around with a forty-thousand-dollar bauble—at the poor taxpayers' expense and making 'em like it?"

With what appeared to be a thawing out of Soviet tactics, Truman decided to address the final session of the UN Charter Conference on June 26. He wrote his mother that he would see her on his way back from San Francisco. "How would you like to be the President des Etats Unis?" he asked. "It's a hell of a life."

Before going to San Francisco, he stopped for a short vacation at Olympia, Washington, with Governor Mon Wallgren. At the red brick governor's mansion, he played piano, went fishing, tried his hand at an organ, joined Wallgren and Charlie Ross in a singing trio that gave forth with "Melancholy Baby" and "Peggy O'Neal," and won a five-dollar bet that his suit was older than Wallgren's. Then he was off for San Francisco where he was cheered by a million persons who lined the streets.

That evening he held a reception at the Fairmont Hotel for the heads of missions and delegates. He had good reason to feel jubilant because he had effected a vital last-minute change in the UN Charter while frolicking with Wallgren. The Russians had opposed giving the General Assembly the right to free discussion of all matters or to make recommendations to the Security Council. By threatening to go over Molotov's head directly to Stalin, he had finally won this major Soviet concession. To promote good relations with Republicans in Congress, Truman gave the credit to Senator Vandenberg for making the General Assembly the "Town Meeting of the World."

At the evening reception, Truman shocked protocol officers when he grabbed the arms of two American newsmen and pulled them into

250

the receiving line to stand beside him. But the next day, when he went to the Opera House for the signing of the UN Charter, he was blandly sedate. He made an excellent speech, closing with: "Let us not fail to grasp this supreme chance to establish a world-wide rule of reason— to create an enduring peace under the guidance of God."

Now he went home for the first time since becoming President. The crowds were enormous at Kansas City on the twenty-seventh. When he rode in an open car with Bess and Margaret along the route to Independence, he remarked, "It swells me up like a p'izened pup." During his four-day stay he made several speeches and collected his first honorary degree. "I can't be President in Jackson County," he exclaimed. "I'm still county judge." To a crowd of 8,000 persons in the Independence auditorium of the Church of Jesus Christ of Latter Day Saints, he pointed out, "Time and again I've tried to fill this hall. This is the first time I've ever been able to do it." He told the Kansas City Jesters at lunch, "When I hear Republicans say I'm doing all right, I know damned well I'm wrong. . . . To keep from going high hat and stuffed shirt, I have to keep in mind Luke 6:26."

Truman also dropped into Eddie Jacobson's haberdashery store. "I want three white shirts, Eddie," he called out, "size 15½—33."

Jacobson was embarrassed. "I don't have any, Harry. You know, the war shortage. But I've got some red-hot bow ties."

Their friendship had never ebbed. On a later visit, he and Jacobson and some of the old gang spent an evening playing poker. Jacobson failed to win a single pot. The next day Truman walked into his store and bought 18 pair of size 11 socks. "I thought you'd need this sale after what we did to you last night," he said.

When he asked how business was, Jacobson replied, "It's wonderful, but you know there's one thing that's worrying me. It's this inflation." Truman agreed with him. "It worries me, too. But, Eddie, I'm watching it all the time."

Truman also spent some time with his mother. When photographers tried to take pictures, she said to her son, "If you're President, Harry, why can't you shoo all these people away?" She had refused to let Secret Service men guard her at home. "It isn't neighborly," she complained. Her eyesight had dimmed now that she was almost ninety-three, and she could no longer read the *Congressional Record* each day or maintain her heavy correspondence with Senators. Before Truman left, she cautioned him: "Don't be too good. I don't like being too good." He promised her he wouldn't.

Back again in Washington, he appeared before the Senate on July 2 and requested the ratification of the UN Charter. Afterward, he began his preparation for the forthcoming Potsdam Conference. He wrote Mamma and Mary on July 3: "Went to the Senate yesterday and you should have seen the carrying on they did. I could hardly shut 'em up so I could speak. . . . I am getting ready to see Stalin & Churchill, and it is a chore. I have to take my tuxedo, tails . . . preacher coat, high hat, low hat and hard hat."

29

WHEN Truman became President, it was Harry Hopkins' opinion that FDR's entire Cabinet should resign except Secretary of War Henry L. Stimson and Secretary of the Navy James V. Forrestal, who he felt should remain until the war was over. "Truman has got to have his own people around him," Hopkins insisted to Robert Sherwood. "If we're around, we'd always be looking at him and he'd know we were thinking, 'The *President* wouldn't do it that way.' "

Upon taking office, Truman had asked Roosevelt's Cabinet to remain. But he soon became aware that their loyalty was to the dead President and not to him. As weeks passed, he came to regard his inherited Cabinet as a "blankety-blank mudhole." According to reporter Bill Helm, Truman was especially peeved at Wallace, claiming that he had come to him one day and said, "I'm going to be your Left Hand in this Administration."

Before going to Potsdam, he replaced Secretary of Labor Frances Perkins with his former Senate colleague, Judge Lewis Schwellenbach. Washington correspondents had predicted that he would replace Attorney General Francis Biddle with Hugh Fulton. But Fulton, who had gone into private practice just before Truman became President, had irked him by sending out announcements, advertising himself as the former counsel of the Truman Committee. In place of Biddle, he appointed Tom Clark. Bob Hannegan replaced Frank Walker as Postmaster General; Representative Clinton Anderson of New Mexico succeeded Claude Wickard as Secretary of Agriculture; and now that the San Francisco Conference had ended, Jimmy Byrnes succeeded Edward Stettinius as Secretary of State.

Truman's original thought in offering Byrnes the post was that the Secretary of State was next in line to succeed him if he died, and he wanted an experienced politician to be waiting in the wings. In addition, he felt he owed a debt to Byrnes because he had won the Vice-Presidential nomination from him in 1944. Later, however, he confessed that his reasoning was less than sound when he told Bill Hassett, his corresponding secretary, "Whenever Jimmy came here and sat where you are now sitting, I could tell that he felt he should be sitting here in my chair."

Truman had a special problem with Secretary of the Treasury Henry Morgenthau, author of the so-called Morgenthau Plan, or "scorched earth" program for postwar Germany, designed to reduce an industrial nation to a rural society. Shortly before Truman was to leave for Potsdam, Morgenthau asked to accompany him, ostensibly to put the Morgenthau Plan into operation. Bluntly Truman told him he had to stay in Washington. But Morgenthau insisted upon going and asserted that if Truman would not take him, he would resign.

"All right," Truman snapped, "if that's the way you feel, I'll accept your resignation right now." To succeed Morgenthau, Truman appointed Fred Vinson as Treasury boss and moved John Snyder into Vinson's old post as War Mobilizer.

Having made these changes, Truman left Washington on July 6 and early the next morning boarded the U.S.S. *Augusta,* at Newport News, Virginia. During the eight-day voyage across the Atlantic, he took part in abandon-ship drill, saw a few movies in Jimmy Byrnes's cabin and stood in chow lines with the sailors. He spent most of his time, however, boning up for the forthcoming conference with Stalin and Churchill. A humorous mishap occurred when the *Augusta* reached Antwerp. One of Margaret's boy friends, a young lieutenant junior grade who was in charge of the harbor, refused to let the ship dock because it was drawing water. But when he learned who was aboard the *Augusta,* he lapsed into a state of shock. Truman later told Margaret that he should have brought her along to Potsdam in order to enter Antwerp.

Truman had ordered Eisenhower to arrange for accommodations and conference space for his party at Potsdam and all was now ready. After he went through the formalities of protocol at Antwerp, he flew to devastated Berlin and rode the autobahn twelve miles to his residence at Babelsberg, a suburb of Potsdam. He was now prepared to confront the gigantic task he had set for himself—peace for Europe and a revitalized continent.

Truman's residence was a three-story, yellow mansion at No. 2 Kaiserstrasse, the former home of the head of the German film colony who had recently been deported to Russia. Despite its color, the house was soon dubbed by Truman's staff as the "Little White House." It sat in a magnificent landscaped setting near a mosquito-infested lake. Not long afterward Winston Churchill, resplendent in the uniform of a colonel in the British Hussars, pulled into Babelsberg. His residence, which he renamed "10 Downing Street," sat at 23 Ringstrasse, two blocks from the yellow "Little White House." When he paid a call on Truman on July 16, it was the first time the two had met. Truman found him weary from his long and arduous wartime duties, and British aides said that he was anxious about the forthcoming British national election pitting him against Laborite Clement Attlee, whom he had brought along to the conference.

It was not until the seventeenth that Stalin arrived at his official residence, a mile from the "Little White House." Shortly before noon that day, he visited Truman and apologized for coming to the conference so late. His excuse was that he had not been feeling well, but actually, he had suffered a heart attack. Truman found Stalin extremely personable and polite, and in a burst of enthusiasm remarked to an aide, "Stalin is as near like Tom Pendergast as any man I know."

Although the Russians had provided a pleasant setting for the conference, Harry Vaughan was hardly impressed by their efficiency in clearing the area. "There are some lovely houses still standing between Potsdam and Berlin," he said. "The Russians gave the occupants an hour's notice to get out. One old lady was so attached to her house that she refused. She is now in the garden, under the flowers."

The first session of the Potsdam Conference got underway at 5 P.M. on the seventeenth. "Colonel Warden" (Churchill's code name), "the Other Admiral" (Truman) and "Uncle Joe" (Stalin) met around a table 12 feet in diameter in a large hall at Cecilienhof Palace, a two-story structure with four wings, which was the former residence of the Prussian Crown Prince.

The initial meeting started off well with Stalin cordially inviting Truman to serve as presiding officer. Nor was there immediate controversy when Truman spelled out his four-point agenda. First, he wanted to establish a Council of Foreign Ministers among the Big Five—the United States, Britain, Russia, France and China—to meet regularly to develop "peace negotiations and territorial settlements," which would be taken up at further conferences by the heads of their governments. He also desired a Control Council for Germany to bring about complete disarmament, eradicate Nazism and try war criminals. Third, he wanted free and unfettered elections in the liberated countries and in former enemy nations. His fourth point called for an easy peace with Italy and her early admission into the United Nations. He made several other auxiliary proposals, such as a TVA for Europe and China and the internationalization of the Rhine, Danube, Bosporus, Strait of Gibraltar and the Panama Canal.

Between sessions, the three leaders entertained each other at lavish affairs. Truman was first and he requested Sergeant Eugene List, the concert pianist, to play Chopin's Waltz in A-Flat Major, Opus 22, plus several Chopin nocturnes. List did not have the score of the Chopin waltz when he was notified to come to Potsdam, and American Army personnel frantically scoured Western European capitals before turning up a copy in Paris. While List played the poorly tuned piano, Truman stood beside him and turned the pages.

To Churchill classical music was torture, and he indignantly exclaimed to Admiral Leahy, "I'm bored to tears. I do not like this music. I'm going home." Stalin, on the other hand, was a Chopin devotee and enjoyed himself immensely. As the evening wore on, Stalin insisted that Truman play, too, and Truman complied with a rendition of Paderewski's Minuet in G. When Stalin was host on another night, Churchill was again in agony, for two Russian male pianists and two overweight lady violinists plowed through a long classical program. But next it was Churchill's turn to entertain and with "puckish malice," said Leahy, he got his revenge. The entire British Royal Air Force Orchestra played at his dinner and they blasted the air with explosive military pieces.

At Potsdam, Truman enjoyed a special link with his past when Colonel Curtis Tiernan, padre of the 129th in World War I and now Chief of Army Chaplains in the European Theater, was his guest at the Little White House. There were stories of the old days to recall with the padre and Vaughan and Fred Canfil, who looked as if he could throw a bull. "At Potsdam, one day after a meeting," Truman said, "I took Fred up to Stalin and I said, 'Marshal Stalin, I want you to meet Marshal Canfil.' Of course, I didn't tell him Fred was only a Federal marshal in Missouri and not a military marshal. Well, after that the Russians treated Fred with some respect. When the conferences were going on, Fred would stand by a window with his arms folded and scowl out the window at everybody who passed in the street. Fred was a little rough, but he was as loyal as a bulldog."

Despite the surface amiability, the meetings did not go well. Truman was irked by Churchill's long speeches on every point. Later he realized that the British statesman was doing this for the record, for future reference when the actual treaty-making parleys were held. Vaughan's interpretation of Churchill's speechmaking was that he was "a garrulous old gentleman who would never say anything in less than twenty words when ten words would do." As for the Soviet dictator, who sat smiling and sipping mild French wine, it became apparent to Truman that he had not the slightest intention of yielding an inch of newly controlled territory or permitting even a suggestion of democracy within his holdings. When Truman inquired about the rights of Catholics in Poland, for example, Stalin replied, "How many divisions has the Pope?" At one point, when Stalin insisted that Poland should acquire East Germany because no Germans remained in that area, Admiral Leahy whispered loudly to Truman, "Of course not. The Bolshies killed them all."

On July 25, after a week without progress among the Big Three, Churchill and Attlee left Potsdam for England to await the results of the British election. There would be a necessary delay until the victor returned to the Cecilienhof Palace, and on the twenty-eighth Truman wrote his mother and sister, "Well, here another week has gone, and I'm still in the Godforsaken country awaiting the return of the new British Prime Minister."

During this interlude, he flew to Frankfurt where he inspected troops and visited with General Eisenhower at his headquarters. On one occasion, he went for a drive with Eisenhower and General Omar Bradley through the bombed-out area. As their vehicle moved along, Eisenhower said, Truman talked about the peacetime future of the war leaders. "I have no ambitions except to retire to a quiet house,"

Eisenhower told him. According to Eisenhower, Truman said, "General, there is nothing that you may want that I won't try to help you get. That definitely and specifically includes the Presidency in 1948."

"Mr. President," said Eisenhower, "I don't know who will be your opponent for the Presidency, but it will not be I."

One of the tasks Truman had given Eisenhower and his command was to insure American access to Berlin, which lay deep within the Soviet Zone of Occupation. Instead of getting a written agreement, however, General Lucius Clay, Eisenhower's deputy, and General John Deane got an oral agreement from Marshal Zhukov, military governor of the Soviet Zone. Zhukov promised unrestricted use by the Western Allies of the railroad line running from Goslar to Berlin via Magdeburg, the use of the Hanau-Magdeburg-Berlin autobahn and a 20-mile-wide air corridor from Berlin to Magdeburg and two corridors connecting Frankfurt and Magdeburg. This oral agreement was later denied by the Russians and brought the United States and the Soviet Union to the brink of war in 1948. Truman placed the blame on Eisenhower for failing to get a written agreement.

When Attlee returned to Potsdam as the new British Prime Minister, Stalin claimed illness and stayed away from the conference table for two days. Truman wrote to his mother, "I really think he's not so sick but disappointed over the British elections." Attlee reported that Molotov was shocked because Churchill had not "fixed" the election.

The revised Big Three did not hold their first conference until 10:15 P.M. on July 30, when they discussed a Japanese request that Russia mediate the end of the war in the Far East on a vague status quo basis. Truman rejected this proposal. When the draft of an agreement to recognize Italy, Bulgaria, Rumania and Hungary came up, Secretary Byrnes reported with exasperation: "The United States has unfortunately found that if it agrees with the Soviet delegation, the British delegation does not agree, and if it agrees with the British, then the Soviet disagrees." On the question of reparations from the conquered nations, Truman flatly announced that the United States would not spend money to rehabilitate countries to help them pay reparations to other countries.

The Potsdam Conference ran through the thirteen sessions before it ended on August 2. Only the slightest beginning was made toward reconverting Europe from war to peace. The conferees had agreed to the establishment of the Council of Foreign Ministers, a compromise on Poland's borders, a formula for reparations, and Allied control principles in the administration of Occupied Germany. There was also Stalin's reaffirmation to enter the war against Japan. But these were the only achievements. Truman gave his impression of the conference in a letter to his mother and sister: "You never saw such pig-headed people as are the Russians. I hope I never have to hold another conference with them."

It was at Potsdam that Truman made a momentous decision. Word had reached him of the successful explosion of an atomic bomb on July 16 at Alamogordo, New Mexico. When he mentioned this horrifying new weapon to Stalin on July 24, Stalin merely shrugged and said he hoped Truman would make "good use of it against the Japanese." Churchill also advised him to use the bomb.

But first, on July 26, Truman issued an ultimatum calling on Japan to surrender, an ultimatum that was beamed continuously over the air waves, passed through neutral diplomatic channels to the Japanese Government and dropped over the Japanese mainland in the form of 27 million leaflets. The official Japanese reply was that the ultimatum was "absurd" and that fighting would continue.

With his military advisers insisting that an invasion of Kyushu and Honshu would result in a half million American casualties, the time had come for Truman to decide whether to use the A-bomb on Japan. He was aware that a poll of 150 American scientists indicated that almost 90 per cent urged dropping the bomb without warning and on an important objective. Truman discussed the matter with his military advisers, including Marshall, Eisenhower, Leahy and Admiral Ernest King. At first Marshall opposed using the A-bomb, although he later yielded to group opinion. Some time afterward he told a reporter that there had been some discussion of staging a nonmilitary demonstration to forewarn Japan of the terror of the new weapon, but "we had only two [bombs] and the situation demanded shock action."

The final decision was Truman's alone. "I did not hesitate to order the use of the bomb on military targets," he later said. "I wanted to save a half million boys on our side and as many on the other side. I never lost any sleep over my decision."

Once his mind was made up, he ordered Secretary of War Stimson to prepare a list of military targets. Four cities were selected for possible A-bomb obliteration: Hiroshima, Kokura, Niigata and Nagasaki. Truman then ordered General Carl Spatz to drop one of the two existing A-bombs on any of these target cities. On August 2, when Truman said good-by to Stalin at Potsdam, the bomb had not yet been dropped. It was 3 A.M. when he told Stalin he hoped they would get together again in Washington. Stalin replied, "God willing." TERMINAL, the code name for the Potsdam Conference, was at an end. Never again were the two destined to meet, although they were to wage long-distance cold war for almost seven years.

At 8:15 A.M. on the morning of August 6, Japanese time, the destruction of Hiroshima initiated the atomic age. Truman was lunching with sailors aboard the *Augusta,* then off the New Jersey coast, when Captain Frank Graham brought him Stimson's message acknowledging "complete success." Excitedly, he explained to the sailors what had occurred. Then he told Captain Graham, "This is the greatest thing in history. It's time for us to get home."

After Hiroshima, Truman expected a quick Japanese surrender. But when the Japanese Government procrastinated, the Air Force dropped the second bomb over Nagasaki on August 9. The Russians, fearful that they might be deprived of war spoils, territory and new political power in the Far East, jumped into the war that same day.

Confronted with the horror of the second atomic bomb, the Japanese finally surrendered on August 14, after Truman agreed with Under Secretary of State Joseph Grew that Emperor Hirohito should remain as titular head of his nation. The postwar world had now arrived.

30

O N V-J Day, September 2, 1945, after almost four years of war, the industrial potential of the United States was at an all-time high. A veritable revolution had taken place in the country. The number of those in the labor force had skyrocketed because millions of women and farmers had gone to work in war plants and factories. Technical skills had improved accordingly because of the complexities and exacting standards required in producing implements of war. In addition, animosities toward minority groups had slackened since Pearl Harbor and a further push in this direction was needed to prevent backsliding. Millions of GIs would soon be returning home and there was the danger of disillusionment setting in if they did not find opportunities for employment, education and housing.

Truman was determined that the country must not be allowed to flounder at this crucial time. There must be no return to so-called pre-war "normalcy" with 10,000,000 unemployed in 1940. There must be no resurgence of the fire-eating isolationism that had saddled the nation during Roosevelt's first two terms. Economists were already warning that unemployment would reach a total of 8,000,000 persons with the cutoff of war production. Nor was the ink yet dry on the Japanese surrender document when the isolationists emerged from their wartime silence to resume their call for avoidance of all foreign entanglements.

Only four days after V-J Day, Truman sent Congress a 21-point program on domestic legislation for the postwar world. It was a 16,000-word message, the longest handed to Congress since Teddy Roosevelt's 1901 message of 21,000 words. Truman's close friend, John Snyder, then in charge of reconversion, had argued strenuously against submitting this far-reaching liberal call for action with the plea that it broke too much fresh ground. But Truman was not to be deterred.

Truman's September 6 message hit Congress like a bombshell. Up to this point the Republicans in Congress had been smugly content with the belief that Truman would be a conservative and innocuous President. Now they stormed, fumed and let out a roar of indignation. They objected to his call for an "Economic Bill of Rights," which Roosevelt had originally stated in January, 1944. These included the right to a job at fair pay, the right of every family to a decent home and adequate medical care, the right to a good education, the right of farmers to raise and sell crops at prices that would enable them to support their families properly and the right of businessmen to trade in an atmosphere not polluted by unfair competition and monopoly. To implement these rights, Truman asked for a full-employment act, increased minimum wages, extension of unemployment compensation to those not covered by existing law, increased farm price supports, private and public housing programs, a national health program, aid to education, increased Social Security payments, power-development programs patterned after the TVA for a number of river valleys and a permanent Fair Employment Practices Committee to provide equal job opportunities for all Americans regardless of race or religion. He also asked for the continuation of the draft of young men into the armed services and the retainment of some wartime controls to fight inflation.

This message ended Truman's honeymoon with Congress. Joe Martin, Republican leader in the House, epitomized the outrage of his party against the supposedly harmless White House occupant when he said, "Now, nobody should have any more doubt. Not even President Roosevelt ever asked so much at one sitting. It is just a case of out-New Dealing the New Deal."

From this time on, Truman's opponents resorted to every means to discredit him. It was a fight that lasted as long as he was President.

Abruptly, editorial tone changed toward him. He was assessed as "bewildered," a "little man" who "never seemed to understand." One author quoted first-term Democratic Senator William Fulbright of Arkansas as saying he went to see Truman and "I didn't make a bit of an impression on the President. He didn't know what I was talking about." Bill Helm, who had covered Truman for a Kansas City paper since 1934, said that one newsman was told by his editor, "When you go to the White House find out all you can about Truman's drinking parties. I hear he drinks like a fish. Find out what he drinks. Find out how much. Find out who puts him to bed when he gets tight." Another reporter wrote, "The President was up at the crack of dawn, six-fifteen. He walked to the Mississippi River and spit in it."

Truman also found himself the butt of jokes. One bright saying went "To err is Truman"; another, "What would Truman do if he were alive?" He was erroneously charged with a variety of misdeeds. Once, in self-defense, he wrote in a letter: "For your information, I never played golf in my life, never had a golf club in my hands to tell the honest truth, except to look at it—so I couldn't possibly have fired a ball on the Independence Golf Course and hit anybody on the head."

Truman felt that he was one of the few Presidents subjected to such vituperation. But his resentment over the attacks made on him was mild compared with his anger at the attacks on Bess and Margaret. "I have never cared about all the lies that were said about me as long as I knew what I was doing was right," he insisted, "but there is no reason to malign the women in the White House." Margaret said that the papers wrote about her as being "phlegmatic" and having a "hunchy" carriage, "crooked" nose, "matronly" figure, "heavy" legs, no "taste" or "style" and wearing "washed-out pastels."

Truman added that "the attacks made on Mrs. Truman were almost as bad as those made on the two most maligned women in the White House, Mrs. Lincoln and Mrs. Franklin Roosevelt." Actually, most of the attacks on Bess were petty and stemmed from resentment because she refused to hold press conferences, express herself on political issues or speak in public.

"Truman never forgave anyone who cast the slightest slur on his womenfolk," Harry Vaughan declared. "Two members of Congress were barred from the White House because of what they said about

263

Mrs. Truman. These were Adam Clayton Powell and Clare Boothe Luce." In the fall of 1945, when the Daughters of the American Revolution refused to let Powell's wife, Hazel Scott, perform at Constitution Hall, Powell insisted that Mrs. Truman reject a D.A.R. invitation. While Mrs. Truman issued a statement deploring the anti-Negro action of the D.A.R. she said she had accepted the invitation before the incident occurred. "Powell referred to her as the 'Last Lady of the Land,'" Vaughan said, "and Truman boiled at his language."

Nor would Truman forgive Mrs. Luce for her attack on Bess during the 1944 campaign. "One time," Vaughan reported, "Henry Luce came to the White House and asked Truman why his wife was barred. 'Mr. Luce,' Truman replied, 'you've asked a fair question and I'll give you a fair answer. I've been in politics thirty-five years and everything that could be said about a human being has been said about me. But my wife has never been in politics. She has always conducted herself in a circumspect manner and no one has a right to make derogatory remarks about her. Now your wife has said many unkind and untrue things about Mrs. Truman. And as long as I am in residence here, she'll not be a guest in the White House.'"

Thomas Jefferson once observed that the American people expect Presidents to be aloof and unsmiling in public. Truman could never achieve such a pose and assume a false front of aloofness. It was his openness and his grin, his love of horseplay and wisecracks, his inability to articulate the decisions he made in lofty phrases and his absolute lack of snobbishness that added mortar to the brickbats thrown at him by opponents.

Bill Hassett, who served as aide to both Roosevelt and Truman, once noted: "Just as Mr. Truman was more earthy, so also he probably was of a warmer nature than the Hudson Valley squire. Mr. Truman was a direct and uninhibited President—not merely of the earth but at times mundane in the extreme." Truman's frankness and friendliness worked to his great disadvantage. He lacked the fatherly public image of Roosevelt. In private both FDR and Eisenhower frequently used barracks language, but in public they wrapped themselves in a mantle of dignity. Unfortunately, Truman used the same language in public as in private.

Truman's simplicity soon lessened Congressional confidence in him. Several weeks after sending his 21-point program to Congress, he attended a Congressional Democratic outing at Jefferson Island in Chesapeake Bay. He might have remained aloof, but he let everyone call him Harry without protest, laughed heartily at off-color stories and joined the game of stud poker on the porch. Instead of establishing the point that he did not consider himself exclusive just because he was President, his behavior resulted in creating an opposite impression—that anyone could be President.

This impression was intensified in October when he attended the Pemiscot County Fair at Caruthersville, Missouri. Reporters were astonished when he mingled with the crowd on a "Harry" basis and discussed local political problems with farmers wearing overalls. When an old American Legion 40-&-8 locomotive came by, he ran into the street to toot its whistle. He played piano for the Methodist Church ladies, and reporters failed to add to their stories that he winked at the ladies as he said, "When I played this, Stalin signed the Potsdam Agreement."

From the outset of his occupancy of the White House, Truman knew that the New Dealers who had been close to Roosevelt regarded him with suspicion. They failed to remember his superb leadership of the wartime Truman Committee and refused to accept the fact that Roosevelt had personally requested him to be his running mate in 1944. To the old New Deal clan, Truman was merely President by accident.

Not even his strong New Deal message to Congress on September 6 allayed their animosity. Nor did their attitude change when he sent a letter on October 4 to his Cabinet members urging them to fight for his proposals and to report to him twice a month on their progress. After all, they whispered among themselves, hadn't he invited the hated Herbert Hoover to the White House and hadn't he sent him on a 35,000-mile mission around the world to report on food needs abroad? Moreover, wasn't he dropping members of the Roosevelt entourage left and right?

In the fall of 1945, Truman sought to ease this formidable opposition from the left wing of the Democratic Party. Jimmy Byrnes said that Truman told him that "there were two persons he had to have on his political team: Secretary Wallace and Mrs. Eleanor Roosevelt—Mr. Wallace because of his influence with labor and Mrs. Roosevelt because of her influence with the Negro voters." Truman pointedly gave Wallace assurance of his continued friendship and support as Secretary of Commerce and named Mrs. Roosevelt to the United States delegation to the United Nations.

Secretary of the Interior "Honest Harold" Ickes, the self-styled "old curmudgeon," posed a special problem. Truman considered him a "troublemaker" as well as a "scold and a gossip and everything that implies." Long before, when Truman had headed the Senate War Investigating Committee, Ickes had confided in him that he had had a verbal free-for-all with Roosevelt and had been barred from the White House for six months. It was too much to expect that Ickes would change his ways with Truman. Every White House suggestion was a challenge to his own sovereignty over the Interior Department. As an original New Dealer, he viewed Truman as an interloper and considered it an indignity that he was his superior.

This situation could not continue, and the break between the two came early in 1946. Before he died, Roosevelt had intended naming Ed Pauley Under Secretary of the Navy with the understanding that he would later succeed Forrestal. Truman now decided to carry this intention out and sent Pauley's nomination to the Senate in January, 1946.

On January 30, Ickes lagged behind after a Cabinet meeting and told Truman he had been asked to testify before the Senate Naval Affairs Committee regarding Pauley's fitness. "You must tell the truth, of course," Ickes claimed Truman said. "But be as gentle as you can with Ed." Ickes promised him he would. Nevertheless, hardly had Ickes taken the witness chair when he testified under oath that Pauley had approached him in 1940 with "the rawest proposition ever made to me." He insisted that Pauley had pressured him against favoring a government suit to claim Federal control of offshore tidelands oil fields. He said Pauley had called it "bad politics" that "might cost several hundred thousand dollars in campaign contributions." He tried to conjure up the picture of an oilman running the Navy's vast oil holdings and let the committee make its own comparison with the Teapot Dome scandal of the Harding days.

In great indignation and also under oath, Pauley denied he had ever made this "rawest proposition" to Ickes. But he soon realized that the committee was opposed to him in any event and requested Truman to withdraw his nomination.

Although Truman was incensed at Ickes for thwarting Pauley's nomination, he made no move to drop him from the Cabinet. Ickes himself provided the opening for his removal by sending Truman a letter of resignation on February 13; the kind of letter, as Truman described it, "sent by a man who is sure that he can have his way if he threatens to quit." During his long Cabinet tenure, Ickes had frequently written letters of resignation to Roosevelt, knowing that FDR would tear up the notes. But Truman did no such thing. He told Ickes that he was through. Taken aback, Ickes demanded that he be kept on for six weeks more to handle unfinished business. "Your resignation is accepted as of tomorrow," Truman wrote him on February 14.

Firing Ickes only served to reinforce the view of the Roosevelt stalwarts that Truman did not favor the New Deal. Coupled with the strong Republican opposition, the defection of the New Dealers left Truman at the head of a very small army. Even before the Ickes episode, *Life* Magazine had noted, "Washington has begun to turn against him." After Ickes, came the deluge.

There is good reason to believe that had Roosevelt lived, his reputation would have been tarnished during the postwar period. For one thing, during his last two years in office his relations with Congress had deteriorated badly. For another, the beginning of reconversion from war to peace led to unavoidable confusion in the nation's life. Basically, the country wanted the depression period's low prices and abundance of consumer goods even as it enjoyed high wages, full employment and large profits. This was a tall order under any circumstances and no President could have filled it.

Given these impossible goals, all the conflicting animosities and demands, repressed during the war years, now burst forth. Labor leaders demanded that wage controls be eliminated but price controls retained. Business and industry wanted wage ceilings but no top limit on prices. Farmers wanted higher prices for their crops; housewives, lower prices; bankers, higher interest charges. There was also a national demand for immediate demobilization despite the threat of Communism abroad. Congress was deluged with baby shoes with cards attached that read: *I want my daddy back.* Much of this organized campaign was Communist-inspired, as a later investigation revealed.

Since there was no way to satisfy all the contending forces, Truman found himself blamed personally for every new problem that arose. With everyone pulling at him for help and special treatment, he frequently lost his temper. In the spring of 1946, for instance, Senator Charles Tobey of New Hampshire sent a telegram urging him to set aside grain for the poultrymen of New England: THIS IS A MACEDONIAN CRY!

Truman, who could hardly forget that Tobey had led the Republicans against Pauley when he was nominated as Under Secretary of the Navy, penned a hasty reply.

> It seems to me that you have been making Macedonian cries or yells ever since I have been in the White House. For what reasons I could never understand. . . . You are still continuing your Macedonian cries, and I hope you will get a lot of pleasure out of them.

The postwar pressures on Truman were so great that at one point he sat down and wrote a memo to himself in which he said he needed four new Kitchen Cabinet Secretaries. One would be the Secretary for Inflation, to convince everyone that no matter how high prices rose or how low wages fell, no real problem existed. The second would be the Secretary of Reaction, to abolish "flying machines" and "restore oxcarts, oar boats and sailing ships." The third would be the Secretary for Columnists, with the function of reading all columns and then giving him the results so he could "run the United States and the world as it should be." Last there would be a Secretary of Semantics to furnish him with "40- to 50-dollar words." This Secretary would also tell him how to keep quiet and say everything at the same time and would put him against inflation in one city and for it in another.

By the end of his first year as President, Truman was to claim that Congress had given him less cooperation and more trouble than any President since Andrew Jackson. He had requested Congress to raise the minimum wage from 40 cents to 65 cents an hour, but Congress killed the proposal. His efforts to set up a permanent Fair Employment Practices Committee were also to no avail. Instead of the full-employment legislation he demanded, Congress, in February, 1946, gave him a watered-down version whose chief accomplishment was the establishment of the Council of Economic Advisers to keep him informed about economic conditions. When he asked for a strengthened U. S. Employment Service, Congress returned this function to the states. Nor did he get anywhere with his demands for public housing, a national health insurance program or the extension of Social Security benefits.

He had requested a strong price-control bill because supplies of basic commodities came nowhere near meeting demand. When Congress passed a weak bill in June, 1946, he therefore promptly vetoed it. Even though he had acted on principle, his veto proved costly. For when price and rent controls were abolished on July 1, landlords across the nation doubled and trebled rents and evicted tenants. Butter rose to a dollar a pound. Within two weeks prices on 28 basic commodities shot up 25 per cent. Instead of being praised for acting on principle, he was vilified. Then, when meat controls were reinstated in August, he was again lambasted because meat dealers held supplies out of regular channels in order to sell on the black market. One writer noted that "a housewife who cannot get hamburger is more dangerous than Medea wronged."

But these were not all of Truman's dilemmas. When he returned from Potsdam, he faced a unique problem that dogged him throughout the first half of 1946. The atomic bombs dropped on Hiroshima and Nagasaki had ended the war against Japan. But what to do now with this monstrous new weapon?

By the end of September, public hysteria about the bomb had developed to a high pitch. Several influential persons denounced the original dropping of the bomb as unnecessary. These amateur military analysts declared that Japan was on the verge of surrender even before the flights over Hiroshima and Nagasaki. The implication of their statements was that Truman had acted barbarously against Orientals. Saber-rattlers at the other extreme frightened the public with demands that A-bomb production be stepped up and that a stockpile of bombs be made ready for drops on the Soviet Union if the Russians continued to misbehave.

With public frenzy at a peak, Truman could no longer delay and he therefore sent a message on this subject to Congress on October 3, 1945. He asked for the establishment of a domestic Atomic Energy Commission, with Congress laying down its basic principles. He also said that he would develop an international atomic policy only after discussing it with England and Canada and then exploring the field with other nations. "The alternative," he said, "may be a desperate armament race which might well end in disaster."

Truman's statement did much to brake the hysteria. But only a few days later he brought on even greater panic by off-the-cuff remarks made at a news conference at Reelfoot Lake, near Tiptonville, Tennessee. When a reporter asked if he planned to share atomic secrets with other countries, Truman replied that there were no secrets about atomic power among the scientists of the world. But, he added, the United States was the only nation possessing the resources and practical ability to produce the atomic bomb at that time. Pressed further, he declared he had no intention of giving the bomb's secrets away to any other country—"not the know-how of putting it together." At this point Charlie Ross cut in and argued with Truman to keep his remarks off the record. "No, I want it on the record," he insisted. He was surprised when the reporters immediately raced to telephones.

The following morning's headlines read: TRUMAN SAYS U.S. TO KEEP ATOMIC BOMB SECRET. Editorials denounced him for having created confusion because his remarks did not jibe with his October 3 Message to Congress. His news conference also created a furor in England and resulted in a hurried Washington conference between Truman, Prime Minister Attlee and Canadian Prime Minister Mac-Kenzie King. At this meeting, the news conference remarks were rescinded and the three leaders issued a joint declaration on November 15. This declaration reaffirmed cooperation among the three powers on atomic energy and a willingness to share information on a reciprocal basis with other members of the United Nations "just as soon as effective enforceable safeguards against its use for destructive purposes can be devised."

But if this settled for the time being public concern over international control, it still left in mid-air the problem of controlling atomic energy production and use within the United States. A new wave of arguments broke out over the May-Johnson Bill, which proposed establishing a permanent Manhattan District Project under complete military domination.

At first Truman stayed out of the fight over this bill on the grounds that Congress should make its own decision. But on November 30, he announced that he favored civilian and not military control of atomic energy. Accordingly, Senator Brien McMahon introduced a bill taking this approach. Truman, however, made the mistake of not muzzling Administration officials. As a result, bewildering chaos followed when they presented conflicting views to Congress. Major General Leslie Groves, who had headed the $2,000,000,000 Manhattan Project during the war, demanded military control under a nine-man independent commission with the administrator appointed by the commission and not by the President. When Secretary of the Navy Forrestal appeared at the Congressional hearing, he was asked if the President should be solely responsible for deciding on the use of atomic bombs. He replied, "That is too big a responsibility to drop on him." Among the scientists, Dr. James Conant and Vannevar Bush supported military control, while Dr. Robert Oppenheimer, the scientist chiefly responsible for the production of the bomb, opposed this.

It was not until January 23, 1946, that Truman finally wrote a memo to Forrestal and his new Secretary of War, Robert Patterson, in which he insisted on civilian control and stated that he expected them to adhere to this view "without modification." On February 2, he also made public a letter he had sent to McMahon in which he called for an Atomic Energy Commission composed "exclusively of civilians. . . . The Government must be the exclusive owner and producer of fissionable material."

The fight to insure civilian control over atomic energy raged until the end of July, when the Atomic Energy Commission was approved by Congress. The civilian AEC would have complete control over its operations, and only the President could decide on the use of atomic bombs.

At the same time that he was beset by the problems of atomic energy, Truman, of course, had to contend with the many reconversion questions crossing his desk. A most vexing concern was the large number of strikes disrupting the economic life of the country. Labor and management were at each other's throats in the oil, lumber, aircraft, meatpacking, aluminum, rubber, automobile and steel industries. The United Auto Workers' strike against General Motors alone idled 175,000 workers in 19 states.

In November, 1945, he brought 36 representatives of labor and management to Washington and insisted they offer him recommendations for a truce. After three weeks of wrangling, however, they came up with nothing and he took action on his own. Despite the opposition of John Snyder, he appeared before Congress on December 3 and asked for legislation to set up fact-finding boards to investigate each dispute, with a 30-day cooling-off period during which strikes would be prohibited.

When Congress refused to act on his proposal, Truman established fact-finding boards by Executive Order, even though Attorney General Tom Clark advised him that they had no legal basis. The first fact-finding board investigated the dispute in the steel industry and recommended a wage increase of 18½¢ an hour. Satisfied that this raise could be granted without a major price increase, Truman helped settle the steel strike on this basis. Soon afterward, the UAW concluded its 113-day strike against General Motors with a similar settlement and other industries fell into line along this pattern.

Then, just when it seemed he had conquered the plague of strikes by this formula, new trouble broke out in the spring of 1946. In the railroad industry, where more than 300,000 workers were on strike, Truman was able to satisfy 18 of the 20 unions with the 18½¢ an hour increase. Ironically, Alvanley Johnson, of the Brotherhood of Locomotive Engineers, and Alexander Whitney, of the Brotherhood of Railway Trainmen, who had worked hard for Truman's re-election to the Senate in 1940, were the two holdouts.

When Johnson and Whitney sent word to their members that a strike would begin on May 18, Truman called them to the White House and told them bluntly, "If you think I'm going to sit here and let you tie up this country, you're crazy as hell. I am going to protect the public and we are going to run these railroads and you can put that in your pipe and smoke it!" Truman later referred to Johnson as a "damned Republican."

After the two postponed their strike until May 23, Truman and his special assistant on labor, Dr. John Steelman, met with them again. When Truman refused to force the railroads to grant them further concessions, they stumbled furiously out of the White House. Johnson told reporters, "Truman listened to the advice of banker John Snyder, the labor baiter, and the suggestion made by fascist Burton K. Wheeler."

Truman was now thoroughly incensed. The following day, when the strike began, he issued an order for the Government to seize the railroads. The railroad workers, however, did not return to their jobs. Drastic measures were called for, and on Friday evening, the twenty-fourth, with the strike one day old, Truman addressed the nation, announcing that he would ask Congress to authorize the Army to run the railroads. In this speech, widely condemned for its angry tone, he said: "The crisis of Pearl Harbor was the result of action by a foreign enemy. The crisis tonight is caused by a group of men within our country who place their private interests above the welfare of the nation."

Early the next morning he began preparing a message he would deliver to a joint session of Congress that afternoon. Charlie Ross said, "He wanted Congress to pass legislation to draft workers on strike against the Government into the Army, and make them run the trains as buck privates." Ross added, "He had two speeches—one to use if the strike was still on, and the other if Whitney and Johnson caved in before he got to the Capitol."

Truman left for the Hill after 3 P.M. When he strode into the Capitol, his mouth drawn into a tight straight line, he was told that the strike was still on. The truth was, according to Whitney, that he and Johnson had agreed to call off the strike long before Truman stepped up to the rostrum of the House. Not aware of this, Truman began reading the harsh version of his speech. At 4:10, he had just finished saying "I request the Congress immediately to authorize the President to draft into the armed forces of the United States all workers who are on strike against the Government," when Les Biffle tugged at his sleeve and gave him the news that Whitney and Johnson had capitulated. "Gentlemen, the strike has been settled," Truman told a cheering Congress.

The railroad workers went back to their trains, but not before Senator Wayne Morse of Oregon, who believed that Truman had known of the settlement before he started to speak, assailed his speech as "one of the cheapest exhibitions of ham acting." Later, however, when he learned the truth, he retracted his statement. Violently bitter, Whitney announced that Truman had "signed his political death warrant." Not long afterward, his Trainmen voted a $2,500,000 war chest to use against Truman if he ran for election in 1948. In New York, the C.I.O. conference labeled Truman "the No. 1 strike breaker of the American bankers and railroads."

Thus, although Truman had acted boldly to keep the economy moving, he added labor to his Republican and New Deal opposition. Not even his veto of the anti-labor Case Bill in June won him back any tangible labor support.

At the same time that Truman was in the midst of his struggle with Whitney and Johnson, he was also engaged in a battle with John L. Lewis. In the spring of 1946, Lewis threatened a strike unless bituminous coal operators set up a welfare fund for the 400,000 soft-coal miners and paid into it a royalty on coal tonnage mined, with Lewis to be sole boss of the welfare fund. It was Truman's opinion that Lewis was trying to impress other labor leaders by showing them "that he could intimidate" the President. Truman took time off from his fracas with the Railroad Brotherhoods to summon Lewis to the White House for discussions, and although Lewis did not recede from his demand, Truman won his agreement "to carrying on negotiations without calling a strike."

On April Fool's day, when Lewis suddenly ordered his miners out on strike, Truman was furious with what he considered the breaking of a solemn promise. But he waited until May 21 before ordering the Department of Interior to take over the mines. During this seven-

273

week shutdown of the mines, the nation lost the use of the normal production of 90,000,000 tons of coal. Nevertheless, Truman did not punish Lewis, except to bar him henceforth from the White House.

In fact, Lewis came out ahead, for Julius Krug, the new Interior Secretary, negotiated a contract with him providing for joint control of the welfare fund. For the time being, Truman's troubles with Lewis subsided. But in September, with Interior still operating the mines, Lewis started several minor disputes with Krug regarding the welfare fund. Then on November 1, Lewis abruptly served notice that he considered his contract at an end and issued a strike call for the twentieth.

This time the strike was against the Government and not against coal operators. Truman wrote in a memo to himself, "Mr. Lewis wanted to be sure that the President would be in the most embarrassing position possible for the Congressional elections on November 6." When the miners left the pits, Truman ordered Attorney General Clark to get a court injunction against Lewis to force him to cancel the strike. Lewis defied the injunction and was hauled into court on December 4 where he was fined $10,000 for his contempt of the injunction and the United Mine Workers $3,500,000. Lewis was no longer defiant when he meekly ordered the miners to return to work. The Supreme Court later cut the UMW fine to $700,000, but this did not raise Lewis's opinion of Truman. At a Cabinet meeting Krug told Truman that "Lewis had boasted he would get Krug first, Clark second and the Navy third, and that he would wait until 1948 to get the President." Some time after that Lewis gave this description of Truman to the UMW convention:

> "He is a man totally unfitted for the position. His principles are elastic, and he is careless with the truth. He has no special knowledge of any subject, and he is a malignant, scheming sort of an individual who is dangerous not only to the United Mine Workers, but dangerous to the United States of America."

Truman learned an important lesson from his early troubles. The greater his attention to the national welfare the more he antagonized the various segments of the population.

31

THE initial period of Truman's term in office would have been extremely difficult even if there were only the problems of reconversion to resolve. But there was still another fundamental problem to consider—the foreign policy of the United States.

With regard to the Western Allies, he lost little time in establishing the principle that selfish national interests were not to hamstring postwar settlements. Among his earliest decisions were those to thwart French efforts to take over part of Italy, to seize a large share of Occupied Germany and to re-establish French colonial domination of Syria and Lebanon. He had also served notice on Churchill that it was not his intention to help Britain continue her traditional role of power politics in the Mediterranean and other areas of the world.

Of course Truman had to act with even more vigor to hold the wartime allies of the Communist bloc in line. During the postwar confusion, for instance, Marshal Tito, the emerging Communist dictator of Yugoslavia, moved to seize the Italian-populated city of Trieste. Swiftly Truman let Tito know that he was determined to oust him from Trieste, by force if necessary, in order to place the city and the western zone of Venezia Giulia under Anglo-American occupation. "I drove Tito out of Trieste, or rather I scared him off from moving in, which he was planning to do with Stalin's backing," he told Cabell Phillips of *The New York Times*. "I did the same thing later with Stalin when he was threatening to settle his forces down for good in Iran. I ordered the Mediterranean Fleet into the Persian Gulf and told Stalin he had better get out before they got there. And he did, too."

During these crucial early months, Truman had to act largely on instinct to make his decisions. As Admiral Leahy put it, "Everyone, including Truman himself, knew that in the field of international relations he had much to learn." But he was highly educable, Leahy added. "He absorbed very quickly."

When Truman returned from Potsdam, he was convinced that the Russians were bent on world conquest. Only a strong deterrent power would prevent them from pushing ahead rapidly and expanding their domain. In Eastern Europe, they had taken over the governments of neighboring countries, while in Western Europe, Communist agents were already laying the groundwork for eventual control. On the far side of the Urals, the Communists were filling the vacuum created by the surrender of the Japanese.

Truman realized that moral suasion would not hold the Communists in check. The United States had used its only two A-bombs on Japan, but more were being produced. Until the Russians had their own bombs, they would not risk a war with the United States. But even the existence of the American atomic weapon would not deter the Russians from using the Hitlerian techniques of divide and conquer, misrepresentation of motives and psychological warfare to gain their ends.

One of Truman's hopes was to maintain a large American military force in Europe so that Stalin would hesitate to make overt military moves on the Continent. But military strategy had demanded that a large share of American forces be shifted to the Pacific theater to finish off Japan. At war's end, when enormous pressures were brought to bear on Congress for speedy demobilization, the Army lost half its strength in a single year and within two years the original 9,000,000-man Army dwindled to a million.

In the face of Soviet policy Truman saw no point in making Russia stronger by offering her generous postwar aid. On August 21, 1945, only a week after the collapse of Japan, he ordered the end of

Lend-Lease shipments. To those who held the view that Russia could be made more cooperative by aiding her in her postwar reconstruction, this action was considered a blunder. Harry Hopkins, who belonged to this school, wrote to Mrs. Roosevelt, "We are doing almost everything we can to break with Russia, which seems so unnecessary to me." When Truman announced that he expected the Soviet Union to make a settlement on the $11,000,000,000 of Lend-Lease aid, howls of the "friendship with Russia" group increased. Nor did their anguish abate when Stalin asked for a $6,000,000,000 loan from the United States and Secretary of State Byrnes first said he had lost the request and later admitted he had put it in his "forgotten file."

The trouble with ending Lend-Lease was that it affected Britain as well as the USSR. England immediately suffered a severe financial crisis, and Attlee asked for a $5- to $6-billion, fifty-year, interest-free loan. Truman agreed to a loan, although his negotiators drove a hard bargain. Fred Vinson recommended only $3.1 billion and Assistant Secretary of State Will Clayton, $4 billion, but Truman finally compromised with an offer of $3,750,000,000 at 2 per cent interest that was not to be charged until a five-year grace period elapsed.

While Truman groped toward a new American foreign policy, he committed a serious administrative error. Dave Niles, assistant to both FDR and Truman, said, "Truman hadn't had time to consider the problems of government administration until after Potsdam. He was in one hell of a rush until then just settling the hundreds of questions piling on top of him. Then, when he was in a position to put his own ideas on government administration to work, he operated on an entirely different basis from FDR's. Roosevelt never clung to staff lines. Often he gave the same assignment to two or three people and had everyone who worked for him competing against each other to get his view across. All day long he sent out dozens of handwritten chits to government people to work on various questions and send him data. In this way, he was his own government and knew what was going on all over Washington. It was a sort of master intelligence system.

"Truman didn't start out like that," Niles went on. "He delegated the work to the departments involved, let them run their own shows and then backed up their decisions. This couldn't last long because the trouble with this policy was that it developed little czars who considered themselves bosses within their own domains. It couldn't last without making Truman look like a Throttlebottom. And he was anything but that."

It was Secretary of State Byrnes who inadvertently led Truman to abandon this approach to government operation. After returning from Potsdam, Byrnes assessed Truman's theory of government administration at face value and seldom consulted him on foreign policy, a situation that soon became known throughout Washington. At one news conference, a reporter went so far as to ask Truman, "Do you support the State Department policy?" Truman's face turned red with anger.

The issue came to a head in December, 1945, when Byrnes went to Moscow for the Conference of Foreign Ministers. After he left Washington, Senators Connally and Vandenberg hurried to tell Truman that the four-point plan Byrnes would present for international control of atomic energy put the cart before the horse by proposing the exchange of information before arranging for such safeguards as inspection and supervision. Truman immediately wired Byrnes to switch the order of the items in his proposal.

The Moscow Conference of Foreign Ministers was a dismal defeat for the Western Powers. The Foreign Ministers unanimously approved Byrnes's atomic-energy-control declaration in its original form and order of presentation. In addition, Byrnes agreed to a five-year United States-Russian Trusteeship in Korea instead of calling for an election of a unified Korean Government; a Far Eastern Commission, including Russia, which plagued General MacArthur's efforts to rehabilitate Japan; and a set of ground rules that favored the Soviet Union at the Peace Treaty Conference to be held in Paris in 1946 on treaties covering Bulgaria, Hungary, Rumania, Finland and Italy.

"Byrnes lost his nerve in Moscow," Truman said when he learned from the newspapers about the terms of the Moscow agreements. Byrnes's defiance of the President's wishes, his refusal to keep him informed, and the fact that the terms of the agreement were so disadvantageous to the United States made Truman realize his theory of government administration was fine as an academic treatise but would not do in actual operation. When Byrnes returned to Washington and, without consulting him, made arrangements for a four-network radio broadcast to report on the conference, Truman's temper exploded.

Truman was aboard the Presidential yacht *Williamsburg,* anchored at Quantico, Virginia, when Byrnes called Charlie Ross to ask if he had got in touch with the radio networks for his nationwide speech. "Tell Jimmy to get down here as fast as he can and report to me before he does a damn thing," Truman told Ross.

There are two versions of what occurred when Byrnes walked into Truman's cabin aboard the yacht. Some years later Byrnes said that when he met with Truman, the President expressed his pleasure with the progress made at Moscow. Byrnes also said that after dinner the table was cleared for poker, but he asked to be excused in order to work on his radio speech. And following his radio address, Byrnes claimed, Truman "commended it."

Truman's version of what took place was at the opposite pole. "Byrnes got the real riot act," he said. Truman recalled that he let Byrnes know in no uncertain terms that he did not like the way he operated. He said that he wrote a letter to Byrnes afterward which he read to him at his desk on January 5, 1946, although Byrnes denied that this occurred. In part, that letter read:

> MY DEAR JIM:
>
> I have been considering some of our difficulties. As you know, I would like to pursue a policy of delegating authority to the members of the Cabinet in their various fields and then backing them up in the results. But in doing that and in carrying out that policy I do not intend to turn over the complete authority of the President nor to forego the President's prerogative to make the final decision. . . . I was completely in the dark on the whole conference until I requested you to come to the *Williamsburg* and inform me. The communiqué was released before I ever saw it. . . . I do not think we should play compromise any longer. . . . I'm tired babying the Soviets.

Truman said that after this letter Byrnes understood that he was to resign as Secretary of State whenever a suitable replacement was found. This did not come about until a year later when Truman named General Marshall to succeed him. In the meantime, Truman dropped his gingerly treatment of Byrnes and became his own Secretary of State.

An important push forward in the development of an American foreign policy came in March, 1946, and emanated from Winston Churchill, then out of power in England. In this instance, Harry Vaughan proved to be the driving force, although he had not the slightest intention of serving in this role.

279

"After we got back from Potsdam," Vaughan said, "Doctor Franc 'Bullet' McCluer, the president of Westminster College in Fulton, Missouri, and my old classmate there, walked into my White House office one day. We called him 'Bullet' because he stood exactly five feet tall and was shaped like a bullet. Bullet told me he understood that Winston Churchill was coming to the United States for a vacation and he wanted him to speak at our college. Westminster had a small endowment fund of four thousand dollars and he wanted to use the proceeds to bring Churchill out to make the Green Foundation lecture.

"Bullet had already composed a two-paragraph letter to Churchill and wanted to show it to Truman. So the two of us went to see the President. Truman knew Bullet because at one time Bullet thought of running for governor of Missouri. Truman's reaction to the letter was that it was a good idea and at the end he added the following: 'Dear Winnie—This is a fine old school out in my state. If you come and make a speech there, I'll take you out and introduce you.'

"Churchill replied, accepting for the following March, and wrote that this would be his only public appearance in the United States. Harvard and Yale went wild."

Churchill came to the United States the following winter. In February, Jimmy Byrnes went to Florida, where Churchill was trying to get rid of a bad cold. Churchill gave Byrnes a copy of his forthcoming Fulton speech and asked him to pass it along to Truman. Byrnes said, however, that Truman refused to accept or read it because "the Soviets would charge the British and Americans with 'ganging up' on them."

"Churchill came to Washington and stayed at the White House," Vaughan said. "Then at three P.M. on March third, Churchill, his aide, President Truman and I boarded the B. & O. at the Silver Spring, Maryland, station. We were riding along when Truman realized that Churchill hadn't had a drink for two hours. I rounded up a whisky and soda and Churchill held it up to the light and said, 'When I was a young subaltern in the South African war, the water was not fit to drink. To make it palatable we had to add whisky. By diligent effort I learned to like it.' On the way out to Fulton, Churchill read his speech to the President.

"Fulton was jammed when we got there," Vaughan went on. "The town's population of eight thousand had swelled to twenty thousand.

Before the invocation, we were at McCluer's home where Churchill had to get into his scarlet Cambridge robe. It was an hour and a half since he had had his last drink, and President Truman beckoned to me to take a drink up to Churchill's bedroom. This was a problem because Fulton is a Presbyterian dry town, but after scouting around I fulfilled my mission. Churchill was sitting on the bed in his red robe and when he spied the drink, he said to me, 'Well, General, am I glad to see you. I was here trying to debate in my mind whether I was in Fulton, Missouri, or Fulton, Sahara.' "

The gymnasium of Westminster College was almost without oxygen that March fifth as a packed audience of 3,000 waited for Churchill to deliver the Green Foundation lecture. Truman introduced him with "I know he will say something constructive." And then came the speech that created a furor throughout the world. "From Stettin in the Baltic to Trieste in the Adriatic, an iron curtain has descended across the continent," said Churchill. "From what I have seen of our Russian friends and Allies during the war, I am convinced that there is nothing they admire so much as strength, and there is nothing for which they have less respect than for military weakness." Churchill called for the United States to lead the bloc of non-Communist countries to check the Russians.

By the time Truman returned to Washington, he found himself under heavy criticism for raising the issue of the Iron Curtain. He tried to fend off the attacks by stating that he was only a bystander and that Churchill had made the speech, not he. He also wrote a letter to Stalin, offering to send the battleship *Missouri* to bring him to the United States and promising to escort him to the University of Missouri at Columbia "for exactly the same kind of reception, the same opportunity to speak your mind." Stalin's reply was *Nyet,* Truman said.

Truman realized that the time was not ripe for an alliance to hold the Communists in check. But airing the problems with Russia was all to the good, for it brought into the open those who believed that the Soviet Union would mend her ways if she were catered to and treated kindly.

Leader of these forces was Henry Wallace, the only remaining New Dealer in the Cabinet. After Churchill's Iron Curtain speech, Truman said that Wallace concentrated on American relations with Russia and put in few hours on Department of Commerce business.

When Truman appointed General Walter Bedell Smith as Ambassador to the Soviet Union, Wallace wrote Truman on March 14:

> We know that much of the recent Soviet behavior which has caused us concern has been the result of their dire economic needs and of their disturbed sense of security. . . . I think we can disabuse the Soviet mind and strengthen the faith of the Soviets in our sincere devotion to the cause of peace by proving to them that we want to trade with them and to cement our economic relations with them. To do this, it is necessary to talk to them in an understanding way, with full realization of their difficulties and yet with emphasis on the lack of realism in many of their assumptions.

Wallace proposed that Truman hold an economic conference with the Russians, and added, "I am ready to make suggestions regarding the composition of this mission."

When Truman ignored the letter, Wallace wrote him another on July 23, a 12-page, single-spaced typed letter which arrived at about the time Yugoslavia shot down an American plane, killing five men. In this letter, Wallace advised Truman to "allay any reasonable Russian grounds for fear, suspicion and distrust," and pointed out that the size of the military budget, long-range bomber production, the Bikini A-bomb tests and American arrangements for air bases abroad "make it appear either 1) that we are preparing ourselves to win the war which we regard as inevitable or 2) that we are trying hard to build up a preponderance of force to intimidate the rest of mankind."

Truman saw red. However, when Bob Hannegan advised him that support from Wallace was important for the forthcoming November election, Truman sent him a note of appreciation for putting himself on record.

Their next encounter came on September 10 when Wallace came to the White House with two copies of a speech he was to deliver at Madison Square Garden on the twelfth. He said he held one copy and Truman the other, and that they spent thirty minutes going over the speech. At the end, Wallace claimed, Truman told him to go ahead, that "it was okay."

Charlie Ross denied that Truman read Wallace's speech, because they were together only fifteen minutes and there was no time to do so. "He just thumbed through it while Wallace told him he was going to be hard on the Russians."

On the morning of Wallace's speech, Truman held a news conference that did him immeasurable harm. Armed with advance copies of the address, reporters asked him if he would confirm the following Wallace remark: "I am neither anti-British, nor pro-British—neither anti-Russian, nor pro-Russian. And just two days ago, when President Truman read these words, he said they represented the policy of his Administration."

Truman replied that Wallace's statement was correct. Asked if he approved of Wallace's entire speech, he said "yes." "Does that represent a departure from the foreign policy Byrnes is carrying out?" No, said Truman.

That night, Wallace read his speech to an audience of 20,000. When he spoke about Soviet faults, the crowd booed and hissed. When he praised Russia, the crowd almost brought down the rafters with cheers and applause. Wallace warned:

> "Enemies of yesterday and false friends of today continually try to provoke war between the United States and Russia. . . . Russia must be convinced that we are not planning war against her and we must be certain that Russia is not carrying on territorial expansion or world domination through native Communists."

By the next morning, the White House was a scene of turmoil. Editorials declared that Truman had committed his worst blunder. What was the American foreign policy? Who expressed it—Truman or Wallace? Truman compounded his troubles by holding another press conference. This time he said he had not approved the speech, only the right of Wallace to make one. *Time* labeled this statement "a clumsy lie."

On September 16, Wallace returned to Washington where he told newsmen that he intended to continue fighting for what he believed was the right way toward peace. He also released his 12-page letter of July 23 to the press. The State Department was flooded with queries from foreign governments: "Was the United States about to change direction?"

Truman's first instinct was to eliminate this new trouble by firing Wallace. Instead of acting immediately, however, he called Wallace in for a talk during the afternoon of September 18. Afterward, Truman wrote a memo to himself: "I am not sure he is as fundamentally sound intellectually as I had thought. He advised me that I should be far to the 'left' when Congress was not in session and that I should move right when Congress is on hand and in session. He said FDR did that and that FDR never let his 'right' hand know what his 'left' hand did.

"He is a pacifist 100%. He wants us to disband our armed forces, give Russia our atomic secret and trust a bunch of adventurists in the Kremlin Politbureau. I do not understand a 'dreamer' like that."

Despite his strong opinions regarding Wallace, Truman still did not fire him. His explanation some years later was that Wallace had a large following, and if he kept him in the Cabinet, he would be able to hold him in check. Proceeding on this basis, he got Wallace to agree not to make any more speeches until after the Paris Peace Conference, which was then in session, adjourned.

In the meantime, foreign concern over American foreign policy continued to deepen. From London, *New York Times* reporter Clifton Daniel, who would one day become Truman's son-in-law, cabled: TOMORROW MORNING'S PAPERS WILL PRINT REASSURING DISPATCHES FROM WASHINGTON TO THE EFFECT THAT MR. WALLACE IS 'NOTORIOUSLY EMOTIONAL AND NOTORIOUSLY INDEPENDENT' AND THAT WHAT COUNTS IS NOT WHAT HE SAYS BUT WHAT THE UNITED STATES IS DOING. In Paris, according to Tom Connally, who was there as an adviser to Byrnes, "Wallace's speech created terrific tension. Nor did this lessen when Wallace later publicly agreed with Truman that he would not discuss our foreign policy again until the Paris conference ended. For what this implied was that the President would not object if Wallace spoke out at a later date."

On September 19, Truman held a teletype conversation with Byrnes in which Byrnes expressed concern that Wallace would resume his criticism of American foreign policy upon the conclusion of the Paris conference. Truman assured him that he had made no commitment to Wallace that he could do so. That afternoon, while Truman sat at his desk, he picked up a copy of the Washington *Daily News* and found a detailed account of his private conversation with Wallace on the eighteenth.

At ten o'clock the next morning he phoned Wallace. "Henry," he said, "I'm sorry but I have reached the conclusion that it will be best if I ask for your resignation."

"If that is the way you want it, Mr. President," Wallace replied, "I will be happy to comply."

Truman wrote his mother and sister that day:

> Well, I had to fire Henry today, and of course I hated to do it. . . .
> If Henry had stayed Sec. of Agri. in 1940 as he should have, there'd
> never have been all this controversy, and I would not be here, and
> wouldn't that be nice? Charlie Ross said I'd shown I'd rather be right
> than President, and I told him I'd rather be anything than President.
> . . . Well, now he's out, and the crackpots are having conniption fits.
> I'm glad they are. It convinces me I'm right.

The last New Dealer was out. And with his departure went any
remaining doubts about the direction of the foreign policy of the
United States.

32

I N the fall of 1946, Truman's popularity showed a steady decline. The first Gallup Poll taken after he succeeded FDR revealed his national popularity as 87 per cent, or 3 per cent above FDR's highest rating. But now his popularity rating had skidded to a skimpy 32 per cent.

Of course, there had been the Republican bitterness after his message to Congress on September 6, 1945; the defection of the New Dealers and labor leaders; mounting inflation and chronic meat shortages; the uncertainties of his foreign policy; and the outpouring of emotions over atomic-energy legislation. Nor was his popularity helped when military services made public war on each other over his proposal to establish a unified Department of Defense. In an unmailed letter, Truman wrote about his problem with arrogant public servants:

> Some of the generals and the admirals and the career men in government look upon the occupant of the White House as only a temporary nuisance who soon will be succeeded by another temporary occupant who won't find out what it is all about for a long time and then it will be too late to do anything about it.

There was still another matter that diminished his standing. Truman had watched the antics of the House Rules Committee with growing anger and was particularly displeased with Democratic Congressman Roger C. Slaughter, whose 5th Missouri Congressional District covered part of Jackson County. Because Slaughter had played the decisive role in the Rules Committee in blocking his proposal for a permanent Fair Employment Practices Committee, Truman opposed Slaughter's re-election in 1946.

Instead of announcing his opposition to Slaughter and letting it go at that, he called Jim Pendergast to the White House and told him to oppose Slaughter. At a news conference on July 18, Truman publicly announced his position. "With his jaws set," wrote a reporter, "and without a trace of a smile, the President said Slaughter as a member of the House Rules Committee had opposed every bit of legislation he, the President, had suggested to Congress." "If Mr. Slaughter is right, then I am wrong," he told newsmen, and he came out for a young Navy veteran named Axtell, whom he called "an old friend." Tony Vaccaro of the Associated Press interrupted to ask for Axtell's first name. Truman could not remember it. When a Kansas City *Star* reporter piped up with "Enos Axtell," he laughed, embarrassed.

Truman went home for the August 6 primary, which by now was receiving national attention. After he voted, he visited his mother before returning to Washington. "Did you vote on your way down?" he asked her. The old woman, who knew how much he counted on Slaughter's defeat, was in an impish mood. "I certainly did, Harry, and also on my way back."

When the primary results became known, Axtell had defeated Slaughter by 2,771 votes. Bob Hannegan, worried by Truman's announced intention to purge Slaughter, said with relief that Axtell's victory signified "a strong vote of confidence in President Truman."

But Truman's troubles were only beginning. Roy Roberts of the *Star,* who had worked for his nomination at Chicago, noted that in the four strong Kansas City Pendergast wards, Axtell amassed 12,000 votes to Slaughter's measly 2,000. Roberts assigned two reporters to uncover evidence of fake votes. On September 27, the *Star* sent its sizable findings to United States Attorney Sam Wear, whom Truman had appointed to succeed Maurice Milligan. Wear forwarded the *Star* findings to Attorney General Tom Clark, who found himself in a quandary. If he refused to act, he would be accused of whitewashing the primary election. He therefore ordered a cursory FBI investigation and later announced that the FBI had uncovered only minor irregularities. Three Federal judges in Kansas City also examined the FBI preliminary report and came to the same conclusion.

But the *Star* persisted in its charges and Truman was tagged as a crook by newspaper innuendo throughout the country. To make matters worse, in the November election Axtell lost to Republican Albert L. Reeves, Jr., son of the Federal judge who had helped bring down Tom Pendergast. Newspapers found the parallel striking. By now Truman realized that it had been a blunder to involve himself in purging Slaughter.

The Democratic campaign that fall was a peculiar one. Across the nation, Democratic candidates for Congress refrained from mentioning Truman. Instead, they used recordings of FDR's voice to conjure up support from the grave. Senator Harley Kilgore, who was up for re-election in West Virginia, said that the mere mention of Truman's name in the hollows country evoked boos from the coal miners. "Here was a man who was actually doing an excellent job as President," Kilgore said, "but about the most you could do was to defend him in a humorous fashion by using the old Western saloon refrain: 'Don't shoot our piano player. He's doing the best he can.' " On their part, the Republicans plastered billboards along the country's highways with ads containing only two words: HAD ENOUGH? Individual Republican candidates tried to break the Democratic silence on Truman by denouncing him as being soft on Communism and the tool of the unions, strange charges considering that both groups opposed him.

Truman attempted to influence the vote in two ways. Three weeks before the election, he removed price controls on meat with the result that the black market ended and outraged housewives were pacified when beef appeared in butcher shops again. He also tried to help New York Democrats by releasing a letter he wrote to Prime Minister Clement Attlee, requesting permission for 100,000 Jewish refugees to enter Palestine. The Republicans denounced this request as a political trick, although Governor Dewey of New York called the 100,000 figure insufficient.

The 1946 election was a resounding Republican victory in both houses of Congress. Senator Robert A. Taft, who was to be chairman of the Republican Steering Committee of the incoming 80th Congress, exultantly proclaimed that the people had flocked to the polls to repudiate Truman. Actually, the total vote was only 34 million, far below the normal vote in an off-year election. Obviously, millions of Democrats had stayed away from the polls.

It was bad enough for Truman to read the uncharitable remarks the Republicans were making about him. Even worse, a few Democrats also joined in the attacks against him. Senator J. W. Fulbright, a former Rhodes Scholar, recommended that Truman appoint Republican Senator Arthur Vandenberg as Secretary of State and then resign, an act that would elevate Vandenberg to the Presidency. Truman fumed at Fulbright's suggestion. His retort was that "a little more United States land grant college education on the United States Constitution and what it meant would do Fulbright a lot of good."

During the early months of the 80th Congress, the purge of Slaughter returned once more to plague Truman. On January 14, the newly elected Republican Senator from Missouri, James P. Kem, wrote to Tom Clark, requesting information regarding the status of the Federal investigation of the Missouri Democratic primary election. Clark replied that no violations of Federal statutes had been uncovered, but Kem's needling letters continued. In the meantime, a local grand jury sifted through some of the ballots and indicted 71 persons. Then, on May 27, burglars broke into the election commissioner's safe in Kansas City and stole the impounded ballots.

"The Senate Republicans were out now for Truman's scalp," Republican Senator William Langer of North Dakota said as he recounted the events that followed. "Kem introduced a resolution to investigate the whole business and it came before a judiciary subcommittee on which I served. We had a continuous fight in the subcommittee whether we were going to crucify Truman, who was only an innocent party. Finally we took a vote. I was the last to vote and I broke the tie. I voted against the investigation and saved Harry Truman.

"The next time I came up for re-election," Langer went on, "Truman insisted I join his campaign train through North Dakota. At every stop, I introduced him and he eulogized me for several minutes. But he finished each eulogy by asking the crowd to vote for Fred Morrison, my Democratic opponent."

One Republican summed up the 80th Congress's approach to the Truman Administration: "Congress opened daily with a prayer and ended with a probe." The attacks on Truman were broadened to take in several people who were close to him. Harry Vaughan, in particular, provided an easy target. Burly, genial Vaughan always spoke his mind as if he were a loose-tongued barber discussing politics with a customer rather than a man close to the President. And every attack on General Vaughan only spurred Truman to a greater show of loyalty. Once Vaughan handed Truman a magazine article that tore the general to shreds. "This guy's so mean," he complained, "he would steal buckshot to shoot his brother." Truman grinned and said, "I guess the boys don't have much to write about. I'll give them something to write about." With that he released to the press the findings of the Army-Navy Inquiry Board on the Pearl Harbor disaster. The newsmen were busy for days afterward writing news stories drawn from this thick, detailed report.

Despite the widespread reports in the papers of everything he said in public, Vaughan found it hard to keep quiet. Frequently, even when he uttered the most innocuous remarks, he landed in the mud. On one occasion, for instance, he was out in Chicago during a heavy rainstorm. When he got into an elevator in an office building, he noticed that one of the passengers was not wearing a raincoat and asked innocently, "Where's your raincoat?"

"It was stolen from me last week in Washington."

Vaughan let out a characteristic guffaw, and slapped him on the back. "That only goes to prove that while we haven't got all the thieves in the world in Washington, we've got the biggest ones," he said, unaware that there was a reporter on the elevator. A few hours later a Chicago paper carried the following heading over a story: BIGGEST THIEVES IN WORLD IN WASHINGTON, PRESIDENT'S MILITARY AIDE SAYS.

The press devoted a great deal of time and space trying to determine how close Vaughan was to the President. Some papers asserted that he was one of the most influential persons in the White House. Columnist Doris Fleeson was nearest the truth: "General Vaughan is not interested in government policy. He is interested in Harry Truman and stands by to joke, berate or damn the world according to the President's mood." Vaughan said, "The job makes a stuffed shirt of the President because he can't lead a normal life. If I can give him a belly laugh a day, I think I have earned my pay. I don't suppose anyone gives him more advice than I do—or has less of it used."

Vaughan frequently embarrassed Truman, but nothing he did ever led to an estrangement, for Truman realized that he was loyal and never capitalized personally on their relationship. On the subject of gifts, Vaughan said after Truman had left office, "All kinds of presents pour into the White House for the President. Eisenhower accepted ten times as much as President Truman. Truman never let anyone capitalize on presents sent him. For instance, he returned a television set to a manufacturer who advertised that the President favored his type of TV set. He even dropped his New York tailor when that fellow held a press conference and bragged. The only things I got were about three hundred boxes of cigars a year, which the President passed on to me because he didn't smoke, and a lot of hats that came to Truman because we both wore the same size."

Truman could get furious with the press when his close associates were attacked. Vaughan recalled, "One time I got a distinguished-service award from the Reserve Officers Association. That morning Truman was very much annoyed because the columnists were suggesting people whom he should fire. The afternoon papers offered still more names. By the time he got up to speak at the dinner that night he was so mad that he said, 'Everyone is telling me who I should have on my staff and in my Cabinet. No s.o.b. is going to dictate to me who I'm going to have!' He didn't mention anyone by name, but Drew Pearson got into the act by nominating himself as an s.o.b."

After Truman finished his talk, he returned to the White House where Bess was waiting up for him to give him a severe dressing-down for using such language in public. Several days later, Bill Hassett, his correspondence secretary, hurried into Truman's office with the news that the rector of "an exclusive Washington church had come to the President's defense and remarked that, under similar provocation, he might have said the same thing." Truman's face lighted up momentarily, then he turned glum. "I just wish that the rector would go talk to my wife!" he said.

At one point, Truman had labeled the Democratic 79th Congress as the "worst," but he now bestowed this dubious distinction on the 80th Congress because of its record on his domestic economic program. His failures with this new Congress exceeded the long list with its predecessor. The 80th Congress refused to appropriate money for public housing or to aid education. It offered only a pittance for soil conservation and ordered price supports after 1949 to be flexible at a reduced rate of from 60 to 90 per cent of parity. It again rejected a permanent Fair Employment Practices Committee, a national health bill and an expanded Social Security program. Its tax bill, passed over Truman's veto, gave 40 per cent of the tax relief to those whose annual incomes were above $5,000.

But the one piece of domestic legislation enacted by the 80th Congress that drained the blood from Truman's face was the Taft-Hartley Labor Act. In his State of the Union message on January 6, 1947, he asked Congress for a labor bill that would end jurisdictional strikes and secondary boycotts, strengthen the Labor Department and establish a commission to examine the general problems of labor-management relations.

In June, Congress responded by presenting him with a strike-curb bill that outlawed industry-wide strikes, the closed shop and mass picketing; made unions liable to suits; required union leaders to file non-Communist affidavits before they could use the facilities of the National Labor Relations Board; set up "cooling-off" periods before any strike was called; prohibited the use of union funds for political contributions; and gave the President the power to obtain injunctions in strikes involving interstate commerce, public utilities and communications. Truman denounced the Taft-Hartley bill as a "slave labor act" and promptly vetoed it. Then, to rally public support to his side and exert pressure on Congress, he took the issue to the country in a nationwide broadcast. But when southern Democrats joined forces with the Republicans, the Senate overrode his veto by a vote of 68 to 25. Truman lost the battle, although he gained a powerful weapon for the 1948 campaign.

On noneconomic matters the 80th Congress was more cooperative. It passed Truman's bill unifying the armed services into a new Department of Defense and changed the line of Presidential succession so that the Speaker of the House followed the Vice-President, and then the Senate's *pro tem*. Congress also established the Hoover Commission to examine government operations and make recommendations for improving efficiency. Truman was especially pleased with Hoover's appointment, for he believed that the talents of former Presidents should not be allowed to rot on the retirement vine.

Truman's chief success with the 80th Congress came in the field of foreign relations. The wartime baby boom, the pent-up demand for consumer goods and the continuing large military budget had given the American economy great impetus to move forward. When the expected postwar depression failed to materialize, the success or failure of Truman's social welfare program was not for the time being a matter of major importance to the country. But Soviet activities were.

"Without Stalin's 'crazy moves,' " Truman said, "we would never have had our foreign policy. . . . We would never have got a thing from Congress."

A new development in foreign policy occurred shortly after the 80th Congress convened, and at the very time the Republican leadership was attempting to pin the Kansas City vote frauds on Truman. In February, 1947, Attlee informed Truman that Britain could no longer continue economic and military aid to Greece. There was trouble in Turkey, too, where the Soviet Union was pressing her demands for territorial concessions and special privileges to guarantee Russian entrance into the Mediterranean. In September, 1944, when the Nazis were driven from Greece, the British had come into that devastated land with an army of 40,000 troops and economic aid. But the country was kept in turmoil by civil war led by Communist-dominated Greek rebels. In addition, the Communist governments of Yugoslavia, Bulgaria and Albania stationed large army forces along the Greek border.

To Truman the issue was clear-cut even though some of his advisers pointed out that neither Greece nor Turkey had democratic governments. Several of his Cabinet members argued that the two governments should start a program of reform before the United States even considered helping them.

The problem, however, was more basic. If the Soviets filled the vacuum after the British departure from Greece, the West would suffer a serious setback. Moreover if Turkey continued, without outside aid, to pay the cost of maintaining a stand-by army of 600,000 soldiers, she would soon be bankrupt. Soviet victory in these countries would seriously damage the prestige of the United States throughout the world, for other nations were waiting to learn whether the American Government would help them withstand Communist pressures both from within and without.

These considerations led to the birth on March 12, 1947, of the "Truman Doctrine." On that day a grim-visaged Truman rode up Capitol Hill to address Congress. It was a "brother's keeper" doctrine that he enunciated in his flat Missouri twang.

> "I believe that it must be the policy of the United States to support free peoples who are resisting attempted subjugation by armed minorities or by outside pressures. I believe that we must assist free peoples to work out their own destinies in their own way. . . . The United Nations and its related organizations are not in a position to extend help of the kind that is required."

He called on Congress to appropriate $250 million for Greek aid and $150 million for Turkish aid.

The Truman Doctrine elicited mixed reaction, for it represented a vital break with the tradition of American isolationism. Walter Lippmann feared that Truman was trying to be too global. Mrs. Roosevelt said that it weakened the United Nations. Senator Kenneth Wherry, who led the Senate fight against the Truman proposal, claimed that it would invalidate George Washington's doctrine of avoidance of all foreign entanglements. The Washington *Post* added in an editorial: "He was asking America to be Atlas, offering to lead his country in that tremendous role, yet his flat voice carried no significance of his fateful recommendation." Henry Wallace, on a tour of England and France, denounced the Truman Doctrine as a further step along the road to war.

Nevertheless, the Truman Doctrine prevailed and Greece and Turkey were saved from Communism.

While the Congressional fight over Greek-Turkish aid was on, Truman received bad news. Martha Truman, now ninety-four, had fallen on February 14 and fractured her hip. Early in May she contracted pneumonia. When her doctors told Truman that they did not expect her to live, he hurried to her side despite the major fight on his aid bill. On May 19, two days after his return to Grandview, doctors told him that this would be her last day on earth. But her constitution was strong and she continued her struggle for life. On May 22, Truman took time off from his vigil to go to the Muehlebach Hotel, where he signed the Greek-Turkish Aid Act, which had cleared the Senate by a vote of 67-23. His mother's crisis broke on the twenty-fourth when she called out for watermelon. Watermelon was out of season, but Truman's friends found one for her.

After this she showed steady improvement. Charlie Ross, who had known her since his childhood, said that he knew she was recovering when she started discussing politics. "Is Taft going to be nominated next year?" she asked her son. She had a strong dislike for the Ohio Republican.

"He might be," Truman said.

She trained a severe eye on him. "Harry, are you going to run?"

"I don't know, Mamma."

Her expression was one of impatience. "Don't you think it's about time you made up your mind?"

Truman remained with her until the end of May, when he returned to Washington. His sister Mary reported to him in June that "Mamma is getting along fine." During the morning of July 26, Truman learned that once again she was not expected to live out the day. At noon he left the White House and boarded his plane, the *Independence,* for home. He was in the air an hour when the pilot received a message: his mother had passed away. "Well, now she won't have to suffer any more," Truman said. But he was overwhelmed by her death. As the plane continued west, he penned a short biography of Mamma. On July 28, she was buried at Forest Hills Cemetery next to her husband, John Truman, dead since 1914.

In March, while Truman was formulating the Truman Doctrine, he was already moving beyond it to a plan of much broader scope. Europe had failed to recover from the ravages of war. The Continent lay prostrate, and the Russians, Truman noted, "were coldly determined to exploit the helpless condition of Europe to further Communism." A way had to be found to revive the European countries and rehabilitate their economies. Truman visualized a cooperative effort by the European nations to do the job with the backing of the United States Treasury.

He had accepted an invitation to speak at the Delta Council in the Teacher's College at Cleveland, Mississippi, on May 8 and it was here that he planned to present his new proposal. But since his mother was seriously ill at the time, he had turned over his speech to Under Secretary of State Dean Acheson, who substituted for him and made the initial appeal for what later became known as the Marshall Plan. The United States, Acheson said, must "push ahead with the reconstruction of the great workshops of Europe. . . . The war will not be over until the people of the world can again feed and clothe themselves and face the future with some degree of confidence." Acheson also expressed Truman's strategy for American aid: "Free peoples who are seeking to preserve their independence and democratic institutions and human freedoms against totalitarian pressures, either internal or external, will receive top priority for American reconstruction aid."

Although Acheson's speech attracted little attention in the American press, it was widely printed and commented upon in English and Continental papers. The London *Times* treated it as one of the major utterances of the postwar era.

In January, 1947, Truman had dropped Jimmy Byrnes as Secretary of State with the usual regrets, a statement of concern about his health and an expression of hope that it would be possible to call upon his services again in the future. In his place, Truman named General Marshall, to whom he referred as "the greatest living American." Marshall had already carried out a diplomatic mission to China for the President, an unsuccessful venture seeking to unite Chiang Kai-shek's Nationalists and the Communists in a coalition government.

Less than a month after Acheson's speech in Cleveland, Mississippi, Marshall again publicized Truman's new foreign policy theme when he spoke at the Harvard commencement on June 5. "The initiative, I think, must come from Europe," Marshall said. "The role of this country should consist of friendly aid in the drafting of a European program and of later support of such a program so far as it may be practical for us to do so."

The response to Marshall's speech was electric. When European nations convened that month in Paris to consider it, even the Soviet Union and her satellites attended the meeting. It was soon evident, however, that Molotov was there to wreck the program. When he failed to win his point that the United States Government should have no say about the way its money was to be spent, he stormed out of the meeting. The Marshall Plan then became what Truman had wanted all along—a program of economic rehabilitation for the Western European nations as a bulwark against Communism.

Truman realized that he faced difficulties in getting the Marshall Plan through Congress, for the Republican legislators were then increasing their attacks on him. Less than two weeks after Marshall's speech, he vetoed the Taft-Hartley Act and the vituperation heaped on him became more abusive and shrill. Senator Kilgore said, "Truman thought it was best to keep quiet that the Marshall Plan was his own idea, so he made it appear that it was entirely Marshall's doing because Marshall was popular with Congress."

Another difficulty was that the Marshall Plan called for gigantic expenditures—$17,000,000,000 for four years with an initial fifteen-month appropriation of $6,800,000,000. This was a serious obstacle because at that time Representative John Taber of the House Ways and Means Committee and Senator Taft were wielding a meat ax on almost all of Truman's other budget requests. Taft led the opposition to the Marshall Plan on the grounds that the United States could not afford it. But while Taft denounced the program in public, Truman stepped up his efforts to cater to Senator Vandenberg, chairman of the Senate Foreign Relations Committee. "The logical man to head the Economic Cooperation Act, as the Marshall Plan became known, was Will Clayton," Senator Connally said. "But to stay on Vandenberg's good terms, Truman accepted Vandenberg's choice, Paul Hoffman, head of the Studebaker Company." Truman's strategy paid off, for the Senate passed the Marshall Plan in March, 1948, by a vote of 69-17.

Despite his diminished popularity at home, Truman had great ability to arouse enthusiasm abroad. In March, 1947, for instance, only a few days before he presented the Truman Doctrine to Congress, he visited Mexico at the invitation of President Miguel Alemán. The long-standing suspicion of United States intentions seemed to vanish before Truman's grin, simplicity and friendliness. Secret Service men were concerned when he mingled with the people. They were also exhausted trying to keep up with him when he climbed the Toltec pyramids and temples outside Mexico City in the rarefied atmosphere at an altitude of 7,000 feet.

Perhaps the single gesture that won Mexico over to him was his impromptu visit to Chapultepec Castle. Here, a century before, when General Winfield Scott's troops stormed the heights and captured the castle, which was Mexico's West Point, the six cadets who were the only survivors of the assault committed suicide rather than surrender to the hated Americans. Displaying deep emotion, Truman approached the monument to "Los Niños Heroes," placed a wreath before it and bowed his head in tribute. The cadets who stood guard wept without shame at the sight of the symbol of the North American conqueror paying his respects. Afterward, Truman was asked why he laid the wreath at a monument which was an ever-present reminder of the United States invasion of Mexico. "I know the history of this incident," he said with feeling. "Brave men do not belong to any one country. I respect bravery wherever I see it." Before Truman left Mexico, President Alemán asked him what he thought of the Paricutín volcano, the world's youngest mountain which had erupted into birth only four years earlier. "Frankly," Truman replied, "it's nothing compared to the one I'm sitting on in Washington."

Truman made another "good neighbor" trip in August, this time to Rio de Janeiro, where twenty Western Hemisphere countries took part in a conference that resulted in a mutual assistance pact. Each agreed that when any aggression occurred against an American nation, whether by an outside power or by signatories to the treaty, the other member states would be obliged to take joint action against the aggressor.

More than a million persons lined the Rio Branca to cheer "Señor Missouri" and bands played "The Star-Spangled Banner" on every corner. As in Mexico, Truman reached the hearts of the people and won tremendous good will for the United States.

Slowly but steadily during 1947, Truman's popularity at home climbed upward. The unrelenting attacks upon him began to boomerang, and he won wide support because of his advocacy of a foreign policy based on humanitarian principles. The attendance of reporters at his news conferences, which had fallen off drastically with the advent of the 80th Congress, picked up and he again received heavy press coverage.

Some of his hitherto most vociferous critics now made overtures to return to his good graces. Truman was quick to forgive them. Harry Vaughan mentioned an instance when Truman considered appointing a man who had once opposed him to a high government post. "Why do you want to appoint that blankety-blank?" Vaughan asked. "Don't you remember what he did to us in 1945?" Truman grinned. "Well, maybe next time he'll be for us."

Most notable among Truman's enemies who made up with him was Al Whitney of the Brotherhood of Railroad Trainmen. In 1946, when Truman broke the railroad strike, he had called Whitney "un-American" and an "enemy of the people." In return, the fiery white-maned Whitney told reporters, "You can't make a President out of a ribbon clerk." But after Truman's veto of the Taft-Hartley Act, Whitney had a change of heart and made an appointment to see him.

On the day they were to meet, Whitney walked determinedly to the White House but lost his nerve when he reached the gate. Only after trudging twice around the Executive Mansion did he get up the courage to enter. "It's good to see you, Al," Truman greeted him. Whitney's eyes grew moist and Truman added, "You look wonderful. Let's not waste time discussing the past. Let's just agree we both received bad advice."

Whitney said apologetically, "Mr. President, I'm a third-generation Irishman who's part Scotch and you know they are kind of hotheaded sometimes." Truman agreed. "I'm made up on the same plan."

After their conversation, Truman escorted him to the door of his oval office and said, "Al, I remember back in Missouri, when I was running for the Senate in 1940 and there wasn't a soul who seemed to care whether I made it or not, that one man and one organization came forward to help. It was the Trainmen and the man named Whitney. I've never forgotten it." Outside, Whitney told reporters, "I propose to devote my time and effort to electing Harry Truman President because I think his election is in the best interest of the nation."

Even though the Gallup Poll showed that Truman's popularity had risen to 56 per cent from the previous year's low of 32 per cent, as the summer of 1947 passed, Truman was still undecided whether to run for election in 1948. A repetition of his lonely situation in the 1940 Senatorial fight was soon to push him to a decision.

33

IN October, 1947, while his popularity was still on the rise, Truman made up his mind to run for President the following year.

At that time there was every likelihood he would have smooth sailing in winning the Democratic nomination. In November, 1947, when the Kentucky gubernatorial election took place, Senator Taft flatly predicted, "The Kentucky election will reflect to a large degree which party will elect a President in 1948." Earle Clements, the Democratic candidate, was the winner. On January 4, Dr. Gallup's poll buttressed Taft's conclusions with the assertion that if the Presidential election were held then, President Truman would win.

But the election was not held then and troubles soon descended upon Truman. On December 28, 1947, Henry Wallace announced the formation of his third party and on February 17, when Leo Isacson, a Wallaceite, won the special House election in the 24th Congressional District of New York, the Democrats grew concerned that Wallace would split the national Democratic vote that fall.

Other doubts about Truman as a candidate had appeared when he delivered his State of the Union Message to Congress on January 7.

The New York Times described his reception as "extraordinarily chilly," while the Washington *Post* labeled his speech "unmitigatingly demagogic." One of Truman's proposals was a tax cut of $40 for every taxpayer, which prompted Representative John Taber of New York to tell reporters, "Tom Pendergast paid only two dollars a vote and now Truman proposes to pay forty dollars." During his address, Truman paused several times for expected applause, but Congress sat on its hands except when he announced that he would enforce the Taft-Hartley Act. Senator William Langer of North Dakota said, "I was the only Republican who clapped for him. Truman saw it and on his way out he stopped to shake hands. From then on, he always made it a ritual to do that whenever he came to the Capitol to deliver a message."

Northern Democratic support was alienated when Truman dropped James M. Landis, an old Roosevelt friend who headed the Civil Aeronautics Board, and replaced Marriner S. Eccles as chairman of the Federal Reserve Board of Governors with Thomas McCabe, a Republican. Together with the firing the previous year of Wilson Wyatt, the head of the Veterans Emergency Housing Program, the Landis and Eccles incidents added fuel to the charge of New Dealers that Truman was out to decimate their forces still remaining in the government.

Many New Dealers and liberals were also displaying mounting concern about his government employee loyalty program. In 1946, when the Royal Commission Report on Soviet Espionage in Canada revealed Red spy rings operating in the American Government, Truman set up a Temporary Commission on Employee Loyalty to investigate the problem. The following March, when he put the Temporary Commission's report into action by executive order, there was an immediate outcry from liberals. In theory, Truman's order was eminently fair. The Attorney General was to issue a list of "totalitarian, fascist, Communist, or subversive organizations." Employees who belonged to any of these organizations or were otherwise accused of disloyalty were to be granted a hearing by their agency's loyalty board. They would also have the right to appeal to a loyalty review board in the Civil Service Commission.

But theory and practice did not jibe. Individual agencies established their own vague standards for defining "subversion" so that what was loyal in one agency was disloyal in another. Furthermore, guilt by association became a common verdict. In the trial process, defendants were not told in advance of the charges against them. Nor were they permitted to cross-examine their accusers. Conservatives in Congress called the loyalty program too weak, while liberals denounced it as an insult to government employees and a curtailment of traditional American freedom. Truman was caught in the crossfire between both factions.

There were still other reasons for the erosion of Truman's newly gained popularity. On October 5, 1947, faced with the spectacle of grain speculators bidding up food prices, Truman had asked Congress for power to control commodity exchanges. In January, 1948, the Senate Appropriations Committee learned that Ed Pauley, then a special assistant to Secretary of the Army Kenneth Royal, had made several hundred thousand dollars in commodity speculation. When it was also discovered that Truman's White House physician, Brigadier General Wallace Graham, had earned $6,165 as a grain speculator, Truman found himself under attack as if he were personally involved. When he refused to fire Dr. Graham, he was denounced in dozens of editorials. Senator Kilgore explained, "Any World War I officer would have done the same thing that Truman did for Dr. Graham. He was a company commander who had to be personally responsible for his men and go to bat for a guy in a jam. It got to be an inherent trait."

Truman later said that Graham had not wanted to be his doctor in the first place, and agreed only after he pulled rank on him. "I knew his father, old Doc Graham, all my life, but I had never met his son. At Potsdam, I learned he was stationed nearby and I asked him to visit me." Truman was impressed with the young doctor and asked him to become his White House physician. Graham objected strenuously on the ground that "I want to take care of as many people as possible—not just one man."

"It's an order," Truman told him.

But if the Graham disclosure was damaging to Truman, other incidents and events, hardly of earth-shaking significance, were also used to hurt him. In mid-January, for instance, he announced plans to build a balcony leading off his second-floor White House study. Several papers called attention to the fact that Mussolini and Hitler had also had balconies. The New York *Herald Tribune* tartly reminded him that he was only a transient guest at 1600 Pennsylvania Avenue with "a lamentable penchant for meddling with a historic structure which the nation prefers as it is." When the Fine Arts Commission,

302

in charge of the exterior structure of government buildings, unanimously opposed the addition of the balcony, Truman blithely ignored its ruling and proceeded with his plans. The South Portico was designed by Thomas Jefferson, he said, and Jefferson intended to have a balcony. "All changes in the White House since Fillmore's time have faced resistance—like gaslights and cooking stoves," he argued. "Mrs. Fillmore put in the first bathtubs and she was almost lynched for doing it." Months later, when the balcony was completed, the storm abated and Truman was generally praised for his addition to the White House exterior.

In February, 1948, Truman once more revealed his enormous knack for stirring up controversy within the Democratic Party. Dave Niles, who handled minority and religious matters for the White House, said, "Roosevelt did not believe in getting out too far in front of the people. He had far greater patience than Truman and planned long-range educational programs to win popular support before he acted. When Truman saw a problem, he wanted it settled on the spot. For instance, after the war Truman thought it long overdue for Negroes to get a fair deal. He ordered integration in the armed services, and though the generals and especially the admirals fought like tigers against it, he made them swallow it." In December, 1946, he had named a Committee on Civil Rights under Charles E. Wilson of General Electric to help him plan a nongovernmental program. On October 29, 1947, when the Wilson Committee submitted its report, "To Secure These Rights," Truman's Cabinet was badly split on the wisdom of asking Congress to act on it.

Without conferring with his Congressional leaders, Truman sent a 10-point civil rights message to Congress on February 2, 1948. He called for the strengthening of existing civil rights laws, a Federal law against lynching, a Federal Fair Employment Practices Committee, an end to Jim Crow laws in interstate transportation, the protection of the right to vote, and the eradication of the Oriental Exclusion Act of 1924. Southern reaction was one of wild outrage.

Senator Richard Russell of Georgia denounced the message as an attempt to create an "American OGPU." A total of 52 Southern Congressmen lashed out at Truman and said that they would not support him that year. At a White House luncheon for the executive committee of the Democratic National Committee, Mrs. Leonard Thomas, a national committeewoman from Alabama, told him, "I want to take a message back to the South. Can I tell them you're not ramming miscegenation down our throats? That you're for all the people, not just the North?" Truman first read the Bill of Rights to her. Then he said, "I'm everybody's President. I take back nothing of what I propose and make no excuse for it." A Negro White House waiter got so excited listening to the argument that he accidentally knocked a cup of coffee out of Truman's hands. At the Jefferson-Jackson Day dinner in Little Rock, Arkansas, on February 19, 750 persons stalked out when Truman's voice came over the loud-speaker. In Washington, Senator Olin Johnston of South Carolina paid for a table to seat ten for that affair, but kept it empty, commenting to reporters that his wife feared she would have to sit next to a "Nigra."

One of Truman's most harassing problems in what seemed an endless siege of difficulties was Palestine, which had been under British mandate since the end of World War I and had emerged as a strong emotional issue at the close of World War II. On April 5, 1945, Roosevelt had written to King Ibn Saud of Saudi Arabia pledging not to make any hostile moves against the Arabs or to assist the Jews against them. "There are serious doubts in my mind," Dave Niles once said, "that Israel would have come into being if Roosevelt had lived."

Truman believed that the Balfour Declaration of 1917, by which Great Britain promised to support the creation of a Jewish homeland in Palestine, should be honored. For the immediate future, however, he wanted to augment the terms of the British White Paper of 1939, which prescribed the issuance of a certain number of immigration certificates to Jews who wished to settle in Palestine. By late summer of 1945, all such certificates had already been used and Zionists were clamoring for the admission of a million more Jews. On August 31, Truman wrote to Clement Attlee that "the granting of an additional 100,000 of such certificates would contribute greatly to a sound solution for the future of Jews still in Germany and Austria. . . . No other single matter is so important for those who have known the horrors of concentration camps for over a decade as is the future of immigration possibilities into Palestine."

Instead of acting on Truman's proposal, Attlee suggested a Joint Anglo-American Committee of Inquiry to determine where to settle Europe's uprooted Jews. Although Truman considered this a delaying tactic, he agreed if the committee focused its inquiry on Palestine. In his reply, Foreign Secretary Ernest Bevin insisted that other possible settlement areas also be considered, but Truman proved adamant and the British finally accepted his position.

When the twelve-man Joint Committee began hearings on January 4, 1946, Truman was denounced by Zionists and Arabs alike. The Zionists charged that the inquiry was part of a plot to avoid establishing a policy; the Arabs insisted that Palestine was theirs and not up for discussion. In April the committee made its report, proposing a United Nations trusteeship over Palestine and recommending that Truman's request for the issuance of another 100,000 immigration certificates be honored.

Both Zionists and Arabs opposed these recommendations, as did the British Government. On June 12, Bevin charged that the Truman Administration wanted 100,000 Jews admitted into Palestine "because they do not want them in New York." Attlee declared that he would not permit further immigration into Palestine until illegal Jewish armed forces operating there were disposed of.

By now Truman found that Palestine had become a festering issue inside his own government. Leader of the anti-Zionist forces was James Forrestal, who insisted that the United States must do nothing to antagonize the Arabs because Saudi Arabia was "one of the three great oil puddles left in the world." Several State Department officials also attempted to undermine Truman's policy. "Almost without exception," Truman noted, the State Department's Near East specialists were "unfriendly to the idea of a Jewish state." Some of his opponents in the State Department, he said, believed that the Arabs should be "appeased" because of their oil resources and "there were some among them who were also inclined to be anti-Semitic."

Britain's refusal to honor the Joint Committee's recommendations resulted in an organized campaign of violence by Jewish terrorists in Palestine. The situation grew more tense when the British began arming the Arabs. In June, Truman suggested to Attlee that still another joint effort be made to find a solution. This time a Joint Cabinet Committee met in London in July, 1946, and came up with new recommendations. Palestine would be partitioned into a Jewish zone, an Arab zone and a central government zone covering Jerusalem, Bethlehem and the Negeb. The Jewish and Arab governments would have a say only on local matters. The central government under British control would not only determine immigration but would also name the executives of the other two governments.

Truman rejected this proposal. Although a humanitarian solution was desperately needed, by the autumn of 1946 he considered the situation "insoluble." The Arabs remained as intransigent as ever, and as Truman noted in a letter, "Not only are the British highly successful in muddling the situation as completely as it could possibly be muddled, but the Jews themselves are making it almost impossible to do anything for them." Later Truman wrote to Dave Niles: "I surely wish God Almighty would give the Children of Israel an Isaiah, the Christians a St. Paul, and the Sons of Ishmael a peep at the Golden Rule."

Early in 1947, Britain tossed the hot potato into the lap of the United Nations but not until Bevin had placed the entire blame for the Palestine troubles on the American Zionists, charging that everything would have turned out all right if Truman "hadn't spoiled my plans with his idea that 100,000 Jews should be given a home in Palestine." On April 2, the British suggested still another study and requested the General Assembly to establish UNSCOP (The United Nations Special Committee on Palestine). As Bevin put it, "After two thousand years of conflict, another twelve months will not be considered a long delay." Truman not only termed this attitude "calloused" but said that it revealed a "disregard for human misery."

Throughout 1947, Truman was subjected to a steady barrage by all parties to the controversy. While UNSCOP worked at its task, illegal entrants supported by funds supplied by American Zionists swarmed into the Holy Land. As President, Truman believed that this private American intervention impaired his efforts to arrive at a fair solution. In August, he wrote to Mrs. Roosevelt, "The action of some of our American Zionists will eventually prejudice everyone against what they are trying to get done. . . . I regret this situation very much because my sympathy has always been on their side."

UNSCOP finally made its recommendations public. It proposed separate Jewish and Arab states bound together in an economic union, with Jerusalem remaining under United Nations trusteeship. The Zionists immediately split on the recommendation for partition, while the Arab League announced threateningly on October 9 that its member nations were moving troops to the Palestine border. Then in November, the partition plan passed the General Assembly by a vote of 33 to 13.

But the American opponents of partition would not give up. At a Cabinet meeting on January 16, 1948, Forrestal argued that without Middle Eastern oil the Marshall Plan would fail and the American economy could not be maintained. He also met with Dean Rusk and Loy Henderson of the State Department on January 29, and Henderson agreed with his view that the General Assembly's vote was only a recommendation and not a final decision.

Despite Attlee's declaration on December 3, 1947, that his government was ending its mandate over Palestine the following May, the British stepped up their delivery of arms to the Arabs. In February, Truman wrote to Mrs. Roosevelt, "Britain's role in the Near East . . . has not changed in a hundred years. . . . Disraeli might just as well be Prime Minister these days."

Unexpectedly, on March 19, came an explosive announcement. On that day Warren Austin, American representative on the United Nations Security Council, flatly declared that the United States was no longer for partition. "My government believes that a temporary trusteeship for Palestine should be established . . . until Jews and Arabs . . . reach an agreement regarding the future of that country."

Truman immediately became the target of enraged Zionists who considered that he had broken a pledge. When Mrs. Roosevelt wrote Truman that she was resigning as a member of the American delegation to the United Nations, he refused to accept her resignation. "The truth of the matter was that Austin had acted on orders from the State Department," Niles said, "and Truman was not even informed of his talk until he read about it in the papers. He was as angry as I ever saw him. General Marshall was out of town, but when he returned, he, Loy Henderson and I had a meeting with Truman. We had a big argument about Austin's speech." When Truman emerged from the meeting, a reporter heard him mutter, "This gets us nowhere!" Later, at his news conference, Truman limply backed the trusteeship proposal and added that this did not mean rejection of partition but merely that it had been postponed. *Time* Magazine called his explanation a "comic-opera performance."

As the May 15 deadline for British withdrawal approached, Chaim Weizmann, head of the Provisional Government of Israel, wrote Truman and requested him to recognize the Jewish Government which would come into existence on the fourteenth. "The day before that deadline we had another hectic session in the President's office," Niles said. "Marshall and Lovett opposed recognition, while Clark Clifford and I urged it." Truman favored recognition of Israel, but the meeting ended without a decision because he did not want to hurt Marshall's feelings. The next day, however, when Niles and Clifford spoke to him again, he decided on recognition and passed word along to Marshall and Lovett. "Ten minutes after Israel came into being that afternoon," said Niles, "I called Eliahu Elath, the Israeli representative in Washington, and told him the good news. He was so excited that he cried." Truman also wrote an explanation to Mrs. Roosevelt:

> Since there was a vacuum in Palestine and since the Russians were anxious to be the first to do the recognizing, Gen. Marshall, Sec. Lovett, Dr. Rusk and myself worked the matter out and decided the proper thing to do was to recognize the Jewish Government.

The aftermath was, of course, war between the Arabs and Jews. But the new nation held its own. A year later, the Chief Rabbi of Israel, formerly the Chief Rabbi of Ireland, wanted to meet Truman and thank him. Niles recalled: "Rabbi Herzog told Truman, 'God put you in your mother's womb so you would be the instrument to bring about the rebirth of Israel after two thousand years.' I thought he was overdoing things, but when I looked over at the President, tears were running down his cheeks."

In the spring of 1948, the turmoil over Palestine, the Southern revolt against his civil rights message, Wallace's third party and the outspoken animosity of the New Dealers heightened activity to ditch Truman as a Presidential candidate. By May, Dr. Gallup issued his statistical summary which indicated that only 36 per cent of the population thought that Truman was doing a good job. In *Time* Magazine, Truman learned that he was "awkward, uninspired and above all mediocre" and that "the country appeared to be getting ready to drop the whole Truman Administration." Columnists advised him bluntly to clear out. *Life* Magazine later explained that the columnists had arrogated to themselves a "superiority complex vis-à-vis Truman." As *Life* put it: "Harry Truman doesn't know as much about diplomatic history as Walter Lippmann, he can't talk economics with *Newsweek*'s Henry Hazlitt, he lacks the dinner table brilliance of the Alsop brothers, he has read less widely than the editorial writer for *Life* Magazine."

It was by now evident to Truman's advisers that his candidacy was in jeopardy. Labor, which had lined up almost solidly behind the Democrats since 1932, turned its back on him. Although the C.I.O. voted 31–11 against supporting Wallace's third party, its president,

Phil Murray, Jack Kroll of its Political Action Committee, as well as Walter Reuther, David Dubinsky and James Carey, would not endorse Truman. Dan Tobin of the Teamsters gave reporters his opinion of Truman: "That squeaky-voice tinhorn. I want nothing to do with him." Al Whitney of the Trainmen was one of the few labor leaders to come out for Truman, but Alvanley Johnston and other Railroad Brotherhood leaders refused to do so. And John L. Lewis was belaboring him in faultless Shakespearean language.

In desperation, Democrats opposed to Truman seized on General Eisenhower as their Moses. Truman, however, had anticipated the pro-Eisenhower clamor and had moved to ease him from the national scene. In October, 1947, Forrestal wrote in his diary that Truman had mentioned Eisenhower's political interest with the acid comment that "everybody seemed to get either 'Potomac fever' or 'brass infection.' " Eisenhower was then Army Chief of Staff. The following month Forrestal reported that Truman was planning to shift General Omar Bradley from the Veterans Administration "to the Army with the idea that it would accelerate the change in the Chief of Staff. He did not want Eisenhower to withdraw but he thought he would take the hint." Eisenhower did take "the hint" by turning over his post to Bradley on February 7 and accepting the presidency of Columbia University.

Before Eisenhower left government service, Truman called him in for a heart-to-heart talk, asking him point-blank if he intended to run for President. Eisenhower replied that he had no such intention. Truman then told him that politics would only tarnish his "splendid career" and that he "was using good judgment."

In January, several Republicans had tried to induce Eisenhower to become their standard bearer. Leonard Finder, publisher of the Manchester *Union Leader,* put him into the Republican primary in New Hampshire, but Eisenhower wrote him on January 23:

> I could not accept nomination even under the remote circumstances that it would be tendered me. . . . The necessary and wise subordination of the military to civil power will be best sustained when life-long professional soldiers abstain from seeking high political office.

Strangely, Eisenhower's letter served as a spur to Democrats who interpreted it to mean that he was only cutting off the possibility of a Republican nomination. Senator Howard McGrath of Rhode Island, who had succeeded Bob Hannegan as Democratic National Chairman

309

after hypertension forced Hannegan to quit politics, was roundly booed at a Democratic dinner in Los Angeles when he praised Truman. When James Roosevelt followed McGrath with a pro-Eisenhower speech, he won prolonged applause.

Truman's future never looked more hopeless. Jake Arvey, the Cook County, Illinois, boss; Bill O'Dwyer, mayor of New York; and Mayor Hague of Jersey City now jumped on the Eisenhower bandwagon. Senator Richard Russell of Georgia announced that he had spoken with Eisenhower several times and was certain he was a states' rights man and therefore acceptable to the South. In the midst of the pro-Eisenhower tumult, Truman called General Marshall and told him that FDR, Jr., had threatened to make a public announcement that "the Democratic Party would have to draft General Eisenhower." Since Truman did not believe he should speak with Eisenhower again to get a reiteration of his stand against becoming a candidate, he asked Marshall to act for him. Marshall preferred not speaking directly to his protégé about this, although he induced Forrestal to do so. Without hesitation, Forrestal telephoned Eisenhower and gave him the news about the revolt "led by the late President's son and namesake against the Truman leadership."

At first Eisenhower was reluctant to telephone FDR, Jr., but Forrestal persuaded him to put the call through. "He called back in about ten minutes," Forrestal reported, "and said that he had got hold of Roosevelt and said that any action of this kind now, in the midst of very delicate situations in various countries abroad, could have the most dangerous consequences and might negate American policy."

Despite the general's unequivocal reply, FDR, Jr., went ahead with his announcement and the Eisenhower boom grew. A long line of Democrats streamed into his university office in the weeks that followed, and rumor spread that he would accept the nomination. Leon Henderson, chief of the Office of Price Administration under Roosevelt, said after his visit in June, "He just joshed me and said he was sure there were a lot of Democrats the Party could turn to without turning to him."

As the Eisenhower boom swelled and the attacks upon Truman increased, the President decided to get out and talk to the people. But he was confronted by the problem of how to finance such a trip, for the Democratic treasury was empty. The solution came when the University of California asked him to receive an honorary degree and speak at its commencement exercises. Since he could charge the expenses of the trip to the Presidential travel allowance on the grounds that it was nonpolitical, Truman promptly accepted the invitation.

Recalling the significance of that trip, Charlie Ross said, "One of our major concerns was that the President was unable to put himself across as a speaker. He sounded uninspired and was always racing for the period. But a change came abruptly on April 17 when he spoke to the American Society of Newspaper Editors in Washington. He gave a dull, prepared radio address, and there was little audience enthusiasm at any point. But when he was off the air, he didn't sit down. Instead he launched into an extemporaneous off-the-record talk on national problems from his own personal point of view. The language was entirely his own, earthy and warm, and the audience went wild." Several editors told Ross afterward, "If Truman campaigned that way, he'd be a hard guy to beat."

It was Truman's intention to speak in just the same direct, forceful way on his "nonpolitical" trip. On June 3, when his 18-car train was being made ready for the long crossing to California, he told reporters, "If I felt any better, I couldn't stand it." Out across the country the train moved slowly, making frequent stops for Truman's extemporaneous rear-platform talks. He seemed to be on fire and the crowds sensed it. Newsmen were amazed at the rapport between him and his audiences. This was a new Truman, out among friends who wanted to touch him and cheer him and claim him as their own. His foes were also their foes, especially when he told them about the prolonged and vicious campaign to make him out a fool. "They've been telling you a lot of things about your President, that he doesn't know what goes on, that he can't handle the Government . . . about my ability or inability, my intelligence or lack of it."

Everywhere he let crowds in on the secret of the "nonpartisan, bipartisan trip we are making." Then he hit at the 80th Congress, making Senator Taft his special target. "I guess he'd let you starve. I'm not that kind." At Gary, Indiana, he denounced the 80th Congress for not acting on his anti-inflation program; at Chicago, for not passing his Displaced Persons bill. In Chicago, 100,000 persons lined the streets to welcome him, and at a banquet at the Palmer House, he looked at his outraged opponent, Colonel Robert McCormick, publisher of the influential Chicago *Tribune,* and said, "In earlier years, I came to Chicago on shopping trips with Mrs. Truman. I enjoyed looking in the windows. No one paid any attention to me then. I suppose a lot of people wish I was looking in the windows again. But they won't get their way because a year from now I'm going to be right back in the same trouble I'm in now."

At Omaha the next day, he took time off to strut eight blocks with his Battery D boys in the 35th Division's annual parade. That evening Eddie McKim made a mess of the arrangements for Truman's speech at the Ak-Sur-Ben Coliseum and *Time* Magazine ran a picture of 8,000 empty seats. There were other mishaps along the way. At Carey, Idaho, because of poor briefing, he misread "William" for "Wilma" and mistakenly dedicated a new airfield "to the brave boy who died fighting for his country." At Eugene, Oregon, feeling folksy, he told the crowd, "I like Old Joe. He's a decent fellow, but he's a prisoner of the Politburo." This remark was to plague him for years.

The crowds were huge wherever he stopped. At Berkeley, where he got an honorary degree, 50,000 turned out to hear his excellent presentation on foreign affairs. A million welcomed him to Los Angeles. While in Spokane, he had first referred to the 80th Congress as the "worst Congress," and the label made a hit whenever he repeated it. At Albuquerque, one excited listener interrupted his recitation of the misdeeds of the 80th Congress to yell, "Lay it on, Harry! Give 'em hell!" Truman stopped momentarily. "I will! I intend to!" he called back. "There is just one issue. It is the special interests against the people."

On June 18, he was back in Washington. Congress was preparing to adjourn and the Washington *Evening Star* made this comment about his trip: "The President in this critical hour is making a spectacle of himself that would reflect discreditably on a ward heeler." Congressional denunciation of his "nonpolitical" trip was fierce. In a last-minute attempt to show who was boss, Republicans passed three bills over his veto.

The Republican National Convention got underway on June 20. Truman wanted Taft to win the nomination because he was the symbol of the 80th Congress. But Taft had too many liabilities. He was the father of the Taft-Hartley Act and the Party wanted some labor support; he had opposed terminal-leave pay for veterans and high price supports for farmers; he was an isolationist, a distinct liability by now; and he was forever getting himself in trouble with undiplomatic and inept language. When Truman returned from his tour, for instance, Taft lashed out at him for "blackguarding Congress at every whistle-stop." Across the nation Republican and Democratic mayors

312

at whose cities Truman had stopped immediately bombarded Taft with irate telegrams denying that their cities were "whistle-stops."

Before the Republican convention, a poll of newspaper correspondents had named Senator Vandenberg as "the most likely Presidential candidate." But neither Vandenberg nor Taft, Harold Stassen nor Governor Earl Warren of California was able to gut the drive of Governor Thomas E. Dewey. Dave Niles said, "After Dewey won the nomination, President Truman reminded me of Dewey's nasty comment about him after the 1944 Democratic Convention. Dewey was talking to reporters and he told them, 'I just can't remember the name of Roosevelt's running mate. Truman, isn't it?' "

On June 24, 1948, the day Dewey was nominated, Truman was confronted with a major international crisis. In April, the Russians had clamped down on all traffic from the Western Occupation Zones in Germany to Berlin deep within the Soviet Occupation Zone. Their excuse for this high-handed action was the "necessity" to inspect all materials being shipped to Berlin. After a few tense days, the Russians suddenly lifted their blockade and traffic was resumed. Despite the uneasiness that lingered afterward, Truman ordered currency reforms in the American Zone on June 18. This act particularly incensed the Russians because they had secured currency plates at the beginning of their occupation and had been flooding Western Germany with "greenback" marks. Now with the currency changed, they could no longer "create" money.

On June 24, only six days after the currency reforms, the Russians retaliated. All access between the West and Berlin was suddenly sealed off. First word from Moscow to Washington was that the Russians would rescind the order if Truman canceled the currency reform. Truman adamantly refused. Now came an arrogant message that the Western Powers had no right to be in Berlin.

At a hastily assembled White House meeting, Under Secretary of State Lovett raised the question: "Are we going to stay in Berlin or not?" Truman's reply was a grim "We are going to stay. Period!" To Truman, the Russian move was more than opposition to currency reform. It was "international Communism's counterattack" for recent setbacks in the Italian and French elections, the defection of Tito in Yugoslavia and the early success of the Marshall Plan. The question was how to maintain communication with the 2,400,000 persons in beleaguered Berlin. Forrestal favored the use of armored trains, others a preventive war, and some a rupture of diplomatic relations. All

313

these courses were wrong, Truman said. "As long as the Russians are willing to continue talks—however futile—there will be no shooting."

He knew, however, that talk would not keep Berliners alive. On June 26, he ordered all planes in the American European Command to service Berlin's needs until the Russians backed down. General Hoyt Vandenberg of the Air Force opposed this move on the grounds that American air strength would be eliminated elsewhere and "an emergency would find us more exposed than we might be able to afford." But Truman refused to accept his argument.

Truman's bold decision paid off. "The Berlin Airlift was important," he later said, "because it proved to the Commies that we weren't fooling about preserving our rights in Central Europe." The Berlin Blockade was not to terminate until May 12, 1949, when the Russians gave up. "It was a dangerous feat," Tom Connally said, "but in the end it paid off. The Soviets held us in higher esteem and the non-Communist European countries knew they could count on us."

During the crucial period of uncertainty regarding the Russian reaction to the Berlin Airlift, the Democrats were engaged in last-minute feverish preparations for their national convention, which was slated to start on July 12 in Philadelphia. Despite Truman's successful whistle-stop trip in June, the uproar had continued among labor leaders, Party bosses and New Dealers to nominate Eisenhower. It was not until nerves were considerably frayed that Eisenhower finally took himself out of Democratic contention. On July 5, with the help of George Allen, he drafted a statement: *I will not at this time identify myself with any political party and could not accept nomination for any political office.*

By the time Democratic delegates began filing into Convention Hall, an aura of abject defeat hung over them. Without Eisenhower, Truman could not be stopped. Yet there was almost complete unanimity that Truman would be swamped by Dewey in November. The 16-year reign of the Democrats appeared to be at an end. To remind delegates of their hopelessness, signs were seen everywhere in the hall: WE'RE JUST MILD ABOUT HARRY. The New York *Post* wrote: "The Party might as well immediately concede the election to Dewey and save the wear and tear of campaigning." The Alsop brothers predicted, "If Truman is nominated, he will be forced to wage the loneliest campaign in recent history."

Although Truman stayed behind in Washington to handle the day-to-day problems of the Berlin Airlift, he watched the proceedings over television and kept in constant touch with National Chairman Howard McGrath over developments at the convention. Otherwise the convention was safely in the hands of Truman's friends, with Sam Rayburn as permanent chairman and Alben Barkley as keynote speaker. Les Biffle as sergeant-at-arms was doling out tickets to make sure that there were no anti-Truman demonstrations.

Everything seemed to go wrong from the minute the convention was called to order. When taps were sounded for the war dead, the bugles hit several sour notes. Lawrence Tibbett sang "The Star-Spangled Banner," but the organist gave him such a high pitch that he sounded as if he were strangling. On Wednesday, when it came to the adoption of a platform, Senator Francis Myers of Pennsylvania presented the usual civil rights plank, designed not to offend the South or make Northern liberals feel too slighted. Instead of quick passage of this plank, however, the convention came to life for the first time when Mayor Hubert Humphrey of Minneapolis offered a much more extreme civil rights plank and exhorted delegates: "I say the time has come to walk out of the shadow of states' rights into the sunlight of human rights."

After a bitter floor debate, Humphrey's plank won by a vote of 651 to 582. And now there was trouble, for 35 Southern delegates walked out of Convention Hall never to return. Before he left, the chairman of the Alabama delegation told the convention, "We will never vote Republican, never vote for Truman and never accept the civil rights program. We, therefore, bid you good-by." A reporter asked J. Strom Thurmond, governor of South Carolina and leader of the Southern revolt, why he was taking this extreme step. "President Truman is only following the platform that Roosevelt advocated," the reporter argued.

"I agree," Thurmond said. "But Truman really means it."

On the question of his running mate, Truman had decided on Supreme Court Justice William O. Douglas. In 1946, after Truman fired Ickes, he had wanted Douglas to become Secretary of the Interior, but Douglas refused the offer. Truman was so certain that Douglas would now become his running mate that he made no effort to work up a list of other possibilities. Douglas was on vacation at a camp sixteen miles from Lostine, Oregon, when Truman reached him by phone and asked him to run as Vice-President. Douglas requested time to think it over, but meanwhile, White House aides urged Mrs. Roosevelt to bring pressure on Douglas. She sent him a note: "Your acceptance would give hope to many for the future of a liberal Democratic Party." Four days later, Douglas called Truman with his decision. "I am very sorry," he said, "but I have decided not to go into politics. I do not think I should use the Court as a steppingstone." Truman was terribly disappointed.

Douglas's refusal to run created a problem. Ed Flynn came up with the name of Wilson Wyatt, whom Truman had fired as head of the Veterans Emergency Housing Program. Another suggestion was Senator Joseph O'Mahoney of Wyoming. Neither man evoked Truman's enthusiasm.

At this point Les Biffle decided to take matters into his own hands and win the Vice-Presidential nomination for Alben Barkley. With impressive competence, in a single day he rounded up enough support to ensure Barkley's victory. Then on Tuesday morning, July 13, he and Barkley telephoned Truman.

"Would you mind if I tried to be named Vice-President?" Barkley asked. Biffle quickly added that he had the votes. Truman's recollection was that Barkley's candidacy came as a complete surprise to him.

"Mr. Truman didn't want me at first," Barkley reported later. (Barkley was almost seventy-one and his age might have been a factor.) In the end, however, Truman asked, "Why didn't you tell me you wanted to be Vice-President, Alben? . . . It's all right with me."

Rayburn's plan was to complete the convention's preliminary business on Wednesday, the fourteenth, and then proceed immediately with the nominations for President and Vice-President. Truman decided it would be best if he appeared in person to accept the nomination. According to Rayburn's timetable, this would be about 9 P.M.

In the late afternoon of that day Truman, Bess and Margaret boarded the Presidential train for Philadelphia. The city was like a furnace when they stepped from the train and entered Convention Hall. Since the voting had not yet begun, Truman and Barkley waited in a dressing room used by show performers on the floor beneath the auditorium. All that evening until 2 A.M. Truman sat on a hard wooden chair facing the alley and held court with visitors. One reported that Truman told him, "They may be mad at me. But I'm not mad at them. I believe in Christ."

When the vote on the Presidential nominee finally came up, Truman beat Senator Russell by 947½ to 263 and Barkley won the Vice-

Presidential nomination by acclamation. The air was stifling when Truman and Barkley walked onto the platform and delegates sat exhausted from their three-day grind.

To brighten Truman's entrance, fifty doves were released from beneath a flower Liberty Bell as a symbol of peace. One banged into the balcony and flopped dead to the floor. "A dead pigeon," one delegate piped up, looking at Truman. The birds, weak from the heat and from being cooped for hours, were a sorry sight. "One perched on Sam Rayburn's head," said Truman. "Was Sam disgusted. Funniest thing in the convention."

Barkley spoke first and made a short acceptance speech, but it was obviously too long for the weary delegates.

Then came Truman's turn. He looked out into the sea of exhausted faces. "Senator Barkley and I will win this election and make these Republicans like it—don't you forget that!" The delegates, electrified by Truman's fighting mood, came to their feet with wild cheers. For twenty minutes he poured it on the Republicans in an extreme, partisan talk, and the Democrats were once more an excited political party. "I made a tough, fighting speech," Truman recalled. "I tore into the Eightieth Congress. . . . I listed in detail the failures and I did not pull any punches." His language was that of the man on the whistle-stop tour.

His trump card came toward the end.

> "On the twenty-sixth of July, which out in Missouri we call 'Turnip Day,' I am going to call Congress back and ask them to pass laws to halt rising prices, to meet the housing crisis—which they are saying they are for in their platform.
>
> "At the same time, I shall ask them to act upon other vitally needed measures, such as aid to education, which they say they are for; a national health program; civil rights legislation, which they say they are for; an increase in the minimum wage, which I doubt very much they are for; extension of the social security coverage and increased benefits, which they say they are for; funds for projects needed in our program to provide public power and cheap electricity. By indirection this Eightieth Congress has tried to sabotage the power policies the United States has pursued for fourteen years. The power lobby is as bad as the real estate lobby which is sitting on the housing bill. I shall ask for adequate and decent laws for displaced persons in place of this anti-Semitic, anti-Catholic law which this Eightieth Congress passed.
>
> "Now, my friends, if there is any reality behind that Republican

317

platform, we ought to get some action from a short session of the Eightieth Congress. They can do this job in fifteen days, if they want to do it. They will still have time to go and run for office. . . . They are going to drag all the red herrings they can across this campaign, but I am here to say that Senator Barkley and I are not going to let them get away with it."

When he made his exit, it was to resounding cheers. He had come an unwanted man. He left, a leader.

34

DESPITE the stir of excitement Truman had injected into the Democratic convention, there was little reason to believe he would win the election. Southern Democrats had organized a States' Rights Party, nominating Governor Strom Thurmond of South Carolina and Governor Fielding Wright of Mississippi to oppose him in the South. The Wallace Progressive Party had also named its ticket with Senator Glen Taylor of Idaho as Wallace's running mate. The Democratic Party appeared to be a splintered political organization.

Moreover, the Gallup Poll, as well as the Crossley and Roper forecasts, indicated an overwhelming Dewey victory. In fact, Elmo Roper announced after his July poll that further polling was a waste of money. *Fortune* Magazine wrote: "The prospects of Republican victory are now so overwhelming that an era of what will amount to one party may well impend." When Harold Stassen paid a courtesy call on Dewey in July at his Pawling, New York, farm, Dewey hauled out a copy of Roper's poll and gave Stassen the pitch for his forthcoming campaign: "My job is to prevent anything from rocking the boat."

The Republicans were furious with Truman's call for the "Turnip Day Special Session" beginning on July 26. Senator Vandenberg, whom he had systematically showered with patronage and favors, turned on him now and called his action "the last hysterical gasp of an expiring administration." After Truman opened the Turnip session, Vandenberg wrote in his diary "All the Republicans and most of the Southern Democrats received him in stony silence. . . . A big group wanted to adjourn *sine die* and go home immediately following his message."

This would have been a wise move, for each day the Special Session sat, Truman bombarded it with broadsides about its "failures" and "feeble compromises." An astute politician, he demanded that the Special Session pass an impossible list of social legislation. When concerned Republicans ordered Administration officials to appear before committees and explain these programs, agency heads procrastinated. Finally, after eleven days of White House ridicule, Senator Taft refused to give Truman any more ammunition against the 80th Congress and brought about adjournment. By the time members dispersed from Washington, Republican leaders were aware that they had blundered.

Nevertheless, Truman's personal triumph in momentarily dispelling the gloom by his fighting speech at the convention and his derisive jibes at the Special Session of Congress did not make the Democrats more confident. Political appointees began a scramble for jobs in private industry and several Cabinet members and sub-Cabinet officials quietly let it be known that their houses were for sale come January. Forrestal wrote to friends that "the end of this year will be the end of my bureaucratic career." In his diary he recorded that Admiral Roscoe Hillenkoetter, head of the Central Intelligence Agency, which Truman had established, was also "assuming Mr. Dewey's election."

Worst of all, the Democratic treasury, like Mother Hubbard's cupboard, was bare. When Senator McGrath called a financial meeting of the Party at the Mayflower Hotel, few showed up, and no one offered to become financial chairman. McGrath sat stunned. Finally, Louis A. Johnson asked him to call a short recess while he went to the White House for a talk with Truman. When he returned to the meeting, he announced that he would take on the fund-raising job. The immediate crisis was averted. Senator Kilgore explained what had happened: "Louie had been hankering after a Cabinet post for years. Roosevelt made him Assistant Secretary of War with the under-

320

standing that he would succeed Secretary Woodring. But Roosevelt never came through on his promise. Now Johnson settled for a promise of a Cabinet post from Truman in exchange for raising campaign money."

Without Johnson, the campaign would never have got off the ground. At the outset, he was forced to pay the Party's initial expenses from his own pocket. Then, when contributions came in, the flow was never more than a trickle.

When McGrath first informed Truman of the financial problem, Truman immediately thought of Bernard Baruch, the old park bench sage who had contributed so generously to the Democrats in the past. But Baruch refused to serve on the finance committee. This was a resounding slap to Truman, who had gone out of his way to provide Baruch with an open door to the White House and a United Nations forum to air the Administration's views on atomic energy control. Angrily, he let it be known that he considered Baruch a publicity seeker, "the only man to my knowledge who has built a reputation on a self-assumed unofficial status as 'adviser.'" On August 31, Truman sent Baruch a letter ending their relationship. "My dear Mr. Baruch," he wrote. "A great many honors have passed your way . . . and it seems when the going is rough, it's a one-way street." In a postcript, he added that he was appointing two women as his official representatives at the forthcoming coronation of Queen Juliana of Holland, even though Baruch's brother was then Ambassador to The Hague.

In August, Les Biffle donned baggy pants and a worn jacket and wandered through West Virginia, Kentucky, Ohio and Illinois to do some polling on his own. After three weeks he returned to Washington and paid a call on Truman. "I think you can win," he told him. "Do you really think so?" Truman asked, with some disbelief.

Truman understood that he was embarking on a lonely venture. "But that didn't bother him," Harry Vaughan said. "He got his baptism in 1940 when he was all alone in that campaign, deserted by his so-called friends. That experience helped give him the terrific confidence in himself that he needed in 1948."

But if he had confidence, he realized that it was not shared by many others. Besides the polls, Dewey had money and the backing of most of the nation's papers. A check revealed that only 20 per cent of the papers with a mere 10 per cent of national daily circulation were on Truman's side. Influential Democrats not only refused to contribute money but refrained from coming out for Truman. The White House made an effort to enlist Mrs. Roosevelt's support, but she refused to take part in the campaign on the grounds that she was a United Nations delegate. In a letter to a friend she wrote:

> I haven't actually endorsed Mr. Truman. . . . Unless we are successful in electing a very strong group of liberals in Congress, in spite of my feelings about the Republican Party and Governor Dewey, I can not have much enthusiasm for Mr. Truman.

By September the Republicans were treating Truman's candidacy as a huge joke. The Berlin crisis was hotter than ever, and while the papers were filled with Republican jibes, Forrestal importuned Truman to turn over custody of the atomic bomb to the military and urged that it be used "if necessary."

Berlin crisis or not, Truman could not remain at his White House desk and let Dewey massacre him. "I want to see the people," he told Charlie Ross. "I'm going to visit every whistle-stop in the United States."

His initial foray took him to Michigan on Labor Day, September 6. Charlie Ross said, "We didn't know what to expect in Michigan because the papers were trying to make it appear we were lepers." It was a six-speech day with the first stop at Grand Rapids at 7:30 A.M. It was pouring rain, yet the crowd that greeted Truman was enthusiastic. "I don't want you to vote for me," he said. "I want you to get out on election day and vote for yourselves—for your interests, your own part of the country—your own friends." At Lansing, the second stop, the large crowd cheered him wildly. Then he went on to Detroit's Cadillac Square where 250,000 persons were assembled for his major Labor Day address. "We are in a hard, tough fight against shrewd and rich opponents." He shook a fist. "They know they can't count on your vote. Their only hope is that you won't vote at all. They have misjudged you. I know that we are going to win this crusade for the right!"

After that he went to Hamtramck, where the entire city turned out to greet him. Then came stops at Pontiac and Flint before he sped back to Washington. Everywhere the crowds called him "Harry"; they applauded Bess and Margaret, and laughed with him when he heaped ridicule on the Republicans. "It was an auspicious curtain-raiser," Charlie Ross said. But the Republicans shrugged off the large crowds as the natural desire of Americans to see a President.

Heartened by this initial success, Truman now planned a cross-country trip that would take him through the cities and towns and into the farm belt and rural America. Barkley and General Marshall came to Washington's Union Station to see him and Margaret off on September 17. Bess was to join the caravan at Des Moines. "Mow 'em down!" Barkley exhorted him, after treating Margaret to his customary Rudolph Valentino kiss.

"I'm going to give 'em hell," Truman assured him.

It was to be a 21,928-mile trip, the most exhaustive campaign tour on land in history. An estimated 12 to 15 million Americans came out to see him and listened to 275 prepared speeches and, as Truman put it, "about 200 more off the record."

He set out from Washington aboard the *Ferdinand Magellan,* a reconstructed Pullman car which had been sold to the Government in 1942 for one dollar by the Association of American Railroads for President Roosevelt's personal use. Covered with armor plate, the *Magellan* weighed 285,000 pounds and had three-inch-thick bullet-proof glass. It contained a lounge, four bedrooms, a dining compartment seating 12, galley and bath. All along the route a pilot train filled with Secret Service men preceded the 17-car Presidential train for security checks. In some places, the President's train had to be run over special routes because bridges could not sustain its tonnage.

At Dexter, Iowa, Truman made his first major speech of the tour before 75,000 persons at the national plowing contest. After a stodgy formal talk, he returned to the platform to speak off-the-cuff as a fellow farmer. "I can plow a straight furrow," he said. "A prejudiced witness said so—my mother." He described how he used to seed a 160-acre wheat field "without leaving a skip." He went on to brag that he did all this with only four mules and a gangplow, not the tractors of the modern era. The farmers whooped and hollered.

Dewey started across the country on September 19 in his *Victory Special.* He, too, spoke in Iowa at the Drake University Field House in Des Moines. Joe Alsop, who heard both Truman and Dewey, reported afterward: "There was something sad about the contrast between the respective campaign debuts here in Iowa. The Truman show was threadbare and visibly unsuccessful—the Dewey show was opulent. . . . The contest was really too uneven."

At Denver the following Monday, cheering thousands lined the streets as Truman rode through the city in an open car. He hit out at the Republicans, called them "a bunch of old mossbacks . . . living back in 1890 . . . trying to sabotage the West." At Reno he got so excited that he called the Republicans "mothbags" instead of "mossbacks." His tone was folksy. "All over the country they call me 'Harry.' I like it. I believe when you speak to me like that you like me."

The hitches in his campaigning techniques had been slowly smoothed out by the time his train rolled into California. Oscar Chapman, Under Secretary of the Interior, served as advance man, working up advance "poop" sheets to inform Truman where he would be stopping en route, what local dignitaries were to board his train and what compliments to pay each locality. When the job grew too exhausting for Chapman, Donald Dawson, a White House aide, helped out. A large group of speech writers were along, some to prepare the longer addresses and some the five-minute talks. Clark Clifford, the chief speech writer, jumped off the train at each stop with Truman's physician, Dr. Graham, and both acted as shills to lead the applause at the proper time.

After a while, the routine became standardized. At each stop the local high school band blared out "Hail to the Chief"; then came the presentation of a gift to Truman, his modest thank you, a welcome to local Democratic leaders and compliments to the community for its new factory or airfield. The climax was an attack on Republicans and the 80th Congress. Republicans gulped to hear themselves referred to as "gluttons of privilege" and "bloodsuckers with offices in Wall Street." Everywhere Truman repeatedly ripped into the Special Session: "When I called them back into session in July, what did they do? Nothing. Nothing. That Congress never did anything the whole time it was in session. If the Republicans win, they'll tear you to pieces." Hoover also came in for some hard raps, even though he and Truman were good friends. "You remember the Hoover cart —the remains of the old Tin Lizzie being pulled by a mule because you couldn't afford to buy a new car or gas for the old one. First you had the Hoovercrats and then you had the Hoovercarts. One always follows the other." Nor was Dewey spared. In town after town, Truman ridiculed him. "Ridicule is a wonderful weapon," he told his aides.

After his political talk, he asked the crowd, "Howja like to meet my family?" Bess came onto the back platform and he identified her as "the boss," with a broad wink at the men in the audience. Then

324

he brought out Margaret and introduced her as "my baby" and "the boss's boss." This was the biggest hit at each stop.

The Secret Service men paled when he climbed off the train to mix with the crowd and shake hands. Once he noticed a cowboy on a skittish horse approach the rear platform in the midst of the crowd. Truman kept an eye on the horse, fearing that it might bolt and seriously injure the people around it. Slowly he descended from the platform and grasped the horses's bridle. "Right nice horse you have there, son," he said, pulling open the horse's mouth. "I see it's eight years old." Then he handed the bridle to a man standing close by and ordered him to lead the animal away.

At Los Angeles the Republicans kept him from speaking at the Hollywood Bowl by renting it for the night he was in town as well as the next night when Dewey was scheduled to speak, claiming that they needed it on Truman's evening to test the lighting. As a result Truman glumly had to settle for the less desirable Gilmore Stadium.

Once he was back on his whistle-stop tour, however, his spirits rose and he began joshing with audiences again. In Barstow a woman called out to him, "Mr. Truman, you sound as if you have a cold."

"That's because I ride around in the wind with my mouth open," he called back.

He moved on to Texas where some Dixiecrats had warned Vic Messall, his former Senate secretary, that "they'd shoot Truman if he went down there, that no-good s.o.b. and his civil rights."

At Dallas, Attorney General Tom Clark, who had been promised the next Supreme Court opening, evoked fits of laughter when he introduced Truman as "the man who stopped Joe Louis."

"No," said Truman, jumping up, "that was John L. I don't have enough muscle to have stopped Joe."

At Waco, Truman received his first booing when he shook hands with a Negro woman. Lyndon Johnson, who had recently won the Texas Senatorial primary from Coke Stevenson by a scant 87 votes, joined the Truman caravan for a while. Campaign or no campaign, Truman could not leave Texas without paying his respects to "Cactus Jack" Garner. He arrived at Uvalde at five A.M. and was surprised by the large gathering waiting to greet him at that miserable hour. He gave the crowd a rousing talk and, at seven, left the train with a small satchel to drive to his old mentor's house. "I've brought something for you," he told Garner. Quickly he opened the bag and pulled out a bottle of whisky. "For snake bites," he advised.

A crisis came at Oklahoma City when there was no money to get the train out of the station. Fortunately, Governor Roy J. Turner and Elmer Harbor of Shawnee, Oklahoma, held a collection party aboard the train and raised enough money to pay for the rest of that tour. Disaster had been averted, but the incident made Truman acutely aware of how precarious his entire campaign was.

While Truman continued to make his way east, Dewey was proceeding according to his plan. He posed as a young elder statesman before the Rushmore Memorial in South Dakota and spoke like a man who already guided the nation's destiny. A reporter accompanying Dewey aptly quipped: "How long is Dewey going to tolerate Truman's interference with running the government?"

With the polls showing him a certain victor, Dewey saw no need to extend himself. He rose late each day and limited his speaking; Truman was up at dawn and drove himself relentlessly until midnight, one day making a total of 16 speeches. Dewey radiated confidence, while Truman personified the underdog who needed everyone's help. Dewey cooed; Truman berated. Dewey exuded calm; Truman, an intense excitement. Dewey's campaign operated with clockwork efficiency; Truman's had an off-the-cuff informality.

Dewey delivered long radio addresses. Truman was often cut off in mid-speech and listeners wondered why he was treated so insultingly. Sometimes this was done on purpose by Louis Johnson "to dramatize the meager funds of the Democrats." At other times there was simply not enough money to pay for precious extra minutes of air time. On one occasion, a radio executive told Johnson, "we'll have to cut him off in a minute unless you agree to put up more money."

"Go ahead." Johnson smiled. "That will mean another million votes."

Truman was back at his White House desk for a short period early in October. While there, he decided to send Chief Justice Fred Vinson to Moscow to talk to Stalin about easing the Cold War. At first Vinson declined, but in the end he agreed to go. When Truman summoned Tom Connally and Arthur Vandenberg to the White House on October 5 to discuss the proposed Vinson Mission, Vandenberg told Connally on the way out, "He must be feeling desperate about the campaign."

Despite the opposition of the two Senators to the Vinson Mission, Truman told Charlie Ross to arrange a half-hour broadcast over the four networks so he could explain its purpose to the American people. But unfriendly papers got wind of his intention and ran long stories about Truman's "appeasement," "unilateral action" and "political stunt." It was only when General Marshall, who was then in Paris, told Truman that he was upset by the idea of sending an emissary to Stalin that Truman called the mission off. Later he complained that it was all right for Roosevelt to bypass the State Department and send Hopkins on special diplomatic missions, but when he wanted to do so, he was accused of "undermining the State Department."

While the Republicans were defending the State Department against him and Vinson, Truman started on his eastern tour. The crowds were even more enormous than before. During his New York swing, 5,000 persons showed up at the Albany station at eight A.M. in a driving rainstorm. "And at every station along the way it was still pouring down rain," Truman said, "but there were overflow crowds everywhere—even in those Republican Congressional Districts." Pennsylvania was more of the same. Here Senator Francis Myers told Truman excitedly, "When they fill even the doorways, windows and rooftops, it could mean victory."

In Ohio, Frank J. Lausche, running for governor, feared that any association with Truman would harm his own candidacy. Lausche reluctantly agreed to board the *Magellan* a few miles outside Columbus and get off when they reached the city. About 7,000 persons were at the station in the tiny town where Lausche climbed aboard. At the next town the crowd was even larger. Then at Columbus the station was not big enough to hold the mob. "Is this the way all the crowds have been?" Lausche asked in amazement.

"Yes," Truman told him matter-of-factly. "But this is smaller than we had in most states."

Lausche stared at him, dumfounded. Finally he muttered, "Well, this is the biggest crowd I ever saw in Ohio." He stayed on the train all the way to Cleveland.

On October 12, Dewey committed a blunder at Beaucoup, Illinois, where a thousand persons gathered at his special train to hear him. Suddenly, without warning, the train backed up into the crowd. People screamed and ran for their lives. Dewey was almost jerked over the platform before the train halted, but fortunately, no one was injured. "That's the first lunatic I've had for an engineer," Dewey said, justifiably. "He probably should be shot at sunrise, but we'll let him off this time since no one was hurt."

The Democrats twisted Dewey's remark to show that he had an anti-union bias. As Truman expressed it: "He objects to having engineers back up. He doesn't mention that under that great engineer, Hoover, we backed up into the worst depression in history."

Truman began more and more to resemble William Jennings Bryan in his charges. There were devils in Wall Street; the Republican Party was "controlled by silent and cunning men who have a dangerous lust for power and privilege." Dewey remained unperturbed as he continued to say, "Our streams should abound with fish," and that he would "cooperate with the farmers to protect all the people from the tragedy of another dust bowl." That fall saw a record crop and Truman railed at the Republican 80th Congress for not providing ample storage space.

As the campaign raced into its final weeks, reporters began to wonder about the differences in the size of the crowds each candidate was drawing. At St. Paul, for instance, Truman drew 21,000 and Dewey only 8,000. Dewey's train traveled in solitude between stops; Truman's train was heralded all along the way by clusters of people waving their hands. *Time* Magazine noted: "Politicians and columnists seem puzzled by the phenomenon." Bob Albright of the Washington *Post* wrote that reporters had begun asking themselves, "Could we be wrong?" Another reporter wrote that the people of the United States seemed "willing to give Truman anything he wanted except the Presidency." Nevertheless, despite Truman's larger crowds, the reporters remained about 8–1 in their belief that Dewey would win. Margaret Truman said, "Many of the reporters who had traveled on our train were condescending. Contempt was lying around in hunks." A few weeks before the end of the campaign, Bess Truman asked Clark Clifford about her husband's self-confidence: "Does he really believe that he'll be elected?" Truman himself admitted that "my advisers were still not optimistic."

The race toward the wire was now on. Republicans showed concern about the farm belt. The price of corn, which stood at $2.36 a bushel in January, dropped to a low of $1.38 on October 15. They felt the sting of Truman's tongue as he hurled his relentless charge that the somnolent 80th Congress was to blame. In addition, Dewey became aware that Midwestern Republicans were not putting out a great effort in his behalf. Chief of the laggards was Representative Charles Halleck of Indiana, who had been told before the Republican convention that he would be Dewey's running mate.

At the last minute, New Dealers began flocking back to the fold. Despite their fight in 1946, Harold Ickes came out for Truman and sarcastically described Dewey as "the candidate in sneakers . . . for unity, Alice in Wonderland and Grimm's Fairy Tales, to say nothing of home and mother." From Paris, Mrs. Roosevelt made a six-minute short-wave broadcast in behalf of Truman at a cost to Louis Johnson's finance committee of $25,721. More contributions came in and the Democratic National Committee flooded the country with comic books on Truman's life. Hollywood New Dealers produced and distributed 2,000 prints of a film on Truman which was shown in movie houses across the nation during the last six days of the campaign.

Audiences continued to welcome Truman with a floodtide of cheers. He drew 50,000 persons at an Indianapolis rally on a cold night. More than 300,000 greeted him in Chicago. At the Chicago Stadium, where four years earlier he had won the Vice-Presidential nomination, 30,000 jammed inside while 10,000 more stood outside and listened to his broadcast. Once again he "poured it on" the Republicans: "Herbert Hoover once ran on the slogan: 'Two cars in every garage.' Apparently the Republican candidate this year is running on the slogan 'Two families in every garage.' "

"Give 'em hell, Harry!" came the cry from the crowd. "I have good news for you," he shouted back. "We have the Republicans on the run. We are going to win."

Toward the end of October, he headed back to Missouri. On the thirtieth, he was exhausted as his train pulled into St. Louis for his last campaign speech at a mammoth rally that evening. His staff worked feverishly polishing his national radio address, but Truman fell asleep and had to be roused just before air time. Because he had not had time to read the speech, he threw it away and spoke extemporaneously. Reporters judged it the best speech of the campaign. The Washington *Post* predicted that if the vote were close, this speech might make the difference for Truman.

The next day he returned to Independence, his campaign over. The plane carrying reporters landed at the Kansas City airport after he had already started off by car for home. They hurried after him in press cars, preceded by a police escort with wailing sirens, but when they reached Delaware Street, he was not there. He finally arrived several minutes later and a newsman asked him why he was late.

"Oh," he replied, "we were stopped by a police car and had to pull over. Seems there were some very important people going through town."

At last, election day, November 2, arrived. Margaret Truman said that when her father announced he would sweep the country "reporters laughed hysterically." Final predictions flooded the papers as Truman left the house to vote. Drew Pearson wrote that Dewey had "conducted one of the most astute and skillful campaigns in recent years." Pearson had already filed his column for the day after the election, informing readers: "I surveyed the closely knit group around Tom Dewey who will take over the White House 86 days from now." *The New York Times* predicted that Dewey would amass 345 electoral votes; the Gallup Poll gave Dewey a 49.5 per cent vote to Truman's 44.5; Elmo Roper held to his final poll in September, which showed a 52–37 per cent victory for Dewey. Walter Lippmann and the Alsop brothers foresaw a black day for the Democrats, as did Marquis Childs. The Kiplinger magazine's cover read: WHAT DEWEY WILL DO. In its November 1 issue, *Life* showed a picture of Dewey and his wife aboard a small vessel and captioned the shot with: *The next President travels by ferry boat over the broad waters of San Francisco Bay.*

For the traditional election night ceremony the Democratic headquarters were at the Biltmore Hotel in New York, while the Republicans gathered a few blocks away at the Hotel Roosevelt. By early evening, the Roosevelt ballroom was jammed with gleeful Republicans. Governor Dewey remained in an upper-floor suite, preparing to come down to the ballroom balcony and announce himself the winner. James J. Maloney, head of the Secret Service, was so certain of a Republican victory that he and five of his men unobtrusively joined Dewey to protect the nation's next Chief Executive.

In contrast to the din at the Roosevelt, the Biltmore headquarters were deserted, except for a few gloomy Democratic party workers and a handful of junior reporters sent as a token gesture. The sad scene promised to grow even more dismal as the hours passed. Audible groans rose when word was received that the four radio networks had sent out alerts to stations to prepare for Dewey's victory announcement at nine P.M. Even when the first scattered returns showed Truman leading, Jim Farley explained over a radio network: "But this is only an early lead. He cannot win—his early lead will fold up."

330

"Late that afternoon," Tom Evans said, "Truman was at dinner at a club in Independence. He told me he was going to sneak away, and after excusing himself to go to the men's room, he ran out the back door. Then with three Secret Service men, he drove to the Elms Hotel at Excelsior, about thirty miles northeast of Kansas City.

"He called me later at the penthouse in the Muehlebach Hotel where his staff and friends were gathered. He had heard the first report over the radio and he said he was going to win. After that we kept in constant touch with each other and his confidence was something to hear. About midnight, H. V. Kaltenborn got on the air with his famous comment—'Mr. Truman is still ahead but these are returns from a few cities. When the returns come in from the country the result will show Dewey winning overwhelmingly.' Then came the bad news that Dewey had won New York because of Henry Wallace's large vote there. I called Harry and told him he had to carry either Ohio, Illinois or California.

"'Tom,' Truman said, 'don't call me any more. I'm going to bed.'

"'What the hell do you mean?' I asked.

"'Just that,' he shouted. 'I'm going to carry all three states so don't call me any more. I'll be over at eight in the morning.'"

In New York, the victorious aura at the Roosevelt had changed to concern when Truman held his national lead. Reporters who had gone there to interview Dewey straggled out toward the Biltmore, which was now filling up with Democrats. Herbert Brownell, Dewey's campaign manager, pale and nervous, said in a shaky voice that Dewey would still win. Close to three in the morning, a reporter looked at Dr. Gallup, whose reputation as a pollster was at stake, and said he resembled "an animal eating its young."

At four A.M., Jim Rawley, one of the Secret Service men with Truman, burst into his room and told him to listen to Kaltenborn. Truman learned that he was over 2,000,000 votes ahead, but Kaltenborn kept insisting, "I don't see how he can be elected. The election will be decided in the House."

"At four-thirty, Matt Connelly and I called Harry," Tom Evans said. "He was awake and in grand humor. 'I'm coming over at six to celebrate,' he told us. The penthouse was a mess when he walked in. We had been up all night and Charlie Ross lay sprawled dead drunk over a bed. We tried to wake him up but he didn't come to. We were screaming like school kids."

Dewey did not concede until 11:14 A.M., when it was certain that

Truman had carried California, Illinois and Ohio with their 78 electoral votes. Truman's total was 304 electoral votes, or a victory margin of 38. The popular vote showed Truman's total as 24,104,836 to Dewey's 21,969,500. The most exciting election in the nation's history was over. Dewey was in a state of shock. He admitted later that he felt like the man who had awakened inside a coffin with a lily in his hand and said to himself, "If I'm alive, what am I doing here? And if I'm dead, why do I have to go to the bathroom?"

Senator Taft exhibited deep bitterness. "I don't care how the thing is explained," he told reporters. "It defies all common sense to send that roughneck ward politician back to the White House." To his staff, Senator Vandenberg said: "You've got to give the little man credit. There he was flat on his back. Everyone had counted him out but he came up fighting and won the battle. That's the kind of courage the American people admire."

Truman enjoyed the perfumed odor of success because he alone had brought it about. At the St. Louis station, on his way back to Washington, he grinned and held aloft a copy of the Chicago *Tribune* with the headline: DEWEY DEFEATS TRUMAN. In Washington, a crowd of 750,000 welcomed him. On Pennsylvania Avenue, the Washington Post Building displayed a sign reading, *Mr. President, we are ready to eat crow whenever you are ready to serve it.* The "Wednesday Morning Club" of Democrats who had been unwilling to contribute to the campaign sent the Party $600,000 in a single day. George Allen told Truman, "I was supremely confident of your defeat." Truman jabbed him in the ribs. "So was everybody else. But you're the first one who's admitted it."

35

SINCE the fall of 1945, Truman had been under almost constant personal attack. And now he found that editors who had previously denounced him with passion were calling him a "master politician." Magazines and newspapers bowed and scraped as they admitted their error in writing him off as a backwoods politician heading straight for oblivion.

One thing was certain: he had no appetite to whistle-stop through another Presidential campaign. "In December of 1948," Harry Vaughan said, "I went into his office shortly before the morning staff conference because I needed his signature on some work I was doing. I asked him point-blank, 'Are you going to run for re-election in 1952?' "

Truman stared at Vaughan in astonishment. "Have you lost your mind? There is only one conceivable way I might be forced to and that is if we were right in the middle of a shooting war—which I don't think we'll be in." He grinned. "By the way, have you got a candidate?"

"Sure," Vaughan replied. "Fred Vinson."

"I'll let you in on a secret," Truman said. "He's mine, too."

The pinnacle of Harry Truman's political career came on January 20, 1949, when he took the oath of office, not as Franklin Roosevelt's number one pallbearer, but as President in his own right. Months before, Republicans had booked most Washington hotels for their expected return to power, and now Democrats had trouble getting rooms. But there was little reason to grumble, because no one expected to do much sleeping. Bars and hotel lobbies were jammed with exuberant Democrats who slapped each other's backs and the air rang with cries of "good old Harry!" The postwar prosperity was evident in the heavy spending and tipping, the sheer number of well-dressed Democrats. Even the inauguration itself was opulent, thanks to the Republican 80th Congress which had generously appropriated funds for what was expected to be Dewey's inauguration festival.

For Truman, January 20 started with breakfast with the 97 surviving members of Battery D. Aging and showing signs of wear, the veterans were nevertheless still a boisterous, spirited bunch. Their old padre, Monsignor L. Curtis Tiernan said grace; then the boys were at it, with loud, continually interrupted tales about Battery D's ballooned exploits.

When the talk simmered down, Truman gave them their battle plans for the inauguration. "I want you to keep sober until the parade," he warned.

"Okay, Captain Harry," several groaned.

He added: "You're going to serve as my guard of honor and march in two long lines beside my car all the way from the Capitol down Pennsylvania Avenue to the White House reviewing stands." (More groans) "I'm sure you can still make one hundred and twenty steps a minute for a mile and a quarter."

After breakfast they sang several songs, including two written for the occasion in honor of Captain Harry. Then they presented him with a gold-headed cane. While one man unwrapped it, another called out, "Don't break it, you clumsy bastard!" Truman promised to use the cane henceforth during his early morning walks around Washington.

At ten A.M., Truman, a Baptist, attended services at Bess and Margaret's church, St. John's Episcopal. Then, escorted by the Joint Committee of Congress, he drove to the Capitol. The Marine Band played "Hail to the Chief" and then he was sworn into office before a crowd of 100,000.

Truman's inaugural address was significant because he introduced a new concept in American foreign policy. In listing a four-point program, he declared the first three points to be "unfaltering support of the United Nations," continued Marshall Plan aid for the economic recovery of Europe and a strengthened military basis for non-Communist countries to withstand aggression. Point Four was "a bold new program for making the benefits of our scientific advances and industrial progress available for the improvement and growth of underdeveloped areas." Arnold Toynbee, the historian, predicted that it would not be the discovery of atomic energy but the solicitude of privileged peoples for the unprivileged as voiced in Truman's Point Four and its implementation that "will be remembered as the signal achievement of the age."

After the inaugural address, Truman and Vice-President Barkley led the long parade down Pennsylvania Avenue with the men of Battery D panting alongside their car. Then in the cold of the White House reviewing stand, they sat through a three-hour parade. Governor Thurmond, the Dixiecrat leader, rode past the reviewing stand and Barkley started to wave to him, but Truman pulled his arm down. In another parade car, General Eisenhower came by. Four years later, at Eisenhower's inauguration, Truman said that the following conversation took place:

Eisenhower: "I did not attend your inauguration in 1949 out of consideration for you, because if I had been present I would have drawn attention away from you."

Truman: "You were not here in 1949 because I did not send for you. But if I had sent for you, you would have come."

After the 1948 election, the Truman's moved into Blair House across Pennsylvania Avenue from the Executive Mansion. Late in 1947 he and Bess first grew concerned about the condition of the White House structure. "The big fat butler brought me my breakfast one morning and the floor shook," he said. The butler recalled that the President told him that he felt the whole floor sway "as if floating in space." A few months later, Truman noticed that his private study "vibrated when any group of people walked up the stairs and it made the great crystal chandelier tinkle in the Blue Room below." Another day the floor beams gave way under Margaret's piano in her sitting room. The final straw was the floor sagging while Truman was in the bathtub. The thought crossed his mind that he would make an odd picture if he fell all the way through during Bess's reception in the Blue Room.

In February, 1948, he requested a committee of experts to examine the entire White House. Their conclusion was that the structure, built originally for John Adams's occupancy, was a rotting hulk. Joists were turning to sawdust, doors had carelessly been cut through support-bearing walls and the entire mansion was sliding into the Foggy Bottom swamp because of improper footings. The heavy ornamental Green Room ceiling was held in place by only a handful of rusty nails. When Truman made the committee's report public, the outcry from tradition-minded editors was as vociferous as when he had built his balcony. Truman's comment on the uproar was that of a defensive Democrat: "Coolidge put on a top floor and a different shape of roof and no one complained."

Fortunately, Congress heeded him and established a Committee on Renovation to decide on the future of the White House. At first the committee considered razing the residence of Presidents. But in the end it decided to save the exterior and rebuild the entire interior at a cost of $5,400,000.

All the while the Trumans resided at Blair House (until the spring of 1952), the Secret Service felt grave concern, for the building sat almost flush against the sidewalk. Furthermore, Truman's bedroom on the second floor faced the street, so that an assassin walking by could actually toss a grenade through the shutter-framed window.

During the years at Blair House, Margaret was seldom home. In May, 1946, she had pleased her father when she graduated from college. On that occasion he made the commencement address and was awarded an honorary LL.D. degree. Still self-conscious over his lack of a college education, he told the audience, "It took Margaret four years, but it took me only four minutes."

After graduation, Margaret was away a great deal of the time busily pursuing her music career. On March 16, 1947, she made her singing debut with the Detroit Symphony Orchestra. Later she admitted, "I was possibly the first unevaluated singer to make a debut with a major symphony orchestra to a radio audience estimated at twenty million persons."

Truman had mixed feelings about his daughter's career. Although he told friends, "I had rather have grandchildren in my family than a prima donna," he was also tremendously proud. When she sang in Washington with the National Symphony Orchestra at Constitution Hall in 1949, he sat in Box 13, the President's box, to the right of the stage. "I wept," he said afterward, "and I almost tore up two programs in the excitement."

The 81st Congress got off to a good start. Joe Martin expressed the opinion of House Republicans when he told reporters, "Mr. Truman ought to be able to get anything he wants from Congress—during the next few months anyway." On opening day, when Sam Rayburn returned to the rostrum as Speaker of the House, the first order of business was to curb the dictatorial Rules Committee which had tied up Truman's legislative proposals in the preceding Congresses. The House agreed that if the Rules Committee failed to clear a bill after 21 days, the chairman of the legislative committee involved could ask the House to bypass the Rules Committee and bring the bill directly to the floor. This was something that not even Roosevelt had been able to accomplish.

Truman's plan was to act fast while the initial stage of his Presidential honeymoon was on. In his State of the Union Message, he provided a slogan title for his "must" program when he told Congress: "Every segment of our population and every individual has the right to expect from our government a fair deal." His was now the "Fair Deal," in contrast to Roosevelt's New Deal, and was given concrete form by his message's list of 24 proposals, including the power to control prices, credit, commodities, exports, wages, rents; to fix allocations and priorities on essential materials and industries in order to fight inflation; to bring about broad civil rights laws, low-cost housing, a 75¢-an-hour minimum wage law, repeal of the Taft-Hartley Act, compulsory health insurance, broadened and extended Social Security, Federal aid to education and a $4,000,000,000 tax increase program that would eliminate tax havens and loopholes.

Sam Rayburn announced to reporters: "We are going to have only one kind of Democrat in this Congress." Bob Albright of the Washington *Post* predicted that the Democrats of the 81st Congress would back Truman's program because they "are not anxious to return to the country with the sort of record they helped Truman campaign against."

But Truman soon learned that the awe at his election "miracle"

337

was like a chunk of ice in the hot sun. By the time he announced his Fair Deal, unemployment rose to 3,200,000, resulting in a drop in the cost of living and weakening his argument for an anti-inflationary program. In addition, the mere presentation of his Fair Deal program solidified his opposition. It was not long before the name-calling was resumed. One morning when he opened the Washington *Times-Herald,* he found himself referred to as a "dishonest nincompoop."

Worst of all, Congressional leaders were unable to exercise any authority over Democratic members. "Campaigns and elections are just preliminary matches," Truman admitted. "The fight in Congress is the main bout."

Percy Priest of Tennessee, Democratic House Whip, explained: "We had 263 Democrats in the House in the 81st Congress, 50 fewer than Roosevelt's 313 in 1933, but still enough to give us our way. However, more than a hundred of the 263 got more votes in their districts in 1948 than Truman did, and they felt they didn't owe him a darn thing."

This situation was also true in the Senate where 14 freshmen Democratic members had joined that body. Most had not expected to win, but now they exhibited strong independence with little desire to organize and take orders from the White House.

Truman realized that his only chance in getting his civil rights program through the Senate was to curb filibustering by Southern Democrats. Under Rule XXII, when 16 Senators signed a petition to close debate upon any pending measure, if two-thirds of the Senators present on the floor voted in favor of such action, cloture went into effect. But Truman's efforts to make it easier to limit debate only brought on a more stringent cloture rule. The Senate approved a change, requiring the favorable vote of two-thirds of the total membership, or 64 Senators, to end debate.

Truman's civil rights program was now doomed in Congress. By executive order, however, he later set up an interdepartmental committee to enforce compliance with nondiscriminatory rules in government contracts. At the end of 1951, this order covered one-fifth of the nation's economy.

The independence of the House and the garrulity of the Senate destined Truman's Fair Deal to failure. Adding to his troubles, Dixiecrats held important committee posts as a result of seniority. Yet he never let up his pressure to get action. "I may even get on the train again and make another tour around the country," he warned Congress in February. Bill Boyle, who succeeded McGrath as chairman of the Democratic National Committee, took the only revenge open to him by purging the national committeemen from the four big Dixiecrat states.

Just as Truman had tangled with Republican Congressional leaders in the 80th Congress, he now became embroiled in pitched battles with Democrats. "I have the right to disagree with Congress," he explained, "and Congress has the right to disagree with me." One of those with whom he fought was Senator Harry Byrd of Virginia, a power on the Armed Services and Finance Committees, who had abetted the Dixiecrats during the election campaign.

Not long after the 81st Congress convened, Truman nominated Mon Wallgren as chairman of the National Security Resources Board, but Byrd succeeded in pigeonholing the nomination in the Armed Services Committee. Finally, at Wallgren's request Truman withdrew the nomination in May. According to Senator Kilgore, "Bernard Baruch really led the fight against Wallgren through Senator Byrd. Baruch said he would call off his dogs if Wallgren promised to do certain things, but Mon refused." Later in the year, however, Truman sent Wallgren's name back to the Senate, this time as a commissioner on the Federal Power Commission, and won confirmation. Byrd also defeated Truman's proposal for a $4,000,000,000 tax boost. In anger, Truman told reporters in May, "There are too many birds [Byrds] in Congress." One unfortunate result of his squabble with Senator Byrd was that Truman struck from the Navy's budget an appropriation for an Antarctic expedition to be led by the Senator's brother, Admiral Richard E. Byrd.

Perhaps Truman's greatest exasperation with a fellow Democrat was directed against Senator Pat McCarran of Nevada, now chairman of the Senate Judiciary Committee, which controlled 40 per cent of the Senate's business.

"Truman's job is merely to execute the laws Congress passes," McCarran argued. "It certainly is not his business to tell Congress what laws it must pass."

Senator Kilgore, who served on the Judiciary Committee with McCarran, said, "Whenever Truman sent the committee nominations of Federal judges, Pat always threatened to sit on the nominations unless Truman let him name one of his own men as a judge. We had a terrible time getting nominations through the committee because you couldn't threaten Truman, and he let McCarran know where he could go."

A major fight between Truman and McCarran during the 81st Congress arose over the issue of displaced persons, a prerogative of McCarran's Judiciary Committee. Truman had campaigned against the "all but unworkable" Revercomb Displaced Persons Act passed by the 80th Congress. Under this Act, only 25,000 of the two-year quota of 205,000 DPs had been able to enter the United States in the first year. One of its provisions, requiring that 30 per cent of all DPs entering the United States be farmers, was aimed specifically at Jewish refugees, for most pre-war European countries did not permit Jews to engage in farming. Other punitive features were directed against orphans, old people and South European DPs. Truman proposed a democratic DP Act to permit 339,000 refugees to enter the United States during the next two years.

Even when Senator Taft joined forces with Truman, McCarran declared his intention to prevent passage of Truman's proposal. After a four-day committee hearing, he closed shop. Then, in October, 1949, when he abruptly left for Europe, he sent back word: "The reason I am against the DP bill is that all these people settle on the East Side of New York and the West Side of Chicago."

Truman's battle with McCarran extended into the second session of the 81st Congress. Early in 1950, McCarran adopted the strategy of promoting his own DP bill, which was in many ways worse than the existing law. Finally, in March, his bill as well as the Kilgore Bill, which was the Truman proposal, were reported to the Senate. In the running debate that followed, McCarran charged that the refugees still remaining in Europe were "criminals, the diseased and those who cannot possibly take care of themselves." On April 5, the final day of debate, McCarran proposed more than 130 amendments to the Kilgore Bill and brought on 20 roll calls, a Senate record for a single day. But just before midnight, after a 13-hour debating brawl on the floor, the Senate passed the liberal Kilgore Bill by a vote of 58–18.

Truman's troubles with Pat McCarran extended even outside the Judiciary Committee, for the Nevada Senator was chairman of the Appropriations Committee subcommittees controlling the budgets of the Departments of State and Commerce as well as the entire Federal Court system, including the Supreme Court. He also held power on the Appropriations subcommittees dealing with Interior, Agriculture and Armed Services allocations. Secretary of the Interior Oscar Chapman once told a reporter, "He always carried on a running battle with Interior to interfere with our operations, threatening to cut our appropriations unless we did what he wanted."

Truman and McCarran also clashed over the problem of how to deal with subversives. The President was having enough trouble trying to administer the Government's loyalty program so that it would not turn into a witch hunt. But matters grew even worse in 1949 when McCarran inserted into the appropriation bills for the Defense and State Departments a provision giving them the power to fire any employee on security grounds without right of appeal. Reports soon reached the White House, said Truman, of how "on the flimsiest pretext people were being fired on security grounds."

In 1950, Truman sent Congress a message calling for remedial legislation so that no individual would be deprived of his rights. McCarran, however, had no intention of permitting this and proposed a much more inclusive program. In his Internal Security bill, he called for the registration of all Communist and Communist-front organizations with the Justice Department, the internment of potential spies and saboteurs, the forced labeling of Communist publications as propaganda and the denial of passports to Communists as well as the right to work in defense plants. McCarran's bill also set up a five-man subversive activities control board to administer the bill and an Internal Security subcommittee in his Judiciary Committee to hold hearings on individuals and organizations it accused of subversion.

"Truman didn't have a chance," Senator Kilgore said. "Many Democrats who opposed McCarran's bill said they had to vote for it because they were up for re-election in the fall and would be falsely charged with being pro-Communist. Even Scott Lucas, our Majority leader, was frightened to death and said he would vote for it in order to be re-elected."

On September 23, 1950, after 22 hours of continuous debate, the Senate passed the McCarran Bill, but Truman vetoed it. In the first place, he said, it would aid potential enemies by requiring the publication of names of vital defense plants from which subversives were barred. In addition, it put the Government in the "thought control" business, deprived the Government of the services of former Communist aliens in intelligence matters, and made the Communists

341

"scurry underground" so that it would become more difficult for Federal agents to keep track of them. Congress ignored his protests and passed the bill over his veto within twenty-four hours.

Later, Truman appointed Admiral Chester W. Nimitz to head a commission to study the entire loyalty program. McCarran opposed the Nimitz Commission and successfully prevented its members from winning confirmation. With deep regret, Truman wrote to Nimitz, "I had hoped that the Congress would be as anxious as I am to make sure that the Bill of Rights is not undermined in our eagerness to stamp out subversive activities."

Despite his failures with Congress over the Fair Deal, Truman made several additions to his program. In the spring of 1949, for instance, he worked closely with his new Secretary of Agriculture, Charles Brannan, on a new farm program which became known as the "Brannan Plan." Instead of existing government support of high consumer prices, farm prices would be permitted to find their natural market level through the mechanism of supply and demand. This meant that consumers would pay lower prices for food. At the same time the 30,000,000 farmers would be paid a direct government subsidy equal to the difference between their market prices and parity support prices.

Truman's enthusiasm for the Brannan Plan led to a unique exchange at a news conference. When he told reporters that he expected Congress to approve the plan, Raymond "Pete" Brandt of the St. Louis *Post-Dispatch* called out, "Wanna bet? I'll bet you a dollar you won't get it through."

Truman studied Brandt. Finally he said, "I've got you covered. It's a bet."

Truman lost, although Brandt never collected.

Strangely, the only piece of Fair Deal legislation to clear Congress in 1949 did so because of the cooperation of his leading opponent, Senator Taft. This was Truman's low-cost public housing bill which faced determined opposition from Southern Democrats and most Republicans. The bill appeared to be dead when Taft suddenly announced that he was for it and successfully shepherded the bill through the Senate despite the barrage of abuse directed against him by the real estate lobby. Afterward the stunned lobbyists, who were the only losers to the Fair Deal, asked: "How did Truman get a Republican floor leader?"

If anyone had told Truman as he stood in the reviewing stand at his

342

inauguration on January 20 that his chief Republican foe would help him win his sole Fair Deal victory, he would have been greeted with a laugh. The facts were now plain. From the crest of triumph early in the year, Truman was back again at his more normal stand on the defensive.

36

EARLY in his Presidency, Harry Truman noted that being Chief
Executive was like riding a tiger. "A man has to keep on riding or be
swallowed," he said. "I never felt that I could let up for a single moment." If there was no burning crisis on any particular morning, he
knew there would be at least one by noon. As Woodrow Wilson once
observed: "The President needs to have the constitution of an athlete,
the patience of a mother, the endurance of an early Christian."

Despite the growing complexity of his job and the constant harass-
ment, the 1948 election produced discernible changes in Truman.
With this vote of approval from the American people, he gained confidence and poise. He appeared more sure of himself and of his ability to handle the crushing burdens that were thrust upon him. He also
took more careful note of the proprieties of the office. When he
traveled or entertained formally, said Bill Hassett, his correspondence secretary, he was a stickler for protocol and was quick to notice
any breach of Presidential etiquette on the part of others. At the same
time, he could not abide snobs. Once, when he was at Williamsburg,
Virginia, Lady Astor, the transplanted Virginian who had acquired

a British accent, derided his flat Missouri twang. "At least my accent is an honest one," he snapped.

Now that his election triumph was in the past, the personal criticism had been resumed with renewed vigor. Most of the time he brushed off these vicious attacks as "a pack of lies." But once he angrily admitted to a reporter, "I'm saving up four or five good hard punches on the nose and when I'm out of this job, I'm going to run around and deliver them personally."

On at least one occasion, however, he had the opportunity to listen to and even enjoy the absurdity of a personal attack. Early in 1950, the C.I.O.'s Ethical Practices Committee accused Harry Bridge's International Longshoremen's Union of following the Communist line. Hearings were held at C.I.O. headquarters in Washington, which adjoined the alley behind Blair House. "While Bridges was in the midst of a foul-languaged attack on President Truman," said Arthur J. Goldberg, the committee counsel, "I leaned back in my chair to the open window. What greeted my eye was Truman standing in the alley only a few feet away eavesdropping with obvious relish. He had a hand cupped over an ear to catch it all and he was grinning like a cat."

The burdens of the Presidency were more than enough to tax the resources of a young man. But Truman, who was sixty-five in May, 1949, seldom tired. "He put in a 16- to 18-hour day and was fresher at the end than I was at the beginning," Charlie Ross said.

After six and a half hours of sleep, he arose at 5:30 A.M., shaved, dressed, and tiptoed downstairs to the first-floor study in Blair House where he scanned the Washington *Post,* the Washington *Times-Herald,* the Baltimore *Sun, The New York Times* and the New York *Herald Tribune.* Then at seven, twirling the gold-headed cane given to him by his Battery D buddies, he rushed down the front stairs of Blair House and set off on a brisk two-mile hike at his normal pace of 120 steps a minute, with Secret Service men scurrying to keep up. Sometimes he walked over the Ellipse and the Mall that stretch in a straight line from the Lincoln Memorial past the Washington Monument to the Capitol. Other times he marched past the shops on F Street and tipped his hat to early risers and weary charwomen returning home after their night's work.

Truman's hike ended at the White House where he headed for the gym to sweat off extra poundage. Then he took a ten-minute swim in the indoor pool that had been built in the West Terrace for President

Roosevelt. Generally, using his own version of a sidestroke, he swam twelve laps, or one fourth of a mile, holding his head out of the water to keep his glasses dry. Afterward he had a rubdown and returned to Blair House at eight o'clock for breakfast. When he ate alone, as he did every summer when Bess took her mother back to Independence for the season, he picked at his food with little appetite.

At eight-thirty, he returned to the White House in a heavily guarded limousine to begin his day's work. Sometimes he paused on his way to inspect the progress being made in reconstructing the Presidential mansion. The West Wing, the business end of the White House which had been erected during Teddy Roosevelt's time, was in good condition and remained operable throughout the rebuilding of the residence next door.

Over the door of Truman's oval office in the West Wing hung a good-luck horseshoe. "He found it while campaigning for re-election to the Senate in 1940," Charlie Ross said. "You couldn't buy that horseshoe from him."

Truman's desk was a seven-foot-long mahogany work table. Unlike Franklin Roosevelt's desk, which was almost completely covered with knickknacks, Truman's held a telephone, a three-sided gadget about six inches long bearing the printed slogan THE BUCK STOPS HERE, a small line engraving of the Chicago *Tribune's* headline DEWEY DEFEATS TRUMAN, six desk calendars, four clocks, his engagement list for the day, a Cabinet folder and a leather-bound book hinged on top and leafed with the names of his staff aides and their activities at that time. "If I disturbed anything on his desk," Charlie Ross said, "he always put it back exactly where it had been." Behind his black leather armchair was a table containing family portraits and a strange hodgepodge of books. One day in 1950 these books included the *Manual* of the state of Missouri; three *Congressional Directories;* Part 2 of the 1950 Hearings before the House Select Committee on Lobbying Activities; *A Practical Commentary on the Code of Canon Law* two volumes of Burton E. Stevenson's *Home Book of Verse; Rules and Manual of the U.S. Senate;* the Real Estate Board of New York *Diary and Manual 1950;* "To Secure These Rights"—the Report of the President's Committee on Civil Rights of 1947; Complete Works of Shakespeare, *Commonwealth of Missouri* by C. R. Barnes, 1877; and an unused diary for 1947.

The day began with a half hour of dictation of personal correspondence to his private secretary, Miss Rose Conway, who had been his brother Vivian's secretary in the Kansas City Federal Housing Administration office.

Many of these letters went out without checking by his staff. He was "an impulsive letter writer," said Bill Hassett, and some letters "did him untold harm" and "offended good taste." Truman wrote to one man in April, 1949: "I feel very much that you still have your economic royalist viewpoint." To a Congressman who importuned him to establish diplomatic relations with the Vatican, he replied that if he did so he would give the Congressman the "rosary concession." To a California Congressman who wrote him regarding the Marine Corps, he answered that "they have a propaganda machine that is almost equal to Stalin's." In 1949, when Jimmy Byrnes attacked the Fair Deal, Truman sent him a letter saying, "Since your speech, I now know how Caesar felt when he said, 'Et tu, Brutus.' " Byrnes replied: "I hope you are not going to think of me as a Brutus, because I am no Brutus. I hope you are not going to think of yourself as a Caesar, because you are no Caesar."

After finishing his dictation, Truman mulled over the vast problems at hand until ten A.M. and made a beginning stab at signing his signature, legally required on a wide variety of government documents, approximately 600 times a day. This relentless chore included signing all the diplomas for the graduating class at Gallaudet College, a school for the deaf which Congress had established, and such local ordinances for the District of Columbia as changes in street names and dog-license rates. When he signed an important bill he used about a half-dozen pens, distributing them as souvenirs to legislators who had promoted the bill through Congress.

"Truman had a passion for weather forecasting," said Charlie Ross. "Every day he went over temperature and rainfall charts sent him by the Weather Bureau." On the occasion of a coal strike in the winter of 1949–1950, Truman held a conference with his labor advisers. "As far as I can see," he said finally, "if it's going to stay warm in the East, we'll have enough coal, but if it's going to turn cold, I'll have to declare a state of national emergency." After studying the weather charts, Truman invoked the national emergency provisions of the Taft-Hartley Act.

Shortly before ten o'clock, Truman's assistants gathered in the office of Matt Connelly, his appointments secretary, whose office was next to the President's. Truman, who always strove for punctuality, liked to spring the door open at precisely ten and wave his aides into his office.

Staff meetings lasted 45 minutes and were never tense or formal. With his aides seated around his desk, he opened a brown leather portfolio containing individual assignments, newspaper clippings and reports. Then after he cleaned out the portfolio he asked each man in turn, "What do you have to do today?" He tried to hew to the staff approach in making assignments but often ignored hierarchal lines in doling out the work.

Anything could come up at staff meetings from matters of international concern to trivia. Vaughan said, "He was grim or smiling, depending on the world situation, and he usually sat with his legs crossed, swinging in his chair and chopping the air with his hands held vertically, two feet apart, to emphasize a point." Charlie Ross reported, "Truman was always dignified with his staff, though sometimes there was some jocularity. Vaughan got off a story now and then. So did Truman. There was the occasion when his burdens seemed especially heavy and he told the following story, which, he said, had been attributed apocryphally to Calvin Coolidge: A President was going over detailed matters of state with his staff. Happening to glance out the window just as the Vice-President sauntered by the White House, he said, 'There goes the Vice-President, with nothing on his mind but the health of the President.' "

Executive Clerk William J. Hopkins wound up the staff meeting by producing papers to be signed. All day long he continued to bring Truman more. Letters from important people and personal friends were culled from the thousands addressed to him each day and were brought to his office. He also saw the human interest mail, answers to which were made public with resulting good publicity. Sorting the stacks of mail that poured into the mailroom was an immense job. Before any parcel was opened it was fluoroscoped and on occasion bombs were found.

On Mondays, staff meetings were delayed until eleven o'clock so that Truman could meet at ten with his Congressional Big Four: Vice-President Barkley, Speaker Sam Rayburn, Senate Majority Leader Scott Lucas and House Majority Leader John W. McCormack. At these meetings he worked from a staff-prepared memorandum showing which legislation was up at the moment, its urgency, probable amendments, who might raise objections, and the likely vote.

Barkley said, "Unlike FDR, Truman did not let legislative matters drift. Besides his Big Four meetings, Truman also wrote letters to the leaders of Congress, used his telephone and frequently called Congressional committees to the White House to meet with him." As an additional source of Senate intelligence, Truman stayed in close touch with Les Biffle, Secretary of the Senate, who had a red, white and blue ribboned telephone connected directly with the one on the President's desk. It was Truman's opinion that Biffle was worth at least ten votes on any issue.

After the staff meeting, Truman was briefed on both national and international security problems by James S. Lay, Jr., executive secretary of the National Security Council, and Rear Admiral Sidney Souers, consultant and former secretary of the NSC. Then he went over his list of appointments with Matt Connelly to see who was on tap for the day.

Appointment hours generally ran from eleven A.M. to one P.M. and from three P.M. until four-fifteen. On an average, Truman saw over 100 persons a week. Most appointments were made through Connelly, although when some individuals had trouble getting past Connelly they prevailed upon Mrs. Truman or Vaughan to make the necessary arrangements.

Truman set aside fifteen minutes for each appointment and only on rare occasions did visitors overstay their time. Appointments were made several days in advance and visitors were asked to present a typed memorandum on the subject to be discussed. Unlike Roosevelt, who dominated conversation, Truman was a listener. As a result, he was able to make marginal notes on their memos while visitors talked. "Sometimes when I came over on short notice and didn't bring a prepared memo," Senator Kilgore said, "Truman would write up our conversation just as a reporter wrote up an interview." Truman wrote on the one side of one typewritten memo, *Baloney peddler;* on another, *This man not only wants to run the country but the universe and the entire milky way;* and on a third, *This 1930 guy should study 1951!*

Sometimes, when the visitor, too, was a listener, the meeting was embarrassingly brief. When this occurred, Truman frequently filled out the time by walking over to a large globe, given him by General Eisenhower, which sat in front of his office fireplace beneath a portrait of George Washington. Here he pointed out the current trouble spots in the world, and thus extended the visit a few minutes. At first Truman would escort each visitor to the door, but when aides told him it wasn't dignified he stopped the practice. Whatever time was left of the allotted fifteen minutes after the caller departed, Truman spent in working on the endless papers that required his personal signature, talking to staff aides or seeing intimates, such as Chief Justice Vinson, who came and went unannounced.

"One of the sorriest problems of being President," Charlie Ross said, "is the amount of time the Chief Executive has to devote to purely ceremonial stuff. An American President has to function as king and prime minister combined." Whole delegations often descended upon Truman in his office. Sometimes they were Gold Star Mothers, or exchange teachers on their way to European schools, or visiting Elks. Generally, these occasions were three-ring circuses and played havoc with his schedule.

At one P.M., Truman returned to Blair House by automobile for lunch and a nap. When he went back to the White House, he continued his appointments and handled his other duties. Certain appointments were fixtures, such as the 3:30 party-politics session on Wednesday with Bill Boyle, chairman of the Democratic National Committee. "Truman ran the Party somewhat like a generous and rather indulgent grandfather," Senator Kilgore said. "As long as he thought the boys were being fair, he didn't get too perturbed over minor antics. But when they did otherwise, he cracked down."

Other fixed appointments were set up for the 12:30 slot on Mondays and Thursdays with the Secretary of State, on Tuesday with the Secretary of Defense and on Wednesday with the chairman of the National Security Resources Board. Actually, the Secretaries of State and Defense were free to come in whenever they pleased. He also met with the National Security Council on Thursdays at 3:30; held his news conferences on Thursday, one week at 10:30 A.M. and the next week at 4 P.M. in order to give an even break to the morning and afternoon papers; and held a regular Cabinet meeting at 10 A.M. on Friday and a Cabinet luncheon on Monday.

"If Truman had a pet agency," Charlie Ross said, "it was the Bureau of the Budget. If anyone dared to run it down, he would take up the cudgel." In terms of time, the Budget Director and his top staff spent more hours with the President than any other officers of the Government. Well aware that many policy decisions were contained in the Government's budget, Truman prided himself on knowing the budget-making process, a dull concern to many Presidents. As each year's new budget was decided upon, he held a seminar for the press in the White House projection room, where he gave a resume of the budget and answered questions on its details.

When Congress sent Truman a bill for his signature, he had the Budget Bureau distribute it to various agencies for their opinions. Occasionally, these opinions conflicted, and Truman had to rely on his own judgment. One instance of major disagreement within the Government came over the Kerr Natural Gas Bill of 1950 which exempted independent companies from control by the Federal Power Commission. Truman, however, considered it class favoritism to exempt the independents from price-fixing supervision and vetoed the bill. Another time, when on the last day of his ten-day-grace period, he vetoed the Basing Point Bill of 1950, which he regarded as a defective attempt to establish a fairer system of pricing in the steel industry, a Congressman asked him if he had trouble making up his mind on the bill. "I intended to veto it all along," Truman said. "In fact, I feel like the blacksmith on the Missouri jury. The judge asked if he was prejudiced against the defendant. 'Oh, no, judge. I think we ought to give him a fair trial. Then I think we ought to take the s.o.b. out and string him up.' "

Truman fully understood that his Thursday news conferences were an important part of his job, even though they were filled with pitfalls. Winston Churchill, who once attended a Presidential news conference, asked afterward, "How does the President dare go before Washington reporters and bare his soul to their boundless curiosity and irreverence?" Nevertheless, Truman knew that these press meetings not only provided him with an excellent springboard for launching ideas and shaping public opinion but also gave him an opportunity to find out what was on the public's mind.

Originally, he held his news conferences in his office, with the newsmen crowding around his desk in a semicircle to ask their questions. But he had to move these meetings to the Indian Treaty Room on the fourth floor of the baroque Old State-War-Navy Building across the street from the West Wing. "In the first place," Charlie Ross said, "more than two hundred reporters often showed up and they were stacked like hard macaroni. There was also an accident one time when the reporters broke for the telephones and one poor guy had his arm broken in the crush. But the final straw was when a reporter spilled ink on the President's rug."

In the Indian Treaty Room, where government officials once met with Indian chieftains to discuss treaties, Truman stood behind a prop

351

desk and faced the seated reporters. He always stood erect, pressing his finger tips on the top of the desk while waiting for questions. He sipped from a glass of water occasionally, and tended to bounce slightly on his heels. Between questions, he twisted a heavy gold ring on the little finger of his left hand, and while a question was asked, he turned from the waist to the reporter and listened, squinting, to his words.

Almost from the outset, Truman had his troubles with his news conferences. Dave Niles said: "FDR treated his press conferences like a poker game, while Truman kept exposing his hand. On purpose, FDR avoided calling on certain reporters who were there only to cause trouble if they could. Truman recognized everyone. FDR was always in control, tossing out trial balloons for public opinion, chiding reporters for asking silly questions and deftly turning aside subjects that he felt shouldn't be brought up. Truman was always direct—a question deserved an answer; he let the reporters take advantage of his low boiling point and his general willingness to please. He could spot a phony much quicker than Roosevelt, but he was still obliging."

Truman's fast answers and snap judgments were of special concern to Charlie Ross because a careless reply could offend allies, build up opposition to one of Truman's programs or provide ammunition for the Soviet propaganda machine. Dean Acheson later said that the State Department "kept on hand, as a sort of first aid kit, a boxful of 'clarifications' for these events." After attending several news conferences, Tony Vaccaro, Truman's reporter friend, made a practice of walking up to him before the question-and-answer period began and asking, "Gonna take it slow today?"

It was after the 1946 fiasco on Wallace's Madison Square Garden speech that Truman decided to meet with his staff a half hour before each news conference and go over questions likely to be asked. Even so, he managed occasionally to get himself in hot water. Roger Tubby, one of his press aides, recalled that in answer to one question Truman replied that he had sent an "ultimatum" to Stalin. This created a sensation. "I went over to the State Department and found the letter in question," Tubby said. "It was certainly a strong letter telling Stalin to keep his hands off Azerbaijan Province in Iran, but it was not an ultimatum. We had to issue a correction." In 1948, when the House Un-American Activities Committee began looking into the Whittaker Chambers-Alger Hiss affair, a reporter added to Truman's problems by asking: "Mr. President, do you think that the Capitol

Hill spy scare is a red herring to divert public attention from inflation?" Truman answered yes instead of shrugging the question off. In doing so he made himself an open target for Senators Pat McCarran and Joseph R. McCarthy and Representative Richard M. Nixon.

At Truman's Friday morning Cabinet meetings, minutes were not kept, nor did any members of his staff attend other than John Steelman and Matt Connelly, who was present primarily to refresh Truman's memory afterward on what had been discussed. The Cabinet Room was dominated by an immense table, an elongated octagon which vaguely resembled a huge coffin. Truman sat at the center, on the window side of the room, facing Vice-President Barkley, while other Cabinet members took leather upholstered armchairs with their nameplates on the backs. Truman had the only telephone in the room —National 1414, extension 33—and occasionally received calls during Cabinet meetings.

Generally these meetings were short but more work was done than in Roosevelt's time, when a Cabinet member had to lag behind if he wanted to discuss business with FDR. Although the atmosphere was somewhat more formal than at his White House staff meetings, Truman followed much the same routine. First he discussed the memoranda before him and then called on those present in rotation. The shape of the table enabled everyone to see all other participants. No votes were taken, and all decisions were left to Truman.

Barkley said, "Every member of the Cabinet felt perfectly free to disagree openly with Truman at the meetings. The President could get off a good aphorism. Once when we were discussing certain matters involving political considerations, I made the observation that where poverty goes in the front door, love goes out the transom. Truman added. 'And where politics goes in the front door, statesmanship flies out the transom.' "

Truman's Cabinets were never a homogeneous group. But, Senator Kilgore said, "President Truman had a pretty good system to keep the department heads in line. When he appointed a Cabinet member, he had him file a letter of resignation. Truman put these letters of resignation in a safe and could pull them out and date them any time he thought it was necessary.

"He did this to Jim Forrestal in the spring of 1949. Jim had not contributed to the 1948 campaign and the Party wanted him out to make room for Louie Johnson as Secretary of Defense. Truman had a high opinion of Forrestal, despite the role he played in the Palestine settlement, and would not have fired him for this reason. What decided Truman was that Forrestal had a mental and physical breakdown and couldn't handle his job. In fact, when Forrestal jumped out of the sixteenth-floor window at the Bethesda Naval Hospital in May, 1949, he had three times earlier tried to commit suicide."

As in most Administrations, Truman's Cabinet members ran the gamut from liberals to conservatives. "The only picture in John Snyder's reception room was that of the Secretary of the Treasury in McKinley's Administration," Senator Kilgore said. "Secretary of State Dean Acheson was always arguing with Charlie Sawyer at Commerce on foreign commerce. When Oscar Chapman took Krug's place at Interior, he and Charlie Brannon at Agriculture were at opposite poles on almost every economic program from Snyder and Sawyer. Often when Sawyer came up to the Hill, he'd tell Senators openly to oppose the Brannon Farm Plan. Then there was Louie Johnson, who undercut Acheson at every opportunity. Johnson went around Washington saying, 'I'll keep asking what our China policy is until I find out.' One time Sawyer testified against a Truman bill to reorganize the Commerce Department and Truman hit the ceiling. He told Sawyer, 'How can I expect anything from Congress when my own Cabinet member does this?' But he didn't fire him. Truman accepted philosophically the fact that Cabinet members would have their differences. But he made it clear that they served at his pleasure and that he was boss."

Sometimes, within a department, there was rivalry among underlings. Up to a point, Truman considered this healthy, although on occasion he waited with supernormal patience before cracking down. In 1949, for instance, he was confronted with the "revolt of the admirals," led by Admiral Louis E. Denfeld, the Chief of Naval Operations. This group fed reams of copy to reporters in an effort to upset Truman's defense balance among the services. In October, when Denfield condemned Johnson in testimony before a House Committee, Truman finally retired him and other officers who were involved.

That year, Air Force generals also attacked Truman openly for permitting them only a 48-group Air Force. When the generals went over his head and won a 58-group Air Force from Congress, Truman reluctantly signed the bill. Nevertheless, he announced his intention to spend money only for 48 groups and to put the rest of the appropriation in reserve. "He hurt his own prestige," Senator Kilgore commented, "by carrying democracy a little too far."

Following his last official appointment of the day, Truman held work meetings with government officials or went over speeches or public statements with Charles S. Murphy, who replaced Clark Clifford as Presidential counsel and principal speech writer. And always there were the never-ending piles of papers to be signed—nominations to various Federal jobs, pardons, military commissions, statutes, documents in triplicate, documents *ad infinitum.*

Truman's speech-writing process was complex. First he met with his staff and discussed his ideas. Then Murphy obtained memos from government officials on the subjects to be mentioned. After further sessions with Truman, who gave them additional material in longhand, Murphy's staff worked up a first draft and sent it to officials directly concerned for comments. Generally, Murphy had to write about a half-dozen drafts and the final one went to the Cabinet for suggestions. Then Truman read the speech line by line to his aides and made comments. Invariably, the President took the speech home and went over it with Mrs. Truman. "She never hesitated to criticize the ideas and language," Charlie Ross said, "and he made further changes accordingly."

When he left his oval office in the White House at 6 P.M. for yet another limousine ride across the street, Truman carried a brief case bulging with papers which he wryly called his "homework." The pile usually measured from four to six inches in depth.

Except for occasions when he gave a dinner for a visiting dignitary —at Blair House if there were fewer than sixteen guests, or at the Carlton Hotel if there were more—Truman dined with his family or alone at 7 P.M. On November 1, 1949, he wrote in his diary: "I take a handbath in the finger bowl and go back to work. What a life." By 8 P.M. or shortly thereafter, he was back in the Blair House study, making notes on his working papers, drawing up memoranda, preparing for the next grueling day.

It always surprised Charlie Ross how Truman managed to find time to do any extracurricular reading. Each year the American Booksellers Association sent him a few hundred books and every now and then he commented on one. He also maintained his interest in history and biography. One day he spent a half hour discussing military history with Edward A. Harris of the St. Louis *Post-Dispatch.* The next day he wrote Harris that he had forgotten to mention Hadrian: "He was the successor of Trajan and was himself succeeded by the Antonines, about whom I talked to you. Hadrian is the greatest of the Roman Emperors according to all the authorities."

After Harris replied, Truman wrote to him again: "Let me call your attention to John Huniades and his operations at Belgrade, Charles Martel the father of Charlemaign (can't spell him) and his battle at Tours which stopped the Moors in Europe." In still another letter Truman pointed out that the greatest military maneuvers of all time were to be found in such battles as Cannae; Arbela, where Alexander the Great's Macedonian Army destroyed the Persians; Austerlitz, where the French under Napoleon defeated the Austrians and Russians; and Chancellorsville.

After four exchanges, Charlie Ross sent Harris a note. "My God," he wrote, "when is all this going to end?"

Truman's killing pace would have soon finished him had he not sought an occasional change in his routine. A few times a year he had lunch at the Capitol with Les Biffle and old Senate cronies. He also enjoyed Masonic gatherings where he wore his little lambskin apron trimmed with heavy gold fringe. During July, 1949, he attended the Shriners' Convention in Chicago but got no rest. "I'd like to get my hands on the guy who kept me awake one whole night singing 'Chloe,' " he said afterward.

Playing the piano was also restful. Once, when Grandma Moses, the celebrated painter, visited him, he played several numbers for her. On another occasion, after he received a Phi Beta Kappa key and an honorary Ph.D. at the University of Missouri, he noticed a piano in the home of the university's president. He quickly pulled his sister Mary to the piano bench and they treated the guests to a rendition of the "Jenny Lind Polka." Eben Ayers, one of his press assistants, said, "Once we were down in Puerto Rico and the governor held a reception for him at the palace in San Juan. When the last handshake was over, he spied a grand piano in a corner of the room and sat down and played."

Truman eschewed regular appointments on Saturdays. Frequently, after a Saturday morning of conferences and staff meetings, he left the White House in time for lunch aboard the Presidential yacht *Williamsburg* and a cruise down the Potomac. Usually, these were stag cruises with his staff and close friends. On Saturday night, the *Williamsburg* anchored in the vicinity of Blackistone Island or Quantico, Virginia, returning to Washington at about 4 P.M. on Sunday. Life aboard the 244-foot seagoing yacht included reading, gossiping, sun-bathing, promenading about the deck and poker. Just after dawn on Sunday, Truman climbed down the ladder to the water and swam for ten or fifteen minutes. Even aboard the yacht the chore of signing documents continued to plague him and mail was brought down from Washington by seaplane and swift cutter.

Each year, Truman spent a weekend at Shangri-la, the Presidential retreat in the Catoctin Mountain of Maryland, which was a favorite hideaway for Presidents Hoover and Roosevelt. But he did not enjoy the two-hour drive to get there or the solitude.

In Washington, it was difficult for a President to drop in on friends or to attend informal gatherings. Senator Kilgore once invited Truman to put aside his cares and accompany him to a party given by the West Virginia State Society. But Truman shook his head sadly and said. "You know I'd love to go, Harley. But they'd only throw five platoons of Secret Service men all over the place. Nobody would have any fun."

Twice a year, in February-March and in November-December, Truman went to Key West, Florida, for vacations. Here at the naval reservation, he loafed, swam, lay in the sun, played horseshoes and wore loud clothes and a cap. Key West was his favorite vacation spot and he brought along such old friends as Les Biffle, Mon Wallgren, Chief Justice Vinson, and Bill Boyle. Once, when some of his fellow vacationers discussed government business, he passed out cards that read: DON'T GO AWAY MAD . . . JUST GO AWAY. When reporters came around, Charlie Ross introduced Truman to them in this fashion: "Gentlemen, we have with us today a distinguished contributor to the *Federal Register*."

At Key West, Truman was boss of the horseplay. Once Joseph G. Feeney, White House liaison aide to the Senate, lay on the hot beach with an arm flung over his eyes. Suddenly ice-cold water poured across his chest. Feeney let out an angry roar and leaped to his feet full of fight. A moment later, as his eyes focused to the brilliance of the semitropical sun, he saw a stocky, gray-haired man with two empty water glasses in his hands, grinning like a Cheshire cat. It was Truman.

Gifted with an extraordinary memory, Truman was forever betting his friends at Key West and elsewhere about the exact wording of literary, historic and Biblical quotations as well as Latin epigrams. Once, Chief Justice Vinson, who considered himself an authority on Latin, got into a heated discussion with him over a Latin quotation: the proper wording of "Carthage must be destroyed." Vinson was smugly certain of his accuracy until a sourcebook was consulted and he learned that Truman was right and he was wrong.

Often Truman and Bill Hassett, whom he called "Bishop" because of his manner and extensive knowledge of religions, made small bets on Biblical questions. One of Truman's specialties was to quote Scripture to clergymen who came to see him in the White House. According to Hassett, whenever Truman won a bet, he would announce, "That's five dollars more for the Boss's pet charity." He gave all such winnings to his wife.

Despite occasional relaxation in the company of his friends, the Presidency was a lonely job. Truman could sail down the Potomac on weekends, lie in the sun at Key West, walk through trains when he traveled and shake hands with everyone aboard, attend the Army-Navy football game or take part in the activities of the Masonic lodge. But the burdensome duties and vast responsibilities of his office were his and his alone.

37

EVEN as he urged his Fair Deal program on Congress, Truman's chief attention was necessarily devoted to foreign affairs. Starting with the Truman Doctrine in 1947, he had inaugurated a major shift in American foreign policy which had moved forward to the Marshall Plan and Point Four. In addition, his airlift to Berlin had forced Stalin to the conclusion that the United States could not be pushed from Berlin or Germany.

Nevertheless, Truman was still dissatisfied with his own efforts to contain Communism. In mid-1947, Stalin had taken over Hungary. Then in February, 1948, a Soviet coup ended democracy in Czechoslovakia. Truman now felt that a corollary to the economic aid of the Marshall Plan was needed to prevent similar disasters in other European nations.

The germ of a new development was sown in March, 1948, when Belgium, Holland, Luxemburg, the United Kingdom and France agreed to the Brussels Alliance. Under this pact, the five nations declared that they would come to each other's aid if any one of them was subjected to an armed attack in Europe.

359

Truman proposed to expand the Brussels Alliance to include the other nations of Western Europe and the United States. When his plan met with strong support in Europe, he asked Senators Connally and Vandenberg to push a resolution through the Senate backing such a European regional defense pact. Known as Senate Resolution 239, this measure passed the Senate on June 11, 1948, by a vote of 64–4.

Assured of Senate support, Truman ordered the State Department to draw up a treaty with the interested nations. The result was the establishment of the North Atlantic Treaty Organization (NATO), and it was with a sense of real accomplishment that Truman addressed the representatives of the eleven signatory nations on April 4, 1949, at a ceremony in the blue-domed Interdepartmental Auditorium in Washington. The Senate then approved the treaty by a vote of 82–13.

But now a battle ensued when Truman sent the Senate his Mutual Defense Assistance Bill, which was the military implementation of NATO. In asking for an initial appropriation of $1,450,000,000 in arms-aid to the NATO countries as well as Greece, Turkey and the Philippines, he told Congress, "We are not arming ourselves and our friends to start a fight with anybody. We are building defenses so that we won't have to fight."

For four days the Senate sharply debated the bill, with Senator Taft leading the opposition. Allied with Taft was Senator Vandenberg, who argued that arms-aid was unnecessary, that the mere existence of the treaty would deter the Soviet Government. He labeled arms-aid to Western Europe "another Lend-Lease business—too costly and too premature." Senator John Foster Dulles of New York insisted that the bill gave Truman dictatorial power in determining what equipment should be sent abroad. In the end, however, both Vandenberg and Dulles came out for the bill after Truman added a large appropriation for Chiang Kai-shek. Finally, on September 22, 1949, the bill cleared the Senate by a vote of 55–24. The United States had taken another long stride forward in foreign affairs.

Afterward, Truman took three steps to make NATO a potent deterrent force. The first was to win acceptance from the NATO nations to work for a united defense force with German participation. Originally, the member nations planned to maintain individual control over their own armed forces and make their own defense plans. After considerable effort, Truman and Dean Acheson convinced them that the NATO deterrent power would be strongest if there were a single NATO defense force "to which each country would contribute its share."

A second vital step was to appoint General Eisenhower as Supreme Commander for the Allied Powers in Europe. Eisenhower's appointment was extremely popular with the NATO nations, and there was every reason to believe he would create an effective military force.

The third step was to commit American troops to Europe as part of the NATO forces. This measure brought on an acrimonious Senate debate with Senators Taft and Wherry questioning Truman's right to send American troops abroad during peacetime. To prove his point, Truman quoted from *Our Chief Magistrate and His Power,* written by Taft's father, former President William Howard Taft. Vehemently, Truman said that he had the Constitutional right to send American troops anywhere in the world without Congressional approval. When Wherry introduced a resolution barring the President from taking such action without Congressional consent, the Senate aired his resolution for three months. Finally, by a vote of 69–21, a substitute resolution passed, permitting four American divisions to be sent to General Eisenhower but advising Truman to ask for the approval of Congress before sending more.

Truman had made his Point Four proposal to Congress in his State of the Union Message on January 5, 1949. But it was not until June, 1950, that Congress implemented his plan for helping the underdeveloped countries. Within six months about 350 industrial and scientific technicians were at work on more than a hundred technical cooperation projects in 27 countries. Greatest needs were to increase the food supply, prevent diseases, provide basic and vocational education, improve transportation, and build dams and irrigation projects. Point Four technicians cut the malaria rate in the Shan States of Burma from 50 per cent to 10 per cent. School systems appeared for the first time in many areas in the Middle East, Asia and Latin America. Since many of the underdeveloped countries had been heavily propagandized by the Communists about the designs of Yankee imperialism, Truman insisted that nations receiving aid had to ask for it in the first place, and then had to help pay for it. By early 1952, Truman proudly told Congress: "There is nothing that shows more clearly what we stand for and what we want to achieve."

Despite his creative efforts to contain the Russian threat through the Truman Doctrine, the Marshall Plan and NATO and to take the offensive with Point Four, Truman was well aware that the Communists were ever on the alert to expand their military control. In 1946, to head off one possibility of immense danger, he had requested Dean Acheson and David Lilienthal, head of the TVA and later the Atomic Energy Commission, to work up a plan for international control and inspection of atomic energy production. That year he also appointed Bernard Baruch to push the Acheson-Lilienthal plan before the United Nations with the additional proviso that the Security Council would not have a veto over the decision of the control body to punish violators. The Russians, however, would not go along with this proposal and instead insisted on a treaty outlawing the atomic bomb and destroying all stockpiles within three months. Truman would not agree to this and the plan died.

Events later revealed why the Russians took this position. The acceptance of the Truman proposal would have prevented them from producing their own bombs. Through the efforts of spies, such as Klaus Fuchs in England, the Soviets already knew the details of atomic bomb construction. All they needed was time to build the necessary industrial apparatus.

On September 3, 1949, an Air Force plane in the American Long Range Detection System collected a radioactive air sample. Study revealed that an atomic explosion had taken place the week before in Asia. Only one conclusion could be drawn. On September 23, Truman told the American people: "We have evidence that within recent weeks an atomic explosion occurred in the U.S.S.R."

Panic gripped the nation while Truman was now faced with another major decision.

Shortly after the first atomic bomb had been dropped on Hiroshima in 1945, Hans Thierring, an Austrian scientist, published the theory of the hydrogen bomb. His paper examined the possibility of producing a thermonuclear weapon which would operate by "fusion" instead of fission and would have an explosive force at least a thousand times more powerful than an atomic bomb. When the Atomic Energy Commision was first organized, Truman pondered the question of starting an H-Bomb project comparable to the Manhattan Project for the A-bomb and referred the matter to a group of top scientists headed by Vannevar Bush. But when Dr. Bush's committee looked into the theoretical possibilities of the H-bomb, they recoiled with horror at its devastating power and recommended that the United States refrain from the attempt to produce it.

Truman accepted Bush's recommendation, but in 1949, after the

Russians exploded an A-bomb, he decided to reconsider the matter. An argument developed at the Atomic Energy Commission over what advice to relay to him. Chairman David Lilienthal and two others on the five-man AEC argued strenuously against producing an H-bomb, while Commissioners Gordon Dean and Lewis Strauss favored it. All during the fall of 1949 Truman listened to the arguments of both sides. The Washington *Post* said that his choice "may be the most cosmic that has confronted any chief of state in war or peace in American history." Admiral Nimitz, in a talk to West Point cadets, said, "I hope I don't live to see an H-bomb developed."

As the controversy raged in the press, Truman delayed his decision until January 31, 1950, when he ordered the construction of an H-bomb. Whatever the cost, the United States had to stay ahead of Russia in the armaments race. If the United States did not proceed with the H-bomb and if the Russians did, the entire Western World would be in jeopardy.

It was not until November 1, 1952, that the first test of a hydrogen bomb took place and an entire Pacific island vanished in the force of its blast. Winston Churchill expressed shock at the hideous power of this new weapon. "I would have been more than happy," Truman agreed, "if our plan for international control had been carried out."

One of the most difficult foreign problems Truman had to grapple with during the 81st Congress was China. This ancient land was a morass that was to bring him only trouble and cloud his activities in other foreign endeavors.

Since China had been opened by the West early in the nineteenth century, relations with the United States had been cordial. During World War II, Roosevelt went so far as to elevate China to the status of a big power in international relations, even though she lay under the Japanese yoke and was torn by civil strife. When Truman became President, he inherited this fiction of China as a big power and helped install her as a permanent member of the UN Security Council.

But he was not long in office when he realized that "China was only a geographical expression." Generalissimo Chiang Kai-shek's Nationalist Government held control only in the southwest corner of China. The remainder of south China and east China still lay under Japanese occupation; north China was dominated by the Chinese Communists; and Manchuria, by the Russians. General Albert C.

Wedemeyer, chief of staff and military adviser to Chiang Kai-shek, made the following report:

> A satisfactory solution to the China problem will never be accomplished by civil war in this area. Based on limited knowledge, neither the Chinese Communist Party nor the Kuomintang [Chiang's party] is democratic in spirit, or intentions. China is not prepared for a democratic form of government with 95 per cent of her people illiterate and for many other cogent reasons. The inarticulate masses of China desire peace and are not particularly interested in or aware of the various ideologies represented.

During the war, Ambassador Patrick Hurley had expressed his opinion that the Chinese Reds were "not in fact Communists. They are striving for democratic principles." After the war, however, he changed his mind, although several members of his embassy staff continued to hold his earlier view. Truman's position was that the Chinese Communists were not just "agrarian reformers" but were out-and-out Communists who followed the teachings of Marx and Lenin and believed in the eventual victory of the proletariat.

The dilemma he faced was enormous. He could refrain from taking any part in Chinese affairs, but he realized that his inaction would result in China being plunged into fratricidal war, with the Russians offering heavy support to the Chinese Reds. China would then be lost to the West. As an alternative, he could commit American military strength to Chiang's side and fight it out with the Communists. But the United States had just come through a major war and the American Army was already in process of demobilization. Had he sent troops to China, he would have met national and Congressional resistance. Furthermore, he was aware that Chiang Kai-shek's Government did not command respect in most of China because of its corruptness.

This left Truman with the alternative of proposing to the Chinese Communists that they become a minority party in a unified government. Then, by giving China large-scale economic aid, he reasoned, the United States would help eliminate the country's substandard existence and Communism would lose its appeal to the people. "Of course the struggle for power would continue," he said, "but there was no reason why the National Government could not be successful in this struggle, as non-Communist governments had been in Europe, if it attended to the fundamental needs of the people."

This approach became the Chinese policy of the United States. At Hurley's instigation, Mao Tse-tung, the Communist leader, came to Chungking, Chiang's wartime capital, for conferences with the Nationalists. On October 11, 1945, the two Chinese leaders agreed to hold a constitutional convention in which all political parties would join in the writing of a new constitution for China. The Nationalists were to receive greater representation in the convention than the Reds. In the interim, Chiang was to appoint a 40-man council to run the government and would have a veto over any of the council's decisions.

Truman immediately ordered American Air Force transports to ferry Chiang's troops into territory held by the Japanese. In addition, 50,000 American Marines landed at strategic ports to evacuate the Japanese. Hurley was back in Washington conferring with Truman when word came that the Communists were not living up to their agreement with Chiang. Not only were they cutting rail lines to hinder troop movements but they had also gone into Manchuria to take over when the Russians departed. There were reports of clashes between the Communists and the Nationalists. Under these circumstances, Truman told both Hurley and Wedemeyer that while it was his policy to support Chiang, he did not intend to put American troops into the field to fight against the Reds.

During the morning of November 27, 1945, Truman again met with Hurley and requested him to return immediately to Chungking. Hurley agreed to do so, but that same day he spoke to the National Press Club, attacking the State Department, the China policy and Truman personally, and announced his resignation. Truman was shocked by his unexplainable turnabout.

Nevertheless, he was more than ever determined to halt civil war in China. The man he selected to attempt this was General Marshall. Before Marshall left for China in December, 1945, Truman gave him as his objectives: "To persuade the Chinese Government to call a national conference of representatives of the major political elements to bring about the unification of China and, concurrently, to effect a cessation of hostilities, particularly in North China. . . . A China disunited and torn by civil strife could not be considered realistically as a proper place for American assistance." According to Jimmy Byrnes, Truman added orally that "in no case was Chiang to be left entirely without help from the United States."

Initially, Marshall met with some success by effecting a cease-fire and getting an agreement from both sides for the establishment of cease-fire teams to arrange on-site peace. But both parties were soon violating the truces. "I am working against time," he cabled Truman in May. By July, the fighting was general and in January, 1947, Marshall abandoned his mission with the statement: "The reactionaries in the government have evidently counted on substantial American support regardless of their action. The Communists, by their unwillingness to compromise in the national interest, are evidently counting on an economic collapse to bring about the fall of the government."

With civil war enveloping China, Truman was forced to reconsider American policy. His decision was to continue aid to Chiang, even though this subjected the United States to the charge of "imperialist meddling." Chiang would have to fight his own battles, although during the next two years he received about $2,000,000,000 of American aid.

By mid-1947, the news from China was bad. On June 26, Marshall reported that the United States was "confronted by the dilemma created by the incompetence, inefficiency and stubbornness of the Central Government—qualities which made it very difficult to help them." He cited "the military ineptitude of their leaders, the cashiering of the only generals who had produced successful campaigns, the instability of their leadership and the appalling lack of an organization to deal with the vast and complex economic and social problems of China."

With each new Communist military success, hatred for the United States mounted in China because of American support of Chiang. Entire Nationalist armies surrendered to the Communists; other Nationalist generals sold the enemy vast quantities of American military supplies which had been funneled to them. Corrupt local Nationalist officials failed to deliver the enormous emergency food shipments sent to Chiang by the United States. On January 22, two days after Truman's inauguration in 1949, the Nationalists surrendered Peking and the eventual fate of China was sealed.

In Washington, the Chinese fiasco resulted in violent attacks on Truman by the Republicans, who charged him with being responsible for Chiang's failure. Some Democrats joined in the attack on Truman, including young Representative John F. Kennedy of Massachusetts. Constant repetition of this theme produced great confusion across the country. In one important respect, the Administration was remiss, for as the Chinese crisis developed, Truman had not taken Congressional leaders into his confidence as he had done in European affairs. For example, Senator Vandenberg announced that it was not his duty to support Truman's policy because Truman had never tried to make it a bipartisan matter. Yet in his diary Vandenberg wrote:

> If we made ourselves responsible for the Army of the Nationalist Government, we would be in the China war for keeps and the responsibility would be ours instead of hers. I am sure that this would jeopardize our own national security beyond any possibility of justification.

By the summer of 1949, the issue boiled over in the press and in the halls of Congress. It grew obvious to Truman that the "China Firsters" were making headway with their propaganda that they were trying to save China while the State Department was sabotaging an anti-Communist government. In early August the State Department finally offered a belated justification in the form of a White Paper:

> The unfortunate but inescapable fact is that the ominous result of the civil war in China was beyond the control of the Government of the United States. Nothing that this country did or could have done within the reasonable limits of its capabilities could have changed that result; nothing that was left undone by this country has contributed to it. . . . The government and the Kuomintang . . . leaders have proved incapable of meeting the crisis confronting them, its troops had lost the will to fight and its government had lost popular support. They did not have to be defeated; they disintegrated.

Two months after the State Department's White Paper, the Chinese Communists announced the establishment of the People's Republic of China. Then on December 8, 1949, Chiang Kai-shek and the remnants of his forces fled to the island of Formosa.

So long as he held office, Truman's opponents were to use China as a propaganda club to strike at him and his policies in entirely unrelated fields.

38

AT THE close of 1949, when Truman looked over the political ledger, there were many more positive entries than negative ones. It was true that China was lost to the Communists, but his foreign policy had advanced on all other fronts. In Europe, the Soviet threat to the Continent appeared to be lessening. And in the Far East, General Douglas MacArthur had achieved notable success in restoring Japan as a useful member of the free world. At home, almost the entire Fair Deal had failed of enactment. Truman realized, however, that his proposals were in the main far in advance of the conservative philosophy of Congressional leaders and only time and a great deal of public education would put them across.

During 1949, his achievements were often obscured by minor events. He could take a bold stand one day on public matters, only on the following day to tarnish the impression he had made by an undignified comment. Newspapers delighted in printing every "hell" and "damn" he uttered, instead of editing copy as they did for his predecessors. Even the staid *New York Times* once ran the following Truman quote: "I knew there would be a lot of stink about it, but I didn't give a damn."

There were mounting attacks on his associates in 1949, especially on General Vaughan. In August, Senator Clyde Hoey of South Carolina undertook an investigation of "Five Per-centers," or the influence-peddlers who knew their way around government agencies dealing in contracts or licenses. Hoey, who wore high top shoes, a wing collar and a frock coat, hardly looked the part of a fire-eating investigator. But he was soon getting daily headlines pointing a palsied finger at Vaughan. John Maragon, a former Kansas City shoeshine boy and Capitol train reservations employee, whom Truman had barred from the White House when he became President, was one of those called to testify. Hoey's subcommittee disclosed that Maragon was drawing $1,000 a month from an importer at the same time that he worked for the Allied Mission to Greece. Subsequently Maragon went to prison, but his unsavory shenanigans besmirched Vaughan, who had found a place for him on the Mission—and even reflected on Truman, who was entirely innocent. Then there was Colonel James V. Hunt, who was shown to have undue influence with the chief of the Army Chemical Corps and the Quartermaster General. Truman immediately ordered the retirement of the first and suspension of the second general, but the uproar continued. The papers made much of the fact that Hunt possessed matchboxes labeled *Swiped from Harry S. Truman.* Although Truman emphatically denied that he knew Hunt, it was not until long afterward that a matchbox manufacturer revealed that Hunt had ordered 2,500 matchboxes from him imprinted with that line.

When Hoey summoned Vaughan to testify, *Time* Magazine reported that the subcommittee had spent several weeks preparing a "barbecue pit" for him. At first Truman refused to let his aide testify because he considered the subcommittee's interest in Vaughan only a subterfuge to get at him. But on second thought he realized that silence would be interpreted as a tacit admission that Vaughan was in league with the Five Per-centers. At the end of August the subcommittee grilled a sweating Vaughan for two days about his relationship with Hunt and Maragon, about some factory-reject deepfreezes that had been given as gifts to the White House, and about lumber priorities that had been granted a race track. Hoey's verdict was that although Vaughan had been careless in his associations, he was not guilty of premeditated wrong, that the deepfreezes were outright gifts and not payment for favors. But the damage was done. Opposition

369

papers used the incident of the deepfreezes as a club to batter Truman's character and label him as corrupt.

The charge of Administration corruption was raised again a short time later when newspapers reported that Secretary of the Interior Julius Krug was involved in a lawsuit over a $750,000 loan. In addition, his name was found on the expense account of a lobbyist. Truman summarily relieved Krug of his duties and elevated Oscar Chapman to Cabinet status.

When Hoey's subcommittee uncovered other instances of Five Per-centers operating in various departments, most newspapers conveyed the impression to their readers that the entire Administration was honeycombed with corruption. But Joseph Alsop, no friend of the Administration, wrote: "There is nothing big in what the Five Percenters' investigation has been unearthing. There is only a kind of small pettiness. There has been no evidence of personal corruption. . . . It has all been on a niggling scale—the hole-in-corner wire pulling, the commercialized 'friendships,' the little favors for little men." Comptroller General Lindsay Warren said that the money which found its way at that time into the pockets of the Five Percenters was small change compared with the "biggest money grab from the U. S. Treasury, which was never publicized. By Congressional action, the responsibility for final settlement of war contracts was placed in the hands of those who gave out the original contracts. The cost of this folly to taxpayers was at least $500,000,000."

With most Presidents, the American press has generally absolved the Chief Executive from responsibility for any wrongdoings uncovered in a governmental department, placing the blame directly on the officials involved. Truman, however, was condemned personally for all misdeeds in the far-flung Federal apparatus. Herbert Hoover called these sweeping accusations silly. He pointed out in 1949 that there were 65 agencies reporting directly to the President, who, if he devoted one hour a week to each, would be putting in a 65-hour week to the disregard of a vast number of basic matters.

Besides the charge of corruption, Truman's opponents developed a new and powerful weapon in 1950. In January, after Alger Hiss was convicted in the Whittaker Chambers affair, Secretary of State Acheson, who had been a friend of Hiss, was quoted publicly as saying, "I will not turn my back on Alger Hiss." Although he also said that he did not condone the crime for which Hiss was convicted, the papers did not play this up. Repeated demands were now made in

Congress and in the press that Truman fire Acheson as being "soft on Communism." Leader of the initial attack was Senator Wherry, who, according to *Time,* demanded Acheson's resignation as regularly as "a factory lunch whistle."

Truman considered this attack on Acheson contemptible. If he fired him, he said, "it would weaken the firm and vigorous position this country has taken against Communist aggression." For Acheson had been in the forefront of every effective action taken against Soviet imperialism, beginning with the Greek-Turkish aid program. Acheson, who had served as Under Secretary of State from August, 1945, to July, 1947, had become Secretary in January, 1949, when General Marshall resigned.

In early 1950, the attack on Acheson broadened when Senator Joseph McCarthy of Wisconsin, a rather quiet and nondescript Senator until then, made a speech at Wheeling, West Virginia, in which he charged: "I have here in my hand a list of 205—a list of names that were made known to the Secretary of State as being members of the Communist Party and who, nevertheless, are still working and shaping policy in the State Department." Truman bluntly denied that any such list had been given to the State Department. He said further that there were no known Communists employed by the Department, and that McCarthy's charge served only to damage the morale of all persons working there.

Nevertheless, the entire lunatic fringe of the nation jumped on McCarthy's bandwagon and he gained anti-Truman adherents with each passing week. Although McCarthy changed the total of his so-called list with each speech, this made no difference to his supporters. Nor did the fact that the State Department's security officers failed to uncover a single bona fide member of the Communist Party cause his movement to falter.

Despite the increasing bitter partisanship in politics, Truman decided in May, 1950, to gain popular backing for his dying Fair Deal and explain his foreign policy by making a 16-state tour across the country, covering 6,400 miles. Although it was described as a "non-political" trip ostensibly to dedicate the Grand Coulee Dam, his opponents knew what he planned. When the Secret Service sent out word that "Potus," the railroad code name for the President of the United States, would soon be passing through various towns, Republicans braced themselves for ringing attacks.

The trip had all the markings of his 1948 campaign whistle-stop

371

tour. This was the Truman of old, explaining to enthusiastic gatherings in his flat Missouri twang that his opponents were "reactionaries, greedy men and calamity howlers." At one stop he told the large crowd: "I am talking to you as your hired man. I have come out here to tell you just exactly what I am trying to do, and I am telling it to you firsthand so it can't be garbled. There is no way to get the truth to you, but to come out and tell you."

Bess and Margaret traveled with him and he introduced them as he had in 1948. He attacked McCarthyism, the new word in the American vocabulary, and defended the patriotism of government employees. Point by point he went through his Fair Deal program, to the cheers of the crowds and yells of "Give 'em hell, Harry." He ripped into the conservatives of Congress who were withholding action on his program and throwing out the smoke screen that it was socialism. At Galesburg, Illinois, he told how he had worn a white Democratic campaign cap to school. "Well, some big Republican boys took my cap away from me and tore it up. And the Republicans have been trying to do that to me ever since." Everywhere, he winked at the crowd and said, "This is a nonpolitical trip. But I may be back later and be a little more interested in politics."

By the time he returned to Blair House, he had talked to 525,000 people. *The New York Times* reported that the trip had helped his cause immeasurably. "He reduced the issues to town-size so any dirt farmer can understand them."

The Democratic National Committee was heartened most of all because of the coming Congressional elections that fall. Chairman Bill Boyle said: "We lived in a big old-fashioned house in Kansas City when I was a boy. And I remember the Trumans used to come over and visit us on Sundays. My mother was active in local politics. What I remember best were the political picnics the Party used to hold every summer at Lonejack, Missouri, outside of Kansas City. These were hell-roaring, rip-snorting affairs with the loudest speeches you ever heard. The President loved those picnics, never missed one." Truman's May, 1950, tour across the country was one long "Lonejack oration."

Boyle looked forward to more "Lonejack orations" in the fall. But there were not to be any. The Communists were to see to this in Korea.

39

AT THE Cairo Conference in 1943, Roosevelt, Churchill and Chiang Kai-shek announced their desire for a Korea free from the Japanese yoke. Korea, in English "the land of the morning calm," was discussed further at the Yalta Conference in February, 1945, where the conferees agreed informally to a period of trusteeship before a Korean Government took over.

In May, 1945, when Harry Hopkins spoke to him in Moscow, Stalin reaffirmed his commitment to a four-power trusteeship over Korea. Then, at Potsdam, the State Department advocated that American forces handle the entire Japanese surrender in Korea. But when military advisers told Truman that it would be impossible to dispatch sufficient troops there, he accepted the military view and agreed that the Russians should handle the Japanese surrender above an arbitrary point, the 38th Parallel, and the United States, below. Once that job was completed, joint control was to extend over the entire peninsula preparatory to the establishment of the trusteeship.

What followed instead was a classic example of Communist tactics. Only a few weeks after V-J Day, General John R. Hodge, in charge below the 38th Parallel, reported to Truman that he was rebuffed in his attempts to negotiate with the Soviets in the north. An Iron Curtain had descended at that line. Moreover, anti-American propaganda was flooding the southern section, blaming the United States for cutting the country in two and depriving the agricultural south of the industry that was almost entirely located in the north.

In December, 1945, when Secretary of State Byrnes went to Moscow, he agreed to a joint United States-Soviet Commission, to establish a provisional Korean Government composed of "Korean democratic and social organizations." Unfortunately, he failed to define the terms concerning the composition of this provisional government.

Byrnes's naïveté was soon apparent. When the Joint Commission met in Seoul on March 20, 1946, an argument immediately ensued regarding the meaning of "Korean democratic and social organizations." The Russians adamantly insisted that any party opposed to Communism was automatically barred from participating. As a result, the Joint Commission adjourned permanently in May with the Americans holding South Korea and the Russians North Korea.

Despite United States economic aid, the situation in South Korea was distressing. Serious floods and strikes produced chaos, and a widespread black market in foodstuffs and manufactured goods sent prices rocketing. Elderly Syngman Rhee, the Princeton graduate and Korean expatriate who had come to the fore as a leader, went so far as to accuse General Hodge of "trying to build up and foster the Korean Communist Party."

When Hodge informed Truman in 1947 that civil war was in the offing unless the United States and Russia found a joint solution to the problem of Korea, Truman proposed a seven-point plan to Stalin that included provisions for an all-Korea vote by secret ballot on a basis of universal suffrage. Stalin disdainfully turned him down.

The argument over Korea had gone on now for two years, and Truman decided that it was time to place the impasse before the UN General Assembly. General Marshall, who was then Secretary of State, went to Lake Success to ask the United Nations to reunite Korea because of "the inability of two powers to reach agreement" there.

In the meantime, Truman ordered the Joint Chiefs of Staff to study the military value of Korea. A report submitted by General Eisenhower, Admiral Leahy, Admiral Nimitz and General Spaatz in

September, 1947, said: "The Joint Chiefs of staff consider that, from the standpoint of military security, the United States has little strategic interest in maintaining the present troops and bases in Korea." General MacArthur also agreed with this view to exclude Korea from the American defense perimeter. MacArthur went even further, saying that anyone who advocated a land war on the Asiatic continent should have his head examined.

When the United Nations established a Temporary Commission on Korea to supervise free elections, the Russian commander in North Korea would not permit the Commission to cross the 38th Parallel. Faced with this impasse, the Commission limited the free election to South Korea, which had a population of 20 million, compared with 10 million in North Korea.

On May 10, 1948, out of some 8,300,000 eligible voters in the south, 7,000,000 went to the polls and elected a National Assembly, which wrote a constitution and selected Syngman Rhee as President of the Republic of Korea. When Truman recognized Rhee in August, the American military government came to an end. In the north, the Russians countered by establishing a "Democratic People's Republic of Korea."

With the establishment of the ROK Government, Truman had three possibilities to consider. He could now forget about Korea; continue military and political responsibility; or train a ROK security force and give the Government economic aid. He chose the last course.

On the military side, he ordered aid to equip and train a 65,000 man ROK army, a 4,000-man coast guard and a 45,000-man ROK police contingent. In addition, he shipped the Rhee Government about a billion dollars of economic aid, despite widespread opposition by an economy-minded Congress.

By 1950, Truman was well aware that Rhee was making no effort to democratize South Korea, despite this aid. Rhee, he said, had "attracted to himself men of extreme right-wing attitudes" and his police used inhuman methods "to break up political meetings and control political enemies." Inflation was also growing worse and Rhee did nothing to improve the lot of the peasants. Taken all together, Truman realized that Korea was hardly a showcase for democracy in the Orient. Yet the United States, as the republic's godfather, had the direct responsibility for maintaining her existence, despite her lack of strategic value.

In January, 1950, Secretary of State Acheson, successor to Marshall, expressed government policy when he told the National Press Club that America's first-line defense perimeter did not include Korea: "No person can guarantee these areas against military attack." However, he added, "Should such an attack occur . . . the initial reliance must be on the people attacked, and then upon the commitments of the entire civilized world under the Charter of the UN."

In the spring of 1950, the Central Intelligence Agency reported to Truman that the North Koreans were strengthening their forces. But the CIA also reported that the Communists were building up strength in a dozen other danger spots in the world. If the United States divided its limited forces to cover each danger point, this widespread dispersal would work to the advantage of the Communists.

On June 24, 1950, Truman dedicated the new Friendship Airport outside of Baltimore and then flew to Independence for what he hoped would be a quiet weekend. That evening at ten-thirty his phone rang and an agitated Dean Acheson was on the other end of the line. "Mr. President," Acheson said, "I have very serious news. The North Koreans have invaded South Korea." North Korean troops spearheaded by 100 Soviet T-34 and T-70 tanks had roared across the 38th Parallel at three separate points. They had also made seven amphibious landings along the east coast of South Korea.

Truman's first reaction was to hurry back to Washington. Acheson said, however, that not enough details had come in yet regarding South Korean defenses and that he need not plan on returning until there was further information. Acheson suggested that in the meantime the United States should request the UN Security Council to meet at once and declare that an act of aggression had been committed against the ROK Government. Some time before, when the United Nations had refused to seat Red China, the Russians had walked out of the Security Council. Owing to this fortunate circumstance, they would not be present to veto any Security Council action.

Acheson called Truman again on Sunday at 12:35 P. M. with the news that the UN Security Council was to meet at three that afternoon. He informed the President that there was little question that the North Koreans were making a major effort to take South Korea. Truman rounded up his aides and took off for Washington at 2:10.

His face was grim when the *Independence* landed at the National

Airport that evening, for his mind was already made up on the most crucial decision of his Presidential years. If the United States let South Korea fall, the Communists would next move against other weak nations and pick them off like ripe plums.

"When the President reached Blair House," said Eben Ayers, Truman's assistant press secretary, "he had dinner with his advisers at eight P. M., though Mr. Truman insisted they refrain from discussing Korea during the meal because the servants were present. Afterward, they held a conference that lasted until ten-forty-five."

At that meeting, Acheson reported that the UN Security Council by a vote of 9–0 had approved a resolution calling for a cessation of hostilities and withdrawal of North Korean forces behind the 38th Parallel. To Truman, this was an innocuous resolution, for it made no counterthreats to the invaders. The line had to be drawn sharper against aggressors, he said. A further resolution was obviously needed.

In the meantime, he ordered General MacArthur to evacuate by air the 2,000 Americans then in Seoul and to supply arms to the ROK forces by airdrop. Because military reports spoke glowingly of the fighting capacity of the ROK army, Truman had every reason to believe that once the initial shock of the surprise invasion was dissipated, the ROK army would repel the North Koreans. He also attempted to localize the fighting by ordering the U. S. Seventh Fleet, then off the Philippines, to proceed into the Formosa Strait. It objective was to protect Formosa from attack by the Chinese Communists and to prevent raids on the Chinese mainland by Chiang Kai-shek's forces.

The next day, Monday the twenty-sixth, the news from Korea was all bad. Red tanks were approaching Seoul and Rhee's Government had fled to Taegu, 150 miles to the south. That evening at nine, Truman held another conference at Blair House. By now it appeared that the ROK forces needed more than American military supplies. At this meeting Truman ordered Secretary of Defense Louis Johnson to call MacArthur on the scrambler phone and instruct him to support Rhee with American air and naval forces. No mention was made of committing American ground forces.

On Tuesday, when the situation in South Korea continued to deteriorate, Acheson succeeded in winning a UN Security Council resolution calling on member nations to "furnish such assistance to the Republic of Korea as may be necessary to repel the armed attack and restore international peace and security."

377

That day Truman invited Congressional leaders for a briefing. "Truman was grimly thin-lipped," said Tom Connally. "After Acheson gave us a résumé of the fighting, Truman discussed the UN, what it meant to the world, why we had to act through it and what would happen if the UN failed to take a decisive stand on the fighting. There was no disagreement that the United States had to help the South Koreans. Nor did anyone object to Truman's remarks about the UN. In fact, the Republicans present insisted that we act strictly according to UN directives. When Truman went into the policy decisions he had made thus far, no one present raised even minor criticism, although a few wondered if Congress should approve them."

At Truman's suggestion, MacArthur took off from Tokyo on June 28 to observe the Korean fighting firsthand. Riding in a jeep to the south bank of the Han River, only a mile below Seoul, he found the city in flames, Red planes strafing the area, and all roads south from Seoul crowded with refugees. More than half the ROK force had evaporated, some killed, some wounded and others trapped on the wrong side of the Han by other ROK troops who had stupidly blown up bridges. What was left of the ROK army was in full retreat.

On Thursday, the twenty-ninth, Truman met with the National Security Council and announced that the American objective in Korea was to push the North Koreans back across the 38th Parallel. Also up for discussion was an offer from Chiang Kai-shek to send 33,000 men to Korea, if the United States would deliver them there and then supply them with arms. Truman's first inclination was to accept the offer, but the Joint Chiefs of Staff pointed out that Chiang's troops were poorly equipped and would only suffer the fate of the ROK forces. Since there was also the risk that if Chiang's soldiers appeared in Korea, the Chinese Communists might join the fighting, Truman rejected the Generalissimo's offer.

The final step along the road to war came in the middle of that night. At four A.M., MacArthur held a telecon (teletype radio conference) with the Joint Chiefs of Staff at the Pentagon in which he declared that the only way to prevent the collapse of South Korea was to commit "United States ground combat forces into the Korean battle area."

Secretary of the Army Frank Pace awakened Truman at five A.M. to tell him of the conversation. Truman did not hesitate. "Inform General MacArthur immediately that the use of one regimental combat team is approved."

378

Seven hours after he made his fateful decision, Truman met again with Congressional leaders. Before the meeting, he talked privately with Senator Connally. "Do you think I'll have to ask Congress for a declaration of war?" he asked.

Connally's reply was in the negative. "If a burglar breaks into your house, you can shoot at him without going down to the police station and getting permission. You might run into a long debate by Congress, which would tie your hands completely. You have the right to do so as Commander in Chief and under the UN Charter." Truman took Connally's advice.

As the Korean involvement got underway, Truman committed two errors. Although he wanted to ask Congress for full wartime economic controls, including price controls, Sam Rayburn advised him that he could get priority and allocation controls within a week if he did not ask for price controls. Knowing how unpopular price controls had been during World War II, Truman accepted Rayburn's suggestion. His mistake was soon apparent, for prices shot sky high. Had he asked for price controls at the outset, there is little doubt that Congress would have approved this authority. As it was, when he finally attempted to stem the wild inflation, Congress did not grant him power to freeze prices until January, 1951.

Truman's second error resulted from a hasty reply at a news conference. When a reporter asked him whether it was correct to refer to the American intervention in Korea as a "police action," Truman unthinkingly agreed to the use of the term. By doing so, he gave isolationists the opportunity to confuse the issue when military casualty lists began appearing and to heap ridicule upon his courageous action.

The fighting in Korea was hardly a police action. With the North Koreans pushing steadily toward Pusan, the heel of the Korean peninsula, MacArthur was in a desperate position. He had only a few troops, but he reasoned that if he could trick the North Koreans into believing he had a large force, he might hold them off until other American units eventually arrived. "I threw in troops by air in the hope of establishing a locus of resistance around which I could rally the fast-retreating South Korean forces," he later explained. "I also hoped by that arrogant display to fool the enemy into a belief that I had greater resources at my disposal than I did. . . . The enemy . . . could not understand that we could make such an effort with such a small force. Instead of rushing rapidly forward to Pusan, which he could have reached within a week without the slightest difficulty, he stopped to deploy his artillery across the Han. We gained ten days by that process." During those precious days, when the North Koreans, who outnumbered MacArthur's forces 100 to one, spread out at the Han for an expected major battle, MacArthur had time to bring in two divisions from Japan and deploy them near Pusan.

In those desperate days, when it looked as if the North Koreans would push the Americans into the sea, the initial bipartisan approval of Truman's action in Korea began to evaporate. With each report of casualties, Truman was ridiculed for labeling the fighting a "police action." Cabinet members also found themselves under siege-gun attack. Senator Wherry fired shots in all directions. Prefacing several of his statements with "It is my unanimous opinion," he sneered at the Joint Chiefs of Staff as the "Chief Joints of Staff" and hurled bloodcurdling charges against Acheson.

The Secretary of State was put through a verbal meat grinder. In the House, Joe Martin introduced a bill to stop Acheson's salary. In the Senate, Taft loudly demanded that Truman fire him. "In January, 1951," Senator Connally said, "Taft, a man of no military background, advised us to abandon Korea and then in April he demanded an expansion of the war to the Chinese mainland. . . . On December 20, 1950, Herbert Hoover publicly advocated that American defenses be limited to the Western Hemisphere plus Japan, Formosa and the Philippines in the Pacific and to England in Europe. He was heartily applauded by Wherry, Bridges, Taft and other Republicans, who were at the same time attacking Acheson's January statement to the National Press Club, for omitting Korea from our Pacific defense perimeter."

Truman's friend Harry Vaughan once commented why he thought Acheson failed to put himself across to the American public. "His elegant appearance and continental manner were against him. I told him he should wear a ratty mustache, wrinkled suit and an American-type hat, drop his British accent and make a grammatical error in each speech."

Secretary of Defense Louis Johnson was also the object of fierce criticism. The man who had helped save Truman in 1948 by raising campaign funds turned out to be a conservative secretary, ever mindful of the budget. It was chiefly his defense budget for fiscal 1951, composed long before the Korean war began, that rendered him a prime target in a hindsight attack by opponents who had earlier considered his budget too high.

To fend off his attackers, Johnson pointed out that General Eisenhower had played a vital role in writing the defense budget for fiscal 1951. He insisted that the "versions of that budget were known at the Pentagon as Ike I, Ike II, and Ike III." When Eisenhower appeared before the Senate Appropriations subcommittee on the Pentagon's slashed budget, he had justified it on the ground that war was not "imminent," and called it "fairly well on the line between economy and security."

Once the Korean war had started, Truman defended Johnson from the vituperation that was rained on him. But he became increasingly disturbed when he began hearing reports that Johnson was criticizing Acheson privately to various Republican Senators. "At a closed committee hearing," Senator Kilgore said, "Johnson stared over at a man from the State Department and inquired, 'Is everyone here cleared for security?' He also went out of his way to criticize the State Department's handling of the China problem and there were stories that he was feeding Senators Brewster and Bridges with anti-Acheson material."

Johnson became expendable, and on September 12, 1950, Truman sent him a "Dear Lou" letter, commending him for his fine work and expressing regret that he was leaving the Government. A newsman reported that Johnson was so upset at being fired that he was "white, choked up." To succeed him, Truman named General Marshall as his next Secretary of Defense.

Although Senator Taft applauded the firing of Johnson, he took a dim view of his successor. The National Security Act of 1947 provided that no military man could become Secretary of Defense unless he had been out of the active service for ten years, and Taft was intent upon preventing a special ruling for Marshall. In the debate on the nomination, he said that Marshall at seventy was too old for the job and charged that he had encouraged the Chinese Reds during his mission to China five years before. But Taft was mild compared with Senator William Jenner of Indiana, who said, "Marshall is a staggering swindle. Marshall is willing to play the role of a front man for traitors. Marshall is a living lie!" The Senate thought otherwise and confirmed the general's nomination.

Despite his brilliant feat in preventing the North Koreans from pushing the Americans into the sea off Pusan, General MacArthur helped muddy the turbulent political waters when he went to Formosa and paid a courtesy call on Chiang Kai-shek on July 31, 1950. Before his visit, MacArthur had informed Generals J. Lawton Collins and Hoyt Vandenberg that he would explain to Chiang that the use of his troops in Korea would be of little value. The two generals had reported to Truman that MacArthur believed Chinese Nationalist troops would require "extensive logistic support from us" and "would be an albatross around our necks for months."

On Formosa, Chiang offered MacArthur command of all his troops, a proposal MacArthur rejected as "not appropriate." But hardly had MacArthur left the island when Chiang broadcast to the world that MacArthur was in complete agreement with him about the Truman policy of a neutral Formosa being entirely wrong. Chiang boasted that MacArthur favored an aggressive role for the Chinese Nationalists against the mainland while the fighting was going on in Korea.

Filled with concern that his Far East Commander was raising havoc with his foreign policy, Truman dispatched Averell Harriman to Tokyo on August 3. MacArthur must be made to realize, said Truman, that the Korean action stemmed from a broad Kremlin plan to destroy unity in the free world, that the Korean war was a Soviet maneuver to draw the United States into military action in Asia and thus prevent effective American participation in NATO for the defense of Europe. To extend the fighting in Asia, where the United States was weakest, merely to further the ambitions of Chiang Kai-shek would put Chiang, not Truman, in charge of American foreign policy.

Harriman held several conferences with MacArthur, and in a long report to Truman, he wrote:

> I asked MacArthur whether he had any doubts about the wisdom of the Korean decision. He replied, "Absolutely none. . . . It was an historic decision which would save the world from communist domination, and would be so recorded in history. . . . I told him the President wanted me to tell him he must not permit Chiang to be the cause of starting a war with the Chinese Communists on the mainland, the effect of which might drag us into a world war. He answered that he would, as a soldier, obey any orders that he received from the President. . . .
>
> I pointed out to him the basic conflict of interest between the U. S. and the Generalissimo's position as to the future of Formosa. . . .

Chiang...had only the burning ambition to use Formosa as a steppingstone for his re-entry to the mainland. MacArthur recognized that this ambition could not be fulfilled, and yet thought it might be a good idea to let him land and get rid of him that way.

Truman assumed that the Formosa issue was now settled. But on August 26, Charlie Ross handed him a statement which MacArthur had sent to the commander of the Veterans of Foreign Wars and had already been printed in the August 28 issue of a weekly magazine. Truman was irate when he read MacArthur's words. The entire statement was critical of his policy to neutralize Formosa, for it advocated a military policy of aggression, using Formosa as an American base of operations.

At a meeting with advisers that day, Truman said that he planned to relieve MacArthur and replace him with General Omar Bradley. On second thought, however, he realized that MacArthur's military genius was essential for conducting the war in Korea. For the time being, therefore, he did nothing except insist that MacArthur withdraw his statement to the VFW. The general complied with this order, although his statement was already public.

Throughout August, the North Korean invaders continued their fierce assault against the Pusan beachhead. Lieutenant General Walton Walker's Eighth Army could do no more than hold on grimly against the enemy, and MacArthur realized that a spectacular move was needed to prevent his forces from being pushed into the sea. The answer came to him one night when he read the account of British General James Wolfe's campaign in 1759 to capture Quebec. Wolfe's staff had argued that an attack up the perpendicular riverbanks to the south of the walled city would fail because it was not possible to scale those heights. But Wolfe reasoned that if his aides considered this attack impossible, so would the French. By utilizing just this daring approach, Wolfe took the French by surprise and captured Quebec.

MacArthur's Quebec became Inchon, on Korea's west coast near Seoul and almost back to the 38th Parallel, where the North Koreans would never expect him to attack. The chief drawback was that Inchon was a hazardous landing spot. Its offshore tides rose and fell more than twenty feet, so that a landing could be made only at high tide, giving invasion ships just a few hours before they would be stranded in mud which extended two miles out from shore.

When Truman sent General J. Lawton Collins and Admiral Forrest

Sherman to Tokyo in mid-August, they attempted to talk MacArthur out of his proposed offensive. They pointed out the dangers of a landing at Inchon and argued that Inchon was too far in the rear of Pusan to relieve pressure on the beachhead. MacArthur turned on them angrily. "Inchon," he insisted, "will save a hundred thousand lives."

Collins and Sherman left Tokyo without expressing approval of an Inchon landing. Truman, however, considered it "a daring strategic conception" and gave his approval.

D-Day at Inchon came on September 15 when Marine assault waves stormed ashore. Then the X Corps, under Major General Edward N. (Ned) Almond, struck toward Seoul and liberated the ROK capital by September 28. On the Pusan beachhead, General Walker noticed one day that the North Korean strength had ebbed. When the enemy attempted to head north, they found their supply lines cut. Caught now between the X Corps and the Eighth Army, the Red forces collapsed and about 130,000 North Koreans were taken prisoner.

MacArthur's generals were now in control of the entire area below the 38th Parallel. And from Washington, Truman sent him a heartfelt message.

> I know that I speak for the entire American people when I send you my warmest congratulations on the victory which has been achieved under your leadership in Korea. Few operations in military history can match either the delaying action where you traded space for time in which to build up your forces, or the brilliant maneuver which has now resulted in the liberation of Seoul. . . . Well and nobly done.

40

ONCE MacArthur's forces regained the 38th Parallel, Truman was faced with a new problem. Was it in the best interest of the United States to call a halt to the fighting now? Or should he order MacArthur north of the Parallel to take all of Korea?

On June 28, when the fighting in Korea had hardly begun, this subject had come up at his meeting with the National Security Council. At that time, when Secretary of the Army Frank Pace had expressed caution in authorizing operations above that line, Truman had agreed with him. But with the success of MacArthur's Inchon strategy, Truman changed his mind. He told Senator Connally, "We have to go beyond the 38th Parallel because it isn't a good battle line. We need a line that can be properly defended. So we have to fight a while longer in order to convince the North Koreans they are vanquished and that further aggression doesn't pay."

Accordingly, Truman sent MacArthur new instructions on September 27. The objective now became "the destruction of the North Korean Armed Forces." In a clarification, he authorized MacArthur to conduct a military campaign north of the Parallel if he found no major Soviet or Red Chinese forces operating there. In a further limitation, MacArthur was told not to cross the Soviet or Manchurian borders contiguous with Korea by land or air and to rely solely on ROK troops at the approaches to those borders.

On October 1, Chou En-lai, foreign minister of Red China, announced: "The People's Republic of China will not stand idly by and see North Korea invaded." At the time this seemed a hollow threat because American intelligence did not find large Red Chinese forces along the Korean border.

Named United Nations as well as United States commander of the forces in Korea on July 8, MacArthur waited until the UN General Assembly passed a resolution on October 7 authorizing him to operate in North Korea. Even then, he made two cease-fire appeals to the enemy. When the North Koreans ignored these appeals, he ordered his forces "to destroy the North Korean army and unify the entire nation."

General Walker's Eighth Army slashed up the center of North Korea toward Pyongyang, the Red capital, while General Almond's X Corps proceeded up the east coast toward Wonsan. Token troop units from 16 United Nations contingents also participated in the drive, as well as recently trained ROK armies. From a military point of view, the separation of Walker and Almond's forces was poor strategy because they were divided by a mountain range and could not easily come to each other's aid in case of trouble. But Walker and Almond were not on speaking terms and there was no other way to utilize the services of both generals. In fact, their rivalry spurred their armies on to outdo each other in the rush northward.

Shortly after the drive across the 38th Parallel began, Truman decided that it was time he became personally acquainted with General MacArthur. "At first Truman wanted to call the general back to Washington for a conference," Senator Kilgore said. "But he listened to his aides who argued, 'If he comes here, everyone will want him to talk and the Republicans will have a field day using him to attack you.' At that time, Senator Knowland was insisting that the President had gagged MacArthur on Formosa policy, and the rest of the China Lobby was using the general as the focal point of their attack on Truman."

Truman finally requested MacArthur to meet him at Wake Island on October 15. When the *Independence* set down on Wake at six A.M. that morning, MacArthur was waiting to greet him. Truman was

386

taken aback by MacArthur's casual wartime garb which included an unbuttoned shirt and his battered cap. "I've been a long time meeting you," he said, shaking hands. Reporters who were present said that Truman did not act like a commander in chief greeting a subordinate. Tony Leviero of *The New York Times* described the meeting of Truman and MacArthur as that of "an insurance salesman who had at last signed up an important prospect . . . while the latter appeared dubious over the extent of coverage."

The best car on Wake Island was an old dilapidated vehicle, and together the two men rode in it through the searing heat for their first private conference in a Quonset hut. Truman later admitted that he had not expected MacArthur to be friendly and was pleasantly surprised at his warmth. During this talk, which lasted an hour, Truman said that the general was optimistic and announced that victory was near in Korea, that the Chinese Reds would not enter the fight and that Japan was quite ready for a peace treaty restoring her independence. MacArthur also mentioned his August statement to the Veterans of Foreign Wars and expressed regret that his remarks on Formosa had offended Truman. The President good-naturedly accepted this apology.

At the close of their private conversation, they moved to another building for a second conference at 7:30 A.M. with staff aides. Truman, who had brought along several top advisers, had expected MacArthur to do the same, but the general was accompanied only by a single aide. Truman later said that MacArthur acted as if he wanted to get this second meeting over with in a hurry. On his part, MacArthur was furious afterward to learn that a secretary sat outside the meeting room and took stenographic notes of what she could hear.

This second meeting was quick and to the point, with Truman referring to a prepared agenda of topics. One was the proposed Japanese peace treaty; another the matter of the postwar reconstruction of Korea. MacArthur also raised the question of a Pacific pact for mutual defense against aggression.

At one point, Truman asked MacArthur, "What are the chances for Chinese or Soviet interference in the Korean fighting?"

MacArthur replied that there was little chance of the Chinese Reds entering the fighting directly, although intelligence data from his own command and the Central Intelligence Agency disclosed a concentration of more than 300,000 Red Chinese troops in Manchuria across the Yalu River boundary. At best, said MacArthur, intelligence reports showed that the Chinese Communists might get fifty to sixty thousand men into Korea, but because they lacked an air force, "if they tried to get down to Pyongyang, there would be the greatest slaughter."

As for Russian intervention, MacArthur continued, there was little likelihood that they could bring in large numbers of ground soldiers before the coming winter. He added that, according to the American Government's own intelligence reports, Soviet planes and pilots were inferior to those of the United States.

When Truman asked him how long the war would last, MacArthur replied that he expected resistance to end by Thanksgiving. At that time he would withdraw Walker's Eighth Army to Japan by Christmas, and leave his other forces in Korea until elections were held, possibly as early as January.

When the meeting ended at 9:30 A.M., Truman invited MacArthur to be his luncheon guest. However, the general glanced at his watch and said that he preferred returning to the war front. Although disappointed, Truman did not press him to remain.

In a speech at San Francisco on October 17, Truman said, "I have just returned from Wake Island where I had a very satisfactory conference with General Douglas MacArthur." But sometime later he declared, "I traveled fourteen thousand miles to Wake Island to get a lot of misinformation."

The offensive in North Korea now proceeded at a sweeping pace in most sectors. General Almond's X Corps captured the important North Korean port city of Wonsan by amphibious action, although two vital weeks were wasted in clearing the harbor of floating mines. Truman was elated when MacArthur once more revealed his genius in capturing the North Korean capital of Pyongyang on October 20 by dropping paratroopers 25 miles north of the capital while ground troops moved on the city from the south. At his triumphant entry into Pyongyang, the entire population turned out to greet him with loud cheers and a display of banners. This bore out his observation, which he had expressed to Truman, that the North Koreans were no more Communists than the South Koreans.

As MacArthur's forces continued to drive north to the border, he had to make a difficult choice. Truman had ordered him to use only Korean troops in the vicinity of the Yalu River frontier. But his ROK units were woefully inexperienced, and he therefore unilaterally ordered American units to spearhead the drive to the border, an action that swiftly brought him into controversy with the Joint Chiefs of Staff, sitting in the Pentagon thousands of miles away.

A much more basic problem was arising, however. On the day Pyongyang fell, the CIA reported to Truman that the Chinese Reds planned to move across the border to protect the Suiho power plant and other electrical installations in North Korea that served China. Acheson wanted MacArthur to issue a statement that he would not attack these installations. But when the general insisted that this would be poor military tactics, Truman agreed with him.

Even though the CIA did not actually say that the Chinese Reds were certain to plunge full-scale into the Korean war, MacArthur now grew apprehensive at this possibility. In an unarmed plane, he flew the length of the Yalu River to make his own observations, but down below he saw only ice and snow—no sign of Chinese troop concentrations.

Yet on October 26, near Wonsan, the X Corps captured a Red Chinese soldier. A few days later several others were taken. They claimed to be "volunteers," but MacArthur's suspicions were aroused. On November 4, he wrote to Truman: "It is impossible at this time to authoritatively appraise the actualities of Chinese Communist intervention in North Korea. Various possibilities exist based upon the battle intelligence coming in from the front." But he cautioned "against hasty conclusions" and said that "a final appraisement should await a more complete accumulation of military facts."

On November 1, when Truman woke, he was filled with concern about the Chinese Reds. After his usual early-morning hike, swim and breakfast, he rode across the street to his oval office in the White House. He dictated some letters and worked on staff and Cabinet memoranda until nine-thirty, when General Bradley came in to brief him as he did each morning on the military situation, using a long pointer and a map set up on an easel about five feet from Truman's desk. Bradley, whose manner was generally serious, called Truman's attention to a dot of an island off the Korean coast which he explained had been captured that morning by twenty American soldiers.

"Now why did they ever bother to do that?" Truman inquired.

"I really don't know unless the boys discovered there was a brewery on that island," Bradley said, smiling.

After the briefing came the staff meeting, and then the visitors. Truman discussed Chopin and Beethoven with Rudolf Friml, then talked about commercial aviation problems with Delos W. Rentzel, chairman of the Civil Aeronautics Board. After Rentzel, he saw Nelson Rockefeller, awarded the Congressional Medal of Honor to a Marine hero at Iwo Jima, conferred with Anthony Eden and Sir Oliver Franks, the British ambassador, and then with Stuart Symington, chairman of the National Security Resources Board.

At one P.M. he returned to Blair House, where he had lunch with Bess and her mother. Afterward he went upstairs for a nap in his second-floor-front bedroom. The temperature outdoors was 84°, an unusually hot day for fall and particularly uncomfortable in Washington because of the high humidity. It was so hot that he took off his suit and stretched out on top of the bedcover in his underwear. He was scheduled to depart from Blair House by way of the alley at 2:50 P.M. for a ride across the river to Arlington Cemetery to speak at the unveiling of a statue of Field Marshal Sir John Dill, the British member of the World War II Combined Chiefs of Staff.

Outside of Blair House, while Truman slept, guards were on duty in white sentry boxes at the east and west ends of the sidewalk. In the east booth, a Secret Service man stood talking to a White House policeman as pedestrians sauntered by. A canopy stretched from the front door to the sidewalk and a policeman also stood guard there.

At 2:20, two Puerto Ricans, Oscar Collazo and Griselio Torresola, suddenly approached Blair House. They were armed with guns and carried 69 rounds of ammunition. Truman had appointed the first native governor of Puerto Rico, given White House support for the island's new constitution, fought for its status as a commonwealth and extended Social Security to its population. But these two men had come to kill him. As Collazo said later at his trial, he hoped that Truman's assassination would spark a revolution in the United States; then, during the upheaval, Puerto Rican Nationalists would declare the independence of their country.

Thirty-one shots were fired in three minutes. The wooden front door of Blair House was wide open, although the screen door was latched. Collazo raced for the entrance, but he climbed only two of the ten stairs before he was shot down. In the exchange of shots, his partner and a White House policeman were slain.

When Truman heard firing, he leaped from bed and ran to the window. While slugs bounced off the building, a guard looked up, spied him and yelled, "Damn it! Get back! Get back!"

As the shooting ended, a reporter for *Time* came running to get the story. A bystander who claimed to have witnessed the firing told him,

"They've broken into Blair House. They've killed the President and seven Secret Service men!"

Truman remained unruffled and went to Arlington Cemetery on schedule to keep his speaking date. "A President has to expect those things," he remarked matter-of-factly. To Admiral Leahy, he said, "The only thing you have to worry about is bad luck. I never had bad luck."

After the assassination attempt, the sidewalk in front of Blair House was roped off. Truman did not mind this so much as the fact that the Secret Service would not let him begin his walk from Blair House each morning. Instead he was driven to a different outlying Washington area each day for his brisk hike.

On Monday, November 6, Truman was in Kansas City to await the results of the Congressional elections the next day. No further word had come from MacArthur regarding Chinese intervention, nor had the CIA made an additional report about this possibility. On that day Truman's worst fears came true.

A message arrived from MacArthur which said in part, "Men and matériel in large force are pouring across all bridges over the Yalu from Manchuria. This movement not only jeopardizes but threatens the ultimate destruction of the forces under my command. . . . The only way to stop this reinforcement of the enemy is the destruction of these bridges. . . . Every hour that this is postponed will be paid for dearly in American and other United Nations blood."

Truman's reply was tempered with caution. "You are authorized to go ahead with your planned bombing in Korea near the frontier including targets at Sinuiju and Korean end of Yalu bridges. . . . The above does not authorize the bombing of any dams or power plants on the Yalu River. . . . Because it is vital in the national interests of the U. S. to localize the fighting in Korea it is important that extreme care be taken to avoid violation Manchurian territory and airspace."

MacArthur's dire report on the Chinese Communists proved to be a factor in the election the next day, November 7. Despite a few speeches by Truman and Acheson on the reason why the war was being waged, the Administration had failed miserably to educate the public on its necessity. The confusion regarding Chiang Kai-shek and Formosa, MacArthur's seeming independence, the repetitive undermining of the State Department by Senator McCarthy, fear of an expanded war with China—all contributed to the lack of public understanding.

391

As a result of the 1950 elections, the large Democratic majority in the House was cut drastically. In the Senate, the new alignment became 49 Democrats and 47 Republicans, with the Republicans picking up six seats, knocking out Senator Scott Lucas, the Majority Leader, and Senator Francis Myers, the Democratic Whip. In Ohio, Senator Taft won re-election by a whopping 400,000 majority and became the frontrunner for the Republican Presidential nomination in 1952.

Only a day after he wired Washington that the Chinese Reds had intervened on a full scale in Korea, MacArthur sent a revised opinion that this was not so. But, he added, "hostile planes are operating from bases west of the Yalu River against our forces in North Korea. . . . The present restrictions . . . provide a complete sanctuary for hostile air immediately upon their crossing the Manchuria-North Korea border. . . . Unless corrective measures are promptly taken this factor can assume decisive proportions."

Besides the right to "hot pursuit" of planes across the Yalu, Mac-Arthur also requested permission "to execute the bombing of the targets under discussion as the only resource left to me to prevent a potential build-up of enemy strength to a point threatening the safety of the command."

In reply, Truman denied MacArthur the right to engage in "hot pursuit" of enemy planes and rejected his plea to bomb bases in Manchuria. As he saw it, such action would not only extend the war to China but would also cause the Russians to intervene as Red China's ally. World War III would then be unleashed upon the globe with all the new horrible weapons of war.

Despite Truman's restrictions, MacArthur began a renewed drive to reach the Yalu. On November 21, scattered units under his command arrived at the border. Three days later he sent Walker's Eighth Army on what was to be its final offensive. "If successful," he said, "this should for all practical purposes end the war, restore peace and unity to Korea . . . [and] enable the prompt withdrawal of United Nations military forces." There was also a report that MacArthur had told one of his commanders that "the boys will be home for Christmas," a report that the general later denied.

Then, on November 26, MacArthur's hope for a quick victory vanished. Across the wobbly planks of Yalu River bridges under cover of darkness, more than 200,000 Chinese Communist troops, well-armed and trained, poured into North Korea. By the twenty-eighth, Walker's army was reeling under a massive, sustained assault; and on the east coast the X Corps found Chinese units both to the north and the south. With utter disregard for life, ignoring gunfire and heavy casualties, the Red Chinese soldiers swept forward in waves of frontal attacks. The X Corps soon lost contact with the Eighth Army, and the competition to reach the Yalu was now forgotten in a headlong retreat and a fight for survival. Bitterly MacArthur complained that the sole reason for this disaster was the order from Washington limiting the fighting to Korea. To reporters, he spoke about "extraordinary inhibitions . . . without precedent in military history."

"After the Chinese breakthrough," said Senator Connally, "the Republicans absolved MacArthur of all blame and loudly demanded Acheson's scalp for the blunder." At the same time, ill-feeling toward MacArthur ran high at the Pentagon. "It was well known in Washington that General Bradley disliked MacArthur," Senator Kilgore said. As for General Marshall, he and MacArthur had not been friends for decades.

While the Chinese Reds continued their savage advance, future military tactics in the Korean debacle became a matter of international concern because of Truman's news conference on November 30, 1950. Speaking to reporters, he remarked that "we will take whatever steps are necessary to meet the military situation, just as we always have."

"Does that mean that there is active consideration of the use of the atomic bomb?" a reporter asked.

"There has *always* been active consideration of its use," Truman replied. "I don't want to see it used. It is a terrible weapon, and it should not be used on innocent men, women and children who have nothing whatever to do with this military aggression."

Most newspapers omitted the words "always" in quoting Truman. The result was that his statement was given an entirely false interpretation. In England, a hundred Labor MP's signed a letter to Attlee protesting the possible use of the bomb, and a long and serious debate on Truman's supposed intention to use the bomb followed in the House of Commons. At the close of the debate, Attlee was loudly cheered when he announced that he was flying to Washington to discuss the use of the bomb with Truman.

By the time the Truman-Attlee talks got underway on December 4, Truman was in possession of a MacArthur note that read: "This command . . . is now faced with conditions beyond its control and strength." Truman promptly pointed out to Attlee that although his advisers did not believe there was a chance to hold the line in Korea, he intended to make the attempt "until the situation improves the chances for negotiation." If the Chinese took Korea, he added, they would next move into Indo-China, then Hong Kong, then Malaya. The Soviet Union was the true aggressor, the two agreed, and would benefit most if Truman listened to MacArthur and extended the war to China proper. As General Bradley later expressed it, such a conflict would involve the United States "in the wrong war, at the wrong place, at the wrong time and with the wrong enemy."

On the fifth, Truman and Attlee, with their advisers, met again on the *Williamsburg* for lunch and further discussion. This was one of Truman's worst days. Afterward, Charlie Ross returned to his office in the White House, where he suffered a heart attack at his desk and died.

Truman was stunned. But he had no opportunity to retire alone with his grief, for that very evening Margaret was giving a concert at Constitution Hall. Concerned that Ross's death would affect her singing, he implored his aides not to inform her. That evening, Margaret said, when she walked onto the stage, "the atmosphere was charged not only with grief but with mystery. I think I should have been told that my friend had died."

The concert went smoothly enough, but its aftermath produced a furor because of a letter Truman wrote to the music critic of the Washington *Post* while under great emotional stress. The statements in Paul Hume's review of Margaret's concert that most infuriated Truman were: "She is flat a good deal of the time. . . . She cannot sing with anything approaching professional finish. . . . She communicates almost nothing of the music she presents."

After Truman read the review early the next morning, he did not wait to reach his office to write a denunciatory letter. Without breakfast, mourning the loss only thirteen hours earlier of Charlie Ross, and with both Clement Attlee and a military catastrophe on his hands, he dashed off a wrathful note in longhand on a White House memo pad. The collector's item Hume received read:

> I have just read your lousy review buried in the back pages. You sound like a frustrated man that never made a success, an eight-ulcer man on a four-ulcer job, and all four ulcers working.

I never met you, but if I do you'll need a new nose and plenty of beefsteak and perhaps a supporter below. Westbrook Pegler, a gutter-snipe, is a gentleman compared to you. You can take that as more of an insult than a reflection on your ancestry.

The letter was widely publicized and editorial after editorial denounced Truman's lack of decorum. When Margaret was first told about the letter, she said angrily, "I am absolutely positive my father wouldn't use language like that." But later, when she learned that he really had written it, she added, "I appreciated my father's insistence on being a human being first, and the Devil take the hindmost."

There were other letters during that period of grave concern over the course of fighting in Korea. When Colorado State Senator N. Bishop wrote to him proposing that John L. Lewis be named ambassador to the Soviet Union, Truman replied that he would not appoint Lewis dog catcher. Then on December 7, before the publication of the diplomatically worded communiqué on his meetings with Attlee, he wrote a blistering reply to Representative Edward Hebert of Louisiana, who had proposed that he ask the churches to set aside a day of prayer "to appeal to Almighty God for guidance and wisdom": "I am extremely sorry that the sentiments expressed in your letter were not thought of before November 7, when the campaign in your state, Utah, North Carolina, Illinois and Indiana was carried on in a manner that was as low as I've ever seen and I've been in this game since 1906."

As the grim days of December dragged by, the news from Korea continued bad. Pyongyang fell to the Chinese Reds. By January 4, 1951, Seoul was also in their hands, and MacArthur regrouped his armies at new positions running about 70 miles below the 38th Parallel. For a time, the Joint Chiefs of Staff warned Truman that there was a probability of a re-enactment of the Pusan beachhead stand of the previous August-September and perhaps a general retreat to Japan. But by the end of January, MacArthur's forces slowly began a forward movement. General Walker had been killed in a jeep accident, and General Matthew B. Ridgway, who replaced him as commander of the Eighth Army, did yeoman work in putting his army on the offensive again. The X Corps had been successfully evacuated from the northeast sector at Hungnam in North Korea and was ready for further action. In March, MacArthur's men were back at the 38th Parallel.

But as a soldier who had contempt for the term "defensive warfare," MacArthur was unwilling to stop here. All of Korea must be set free. He could not move much farther beyond the Parallel, however, because of Truman's interdiction, which barred bombing of Chinese supply bases outside of Korea and chasing enemy planes across the border. All that was left to him, MacArthur complained, was an "accordion war," with first one side advancing until its supply lines became overextended, and then the other side taking the offensive until it moved too far ahead of its supplies. MacArthur told reporters that the accordion war could not continue for long without a "tremendous expense of American blood."

In overflowing anger at the restrictions placed upon him, MacArthur dictated a strong statement to reporters on March 7. He now proposed a blockade of the coast of China, air bombardment of her industrial centers, the use of Chiang Kai-shek's Nationalist forces in Korea and an invasion of South China by Chiang's army.

When word of this statement reached Truman, he was deeply disturbed, for with South Korea cleared he was making his first move to negotiate a cease-fire. MacArthur's aggressive remarks could jeopardize his entire policy. The crisis between Truman and MacArthur was now nearing its climax. On March 20, the Joint Chiefs of Staff informed MacArthur: "State Department planning a Presidential announcement shortly that, with clearing of bulk of South Korea of aggressors, United Nations now preparing to discuss conditions of settlement in Korea."

Before Truman could issue this statement, however, MacArthur released one of his own on March 24:

> "The enemy [Red China], therefore, must by now be painfully aware that a decision by the United Nations to depart from its tolerant effort to contain the war to the area of Korea, through an expansion of our military operations to its coastal areas and interior bases, would doom Red China to the risk of imminent military collapse. ... Within the area of my authority as the military commander ... I stand ready at any time to confer in the field with the commander in chief of the enemy forces to find any military means whereby realization of the political objectives of the United Nations in Korea ... might be accomplished without further bloodshed.

Instead of Truman's proposed cease-fire, MacArthur threatened Red China with general attack. Instead of negotiations with the enemy through the United Nations, MacArthur proposed that North Korea be surrendered to him personally.

"By this act," Truman said, "MacArthur left me no choice—I could no longer tolerate his insubordination." For if he did, he would have relinquished civilian control of the government to the military. Yet to the bitter end, MacArthur did not view his controversy with the President as having any Constitutional significance. "It was not the soldier who had encroached upon the realm of the politician," he insisted, "but rather was it the politicians who were encroaching on that of the soldier."

As angry as he was, Truman nevertheless took no action for two weeks. During this time foreign governments beset the State Department to learn if the United States had shifted its policy in the Far East. Senator Kilgore reported that Truman was beside himself with fury, exploding, "I'll show that s.o.b. who's boss" and "Who the hell does he think he is—God?"

The last straw finally fell on April 5 when he learned that Joe Martin read a letter in the House which MacArthur had written to him:

> My views and recommendations with respect to the situation created by Red China's entry into war against us in Korea have been submitted to Washington in most complete detail. . . . Generally these views are well known and generally understood, as they follow the conventional pattern of meeting force with maximum counter-force as we have never failed to do so in the past. Your view with respect to the utilization of the Chinese forces on Formosa is in conflict with neither logic nor tradition. . . . As you point out, we must win. There is no substitute for victory.

MacArthur's insubordination could no longer be ignored. At one A.M. on April 11, after long sessions with his military advisers, Truman called a special news conference. Reporters drifted in sleepily and were handed several announcements and background sheets by Joseph Short, Truman's new press secretary. One announcement read:

> With deep regret, I have concluded that General of the Army Douglas MacArthur is unable to give his wholehearted support to the policies of the United States Government and of the United Nations in matters pertaining to his official duties. In view of the specific responsibilities imposed upon me by the Constitution of the United States and the added responsibility which has been entrusted

to me by the United Nations, I have decided that I must make a change of command in the Far East. I have, therefore, relieved General MacArthur of his commands and have designated Lieutenant General Matthew B. Ridgway as his successor.

MacArthur was eating lunch in the American Embassy in Tokyo when a tearful aide told his wife that word of MacArthur's firing had just come over the radio. She leaned toward the general and whispered the news in his ear so that the other guests would not hear. His face grew stiff and he paled. Finally he glanced up and said, "Jeannie, we are going home at last."

41

WHEN Truman fired MacArthur, he was greatly concerned that the general might become a provocative figure at home. But Senator Connally told him, "National sympathy will be on MacArthur's side at first, even though his proposals would have plunged us headlong into World War III. After a while, however, national interest in the general will pall and the affair will blow over."

This is exactly what happened. As soon as he returned to the states, MacArthur was greeted with enormous parades and elaborate welcoming ceremonies. Wearing his old trench coat and battered gold-braided military cap, he accepted the acclaim of cheering millions from coast to coast. He was invited to address a Joint Session of Congress, and the Senate Foreign Relations and Armed Services Committees held joint hearings to air his dismissal and unravel the details that had led to his recall. Although the Republicans were intent upon open hearings to give MacArthur a ready platform from which to express his views to the nation and the world, Senator Connally won a vote for closed hearings, with only nonclassified testimony released to the press each day. The effect of MacArthur's oratorical brilliance was thus watered down and the proceedings soon produced public apathy.

During the period of MacArthur's homecoming tumult, Truman suffered through one unhappy afternoon when he took Bess to a baseball game at Griffith Stadium. In the eighth inning, according to custom, a loudspeaker announcement requested the crowd to remain seated until he left the park. A crescendo of boos rose from the spectators and Truman had to sit through a half inning of steady jeering.

After recalling MacArthur, Truman continued his efforts to obtain a cease-fire in Korea. Finally, on June 23, Jacob Malik, Soviet representative on the UN Security Council, suggested that his government might be amenable to a negotiated armistice. Truman was then in Tennessee dedicating an aviation engineering development center, but he ordered Ambassador Alan G. Kirk in Moscow to learn whether the proposal was official. With Stalin's affirmation, serious negotiations were begun and liaison officers from both sides met in a tent at Kaesong, near the 38th Parallel, on July 7. Having been stung by his experiences with MacArthur, Truman insisted that General Ridgway take no major steps in the negotiations without his specific approval.

By 1952, Truman was optimistic that a satisfactory agreement was attainable. But when the Communists suddenly demanded forced repatriation of prisoners, he refused to agree. "We will not buy an armistice by turning over human beings for slaughter or slavery," he insisted. On this single issue the truce negotiations continued fruitlessly throughout the rest of Truman's term in office.

The cost of Stalin's truce demand was enormous. For the fighting continued throughout the prolonged negotiations, and American casualties during that time numbered 80,000, or more than during the previous period when MacArthur was in command. It was a grim struggle for worthless hills, while negotiators haggled endlessly in tents. It saw inhuman treatment of prisoners by the Chinese and their large-scale efforts to brainwash young Americans. The result was at first public perplexity and then revulsion. It was to sweep Eisenhower into the White House in 1952.

If Truman had the Korean fighting and the vexing negotiations for a cease-fire constantly before him, there were still dozens of other problems to plague him. Late in 1951, for instance, the United Steelworkers of America announced a strike call unless the industry granted a substantial wage increase and improved working conditions.

Truman first entered this situation when the industry refused to bargain over these demands. From the national point of view, a steel strike would affect the Korean campaign as well as the development of the NATO forces in Western Europe. Truman might have invoked the Taft-Hartley Act, but instead, he ordered the Wage Stabilization Board to make a fact-finding study. Late in March, 1952, the Board recommended a wage boost of 26.4 cents an hour. But when the industry refused to accept this unless granted an increase of $12 a ton in the price of steel, Truman was outraged.

"If the steel companies absorbed every penny of the wage increase," he said, "they would still be making profits of seventeen or eighteen dollars a ton. During the three years before the Korean outbreak, steel profits averaged a little better than eleven dollars a ton. The companies could absorb this wage increase entirely out of the profits and still be making much higher profits than they made in the three prosperous years before Korea."

Nevertheless, he attempted to mediate the dispute in a long series of White House conferences. The meetings were held in the Truman Fish Room, across the hall from Matt Connelly's office, which derived its name from the few guppies in the two-foot aquarium on a table in the corner. "The companies never really bargained," Truman said. Failure of the talks was signified on April seventh by the union's call for a strike to begin at midnight the following evening.

Only 90 minutes before the strike was to begin, Truman went on radio and announced that the Government was seizing the 92 steel mills in order to keep them operating. "I have to think about our soldiers in Korea," he said, "facing the Chinese Communists, and about our soldiers and allies in Europe, confronted by the military power massed behind the Iron Curtain. . . . I would not be living up to my oath of office if I failed to do whatever is required to provide them with the weapons and the ammunition they need for their survival."

A fierce argument raged in the press and in legal circles regarding Truman's authority to seize the steel industry without specific legislation from Congress. To cover his action he sent a message to Congress the next day requesting legislation for government operation of the steel mills, but Congress refused to grant this. In the House, Representative George Bender of Ohio proposed that Truman be impeached. Other Congressmen demanded that Congress censure the President. But neither impeachment nor censure was seriously pushed by the Republican leadership, who believed that this might make Truman angry enough to run for re-election in 1952. "As of today," one Republican strategist reasoned, "Harry Truman is worse licked than he was in April, 1948. Let it stay that way."

Truman insisted at his news conference on April 24 that the President had inherent powers under conditions of national emergency to seize the steel industry. This inherent Presidential power, he maintained, was used by Jefferson in the Louisiana Purchase, by Polk in the territorial annexation in the Southwest following the Mexican War, by Lincoln in his response to the outbreak of the Civil War, and by Franklin Roosevelt during the depression emergency and World War II.

Truman became so heated in his explanation, however, that he did not know when to stop. A needling reporter asked, "Mr. President, if it is proper to seize the steel mills, can you, in your opinion, seize the newspapers and radio stations?"

Without waiting to think this over, Truman blurted out, "Under similar circumstances, the President has to act for whatever is for the best interests of the country."

This hasty reply confused the entire issue, for the press ignored his main point and played up only his remark that he could seize papers and radio stations. The charge of "Dictator" was now hurled at him. At his next news conference, Truman tried to undo the damage. "There has been a lot of irresponsible talk," he chided reporters, "about the seizure of the press and radio. That was a lot of hooey." But nothing he said now could win popular support for his steel seizure.

On April 29, Federal Judge David Pine ruled that Truman's order was unconstitutional and ordered the mills returned to the companies. The next day, however, the Circuit Court of Appeals stayed Pine's order and passed the case to the Supreme Court. When the Supreme Court failed to hear the case immediately, Truman called in Ben Fairless, president of United States Steel, and Phil Murray, head of the Steelworkers and the C.I.O. On May 2, he told them, "Gentlemen, the eyes of the nation are upon you. Work out your differences and let's have a settlement."

In a single day, the two men chipped away at their differences, but on May 3, when the Supreme Court announced it would hear the case promptly, the negotiations ended. "If the Court had not made the announcement for perhaps twenty-four or forty-eight hours," Truman said, "there is a strong likelihood that agreement would have been obtained."

While the case was before the Supreme Court, daily news stories and editorials attacked seizure and Truman personally, and full-page ads by the steel companies denounced him in scathing terms. Finally, on June 2, by a vote of 6–3 the Supreme Court upheld Judge Pine and ruled that Truman's seizure violated the Constitution. In his dissent, Chief Justice Vinson vitriolically attacked the majority for requiring six separate opinions and for "the lack of references to authoritative precedent . . . and the complete disregard of the uncontroverted facts. . . ." For this dissenting opinion, Vinson found himself attacked as a "Truman crony" and as an "unlearned lawyer" who did not deserve his position on the bench.

The aftermath of the Supreme Court's decision was that the steel companies regained immediate control of their mills. But the union went out on a seven-week strike that resulted in a daily loss of $40,000,000 in wages and production. Truman finally approved a price increase of $5.65 a ton, a price agreed to by the companies as a condition for settling the strike.

The Washington scene was confused and turbulent during Truman's last two years in office. With the Korean war ever present to dampen his spirits, he also had his hands full with a Congress that derived pleasure in feuding with him. McCarthyism was on the rise with shrill and continuous charges against Acheson and the State Department, and the few Senators who dared to challenge McCarthy found themselves no match for his invective. Senator William F. Knowland of California hardly let a day go by without attacking Truman for his policy regarding Chiang Kai-shek and Formosa. Senator Taft was already campaigning for President and had something dismal to relate about Truman every time he stepped off the floor to meet with reporters. Senator McCarran was as busy as ever, writing a new immigration bill and passing it over Truman's veto, interfering with Marshall Plan operations from his perch as chairman of the Senate's special "watchdog" subcommittee on foreign aid, championing loans to Franco, forcing the Administration to permit importation of cheap-labor Basque sheepherders for Nevada ranchers, hauling American United Nations officials before his Internal Security Subcommittee on charges of subversion, and interfering with the operations of a half-dozen agencies in his capacity as chairman of the Judiciary Committee and of subcommittees in the Appropriations Committee.

A kettledrum attack was now launched against Truman for incidents of public immorality that came to light. World War II had seen the rise of Big Government, Big Labor and Big-Big Business, and with these mammoth concentrations had come a looseness of postwar morals because of the large amounts of money that were available to the dishonest. By 1951, the Truman-haters were neatly tying the various wrongdoings into a package and labeling it "the Truman Scandals."

The Reconstruction Finance Corporation became a major item in this package. After whispered reports concerning unsavory RFC loans made the rounds of the Capitol, Democratic Senators William Fulbright and Paul Douglas undertook hearings on this lending agency in the spring of 1950. Among their first disclosures was the fact that Bill Boyle had combined his activities on the Democratic National Committee with private law practice. One of his clients, the American Lithofold Company of St. Louis, was granted an $80,000 RFC loan and within a year added $565,000 more.

Another person of interest to Fulbright and Douglas was Donald Dawson, Truman's aide on patronage, whose wife worked at the RFC. When the committee asked Dawson to testify, Truman, who believed it was embarked on a witch hunt, refused to let him appear before the committee, for two months. Committee investigators learned that Dawson had accepted 22 days of free lodging at a Miami hotel which was involved in RFC business. One RFC examiner had turned down the hotel's request for a $1,500,000 loan, but a new examiner approved it. When newspapers wrote that Truman was trying to hush up a scandal, he realized that he had overplayed loyalty to his aide and ordered Dawson to appear before the committee. Dawson, however, acquitted himself of all charges of wrongdoing except for his indiscretion in accepting the free hotel stay from an RFC borrower.

Boyle and Dawson were not the only ones who came under the committee's fire. One RFC director testified that he had a friend who wanted a $300,000 loan and that he had helped him by assigning a special RFC examiner who favored the loan. It turned out that the friend subsequently became an RFC director too, and was then serving as vice-chairman of the agency. There was also a $4,500 a year RFC employee named Merle Young whose wife was a White House stenographer. Claiming to be a cousin of the President and thus with White House influence, Young went to work for a company borrowing money from the RFC. The committee found that his salary was now $46,000 and that his wife went to work wearing a $9,500 mink coat.

"Mink coats and deepfreezes" became the battle cry of the anti-Truman forces.

In August, 1950, Truman took action and dropped the RFC chairman and two directors. This did not satisfy Fulbright and Douglas, however, and they insisted that the other two RFC directors must also be fired. The two Senators, accompanied by Senator Charles Tobey, paid a call on Truman. Upon leaving the White House, they agreed that Truman had treated them like schoolboys with his insistence that he knew best how to handle the RFC mess.

Senator Tobey especially was incensed when Truman walked them to the door, telling them not to worry, and he began rising frequently in the Senate to condemn White House influence with the RFC. It was Truman's turn now to become angry and he ordered the RFC to send him its ten-year accumulation of letters from Congressmen seeking favors for prospective borrowers. Then one day, his anger boiling over, he called Tobey on the telephone. "You Congressmen aren't free from lobbying," he said. "I have the goods on a great many Congressmen who have been taking fees for influencing RFC loans."

Tobey, whose tone was moralistic, shouted back that another RFC scandal must be developing or else Truman was attempting to head off the investigation. Later he repeated this allegation to the Senate.

Some weeks afterward, Truman learned that Tobey had a recording device on his telephone. According to Tobey, Truman called him again and gave him unshirted hell for recording their conversation. "Tobey," Truman finally shouted into the phone, "you're talking impeachment!"

"That's not a fact," said Tobey.

"I've got it from reliable sources," Truman snapped. "And let me tell you, Senator. If you want me impeached, you go right ahead and I'll help you!" With that he hung up.

On February 5, 1951, Fulbright's committee issued its report: "Favoritism and Influence." Its broad conclusion was that there was "an influence ring with White House contacts" involved with RFC irregularities." After Truman read the report, which centered its attack on Dawson, he angrily labeled it "asinine" and called Fulbright "an overeducated s.o.b."

When Senators John Bricker and Homer Capehart of Fulbright's subcommittee issued their own minority report, however, Fulbright came to Truman's defense. The two Republicans charged that Truman and Boyle had "transferred Pendergast politics to the highest level." Fulbright denounced this conclusion as "scurrilous."

Despite his own attack on Fulbright's report, Truman decided now, belatedly, that he should straighten out a situation which *The New York Times* so aptly defined as "a potential paradise for political shysters and chiseling businessmen." He dropped the five-man RFC board and named Stuart Symington as the agency's single boss. Symington's orders were to clean house.

Still other troubles involving public morality beset Truman in these hectic days, and although he was in no way personally responsible, they were also put into the package so conveniently tagged the "Truman Scandals."

The worst of these had to do with tax evasion. With personal rates rising to 90 per cent of net earnings for the rich, there was little wonder that some members of this group sought ways to avoid paying what they owed the Government. When it was not possible to make use of such tax loopholes as depletion allowances, collapsible corporations and capital gains arrangements, illegal means were resorted to. Sometimes this meant submitting false records or bribing Internal Revenue Bureau employees, most of whom were notoriously underpaid.

Senator John J. Williams of Delaware first uncovered what became known as the "Truman tax scandals." He found, for instance, that the Government had settled tax claims of $40,000,000 against 48 companies for only $10,000,000. One of these claims—for $800,000—was settled for a mere $1,000. When Truman learned of the corruption in various Internal Revenue offices, he ordered the removal of the Collectors in those cities. Among those who either resigned under pressure or were dismissed were the Collectors in Brooklyn, Boston, St. Louis and San Francisco. Then the Commissioner of Internal Revenue himself was accused of failing to pay taxes of $176,000, and the Assistant Commissioner was indicted for evading taxes. Secretary of the Treasury Snyder acted to remove about a dozen Collectors and almost 200 Internal Revenue employees. His investigation revealed that 55 had taken bribes, 24 embezzled government funds, and 21 did not pay their taxes.

Late in November, 1951, Truman sent a strongly worded letter to Democratic leaders demanding that they make the Democratic Party morally strong for the next year's campaign. And at his news conference on December 21, he told reporters: "Wrongdoers have no house with me, no matter who they are, nor how big they are." But the slogan of "mink coats and deepfreezes" had already made its mark and he failed to turn the rising tide of resentment against government grafters.

In January, 1952, the House Judiciary Committee recommended an investigation of the Justice Department for its laxity in prosecuting corruption in the Bureau of Internal Revenue. Truman had personally removed T. Lamar Caudle, the Assistant Attorney General in charge of the Tax Division, in order to speed up prosecution. But when he realized that this action in itself was not sufficient to remedy the situation, he decided to bring in outside help. The man he selected to investigate corruption was Newbold Morris, a Republican from New York.

Morris had hardly arrived in Washington when he devised a long, detailed questionnaire calling for minute information about personal income from all Justice Department employees. Attorney General Howard McGrath unfortunately regarded Morris's appointment as an attack upon his own integrity, and hotly insisted that he had no right to distribute the questionnaire. One morning, while Truman and his Cabinet were at the airport to greet Queen Juliana of the Netherlands, McGrath stood beside Truman and argued vehemently with him to cancel Morris's questionnaire. Truman's face was set in hard lines as he listened to McGrath, who stopped pleading only when Juliana stepped from the plane. When McGrath returned to his office, he notified Morris that he was dismissed. Truman then turned around and fired McGrath, replacing him with James P. McGranery. But what remained firmly fixed in the public's mind was the fact that Morris had come to Washington to do a job and had been fired.

In a speech on March 29, 1952, Truman went into the question of corruption.

"I stand for honest government. I have worked for it. . . . I hate corruption because it is the deadly enemy of all the things the Democratic Party has been doing all these years. I hate corruption everywhere, but I hate it most of all in a Democratic officeholder. . . .

"The Republicans make a great whoop and holler about the honesty of Federal employees, but they are usually the first to show up in a government office asking for special favors for private interests and raising Cain if they don't get them. These Republican gentlemen can't have it both ways—they can't be for morality on Tuesday and Thursday, and then be for special interests for their clients on Monday, Wednesday and Friday."

To his vociferous opposition Truman now also added the Southern Democrats from the oil states. This fight erupted over the issue of whether the Federal Government or the states owned the tidelands oil in the submerged "continental shelf" beyond the three-mile territorial limit.

The battle had begun on September 28, 1945, when Truman issued an executive order claiming Federal jurisdiction over the resources of the continental shelf. In a court case in 1947, the Supreme Court ruled that the Federal Government "held dominant rights." Then, in 1950, when violations recurred, the Court twice reaffirmed its earlier decision.

With an estimated 15,000,000,000 barrels of oil at stake, however, the oil lobby put pressure on Congress to pass legislation that would negate the Supreme Court decisions. In early May, 1952, Senator McCarran introduced and won passage of a joint resolution to give the tidelands oil to the states. "It would have been a gift to three states," Truman said, "at the expense of the other forty-five." And in a stinging veto message on May 29, he condemned the resolution. So far as he was concerned, "it would be the height of folly" for the Federal Government to give away the continental shelf oil and then buy it back "at stiff prices" for the military services. McCarran rounded up his forces to override the veto but failed to muster the necessary two-thirds vote in the Senate.

Truman's victory, however, was won at great cost to the stability of the Democratic Party, especially in the South. In Texas, for example, Governor Allan Shivers and Price Daniels, a candidate for Tom Connally's Senate seat, sought a deal with Republicans to support the Republican Presidential candidate in that year's campaign in exchange for the promise to turn over tidelands oil control to the states.

And so, amid charges of corruption and countercharges of obstruction, while the fighting and negotiations in Korea dragged on and on, the confusion and turbulence in Washington reached a crescendo as the 1952 election race approached.

42

ALMOST immediately after his victory in 1948, Truman had confided to General Vaughan that he would not run again. Later he reaffirmed this decision when he remarked jokingly to Vaughan, "If you don't like the heat, get out of the kitchen. Well, that's what I'm doing." Frequently, he referred to the office of President as a "man-killer" and on one occasion bluntly stated that he did not plan to run again because he "didn't want to be carried out of the White House in a casket." It was not until November 19, 1951, however, when he was at Key West, that he broke the news to his staff that he would not seek another term and swore them all to secrecy.

The problem now was to select a candidate to succeed him. "I had suggested Fred Vinson to Truman," Vaughan said, "and Truman believed that Vinson would make the best candidate. The President first broached his offer to Vinson at Key West in the fall of 1951. Then later, back in Washington, Vinson came over to the White House with his decision. 'I can't accept your offer,' Vinson told Truman. 'The doctors say I must take it easy because my heart isn't good. So I'll stay on the Supreme Court.' The President was deeply disappointed."

With Vinson out as a possibility, Truman was in a quandary about whom to support. Arthur Krock of *The New York Times* reported that Truman offered to back General Eisenhower for the Democratic nomination, but that the general had implied he would refuse it. Truman denied ever making such an offer. He later asserted, however, that Eisenhower naïvely believed he would get not only the Republican nomination but the Democratic nomination as well.

As Truman scanned the field of available Democrats, his aides and Frank McKinney, the Democratic National Chairman, begged him to reconsider and run again, but he rejected their entreaties. Although he was concerned at the time with the truce negotiations in Korea and the impending steel strike, he began his search for a new candidate. There was Averell Harriman, who had broad experience in the field of foreign affairs, but Harriman, he decided, lacked experience in campaigning for office. Senator Robert Kerr was an effective Senator and had gained administrative experience as Governor of Oklahoma, but he represented the oil and gas interests and Truman felt that this disqualified him. Senator Estes Kefauver was making a big splash as a Senate committee investigator, but Truman disliked his methods. Then there was Senator Richard Russell of Georgia, but since he was from the South he could not possibly get the nomination because of the civil rights issue.

By a process of elimination, Truman decided that Governor Adlai E. Stevenson of Illinois was the man. In 1948, when Truman carried Illinois by only 34,000 votes, Stevenson had won by 572,000. Stevenson was also well trained in national affairs, having worked for the Navy and State Departments as well as with the United Nations as a prime mover in writing and implementing the Charter. In addition, as a student of history Truman was impressed that one of Stevenson's grandfathers had played a leading role in Lincoln's first nomination while the other had served as Grover Cleveland's Vice-President. "It seems to me now," Truman wrote in a memo to himself early in 1952, "that the Governor of Illinois has the background and what it takes. Think I'll talk to him."

In January, 1952, Truman invited Governor Stevenson to come to Blair House for a chat. Stevenson arrived about 8:30 P.M. on the twenty-second and stayed until eleven. During their conversation Truman asked him to accept the nomination and assured him that if he agreed he could be nominated. "But he said: No!" Truman wrote in his diary. "He apparently was flabbergasted." Truman was evidently even more flabbergasted by Stevenson's refusal.

On March 4, he again invited Stevenson to come by for another talk. But once more Stevenson refused to seek the Presidency, declaring that he was obligated to run for re-election as governor in order to complete the state program he had begun.

Twenty-five days later, Truman attended the annual Jefferson-Jackson Day Dinner in Washington. Even though he still had no candidate, he told the 5,300 Democrats present that he would not run again. A silence fell over the hall, and then came wails of "No! No!" When he returned home, all the servants were congregated near the entrance sobbing. Embarrassed, he chided the two maids who were assigned to Bess's mother and asked them to get back to their jobs.

Early in April, he made his last effort to persuade Stevenson to become a candidate. National Committee Chairman Frank McKinney visited the governor and reported back that Stevenson would not run under any circumstances. Truman would have to look elsewhere.

An unexpected candidate appeared about two weeks before the Democratic National Convention got underway when Vice-President Barkley let word trickle to the White House that he wanted to be the nominee. Barkley, whom Roosevelt had rejected as his running mate in 1944 because of his age, had gained national popularity with his December-May marriage to a young St. Louis widow. He was now the beloved "Veep," a man with a humorous story for every occasion. Although he was in his seventy-fifth year, he pointedly told visitors that a fortuneteller had predicted he would live at least thirty more years.

When Barkley persisted in his candidacy, Truman invited him to the White House for a discussion. Despite Barkley's age he agreed to support him, but he made it plain that this was not to be noised about in advance of the convention.

With this pledge, Barkley went jauntily out to the Chicago convention. In their strategy talk, Truman had advised him to win the support of the labor leaders at the convention. But it was essential, Truman said, that he see them individually, because each one considered himself a great political power and they would not commit themselves as a group. Feeling self-confident, Barkley blithely ignored Truman's advice and invited 16 labor leaders to meet with him at

411

breakfast on July 21, the day the convention opened. The result was disastrous. The labor leaders rejected him unanimously to his face.

That afternoon, shaken to his roots, Barkley called Truman in Washington. When he told Truman that he had decided to withdraw from the race, Truman insisted that he stay in. "It's too late," said Barkley despondently, "because I've already told the press." All further urging failed to convince him to remain in the fight. Once more Truman was without a candidate.

On the twenty-fourth, the day the Presidential candidates were to be placed in nomination, the phone rang on Truman's desk. It was Adlai Stevenson. "Hello," Stevenson said airily. "My friends want to nominate me for President. Would you object if I agreed to run?"

"Well, I blew up," Truman said afterward. "I talked to him in language I think he had never heard before." After unleashing this Battery D barrage, Truman added, "I have been trying since January to get you to say that. Why would it embarrass me?"

A strong movement was already in progress to draft Stevenson, but his protracted reluctance to put his name forward created the danger of a deadlock in the convention. In fact Barkley, who had delivered his farewell address to the convention on the twenty-third, a talk that produced loud cheers and flowing tears, suddenly changed his mind and allowed his name to be placed in nomination. Truman, however, did not believe that his earlier commitment to Barkley was still in force.

When other candidates began a wild scramble for Truman's support, Truman's alternate delegate at the convention, Thomas J. Gavin, found himself treated royally. At Harriman's headquarters, when a Mr. Gavin was announced, the man was ushered in with great deference, treated to drinks and asked his opinion on a variety of subjects. After a while, he stared at the politicians who surrounded him and asked, "Why are such important people putting themselves out so for a man who merely came to fix the TV set?" This Mr. Gavin was a repairman.

When the deadlock that Truman feared did develop, he and Bess boarded the *Independence* on July 25 and flew to Chicago. Tensely, he watched the second disappointing ballot on the plane's television set. Kefauver had 362½ votes; Stevenson, 324½; Russell, 294; Harriman, 121; and Barkley, 78½. As soon as he arrived, he met with the convention's leaders and insisted upon Stevenson's nomination. Harriman was ordered to throw his support to Stevenson. "If I had not flown to Chicago from Washington," Truman admitted afterward, "Stevenson would not have been nominated." Even before the third ballot began at nine P.M., Stevenson was already in. Truman also suggested that Senator John Sparkman become the Vice-Presidential nominee, and the convention unanimously supported his choice.

But Truman's control over the Party ended at this point, and he was to have nothing but misgivings about the campaign that followed. At the start Stevenson made his intention clear to manage his own campaign without the advice and strategy of the old political war horse in the White House. One of his first moves was to establish his campaign headquarters at Springfield, Illinois, a pointed effort to dissociate himself from Washington. "And perhaps from me," Truman said. The result was chaos, with two campaigns being waged independently: one from Stevenson's Illinois headquarters and the other from the Washington office of the Democratic National Committee. Stevenson also decided to ignore most of the big city bosses. Certainly this revealed a high-minded political attitude, but its dismal consequence was to nullify the tremendous vote-getting edifices erected by these political professionals.

Truman had hoped that Stevenson would run on the record of his Administration, but the Presidential nominee chose not to do so. Stevenson's silence on this score incensed Truman because of the years of hard work he had devoted to saving the free world with his Truman Doctrine, Marshall Plan, NATO, Japanese Peace Treaty and his decision to halt Communist aggression in Korea. Instead, the Stevenson strategists were very much influenced by the Gallup Poll, which had reported in November, 1951, that Truman's popularity had fallen to a low of 23 per cent from his July, 1945, high of 87 per cent.

In fact, on several occasions Stevenson seemed to be running against Truman as well as against Eisenhower. In Oregon, he made a bad slip in a press interview when a reporter asked if he planned to clean up "the mess in Washington." Stevenson inadvertently quoted the reporter's exact words and said yes. What he intended to say was that he opposed corruption, but, as Truman said, his hasty reply made it appear that Stevenson had been taken in by the "Republican fraudulent build-up of flyspecks on our Washington windows into a big blot or 'mess.' "

Then, in Cleveland, Stevenson again appalled Truman when he spoke defensively on the issue of Communists in government. Truman had hoped that he would go on the offensive, emphasizing how the Administration had taken strong steps to combat Soviet imperialism abroad and had prosecuted Communist conspirators at home through the courts. By his defensive approach, Truman said, Stevenson lent credence to "the most brazen lie of the century—that Democrats were soft on Communists."

But if Truman had his doubts about Stevenson's campaign, the Eisenhower-Nixon campaign moved him to rage. Once he explained away his $18,000 slush fund by appearing on television and telling the world how much he loved his little dog, Nixon roamed the country, running against Alger Hiss, Stalin and Truman. Nixon's campaigning, however, was a minor nuisance to Truman when compared with Eisenhower's. He boiled when he saw a picture of Eisenhower and Senator William Jenner together on the same platform. "Here was a man who called General Marshall a traitor and Ike didn't open his chops," he said. Later, in Milwaukee, Eisenhower agreed to delete a personal tribute to General Marshall because Senator McCarthy, Marshall's chief detractor, was scheduled to appear on the platform with him. "How can he do that to the greatest living American?" Truman demanded. "General Marshall recommended him three times for important jobs. You don't kick the man who made you."

Not until late in the campaign did Stevenson finally ask Truman to make some speeches. Truman accepted with alacrity and roared out on the hustings to do battle against Eisenhower. On October 4, at Oakland, California, he blamed the general for his failure to take Berlin before the Russians did and named him as the direct cause of the Berlin Blockade; in other speeches he quipped: "Ike has a brass halo." Coming down the homestretch of the campaign, Eisenhower capitalized on the immense unpopularity of the Korean fighting, and took time off from his promises to "clean up the mess in Washington" to make the announcement that assured him of victory. At Detroit, he proposed to "go to Korea in person if elected and put an end to the fighting." Truman rejoined with the angry comment that "any man who talks like a superman is a fraud." For he knew that the Communists would not drop to their knees and quake at the sight of Eisenhower in Korea. But the proposal had tremendous appeal to the war-weary nation.

The Republicans revealed a healthy respect for Truman's campaigning abilities by assigning a "truth squad" to issue discrediting statements wherever he spoke. At Buffalo, they pulled a degrading stunt when they employed hundreds of children to break up the meeting by yelling Truman down so he could not be heard. Truman's whistle-stop tour with Bess and Margaret took him across the country and to both coasts. The one bit of humor occurred in Ohio when Mike DiSalle made the introduction from the platform and said, "I would like all you people to meet Margaret Truman's father." After the laughter, Truman told the crowd, "I'm a back number already."

Although he was not surprised when Eisenhower won on November 4, he hardly expected the general's plurality to be in excess of six million votes. In an interesting post-mortem, Truman concluded that if he had run instead of Stevenson, he would have been re-elected President. Had he announced in 1951 that he was a candidate, Truman reasoned, Eisenhower would not have been the Republican candidate, for the general made himself available because he believed that the Democrats would nominate him, too. With Eisenhower out, Taft would have become the Republican nominee, and Truman felt certain that he could have easily defeated the Senator.

But the fact of the situation was that Eisenhower was now the President-elect, and Truman was determined to effect a smooth transition from his own to the next Administration—up to a certain point. On his way back to Washington by train, he sent the general a message of congratulations, the last sentence of which read: THE INDEPENDENCE WILL BE AT YOUR DISPOSAL IF YOU STILL DESIRE TO GO TO KOREA.

Eisenhower was at first stunned and then infuriated by this sentence, which he interpreted to mean that Truman considered him a charlatan. Nevertheless, he held his peace and replied, "I deeply appreciate your courteous and generous telegram." On November 5, Truman wired Eisenhower again, inviting him to the White House "so that it may be clear to all the world that this nation is united in its struggle for freedom and peace." At that time the general was at the Augusta, Georgia, golf course where his aides, reacting with suspicion, tried to determine whether Truman hoped to force his hand as President. But Eisenhower, deciding that a meeting was worthwhile, agreed to fly to Washington on November 18 to confer with Truman. He also agreed to send Senator Henry Cabot Lodge, Jr., who had just lost his re-election contest in Massachusetts to Representative John F. Kennedy, and Joseph M. Dodge of Detroit as his liaison aides to arrange for an orderly transition of government.

When Eisenhower arrived at the White House on schedule at two

P.M. on the eighteenth, his famous smile was missing. At the first meeting, a private conversation, Truman said that he tried to put Eisenhower at ease by thanking him for giving him the office globe the general had used during World War II. When Truman offered to leave the globe behind when he left the White House, he said that the general "accepted, although he remained unsmiling."

Matt Connelly later told Ed Folliard of the Washington *Post* that he overheard an exchange between Truman and Eisenhower at this private session that perturbed Truman because it foreshadowed a weak President. "Who is your chief of staff around here?" the general demanded. Truman replied: "I don't have a chief of staff in the sense that you mean it."

Afterward, John Steelman, Assistant to the President, substantiated Truman's initial concern. "In talking to Eisenhower," Steelman said, "I got the impression that he didn't want to be told about any problems until the staff had worked on them. I got the further impression that he didn't want his staff to bring him any problems unless they also brought along solutions for those problems. The new Chief Executive just couldn't imagine any other approach."

After a stilted conversation of twenty minutes at their first meeting, Truman took Eisenhower to the Cabinet room for a briefing. Joining them around the coffin-shaped table were Acheson, Lovett, Snyder, Harriman, Lodge and Dodge. Truman opened this second session with a statement of purpose: "I have invited you gentlemen to meet with me here to establish the framework for full understanding of our problems and our purposes in the interim until January twentieth. So far as our relations with other countries are concerned, I think it is important during this period to avoid needless differences between this Administration and its successor." He went on to say that the meeting "will show the world national unity in foreign policy as far as politically possible." When he concluded, Eisenhower pointedly requested a memorandum of his earlier private conversation with Truman.

After passing out copies of a two-page memorandum on taxes and debt management prepared by the Treasury Department, Truman called on Acheson to bring Eisenhower up to date on urgent foreign-policy questions. Before Acheson could begin, Eisenhower asked whether he should take notes, but Acheson told him that he would send him a memorandum later. Then Acheson went into an analysis of the current United Nations discussions on Korea, emphasizing the prisoners-of-war issue on which Truman refused to compromise. There was then pending at the United Nations an Indian truce proposal that callously called for forced repatriation of prisoners. Truman had already prepared a statement expressing his opposition to the proposal and he suggested to Eisenhower that they issue it jointly. Lodge, however, insisted that Truman delete the sentences opposing forced repatriation before it was issued. When the meeting broke up, Truman said, he was "troubled" by a feeling that the general "had not grasped the immense job ahead of him."

Nor was he happy about Eisenhower's belief that a President should operate like a general. "He'll sit right here," Truman told his aides one day in his office, "and he'll say, 'Do this! Do that!' And nothing will happen. Poor Ike—it won't be a bit like the Army. He'll find it very frustrating."

Truman's animosity toward his successor grew sharper when Eisenhower went to Korea. Eisenhower had wired MacArthur that he would meet with him to discuss MacArthur's so-called solution to the struggle in Korea, which did not involve "increased danger of provoking universal conflict." Madge Wallace, Bess's mother, had died in the White House on December 5, and Truman had accompanied his wife to Independence for the funeral. On the return trip to Washington, he read Eisenhower's message to MacArthur in a newspaper. Exploding in wrath, he told reporters, "If MacArthur has a solution he should present it to me!"

Back in Washington, he strode into his news conference with eyes ablaze. After expressing doubts that MacArthur had any solution to the conflict in Korea, he turned his fire on Eisenhower, calling his trip to Korea "a piece of demagoguery merely to carry out a campaign pledge." When the general heard about this latest blast, he in turn was furious. The relationship between the two men had reached the point of no return.

With only a few weeks now remaining before he left office, Truman decided that his personal feelings must not hamper full cooperation with the incoming Administration. He allowed Sherman Adams, who was to be Eisenhower's White House chief of staff, to begin a pre-inaugural redecoration of the Executive Mansion. He also wrote to the House Ways and Means Committee and the Senate Finance Committee, suggesting a reduction in the tax liability of future Presidents, ordered Major John Eisenhower to return from Korea to witness his father's inauguration, and instructed his aides, Cabinet members and agency heads to prepare an orderly transfer of responsibility to the incoming officials. Packing his belongings became a tiresome chore because his personal files were so immense. When Senator Kilgore visited him during this period, Truman said wearily, "If I had known there would be so much work leaving this place I'd have run again."

On January 15, he made his final report to the people in an informal television and radio speech. He recalled his emotions on that April afternoon in 1945 when he succeeded Roosevelt and described how his life had been changed by his new office. Then, in detail, he reviewed the major events of his Administration, affirming strongly that the decisions he had made were morally right. He added that he was fully confident that the free world would not only survive but would triumph over totalitarianism.

Despite this farewell address, he did not forget that he was still President until noon on January 20, 1953. Aware of the deal between the incoming Administration and the tidelands oil states, he issued an executive order on January 16 setting aside the submerged offshore oil lands as a petroleum reserve for the Navy.

The press vituperation which had continued for so many years abruptly lessened during those last days as editorials declared affection for "good old Harry." It was an unexpected bonus that he enjoyed. In a note to Margaret, he provided a modest summation of his political career. "Your dad will never be reckoned among the great," he wrote. "But you can be sure he did his level best and gave all he had to his country. There is an epitaph in Boothill Cemetery in Tombstone, Arizona, which reads, 'Here lies Jack Williams; he done his damndest.' What more can a person do?"

As Inauguration Day approached, it became obvious to Truman that Eisenhower's aides regarded him with contempt. One indication of their attitude was the controversy over inaugural hats. Truman considered it proper that the traditional top hat be worn. When the Republicans decreed that the hat would be a Homburg, he expressed his displeasure but finally agreed. Then the Republicans informed him that, on Inauguration Day, he was to ride in a parade car to the Statler Hotel, pick up Eisenhower and proceed with him to the Capitol for the inaugural ceremonies. Once more Truman was provoked, for the proprieties demanded that the President-elect call for the outgoing President at the White House and then ride with him up Capitol Hill. "If Ike doesn't pick me up," Truman snapped, "then we'll go in separate cars."

On January 20, a reluctant Eisenhower arrived at the Executive Mansion but sat in his car at the portico of the White House, refusing to go in. Finally, to break the impasse, Truman emerged, greeted Eisenhower and joined him in the car. The last thing he did before leaving the White House was to return a pad of paper to the desk of an aide.

After Warren Harding's inauguration, President Wilson complained that his successor talked incessantly about elephants on the way to the Capitol. Truman and Eisenhower, however, made their trip almost in silence. According to Truman, at the Capitol, when they were waiting in the office of the Senate sergeant at arms before going out onto the platform, Eisenhower suddenly turned toward him and asked angrily: "I wonder who is responsible for my son John being ordered to Washington from Korea? I wonder who is trying to embarrass me?"

Truman replied coldly, "The President of the United States ordered your son to attend your inauguration. . . . If you think somebody was trying to embarrass you by this order then the President assumes full responsibility."

After this exchange the two men, wearing their Homburgs, passed through the ranks of Homburg-adorned dignitaries to the front of the platform, where one became "Mr. President" and the other "Mr. Citizen."

When the ceremony was over, the Trumans lunched at Dean Acheson's house where 300 persons gathered out front and cheered, "We want Harry!" Then at the railroad station a crowd of 5,000 persons came to see him off, and so many women kissed him that his face was red with lipstick before his train departed.

On the train going back to Missouri, he had time to think about his long political career that had taken him from Jackson County to the White House. Perhaps his note to Margaret was a good summation after all—"He done his damndest."

43

ONCE Truman was out of office, the growing esteem and good will of the nation surprised him. For a man who had been accustomed to a daily barrage of brickbats, he expected, as he said, to be "cussed and discussed" for a long time to come.

"Did I tell you about those crowds that greeted us at the railroad stations on the way home?" he said to a reporter. "Time after time thousands of people turned out. You'd think I was President—or something. That welcome-home dinner here in Independence—room for less than a thousand but they could have sold more than 10,000 tickets. Bess told me that the 'welcome-home' ceremonies were more than worth the thirty years of hell she's gone through with me in politics. It's hard to believe, but I've received more than 70,000 letters here in Independence in the last two weeks. Almost all were favorable. I even got some kind editorials. Some editors ate crow and left the feathers on."

Only in election years did die-hard Republicans revert to Truman-hating. There were, of course, some exceptions. In San Francisco early in 1953, for example, Truman was on his way to dinner at the home of George Killion, the steamship executive. When his chauffeur lost his way, Truman got out of the car to ring a doorbell and ask for directions. "An unmistakenly Republican-looking gentleman," as Truman put it, opened the door and he inquired if the man knew where Killion lived.

"No," the man replied, backing away a few steps and scrutinizing Truman's face. "By the way, I hope I'm not hurting your feelings but you look exactly like that old s.o.b. Harry Truman."

"I hope I'm not hurting your feelings either," Truman said. "But I *am* that s.o.b."

There was at least one other Republican who could not abide him —his successor in office, who on occasion gave vent to anger at the mention of Truman's name. Only a few days after he moved into the White House, he ordered every lingering trace of Truman removed. This included a piano, the office globe, Truman's favorite chandelier, and various portraits. Even Secret Service men who were known to be fond of Truman were suddenly shunted off to other assignments or retired.

At first, Truman made a few attempts to observe the amenities, but the new President was unforgiving because of Truman's castigation during the campaign the previous year. In October, 1953, when Eisenhower stopped in Kansas City, Truman called his suite at the Muehlebach Hotel and told Jim Hagerty, his press secretary, that he would like to pay his respects. Hagerty promised to pass word along and then telephone back, but no return call came. The two finally did meet some years later at the funeral of General Marshall, where they solemnly shook hands. On one occasion, when Winston Churchill came to Washington, he asked Eisenhower to invite Truman to the White House dinner in Churchill's honor. Much as he admired the former British Prime Minister, however, Truman declined the invitation. Eisenhower, whose boiling point was as low as Truman's, angrily offered the following toast at the dinner: "There are several men here who said to me, when I asked them to come to this party, 'I have some very important engagements, but to see Sir Winston again is one of the greatest things that could happen to me, and I have broken the important engagement in order to do so.'"

Not until November, 1961, did the two men meet again. That month they saw each other twice, once when Eisenhower visited the Truman Library at Independence and another time when both attended the funeral of Sam Rayburn at Bonham, Texas.

421

Once he was back in Independence, Truman could not stay put. In March, 1953, he took Bess and Margaret to Coconut Island in Hawaii, where they were guests of Ed Pauley. "I want a vacation, but Bess deserves one," he said. There was little to do on Coconut Island, except rest. Free of the cares of office, Truman and "the Missus" were like two children out on a lark. He caught frogs and dropped them on Margaret's lap. "Here's a friend of yours," he would announce while she "screamed bloody murder."

When they returned to Independence, the Trumans found that their town had become a tourist's mecca. Crowds gathered at the fourteen-room house at 219 North Delaware, waiting for him to come outdoors, and on rare occasions he permitted tourists to photograph him. In time, his need for some privacy forced him to put a lock on the front gate, which was controlled from inside the house by a buzzer. Once he and Bess slipped across the street to visit his cousins, Nellie and Ethel Noland. Almost as soon as they got to the opposite side walk, a crowd collected outside their house and they had to wait until the people dispersed before trying to return. Bess later told Margaret, "We had to spend most of the evening on the front porch all by ourselves because our cousins weren't at home."

Truman was genuinely fond of the old house that had been built shortly after Lincoln's assassination. In view of the decades which Bess had devoted to caring for her ailing mother, friends assumed that Madge Wallace would leave the house to her when she died, but Mrs. Wallace gave her surviving sons equal shares in the dwelling. Truman had to buy them out in order to acquire the house for himself.

The house contained several mementos of his political career. On one occasion, Truman fondly showed visitors an icon and said, "The Government of the United States, at my direction, sent 200,000 tons of wheat to the starving Moravians, and the Queen of Rumania presented me with this icon, which came out of the mosque of St. Sophia —Constantinople, it was then."

The creaks and groans in the old building reminded him of the White House, where several Presidents insisted that the ghosts of their predecessors roamed about at night. Even Truman held this opinion. He recalled one eerie night in the Executive Mansion when he heard a persistent rapping on his bedroom door. "I got up and answered it about three o'clock in the morning. There wasn't anybody there. I think it must have been Lincoln's ghost walking up and down the hall."

During Truman's first few years back in Independence, he maintained an office in the Federal Reserve Bank Building in Kansas City, a half-hour drive from home. He threatened jokingly to use this office as his campaign headquarters to run for the Senate when he was ninety-one. "But I got a letter from a fellow who looked it up," he said, "and that year wouldn't be an election year. So maybe I'll push it up and run when I'm ninety." Every morning after his two-mile hike, breakfast, and perusal of the morning paper, he backed his car from the rear driveway and drove into town along Truman Road. Renamed in his honor, Truman Road wandered through a seamy area glutted with shops named Truman's Car Wash, Truman's Pharmacy, Truman's Palmistry, Truman Road Hamburger Shop and Harry's Tavern, Harry's Café and Harry's Used Furniture.

At his office, he handled the enormous flood of mail that came in daily, saw a steady stream of visitors, listened without interest to purveyors of get-rich-quick schemes and negotiated for the publication of his memoirs. He complained with a wink that "Democrats treat me like a two-headed calf." One thing he found both amusing and odd was the assumption of his friends that because he had been President he was helpless to do things for himself. One close friend, he said, was "astonished" when he dialed a telephone number. Back in 1948, Truman had sadly admitted that the cost of maintaining his high office took $72,000 of his $75,000 annual salary. In 1949, however, when Congress increased his salary to $100,000 and his expense account from $40,000 to $90,000, making this last increment tax free, he was able to set aside a nest egg by the time he returned to Independence in 1953. As a retired President, he also drew an annual pension of $25,000 and possessed the franking privilege, which saved him thousands of dollars each year on postage stamps. The sale of part of his mother's farm at Grandview for the construction of a large shopping center, known as Truman's Corner, also improved his financial status. Then, of course, he earned a substantial sum from his memoirs, which were reprinted in *Life* Magazine and syndicated in newspapers. He also had income from lecturing and writing columns on current political questions for the North American Newspaper Alliance.

In all his years as President, Truman's health had been amazingly good. Except for an intestinal cold that sent him to Walter Reed Hospital for a few days late in 1952, his chief physical complaint was periodic weariness. Since early youth, he had had an unusually slow heartbeat, which doctors agreed contributed to his lack of internal tension. Then, unexpectedly, in June, 1954, he gave his wife a bad fright when he suffered a severe gall bladder attack and was rushed to the hospital for surgery. On the way there, he added to Bess's concern when, between gasps of pain, he wrote out a codicil to his will on a pad of paper.

When word of his operation was flashed to newspapers, reporters set up a news headquarters at the hospital, which was inundated with get-well notes and telephone calls. There was even a cable from Moscow's Russian Baptists who informed him they were praying for his recovery.

For a while Truman's condition was so grave that he had to be fed intravenously. Dr. Graham, his former White House physician, grew so concerned that he called in three specialists. Other doctors throughout the country telephoned Graham to tell him that they were prepared to fly to Kansas City for consultation. But Truman's strong constitution enabled him to pull through. "They are all trying to hold me down," he told a friend when the crisis was over. "The doctor still has his foot on my neck and he's getting a lot of help from Bess." Although Dr. Graham advised him that it would take a year for full recovery, within a few months he was back on a six-day-a-week work schedule.

Truman was too much the political animal to subside into the role of a hoary elder statesman to be trotted out at party conclaves to utter meaningless banalities. Now that Eisenhower had been in office for some time, he did not hesitate to offer criticism when he thought that the Administration was not "as clean as a hound's tooth," the expression which his successor vowed to be his standard of operations. In foreign affairs, he generally abstained from taking a critical stand. One exception was when Eisenhower "unleashed" Chiang Kai-shek from the neutralized Formosa that Truman had created. But nothing came of this unleashing and Chiang was "released" by a mutual defense treaty which barred him from taking action against Red China without American sanction. Another exception was Korea. Following Stalin's death early in 1953, the Communist line changed to permit voluntary repatriation. In April, the new Administration was able to begin truce negotiations on this basis and the truce was finally signed on July 26, 1953, after two years of almost daily conferences. To those on the inside, it was obvious that any administration then in power could have got the same terms. Truman's objection was that under the circumstances the terms should have been better.

Truman's lingering political potency was highly disturbing to the Administration for a while, and attempts were made to "get" him. Truman once remarked at a Boston dinner, "They put investigators on me and everyone around me to find something wrong. The former governor of Washington and Secretary of the Treasury were hounded to death." Attorney General Herbert Brownell, who had been Dewey's campaign manager in the ill-fated 1948 contest, launched the attack by telling a luncheon group that Truman had promoted Harry Dexter White, the Treasury's top economist, to the World Bank, even though he had been told that White was a Russian spy. Then Representative Harold Velde, chairman of the House Un-American Activities Committee, subpoenaed Truman to appear before the committee to defend himself. Since it was obvious to Truman that the Republicans planned a field day to defame him, he refused to honor the subpoena. Instead, he appeared on television and said, "I have been accused, in effect, of knowingly betraying the security of the United States. This charge is, of course, a falsehood." Editorial opinion throughout the country agreed that the Republicans had pulled a low stunt.

Nevertheless, some Republicans refused to give up. In the 1954 Congressional election campaign, Vice-President Nixon charged that the Communist Party "had determined to conduct its program within the Democratic Party." Nixon boldly implied that Truman was a traitor by asserting that he had been responsible for coddling Reds and for covering up the Communist conspiracy during his Administration. Truman's retort was, "I don't like Nixon and I never will. I don't want to even discuss him. He called me a traitor, and if I'm a traitor the United States is in a helluva shape." Eisenhower finally stepped in and backed Truman.

A vital event in Truman's life took place in the spring of 1956. Some time after he was again settled in Independence, he and Bess visited Mize and Lucy Peters, family friends who lived a few blocks away. Lucy Peters noted that he looked depressed. During the visit he confided to her: "I envy you, Lucy, because you're a grandmother. I'm afraid Margaret isn't going to marry, but will follow the family pattern of my sister, my aunts and my cousins by the dozens." He was proved wrong, however, when at the age of thirty-two, Margaret married Clifton Daniel, a reporter for *The New York Times,* on April

21, 1956. The next year Truman had his first grandson, Clifton Truman Daniel, and in 1959 his second, William Wallace Daniel.

Truman's popularity abroad was apparent when he and Bess went to Europe in the spring of 1956. In England, a high light of his trip was a visit with the Churchills at their estate, Chartwell, which Sir Winston's friends had purchased as a national memorial, providing him with a tax-free residence for the rest of his life. He also went to Oxford to receive an honorary degree and reported to friends, "You ought to see me in this rig—with a red coat and beefeater hat." On another occasion when he accepted an honorary degree, he tripped over his academic gown and exclaimed, "Whoops! I forgot to pull up my dress!"

In the summer of 1956, he learned that he was no longer the dominant force in the Democratic Party. At the national convention in Chicago, he supported Averell Harriman and criticized Adlai Stevenson, charging that he had no heart for the necessary battle and was a "defeatist" who would not carry more than nine states. But Stevenson won handily, although once again he was reluctant to run. Afterward, Truman tried to make his peace by telling the convention, "Governor Stevenson is a real fighter and I ought to know. He's given some of us here a good licking."

Stevenson took it in good humor. "I salute President Harry Truman," he told the delegates. "I am glad to have you on my side again, sir."

When the Republicans held their convention in the San Francisco Cow Palace, Truman commented, "Don't worry. They'll soon convert the Cow Palace into a hog run."

Truman's life took a new turn in 1957 with the dedication of the Harry S. Truman Library, a magnificent edifice of Indiana limestone 525 feet long. Situated on the outskirts of Independence, a short walk from his house, the library was built by his friends at a cost of about $2,000,000. Here he housed the estimated 3.5 million documents comprising his personal papers, as well as those of his political associates who were willing to make them available to research workers. In addition, the library, which is operated by the Federal Government's National Archives, began the microfilm collection of the papers of the thirty-one Presidents who preceded Truman.

At the library, Truman acquired ample working space for his own writing, a process which consisted chiefly of dictation. Down the hall is an auditorium where he frequently speaks to visiting contingents of high school pupils and answers their questions in a manner reminiscent of his Presidential news conferences. His attitude toward these youngsters is fatherly and he attempts to stir in them an enthusiastic interest in their country's history. "You can still do something with high school youths," he said, "but the college kids are different. They think they know everything."

The library is large enough to house many displays commemorating his political career. In the lobby, for example, is the table on which the United States Charter was signed at San Francisco in 1945. The library also has Truman's piano, the rough draft of his Fair Deal message to Congress, pictures of the Potsdam conferees, and mementos of the bitter 1948 Democratic National Convention and his whistle-stop campaign. One room is an exact replica of his oval office in the West Wing of the White House. Truman enjoys acting as guide to visiting dignitaries, and generally maintains the serious mien of an elder statesman. On one occasion he conducted two visitors into the main museum room where he made use of wall exhibits to outline the six jobs of the President—Chief Executive, ceremonial chief of state, legislation planner, political party boss, director of foreign policy and Commander in Chief of the Armed Forces. Afterward he led them into the nonpublic lobby and played a classical piece on the piano there. The visitors were by now greatly impressed with the range of his accomplishments. But he spoiled the illusion by turning to them with a broad grin and exclaiming, "If I hadn't been President of the United States, I probably would have ended up as a piano player in a bawdyhouse."

Generally when he leaves his library on trips east, Truman reverts from the historian to the politician, stirring up hornets' nests as of old. Even on nonpolitical subjects he is able to arouse strong emotions. When he visited Washington in January, 1960, for instance, he told reporters who tagged along on his morning hike: "The horse in the General George Thomas statue at Thomas Circle on Fourteenth Street was converted to a stallion after the sculptor discovered the general never rode a mare. But the head and neck are still a mare's."

His statement produced howls of protest from art lovers, similar to the uproar he set off among admirers of modern art when he was President. On that earlier occasion, he had publicly lambasted modern artists as "ham and eggers" who "just throw an egg at the canvas and mix in a little ham." This time, however, experts examined the bronze animal in the General Thomas statue and pronounced Truman correct.

427

Fully vindicated, he then added a historical footnote by pointing out that General Thomas died of apoplexy after reading a letter to the editor in *The New York Times* which was critical of him.

When the 1960 Democratic National Convention approached, Truman, despite his seventy-six years, again attempted to play a decisive role in the proceedings. But he met with as little success as he had in 1956. Promoting Senator Stuart Symington, whom he had originally opposed as a Senate aspirant from Missouri by calling him "Little Lord Fauntleroy," he said that frontrunner John F. Kennedy was "unready" for the Presidency and that the United States was "unready" for him. There were no religious undertones to Truman's opposition which stemmed from concern about Kennedy's lack of administrative experience and the influence his father might have on him. As Truman put it, "It's not the Pope who worries me, it's the pop." Regarding the elder Kennedy, who held the American distributorship for Haig and Haig, Truman once told ex-Senator William Benton, "Don't drink Scotch. Drink bourbon. Every time you drink Scotch it's money in Joe Kennedy's pocket."

Before the convention opened, Truman made a last-minute attempt to block the Kennedy steamroller by holding a news conference in the Truman Library auditorium. He declared that the convention was already rigged and that he would not honor it with his attendance. When Kennedy won the nomination on the first ballot, however, Truman promptly closed Party ranks and offered to campaign for him.

In an otherwise unexciting campaign between Nixon and Kennedy, Truman created the only commotion when he told an audience of San Antonio that any Texan who voted for Nixon ought "to go to hell." Republican National Committee Chairman, Senator Thruston Morton, immediately wired Kennedy, "This registers the strongest protest possible at the despicable campaign tactics of your colleague and cohort, Harry S. Truman. . . . Such profanity in your campaign is outrageous." When Nixon self-righteously asserted that Truman's language was a menace to American children, hoots of derision erupted against him even in Republican quarters. During the rest of the campaign, Kennedy kept the incident alive. In Detroit he told a crowd, "I have to be careful of what I say in view of what Vice-President Nixon said. There may be children here."

As columnist George Dixon put it, Nixon's concern with Truman's language evoked "the dire picture of impressionable little ones innocently repeating Trumanisms and having their little mouths washed out with bourbon." An apocryphal story made the rounds that after the birth of his first grandchild, Truman told Margaret, "When he gets older, I'm going to teach him to talk."

"The hell you are!" Margaret was supposed to have replied.

There are those prudish souls who have always been appalled by Truman's language; ultraconservatives who say that he promoted radicalism while in office; McCarthy die-hards who maintain he was "soft on Communism"; academicians who aver within their cloisters that he had no grasp of public affairs; and New Dealers who still dislike him because his name was not Franklin Delano Roosevelt.

But when the veneer of his tumultuous era in office is stripped away, and his frank language along with his excessive loyalty are forgotten, what remains is a man of strength and patriotism who made great and courageous decisions. Within his lifetime, he can already be called the most underrated President in his country's entire history. If Truman had a major failing in office, as Bill Hassett said, it stemmed from the fact that he was "utterly human under agonizing burdens."

From a piano-playing youth, to bank clerk, farmer, wildcatter, Captain Harry of Battery D, haberdasher and savings and loan bank executive, through the Pendergast years as county judge, then on to United States Senator, war program investigator, Vice-President and finally President, Harry S. Truman has traveled a long and exciting route. His is the story of the uncommon man whose blessing was that he considered himself the common man.

General Marshall once attempted to assess Truman while he was still in office. "The full measure of this man," Marshall said, "will only be proved by history. But I want to say here and now that there never has been a decision made under this man's Administration . . . that has not been made in the best interest of his country. It is not only the courage of these decisions that will live, but the integrity of them."

It was characteristic of Harry S. Truman that as he listened to Marshall speak these words of praise, tears ran down his cheeks.

BIBLIOGRAPHY

Abels, Jules, *The Truman Scandals*, 1956
—————— *Out of the Jaws of Victory*, 1959
Alinsky, Saul, *John L. Lewis*, 1949
Allen, George E., *Presidents Who Have Known Me*, 1960
Allen, Robert S. (and William V. Shannon), *The Truman-Merry-Go-Round*, 1950
American Guide Series: *Missouri, A Guide to the "Show Me" State*, 1941
Attlee, Clement R., *As It Happened*, 1954
Barker, John T., *Missouri Lawyer*, 1949
Barkley, Alben, *That Reminds Me*, 1954
Beach, Marjorie, *The Mayor's Wife*, 1953
Bell, Jack, *Splendid Misery*, 1960
Bendiner, Robert, *White House Fever*, 1960
Bloom, Sol, *Autobiography*, 1948
Bolles, Blair, *Men of Good Intentions*, 1960
Boorstin, Daniel J., *Genius of American Politics*, 1953
Brandeis, Louis D., *The Curse of Bigness*, 1934
Brown, A. T., *Politics of Reform*, 1958
Bryan, William Jennings, *The Memoirs of*, 1925
Bundschu, Henry A., *Harry S. Truman—The Missourian*, 1948

Burch, John P., *A True Story of Charles W. Quantrell and His Guerilla Band*, 1923

Busch, Noel F., *Adlai E. Stevenson*, 1952

Byrnes, James F., *Speaking Frankly*, 1947

—— *All in One Lifetime*, 1958

Carr, Robert K., *The House Committee on Un-American Activities, 1945–1950*, 1952

Churchill, Sir Winston, *Second World War*, 6 vols., 1948–1953

Clemens, Cyril, *Truman Speaks*, 1946

Coffin, Tris, *Missouri Compromise*, 1947

Connally, Tom, and Steinberg, Alfred, *My Name Is Tom Connally*, 1954

Coyle, David C., *Ordeal of the Presidency*, 1960

Daniels, Jonathan, *The Man of Independence*, 1950

David, Paul T. and associates, *The National Story (Presidential Nominating Politics in 1952)*, 1954

Dayton, Eldorous L., *Give 'Em Hell, Harry*, 1956

Dillon, Mary E., *Wendell Willkie*, 1952

Donovan, Robert J., *Eisenhower: The Inside Story*, 1956

Douglas, Paul H., *Economy in the National Government*, 1952

Douglass, Robert S., *History of Missouri Baptists*, 1934

Dulles, John F., *War or Peace*, 1950

Eisenhower, Dwight D., *Crusade in Europe*, 1948

Eccles, Marriner, *Beckoning Frontiers*, 1951

Farley, James A., *Behind the Ballots*, 1938

—— *Jim Farley's Story*, 1948

Feis, Herbert, *The China Tangle*, 1953

—— *Between War and Peace*, 1960

—— *Japan Subdued*, 1961

Finer, Herman, *The Presidency*, 1960

Flynn, Edward J., *You're the Boss*, 1947

Forrestal, James, and Millis, Walter, *Forrestal Diaries*, 1951

Garwood, Darrell, *Crossroads of America*, 1948

Goldman, Eric, *The Crucial Decade*, 1956

Gunther, John, *Inside USA*, 1947

Haskell, Henry C. and Fowler, Richard, *City of the Future*, 1950

Hassett, William D., *Off the Record*, 1958

Helm, William P., *Harry Truman*, 1947

Hillman, William, *Mr. President*, 1952

Hunt, Frazier, *Untold Story of Douglas MacArthur*, 1954

Hyman, Sidney, *The American President*, 1954

Ickes, Harold, *Secret Diary*, 3 vols., 1953–54

Johnson, Walter, *1600 Pennsylvania Avenue*, 1960

Koenig, Louis W., *Truman Administration*, 1956

Leahy, William D., *I Was There*, 1950

Lee, Jay M., *The Artilleryman*, 1920

Lord, Russell, *The Wallaces of Iowa*, 1947

Mayerberg, Samuel, *Chronicle of an American Crusader*, 1944

McNaughton, Frank, and Hehmeyer, Walter, *This Man Truman*, 1945

—— *Harry Truman, President*, 1948

Miller, W. H., *The History of Kansas City*, 1880

Milligan, Maurice M., *Missouri Waltz*, 1948

Missouri Crime Survey, 1926

Neustadt, Richard, *Presidential Power*, 1960

Norris, George W., *Fighting Liberal, An Autobiography*, 1945

Parkman, Francis, *The Oregon Trail*, 1849

Parrington, Vernon L., *Main Currents in American Thought*, 1926

Political History of Kansas City, 1902

Political History of Jackson County, 1902

Pollard, James E., *Presidents and the Press*, 1947

Powell, Gene, *Tom's Boy Harry*, 1948

Reddig, William M., *Tom's Town*, 1947

Redding, John M., *Inside the Democratic Party*, 1958

Richberg, Donald, *My Hero*, 1954

Rovere, Richard, and Schlesinger, Arthur M., Jr., *The General and the President*, 1952

Schauffler, Edward R., *Harry Truman—Son of the Soil*, 1947

Schlesinger, Arthur M., Jr., *Politics of Upheaval*, 1960

Sherwood, Robert E., *Roosevelt and Hopkins*, 1948

Shoemaker, Floyd C., editor, *Missouri Day by Day*, 1942

Smith, Ira, *Dear Mr. President*, 1949

Smith, Merriman, *Thank You, Mr. President*, 1946

—— *A President Is Many Men*, 1948

Spanier, J. W., *The Truman-MacArthur Controversy*, 1959

Steinberg, Alfred, *Mrs. R: The Life of Eleanor Roosevelt*, 1958

—— *Douglas MacArthur*, 1961

Stettinius, Edward R., *Roosevelt and the Russians*, 1949

Timmons, Bascom, *Garner of Texas*, 1948

Truman, Harry S., *Year of Decision*, 1955

—— *Years of Trial and Hope*, 1956

—— *Mr. Citizen*, 1960

Tully, Grace, *FDR, My Boss*, 1949

U. S. Congress, Senate, Special Committee Investigating National Defense Program, 1943–1944, 20 vols., 1944

Vandenberg, Arthur, and Vandenberg, Arthur, Jr., *Private Papers of Senator Vandenberg*, 1952

Weizmann, Chaim, *Trial and Error*, 1949

Weyl, Nathaniel, *Battle Against Disloyalty,* 1951

White, William Allen, *The Autobiography of,* 1946

Whitney, Alexander Fell, *Railroad Rules-Wage Movement in the United States,* 1946

NEWSPAPERS *The New York Times,* New York *Herald Tribune,* Washington *Post,* Washington *Star,* Washington *Times-Herald,* Chicago *Tribune,* Kansas City *Star,* Kansas City *Journal-Post,* The Independence *Examiner,* St. Louis *Post-Dispatch,* St. Louis *Globe-Democrat, Congressional Record*

MAGAZINES *Time, Newsweek, Life, Look, The New Yorker, Reader's Digest, Harper's, Atlantic Monthly, Forum and Century, Fortune, Collier's, Tomorrow, Common Sense, Foreign Service.*

Index

436

437

Hall, Ella, 34
Halleck, Charles, 328
Halsey, Colonel, 232
Halsey, Ed, 137
Hannegan, Robert, 169, 175, 176, 194-95, 200-01, 202, 203, 204, 205, 206, 207, 208, 209-10, 211, 212-13, 214, 215, 216, 217, 218, 222, 254, 282, 287, 309-10
Harbor, Elmer, 326
Hardin, Ardelia, 124
Harding, Warren G., 69, 143, 160
Harriman, Averell, 241, 382, 410, 412, 416, 426
Harris, Edward A., 355-56
Harrison, Benjamin, 25
Harrison, George, 210
Harrison, Pat, 157-58
Harrisonville, Missouri, 20, 21
Hart, John, 221
Hassett, William, 226, 254, 264, 291, 347, 358, 429
Hatch, Carl A., 128, 175, 183
Hawes, Harry, 113
Hayden, Carl, 127, 142, 210
Hayes, E. W., 74
Hebert, Edward, 395
Helm, Bill, 113, 122, 181, 183, 190, 192, 253, 263
Henderson, Leon, 310
Henderson, Loy, 307
Henry Stanley, 223, 225
Herring, Clyde, 158
Herzog, Rabbi, 308
Higgins, Otto P., 163
High, Stanley, 197
Hill, A. Ross, 110, 111
Hillenkoetter, Admiral Roscoe, 320
Hillman, Sidney, 190, 210, 212, 213
Hinde, Edgar G., 62, 64
Hirohito, Emperor, 260
Hiroshima, Japan, 259, 260
Hirth, William, 116-17, 118
Hiss, Alger, 352, 370
Hitler, Adolf, 244
Hodge, General John R., 373-74
Hoey, Clyde, 369
Hoffman, Harry, 64
Hoffman, Paul, 297
Holland, Al, 137
Holland, Lou, 81
Holmes, Nancy Tyler, 16
Hood, Robert L., 78

Hoover, Herbert, 246, 265, 324, 328, 329, 357, 370, 380
Hoover, J. Edgar, 163
Hoover Commission, 292
Hopkins, Harry, 106-07, 134, 222, 253, 247-48, 277, 373
Hopkins, William J., 348
Horne, Charles Francis, 25
Houchens, B. M., 81
Houchens, Fielding, 29
House Rules Committee, 287, 337
House Un-American Activities Committee, 352
Housing, public, low-cost, 342
Howe, Louis, 104
Howell, Charles M., 105
Huber, Brownie, 33
Hume, Paul, 394-95
Humphrey, Hubert, 226, 315
Hunt, Colonel James V., 369
Hurley, Patrick, 364, 365
Huston, Luther, 230
Hydrogen bomb, 362-63

Ibn Saud, King, 304
Ickes, Harold, 130, 134, 172, 173, 187, 205, 206, 265-67, 329
Igoe, Bill, 115, 119
Independence, Missouri, 12, 22, 23, 53, 75, 124, 138, 207, 219, 222, 226, 250, 251, 329, 346, 376, 417, 420, 422, 423, 426
Independence, presidential airplane, 412, 415
Independence *Examiner,* 61, 242, 243
Independence Junior Militia, 26-27
Independence *Observer,* 101
Inflation, 379
Integration of armed forces, 303
Internal Revenue Bureau, 406-07
Internal Security Bill, 341
Interstate Commerce Commission, 167
Iran, 12
Iron Curtain issue, 281
Isacson, Leo, 300
Israel, State of, 307-08

Jackson, Andrew, 23, 221
Jackson, Samuel D., 211, 214, 216
Jackson, Robert H., 183
Jacobson, Eddie, 42, 43, 53-54, 55, 56, 57, 58, 80, 223, 226, 251
James, Jesse and Frank, 23

442

444

cation of Defense Department, 286, 292; Vice-President of the U.S., 228-34; West Point appointments, 134; White House reconditioning and, 302-03; working-day program, 345-58; World War I and, 41-51

Truman, John Anderson (Harry Truman's father), 15, 16-17, 19, 20, 22, 24-25, 27, 29, 30, 32, 33, 34, 79, 221, 295

Truman, Joseph, 15

Truman, Martha Ellen Young (Harry Truman's mother), 17, 19, 20, 22, 23, 24, 26, 29, 32, 34, 39, 41-42, 53, 76, 97-98, 116, 119, 138, 168, 171, 177-78, 217, 223, 228, 240, 246-47, 251, 252, 294-95

Truman, Mary Jane (Harry Truman's sister), 22, 24, 30, 34, 39, 42, 55, 76, 98, 178, 246, 252, 295, 356

Truman, Mary Jane Holmes (Harry Truman's grandmother), 16

Truman, Mary Margaret (Harry Truman's daughter), 38, 77, 80, 85, 93, 98-100, 119, 121, 124, 125, 127, 136, 138, 176, 189, 192, 207, 208, 217, 218, 222, 223, 230, 231, 234, 240, 249, 250, 251, 255, 263, 316, 322, 323, 325, 328, 330, 334, 336-37, 372, 394-95, 415, 418, 422, 425-26, 429

Truman, Matt (Harry Truman's aunt), 16

Truman, Vivian (Harry Truman's brother), 21, 24-25, 26, 30, 32, 39, 58, 65, 79, 168, 217, 247, 347

Truman, William (Harry Truman's uncle), 16

Truman & Jacobson, 54-58

Truman-Austin Bill, 146

Truman Committee, 180-91, 192-94, 196-98, 223, 265

Truman Doctrine, 293-94, 295, 297, 359, 361, 413

Truman Library, Harry S., 426-27, 428

Tubby, Roger, 11, 352

Tully, Grace, 209, 213

Turner, Roy J., 326

Twenty-one Point program, 262, 264

Twyman, Dr., 24

Twyman, Elmer, 26, 27, 29

Tyler, John, 16

Union Station Massacre, 106

United Nations, 200, 245, 248, 265, 306, 307, 335, 362, 363, 374, 376, 377, 386, 396, 410, 416-17

United Nations Charter Conference, 235, 239, 240, 241, 243, 246, 247, 250-51

Vacarro, Tony, 238, 287, 352

Vandenberg, Arthur, 127, 184, 239, 241, 250, 278, 289, 296-97, 313, 326, 332, 360, 367

Vandenberg, General Hoyt, 314, 382

Van Devanter, Willis, 156

Vaughan, Harry, 22, 43-44, 49, 56, 76-77, 100, 138, 139, 170, 173, 174, 184, 190, 222-23, 231, 242, 255, 257, 263-64, 279, 280, 289-91, 298, 321, 333, 348, 349, 369, 380, 409

Veatch, N. T., 88, 89, 90

V-E Day, 244, 245, 246

Velde, Harold, 425

Vest, George, 139

Veterans of Foreign Wars, 383

Villa, Pancho, 41

Vinson, Fred, 254, 277, 326, 333, 350, 357, 403, 409

V-J Day, 261

Wade, Jim, 178

Wage Stabilization Board, 401

Wake Island, 386-87

Walker, Frank, 199, 200, 204, 212, 215, 254

Walker, Lieut. General Walton, 383, 386, 392, 393, 395

Wallace, David W., 36

Wallace, Frank, 26, 38, 98

Wallace, Fred, 99

Wallace, George, 26, 38, 98, 176, 209, 212

Wallace, Henry A., 130, 173, 183, 199-200, 201, 202, 203, 205-06, 210-11, 214, 216, 217, 218, 226, 228, 229, 253, 265, 281-85, 294, 300, 308, 319, 331

Wallace, Madge Gates, 12, 36, 37, 38, 53, 85, 98, 99, 138, 230, 248-49, 250, 346, 390, 417, 422

Wallace, May, 98

Wallace, Natalie, 98

Wallgren, Mon, 183, 188, 192, 202, 250, 339, 357

B TRUMAN, H.
Steinberg, Alfred, 1917-
The man from Missouri; the
life and times of Harry S.
Truman.

	DATE DUE